Anne-Marie Ambert, PhD

Parents, Children, and Adolescents: Interactive Relationships and Development in Context

Pre-publication
REVIEWS,
COMMENTARIES,
EVALUATIONS . . .

"**A**mbert's book is clearly written, well-researched, and timely. It is carefully balanced in that it is interdisciplinary, and the author does not overstate empirical findings to support a specific value or point of view. I am particularly impressed with the fact that the book is not only interdisciplinary but also multicultural in nature, an important aspect of human development that is often ignored.

Of particular importance is the inclusion of information on genetics as this research relates to each topic. Most of this research is quite new, and Ambert skillfully incorporates rather complicated information into a very understandable format.

Good questions are raised throughout the book. Ambert's approach to the important topic of parenting is fresh and very interesting."

Marilyn Coleman, EdD
Professor of Human Development and Family Studies,
University of Missouri-Columbia

"**A**mbert abolishes boundaries between disciplines and age groups in her book on the parent-child relationship over the life cycle. She proposes a truly integrative perspective, drawing together the most recent literature from disciplines such as sociology, psychology, criminology, and behavioral genetics. In addition, unlike most reviews on the parent-child relationship, she considers simultaneously four phases of the life cycle: infancy, childhood, adolescence, and young adulthood. Another important feature of this book is the discussion of the normative development to lighten many negative parental and children outcomes.

Not only is the book a rich review of all aspects of the parent-child relationship over the life span, it is also full of ideas that are likely to stimulate further research. The book is undoubtedly the most important review on the subject of child socialization. Because of these characteristics, it will be of interest to the specialist of the parent-child relationship for a particular age group and others seeking information on the subject. Students will benefit from a book that is concise, comprehensive, and readable. Professionals will find the book an excellent instrument to update their knowledge and review their practice accordingly. The glossary is an important addition to develop common definitions in the field."

Marc Le Blanc, PhD
Professor,
University of Montreal,
Montreal, Quebec

"**A**nne-Marie Ambert has written a very interesting and highly readable text examining the family relationships of children and adolescents with their parents and the effects on development within the context of the family as well as peers, the school, and the wider society. This emphasis on context is a major strength of this volume, as this material is often either ignored or embedded within other topics in various existing texts. Further, Ambert has taken a multidisciplinary approach to the topics considered in this volume, not limiting herself to the perspectives and approaches of any single discipline.

The Haworth Press, Inc.

Parents, Children, and Adolescents
Interactive Relationships and Development in Context

HAWORTH Marriage & the Family
Terry S. Trepper, PhD
Senior Editor

Parents, Children, and Adolescents
Interactive Relationships and Development in Context

Anne-Marie Ambert, PhD

The Haworth Press
New York • London

The Haworth Press, Inc., 10 Alice Street, Binghamton, NY 13904-1580

Cover design by Marylouise E. Doyle.

Library of Congress Cataloging-in-Publication Data

Ambert, Anne-Marie
    Parents, children, and adolescents : interactive relationships and development in context / Anne-Marie Ambert.
        p.   cm.
    Includes bibliographical references and index.
    ISBN 0-7890-6034-5 (alk. paper)
    1. Parent and child. 2. Parent and teenager. 3. Child development. 4. Developmental psychology. 5. Family–Psychological aspects. 6. Problem families–Psychological aspects. 7. Context effects (Psychology) I. Title.
HQ755.85.A45   1997
306.874–dc20   96-24646
                                                                                                              CIP

CONTENTS

ABOUT THE AUTHOR

Anne-Marie Ambert, PhD, is Professor in the Department of Sociology at York University, Toronto, where she has taught for well over two decades. In addition, she is currently an Associate Fellow at the LaMarsh Centre for Research on Violence and Conflict Resolution. Prior to joining the faculty at York University, Dr. Ambert taught at three different American universities. The author of six books and the editor of two volumes, she has published widely on child development and family relations in journals such as *Criminologie*, the *American Journal of Psychiatry,* the *Canadian Review of Sociology and Anthropology,* the *Journal of Divorce and Remarriage,* the *Journal of Marriage and the Family*, and the *Journal of Personal and Social Relations*. Her areas of research expertise fall within various domains of family studies. Dr. Ambert is a member of many professional sociological and psychological associations.

Preface

The psychotherapy disciplines have for years been interested in the relationship between parents and their children. This interest, unfortunately, usually is in the form of *pathologizing* some aspects of that relationship. For example, beginning with the early psychoanalysts and continuing until today, many therapists have ascribed the various presenting problems seen in their clinical practice to deficiencies in parenting. Besides the *negative* focus, almost all of the major developmental theories focus on the *linear* relationship between parents and children.

In contrast, Anne-Marie Ambert, one of Canada's leading sociologists, has dedicated her professional career to the study of the *interactions* between parents and children. Her work is characterized by an interest not only in those interactions that result in psychological and family problems, but those that are resilient and strength producing. Another difference in Dr. Ambert's work is her unceasing interest in the *systemic* interactions that, although far more difficult to study than the simpler linear interactions, are the ones that really matter. Parents and children do not influence each other in a vacuum. Instead, their interactions are embedded in social *contexts* consisting of siblings, peers, schools, neighborhoods; are delimited by family structure; and are constrained by poverty.

Parents, Children, and Adolescents: Interactive Relationships and Development in Context represents the most current, up-to-date information source of research on development within an interactive perspective. This interdisciplinary book will be of interest to developmental researchers, family studies scholars, clinicians who work with families, and students who plan careers in psychology, social work, marriage and family therapy, and related fields. It is extremely well written and documented, meticulous in its material, and highly original in its theoretical framework. Dr. Ambert is to be commended for this book, which is the culmination of years of research on interactions within the family.

Terry S. Trepper, PhD
Executive Editor
Haworth Marriage and the Family

Acknowledgments

The research necessary for this book took several years to gather and this enterprise would not have been possible without a grant from the Social Sciences and Humanities Research Council of Canada (grant #410-91-0046). I am grateful for Tonda March's copyediting. In her capacity as Managing Editor for the *Journal of Marriage and the Family*, she had worked on several of my publications before. It seemed natural to turn to her. I also benefited greatly from Peg Marr's patient editing at Haworth. Again, as was the case for my previous book, *The Effect of Children on Parents*, also published by The Haworth Press, in 1992, I am indebted to my daughter Stéphanie for preparing the author index, a daunting task during which she has grown from a then young adolescent to what we now call the period of late adolescence. Terry Trepper, the Series Editor, and Bill Palmer, Haworth's Vice President, have encouraged my ideas for books with their repeated confidence. It is worth mentioning that I have stayed with The Haworth Press because a good relationship with an attentive publisher is a pleasure for any author.

Introduction

THEORETICAL ORIENTATION

This text straddles the disciplines of sociology, psychology, behavior genetics, family studies, and to some extent psychiatry and criminology. It contains materials that are generally published in different journals with different readerships, and with little cross-fertilization among the various authors, even when parallel lines of research have emerged. It has become very difficult to keep abreast of the literature in one's discipline, so that forays into complementary or adjacent fields are prohibitive in terms of time. The disciplinary nature of scholarly publications contributes to isolation. Therefore, the first goal that guided the writing of this volume was to bring various disciplines together on selected topics and issues pertaining to the parent-child relationship and child development.

The theoretical orientation begins with an interactional perspective (see Magnusson, 1995) that is complemented with behavior genetics and a substantial element of ecological or contextual grounding. The parent-child relationship is also examined from a life course point of view, following both children and parents as they age, although the emphasis is by necessity on the first 20 years of life. Therefore, the parent-child relationship and child development are examined within a perspective that links the biological organism, behavior, and personality with the multiplicity of contextual variables, including time, that surround individuals. These variables interact with each other to influence relationships and determine development.

I have avoided the temptation to label this integrative perspective a "theory" and to add a new layer of concepts. The concepts already available are used and jargon is left aside inasmuch as feasible. There is much that is new in this text: Its originality resides in linkages that are established between disciplines and topics, in suggestions for further research, and in relevant critiques rather than in conceptual innovations. The latter, in my opinion, often contribute to further disciplinary fragmentation.

The perspective presented is that parents cannot educate or socialize their children without regard for the latter's personalities, predispositions, cognitions, and the contexts in which they live. Moreover, parents and children are considered from the vantage point of how both affect each other (Bell, 1968). We look at how parents and children interact, and react to each other's personalities and behaviors–both over time and within various contexts–and, in turn, how this circularity of effect contributes to human development. We discuss children, not as passive recipients of parental effect, but as active participants in a relationship, as co-producers of their own development, and as co-agents in the production of their family's quality of life (Belsky, Gilstrap, and Rovine, 1984; Lerner and Busch-Rossnagel, 1981). The traditional focus on parents as the producers of their children's personalities, happiness, success, and emotional problems–what Skolnick and Skolnick (1994:9) appropriately call "the assumption of parental determinism"–is still followed in most empirical research although it is no longer accepted at the theoretical level. At this time, there is obviously a lag between theory and research in child and adolescent development (Ambert, 1995). In addition, this book situates the parent-child relationship within some of its many contexts, such as siblings, peers, neighborhoods, and family structure. The combination of the various perspectives allows us to raise research questions and hypotheses that may have been overlooked because of the disciplinary constraints that have existed to this point.

INTENDED AUDIENCES

This text was designed for two audiences; first, for researchers and professionals interested in a multidisciplinary approach and, second, for advanced undergraduate as well as graduate students. To researchers and professionals, this text offers an integrated theoretical framework within an interdisciplinary context, new research questions and suggestions, reviews and critiques of some of the extant empirical literatures, as well as issues that are rarely raised. The book contains perspectives and data, or, if you wish, an amalgamation of theory and information. In addition to in-text references, endnotes provide further references that can help both established researchers and graduate students. The references are up to date, but a few citations of work from the 1970s or even earlier have been included when they are important, or when they represent a type of research that is no longer carried out. Moreover suggestions for research are combined together under "Research–gaps in" in the subject index.

Instructors who use this work as a class text for their advanced courses at the undergraduate level will find several pedagogic features designed to facilitate their task in an accompanying Instructor's Manual. Some of these features are commonly found in such manuals but others are unique to this text. In addition, a glossary of terms is included at the end of the book: Concepts covered are indicated in bold type in the text. This glossary, however, cannot substitute for basic knowledge in sociology and psychology. Hence, this text is not suitable for introductory courses. Another feature is listings in endnotes of scholarly journals that carry some specific types of research. This feature, along with a detailed index, could help advanced students locate topics and references for essays.

VOLUME CONTENTS

There are four sections covering 15 chapters. The first section examines certain aspects of the parent-child relationship and of human development from infancy through adulthood. The second section covers various contexts within which the parent-child relationship evolves and that influence, constrain, or enhance human development. The third section examines the parent-child relationship and human development in families where emotional or behavioral problems afflict one or more of their members. The last section is composed of two concluding chapters. One explains in detail some aspects of behavior genetics and highlights the importance of the nature-and-nurture framework in human development. (It should be emphasized from the start that behavior genetics has nothing to do with assumptions about genetic differences between racial groups or between men and women.) The last chapter discusses the role that parents play in their children's outcomes and the factors that limit parental influence.

Each of the four chapters in Part I serves as a building block for the remainder of the volume; each introduces theories and contexts that recur throughout the text. Hence, the first four chapters serve as a medium to discuss at greater length the origins of personality, its role in the parent-child relationship and in human development, and the impact of young maternal age and poverty (Chapter 1); the effect of the media, the interactional perspective, resilient children, and gender (Chapter 2); parenting practices and influence (Chapter 3); and personality stability and exchange with older parents (Chapter 4). Throughout, an effort has been made to avoid studying the parent-child relationship as if it were a socially isolated dyad: It is located within its multiplicity of contexts (Bronfenbrenner, 1979).

These contexts or interfaces for the parent-child relationship and child development are detailed in Part II of the text. They include siblings (Chapter 5) and peers (Chapter 6). The school, along with its impact on underprivileged and minority families, is the focus of Chapter 7. Chapter 8 discusses the impact of various professionals on the parent-child relationship and on the definition of the parenting role. Finally, the effect of family structure, including divorce, remarriage, and single-parent families, is presented in Chapter 9. Other important contextual variables such as poverty, quality of neighborhoods, and race/ethnicity are woven into the text.

Psychologists consider the various results of human development and call these "outcomes." In Part III, the following outcomes are examined to see how they affect the parent-child relationship: abusive as well as drug dependent and emotionally disturbed parents (Chapter 10), children/ adolescents who suffer from emotional problems (Chapter 11), conduct disorders (Chapter 12), and delinquency (Chapter 13). Matters of etiology and development are critically investigated in each case.

In Part IV, the two concluding chapters present overarching themes in terms of theory and intervention as well as social policy. Chapter 14 explains more thoroughly than in previous chapters the role that genetics and environment play in human development and in the parent-child relationship. Chapter 15 examines not only the extent to which parents can influence their children, but the limits to this influence, as well as the cultural and social roadblocks adults encounter in their parenting role. The book concludes with suggestions for strengthening parental influence. This last chapter clearly indicates that, although genetics is an important element in child development, as are extra-familial influences, parents are children's key proximal context. It is further argued that in this type of rapidly changing society, attentive parenting may have become more necessary than it was in the recent past. These last two chapters have practical implications for social policy as well as for intervention.

The context of parental employment, for which a chapter had originally been planned, had to be abandoned because of space considerations. This context is, however, integrated within the various chapters (Rogers, Parcel, and Menaghan, 1991). The available literature on religion as a context in child development and particularly for the parent-child relationship is sadly underdeveloped in the social and behavioral sciences, and had to be left aside (Thomas and Carver, 1990; Thomas and Cornwall, 1990). Other issues such as those pertaining to attachment, homosexuality, and adoption, for instance, would have required substantial digressions. Overall, in order to introduce a more integrative theoretical perspective, and to focus on some issues that have been previously neglected, I have had to skip many interesting subjects while only skimming the surface of others. I apologize if in the process I have left out your favorite subjects, or have treated them too cursorily, in your opinion. But it has to be kept in mind that these same topics are likely to be ones I regret not including. All in all, it is my hope that readers will learn as much as I have during the year I have just spent wedded to the library researching the contents of this book. Yet so much remains to be learned.

HISTORICAL PERSPECTIVE

Had this book been written 30 years ago, its contents and theoretical orientation would have been far different. One can also presume that the contents of such a text will differ substantially 20 years from now. This stems from the fact that there are trends or "fashions" in research themes, so that the focus of research changes with the decades, and is often recycled at a later date (McCall, 1987:25). But, above all, the parent-child relationship and child development are topics that are very sensitive to cultural, social, and economic changes (Elder, 1993; Gergen, 1973). Family relationships and human development take place within a specific cultural context, at a given period of social change or stability, and under specific economic conditions (Hareven, 1994; Rossi and Rossi, 1990). It is one of the emphases of this work that children's contexts have changed drastically within the past 20 years (Elder, 1995). Parents learn their role within a particular socioeconomic environment, and are forced to make concessions to the conditions they live in and raise their children accordingly (Alwin, 1990), although much of this takes place unconsciously.

For their part, children react to their parents according to the expectations of their environment, including peer group pressure and the messages they receive from professionals as well as from the media. These social pressures change over time so that children's attitudes and behaviors toward their parents evolve. So does their receptivity to parenting efforts. Moreover, the environment we live in encourages the development of certain personality traits while it discourages others (Demos, 1971). At this juncture, the middle-class culture encourages independence in children (Alwin, 1986). Yet not all children can be independent and function equally well: Their own personalities may not fit such requisites, or their neighborhood may be too dangerous to allow independence. Thus, not all environments provide a good person-context fit (Bronfenbrenner, 1986), and not all personalities are equally adaptable to a given context. As the decades move on, different person-context adaptations evolve (Clausen, 1986). Child development as well as the parent-child relationship are thus topics of research that have to be studied within the sociohistorical period to which they belong (Bronfenbrenner, Kessel, Kessen, and White, 1986; Elder, Modell, and Parke, 1993a,b). Each century and each culture has its own social construction of children, normality, and what is an appropriate parent-child relationship (Aries, 1962; Kessen, 1979; Wartofsky, 1983).

Researchers must move quite rapidly to document and explain differences between the present and the past. In North America, certain contexts of children's and adolescents' lives now change every five years or so. One can think here of the content of mass media, technological toys, and the incidence of, as well as the prevalent attitude toward violence. In this text, we try to capture the latest moments and movements in the areas of the parent-child relationship and child development.

PART I:
THE PARENT-CHILD RELATIONSHIP
AND DEVELOPMENT
OVER THE LIFE CYCLE

Chapter 1

The Relationship Between Parents and Their Small Children

Part I focuses on child development and the parent-child relationship throughout children's life course, and serves as a building block for the remainder of the volume as each chapter introduces theories and contexts that are then utilized throughout the text. Because this book has a psycho-sociological orientation, Chapter 1 opens with the first building block–personality.

The relationship between a newborn and its parents begins to take shape well before the birth and even the conception of the baby. When a baby is born into a two-parent family, the mother and the father each have established a way of relating on the basis of their own personalities. It is these personalities, with all their characteristics, that guide in part how the mother and father interact with their infant. In addition, the ecological context in which parents live contributes resources and limitations that impact on their ability to parent (Bronfenbrenner, 1986). The environment in which babies are born may change during their young years so that the quality of care they receive, although within the same family, is not necessarily stable. Parents may change jobs,[1] or may become unemployed; they may go on welfare or off; they may move to a different neighborhood; a sibling may be born; and divorce may take place. These are the most common family transitions that can affect the quality of the parent-child relationship as well as child development (Menaghan and Parcel, 1995).

This chapter examines four key factors that impact the parent-child relationship as well as child development.[2] These are personality, young maternal age, poverty, and the quality of the parents' marital relationship. The context of poverty constitutes an important element in this book and is pursued in other chapters. Specific contexts, both intra- and extra-familial, that are important to the parent-child relationship and child development are discussed in Part II. Because a holistic framework is presented, a consideration of behavioral genetics throughout is also included, and this chapter lays the foundations for this perspective.

PERSONALITY DEFINED

In order to avoid the interminable discussions concerning what "really" constitutes personality, temperament, and traits,[3] we adopt a layperson's definition, or practice some "naive psychology" (Baldwin, 1965). When describing an acquaintance, we may say that she is friendly, cooperative, intelligent, and happy-go-lucky, yet stubborn and at times moody. We are enumerating traits (friendliness, moodiness) that, taken together rather than separately, form a configuration of fairly stable characteristics or temperament (Rutter, 1994). The temperament is probably the most important aspect of personality, along with abilities, intellectual or otherwise (Goldsmith et al., 1987). Physical appearance can also be considered to be part of personality because we are all affected by the way we look; our appearance serves as a stimulus in terms of reactions from others who meet us for the first time (Zuckerman, Miyake, and Elkin, 1995). In addition, someone's general and chronic state of health is part of personality, although specific **acute illnesses*** are not because they do not last.

Unless individuals possess an extreme trait that is overpowering or distracting, such as being very aggressive or very charitable or even extraordinarily beautiful, we tend to perceive people, once we know them, in terms of the sum of their qualities. That is, we react to their overall personality, rather than in terms of just one trait.

ORIGINS OF PERSONALITY

A newborn baby is a tiny physical constitution and a budding personality that, apart from intrauterine factors (such as maternal malnutrition, smoking, alcoholism, or drug abuse), is the result of the genes it has inherited. At birth, a baby is naked in more ways than one, for that baby is yet to be touched by its new environment. We first consider briefly the matter of genetics, explained in far greater detail in Chapter 14.[4] Each baby inherits its genes, half from each of its parents: one set originates from the mother's ovum, the other from the father's spermatozoid that fertilized the ovum.[5] Therefore, a newborn has the potential to resemble its parents in many ways. One baby may inherit its father's physical appearance and some aspects of his temperament, but it may inherit its mother's intellectual abilities as well as aspects of her temperament. Or the reverse. Although some of these characteristics may be apparent at birth (height,

---

*Glossary terms are set in boldface type upon first mention.

facial features, and traits such as fearfulness and restlessness), *others will not appear until later on in life. Hereditary predispositions do not necessarily become actualized at birth* (Riese, 1990). They appear at their appropriate time (Loehlin, 1992). For instance, the best predictor of a woman's age at menopause is the age her mother was when *she* became menopausal. Age at menopause is partly genetic; yet menopause does not occur until the female organism is mature enough to undergo this transition.[6] Moreover, the heritability of some traits increases over time while that of others decreases (McCartney, Harris, and Bernieri, 1990). It is also important to recognize that not all inherited predispositions necessarily materialize or are activated. *Some predispositions have to be exposed to a conducive environment in order to develop* (McGuffin and Gottesman, 1985) or, at the negative level, some predispositions need to be triggered by an aversive and stressful environment in order to appear (Plomin and McClearn, 1993).

There are children who seem to resemble their parents very little, whether physically, psychologically, or intellectually. This may be because the **configuration** of their traits does not resemble that of either parent; the genes they have inherited form a personality profile that, taken in its entirety, differs from that of the parents, even though the particular genetic material comes from them. For instance, a child who has received genetic material from the father predisposing her to aggression may also have inherited a high level of impulse control from the mother. The two predispositions may cancel each other or may combine and result in outcomes that are far different from those encountered in each individual parent. The pattern or configuration the child inherited, coupled with the environmental factors she encounters in her lifetime, make her a very different person from her parents.

THE EFFECT OF PERSONALITY
ON THE PARENT-CHILD RELATIONSHIP

The effect of personality on the parent-child relationship and on child development is examined both in terms of the parents' and the infant's personalities. Basically, people have personalities before they become parents. They also hold various beliefs and attitudes concerning the nature of children and what is desirable in a baby.[7] They may have ideas about "child-rearing practices."[8] The quality of their relationship or marriage[9] is also important in determining their future adaptation to the coming baby (Heming, 1985). Prospective parents have a family, friends, jobs, material resources that all impact, to a greater or a lesser extent, on the way they will interact with their baby. Therefore, a newborn's environment begins to take shape throughout the development of its own parents. Its parents' personalities, beliefs, and relationships form part of this environment. In turn, this environment contributes to determine the baby's interaction with its parents.

At birth, depending on genetic inheritance and intrauterine influences, each newborn is different. These differences may be observed in the nursery of a hospital maternity ward. One newborn, Salina, cries constantly, even when picked up, is agitated, and difficult to feed. Baby Roberto in the next crib may be a total contrast: He sleeps contentedly, nurses avidly, cries momentarily but stops when fed, changed, or picked up. A third baby, La-verne, takes little milk, is small, quiet, does not cry, and sleeps most of the time. Each baby requires different types of care or approaches on the part of the nursing staff and from parents (Super and Harkness, 1994).

Baby Salina requires more attention because she *calls* for more of it via her cries. In contrast, Baby Roberto demands little attention and is actually easy to care for; all that nurses have to do is feed, change, and cuddle him. That baby allows his caretakers more free time and *makes his parents feel competent because it seems to them that everything they do for him is rewarded with success*. Baby Roberto is already poised to have good behavioral outcomes later on because he will adapt easily and will not stress his parents (Lerner and Lerner, 1994).

Baby Salina's temperament presents at the outset the potential for a "poorness of fit."[10] Her parents may feel less competent and more tense, especially if this is their first child and if they had not expected such a bundle of nerves (Sirignano and Lachman, 1985). If they happen to be preoccupied by poverty and marital conflict, Baby Salina may be very taxing indeed and may not elicit parental reactions that are always positive (Wachs and Gruen, 1982). She may therefore grow up with less positive impressions of her environment and may not find interpersonal relation-ships as rewarding as Roberto (Lerner and Lerner, 1994:175). Belsky and Rovine (1990) have even found that babies such as Salina may contribute to a decrease in their parents' marital happiness. For her part, Baby La-verne will arouse her caretakers' concern because of low birth weight and minimal appetite. At the same time, her parents are likely to feel quite at ease because she is an easy baby. If fed regularly, she will eventually thrive and will not make too many demands on her parents. However, in a deprived environment and with a mother who does not know much about baby care, tiny Laverne may deteriorate, waste away, and even die because she may not cry enough to indicate that she is hungry. In times of famine, food may go to her more demanding siblings, a situation observed in Africa by de Vries (1987). Infant demandingness or difficultness may be particularly well suited for survival in the harsh Masai environment.

Parents perceive that their baby is difficult or easy, in part depending on their own characteristics and level of tolerance. Nevertheless, several studies indicate that the frequency and intensity of a baby's crying or fussiness can be objectively assessed by detached observers who rate infants on a scale of difficultness. For instance, Lounsbury and Bates (1982) taped the hunger cries of infants who had already been described by their mothers as being either difficult, average, or easy. The tapes were played to unrelated mothers who judged the cries of the more difficult infants to be more irritating (Bates, Freeland, and Lounsbury, 1979). The correlations between the biological mothers' judgement of their baby's difficultness and the observers' rating were quite substantial.

What emerges from the above paragraphs is a perspective of interaction occurring on two levels. First, each baby has a personality to which nursing staff and parents react, depending on their own personalities and life circumstances. The infant initiates many of the parental gestures that form the cornerstone of the relationship (Breitmayer and Ricciuti, 1988).[11] When parents have rigid personalities, or are stressed by marital conflict, unemployment, or poverty, their own characteristics and situation may be the determining variable (Crockenberg, 1986). Such parents may overlook their babies' needs or misinterpret them (Mangelsdorf et al., 1990). While appropriate parenting practices are no guarantee of success, even difficult children benefit from them.[12] Conversely, less adaptable infants are likely to become more disorganized with parents who are similar to them in terms of irritability. Moreover, problematic parents can produce a negative effect on the child's ability to form attachments.[13] Van den Boom (1989) concludes that mothers experience more problems adjusting to irritable infants, and can be trained to increase their responsiveness to them. According to the perspective adopted in this text, both parental and child characteristics are important and interact with each other as well as with various other contexts in the environment (Belsky, 1984; Lerner, 1982).

Second, in discussing the parent-infant relationship, we enter the realm of interaction between nature and nurture, or between genetics and environment. The environment resides not only in the hospital, the home, and the parental personalities, but also in the parental reactions babies elicit because of their predispositions. Babies evocate reactions (being fed, changed, caressed, or discouragingly ignored) and these reactions become part of their environment, hence the close relationship between genetics and environment (Plomin and Bergeman, 1991). Parental reactions also mark the beginning of the parent-child relationship. When the infant is a bit older, child temperament (e.g., attention span and low impulsivity) is a factor that may foster self-regulation and compliance to socialization requests.[14] A child who easily internalizes family norms requires less supervision (Maccoby, 1984). Such children may form stronger attachments to their parents; this would also contribute to increasing their ability to comply and internalize rules of appropriate behavior (Kochanska and Aksan, 1995).[15]

THE ROLE OF SOCIODEMOGRAPHIC CHARACTERISTICS

Parents' sociodemographic characteristics are key elements in the parent-child relationship and human development. They include the parents' gender, age, marital status, social class (occupation, education, and income), ethnicity or race, and geographic location.[16] These parental variables recur throughout the text. In this chapter, we focus on young maternal age and poverty.

Young Maternal Age

Stages of family development have generally been defined in terms of children's age or the age of the youngest child, rather than parental age (Rossi, 1980). Yet parents of newborn babies vary greatly in terms of age and personal development (Seltzer and Ryff, 1994). It is actually difficult to discuss the impact of parents' age, marital status, and poverty separately because these variables are often closely intertwined. For instance, adolescent parents are generally poor and unschooled: their young age has not yet allowed them to complete their education. Therefore, a baby born to 12 to 18-year-old parents is likely to be placed at a triple disadvantage, each disadvantage compounding the other. Such a newborn is often labelled an "at-risk" infant–an infant at risk of being deprived of an optimal development because of its parents' characteristics.[17] Other infants are at risk because of their own characteristics: low birth weight, hyperactivity, or poor motor skills. A combination of at-risk parental characteristics, at-risk infants, and a deprived environment is most detrimental to child development. Such a combination contributes to maximize negative potential and prevents the actualization of positive potential.

Very young families are much in the news these days, as well as much in the minds of politicians in their efforts to curtail the budgetary deficits at the national and local levels.[18] Government expenditures for families that began with a birth to an adolescent reached $16.65 billion in 1985 (Hayes, 1987).

Adolescent mothers constitute the group of mothers most likely to remain on welfare for an extended period of time (Bane and Ellwood, 1986). The proportion of infants born to *single* adolescent women has risen steadily, as is also the case among older single women compared to married women (Furstenberg, 1991).[19] This trend can be problematic because babies born to very young mothers are likely to begin life with fewer social and material resources than babies born to older, more educated, and married parents who hold at least one job (Klerman, 1991). Very young parents have yet to acquire maturity and a stable personality. Hence, a young mother is quite unlikely to be as knowledgeable about child care or as mature psychologically as an older mother (Helm et al., 1990). Although there is a great deal of variety among adolescent mothers, and many are quite competent,[20] on the average, they have more unrealistic expectations than older mothers (Haskett, Johnson, and Miller, 1994). Therefore, such mothers may be less able to perceive their baby's needs with as much empathy as older mothers,[21] and may be less able to help their child develop cognitive skills that could be used in the school environment.[22] Children of young mothers are likely to develop more behavioral problems and tend to be more impulsive (Brooks-Gunn and Furstenberg, 1986).

Adolescents do not seek prenatal care as frequently as older women, and often their diet is not suitable to healthy fetal development. Consequently, a greater proportion of their infants are born underweight or with other health deficits (Strobino, 1987).[23] The combination of a frail baby and an immature mother may result in both a less positive mother-baby relationship and poorer child outcomes, as well as the possibility of child maltreatment (Massat, 1995). Because teen mothers begin childbearing so early, they are more likely than older women to experience multiple life transitions that may make their lives and those of their small children less stable (Capaldi and Patterson, 1991), thus far more difficult in terms of the degree of adjustment required.[24] Even at-risk children develop more optimally in a stable home environment (Escalona, 1982), and the resulting parent-child relationship is less conflictual on the average. Yet another disadvantage of teenage parenting is that, in many cases, the adolescent tries to delegate many of her maternal duties to her own mother or even grandmother. However, this expectation materializes in only 17 percent of the cases (Elder, Caspi, and Burton, 1988), even though a majority of adolescent mothers reside with their families (Wasserman, Brunelli, and Rauh, 1990).

Furstenberg, Brooks-Gunn, and Morgan (1987) report that adolescent mothers who remain with their parents for the first few years are definitely at an advantage. Beyond that, they become dependent.[25] In the mid-1980s,

12 percent of all grandmothers coresided with grandchildren (Baydar and Brooks-Gunn, 1991). Thirty percent and 9 percent respectively of black and white grandmothers were in such arrangements. This pattern was more evident with adolescent mothers present in a family: In the late 1980s in Baltimore, 60 percent were coresiding with their mothers (Chase-Landsdale, Brooks-Gunn, and Zamsky, 1991). Despite these figures for Baltimore, nationally, 31 percent of black single mothers with small children receive no help from their parents compared with 23 percent of similar white mothers (Eggebeen and Hogan, 1990).

Stevens (1984) notes that grandmothers are more responsive than teenage mothers to infants' needs. McNair (1991) correlates this higher level of sensitivity to a secure attachment of infants to their adolescent mothers. On the whole, recent research seems to indicate some similarity between young mothers and grandmothers in child-rearing practices (Chase-Landsdale, Brooks-Gunn, and Zamsky, 1991). This finding is quite consonant with the perspective whereby parents and children share certain personality traits and home environments that can affect child-rearing practices. It could actually be expected that as the adolescent acquires experience, her skills in this domain will come to resemble more closely those of her mother— both because of the increasing effect of shared genes and what she learns from her mother. Chase-Landsdale, Brooks-Gunn, and Paikoff (1991:400) state that "More research is needed to specify the ways in which grandmothers' parenting may influence mothers' parenting, as well as to ascertain which subgroups of grandmothers may provide superior parenting than adolescents and why."

The focus of research is unfortunately placed strictly on the young mother. Relatively little is known about the father, largely because he often plays a peripheral role in his infant's life. Few studies include him, not only because relatively few studies include fathers in general,[26] but also because these nonresident fathers can be difficult to locate. (For an exception, see Elster and Lamb, 1986.) Their involvement with their child is generally positive both for mothers and infants.[27] Nevertheless, a baby's father can be a salient source of conflict in a young mother's life (Nitz, Ketterlinus, and Brandt, 1995). When the mother is a teen, the father is not necessarily an adolescent himself (Hardy et al., 1989). The older he is, the less likely it is that he has contact with his baby: An older father may already have other children.[28] Moreover, studies find that a young father's involvement is greater when the child is an infant (Sullivan, 1989a). This occurs in part because of the status significance of the transition to fatherhood, particularly among inner-city youth (Anderson, 1989). The baby may be no more than a symbolic object for masculine status and may be soon forgotten.

There is little research on the impact of a father's age on the father-child relationship. The few studies available indicate that fathers who have their first child later than average–that is, above age 30–are more involved with their children than other fathers (Cooney et al., 1993). Moreover, these fathers have more positive feelings about their involvement than younger fathers. Several studies indicate that positive father involvement highly benefits children (Lamb, Pleck, and Levine, 1986). Moreover, some literature has emerged on the role of fathers in black families (McAdoo, 1988; Mirande, 1991), and, for *intact* families, the results are similar to those for white families, both in terms of child outcomes and resources available to parents.[29] In view of the salience of nonmarried fatherhood in black communities, particularly in disadvantaged neighborhoods, much more research is needed on the father-child relationship and on its impact on child outcomes.

Poverty

Currently, many families are being negatively impacted by the swings in the reconstruction of the global economy.[30] Some neighborhoods in inner cities have such a high **concentration** of poverty (Kasarda, 1992) that one can fear the establishment of a permanent underclass that is also mired in violence and criminality.[31] Hence, poverty and economic hardship as environmental factors in family life have become salient in research and policy writings. Among children, economic well-being is decreasing.[32] Well over 25 percent are poor, and children constitute about 40 percent of the population below the poverty level.[33] Minority groups are more affected than others.[34] Child poverty is caused by unemployment and jobs that do not pay enough, both for mothers and fathers (Lichter and Eggebeen, 1994). It is also amplified in one-parent families.

Poor people do not constitute a homogeneous mass; there is a great variety among them (Furstenberg and Hughes, 1995). They have different personalities, live in diverse environments, and the *source* of their poverty is not necessarily identical. First, people who are chronically poor and whose own parents were poor constitute a seemingly permanent underclass; yet, as many manage to climb out of poverty as remain poor (Duncan, Hill, and Hoffman, 1988). Second, other individuals become poor, either because of premature and unsupported child-rearing, layoff, and unemployment, ignorance, illness, alcoholism, and divorce. Third, families stay on welfare for varying periods of time, although there are also differences by race. Duncan and Yeung (1995) indicate that 24 percent of all American children spend at least one year in a family on welfare; one-fourth of these children's families receive welfare for 11 or more years. Long-term dependency may be increasing. Moreover, there is the phenomenon of homelessness, which due to its nature cannot be well documented (Link et al., 1994).[35] More family violence and negative childhood experiences occur among the homeless than among the poor who live at home (Shinn, Knickman, and Weitzman, 1991). The levels of distress are high and substance abuse may be a direct precipitant to homelessness.[36] All of these factors create many differences among disadvantaged people.

Poverty constitutes perhaps the most pervasive stressor in adults' lives, especially when it is combined with unemployment (Wilson, 1987). Economic disadvantage presents chronic stressors and insecurity as well as daily stressors or irritants (McLoyd, 1990). These stem from inability to plan ahead, sense of loss of control over one's life, feelings of **relative deprivation** in terms of material possessions, poor housing, lack of food, cold in the winter and heat in the summer, ailments and illnesses that go untreated, lack of healthy leisure activities, and even criminogenic and dangerous neighborhoods, as well as lack of access to quality day care and schooling for one's children (Jencks and Peterson, 1991). It is not surprising that depression and other mental illnesses are more prevalent in the lower class.[37]

Persons who become poor have to acclimate themselves to deprivation; such a situation strains marital relationships as well as childrearing practices (Liem and Liem, 1989). Adults become more easily irritable and tempers flare. Recriminations are exchanged and mutual support fails at a time when it is most needed. Husbands often withdraw from family life as a result of feeling that they cannot contribute to it because they have failed in their role as provider–even though it is often the economic system that has failed them. Child-rearing practices become harsher, less sensitive, and more inconsistent (Conger et al., 1992; Elder, 1979).

With poverty in general, parent-child relationships are less rewarding, more erratic due to the preoccupations of parents, and, at times, more distant.[38] Infants born prematurely or in ill health do not develop optimally in such an environment (Wille, 1991). The small child, such as Salina, who is more fussy or difficult than another might evolve a particularly conflictual relationship with her stressed parents. Other small children whose cognitive skills are not well developed are less able to make sense of a chaotic situation and may become difficult. *An environment strained by poverty can be detrimental to adults who are less adaptable than others and to small children who have a more difficult temperament–*

the combination of environment and personality. Such vulnerable children also constitute another stressor for their already burdened mothers and, as a consequence, may not receive enough attention from mothers to help them overcome their predispositions or develop adequate coping skills.

Poverty affects children before birth. It deprives many infants of a healthy fetal development and of a wholesome diet after birth; for babies born to urban poverty, their fragile physiological system may be burdened by the noise of an overcrowded apartment.[39] Conditions of overcrowding exist in rural areas as well, where large families may live in cramped quarters in a shack; but here at least, as children grow, they may have more open and less dangerous space to explore and move into beyond the family dwelling. Moreover, poverty in rural areas is less mired in neighborhood violence, gang activities, and homicides with firearms (Fingerhut, Ingram, and Feldman, 1992). A vast literature has accumulated indicating a causal relationship between poverty and negative child outcome.[40] To balance this, more studies are needed that examine what happens to parents and children when they escape poverty. Indeed, research indicates that young children who live in persistent economic hardship develop more problems than those whose poverty is temporary (McLeod and Shanahan, 1993). In turn, the latter have more problems than children who have not experienced poverty (Bolger, Patterson, and Thompson, 1995).

Another important element interacting with family poverty is the extent to which the neighborhood itself consists of economically deprived households (Jencks and Mayer, 1990). Mothers who are poor have little choice as to the quality of the neighborhood they move into.[41] Klebanov, Brooks-Gunn, and Duncan (1994) show that in addition to being disadvantaged themselves, mothers who live in a poor neighborhood provide a less optimal physical environment for their three-year-olds, and are less warm and responsive toward them than poor mothers who live in a neighborhood that is economically mixed. However, maternal characteristics and resources available to the household were more important variables than neighborhood poverty in terms of promoting the small child's learning experience, which, as discussed in Chapters 6 and 7, is also disrupted when adolescent children attend very disadvantaged schools or live in a particularly deprived neighborhood (Brooks-Gunn et al., 1993).

The level of community violence also has a tremendous impact on child development,[42] and on the parent-child relationship (Osofsky, 1995). In disrupted inner city neighborhoods, perhaps one-third of all school-age children have witnessed a homicide and perhaps as many as two-thirds have witnessed an assault (Bell and Jenkins, 1993). Mothers feel helpless about protecting their children,[43] and often have to resort to overprotectiveness to achieve this goal.[44] Osofsky and Fenichel (1994) are concerned about an increased risk of psychological vulnerability among such children. Moreover, these same youth also become potential recruits for gang and drug activities where the cycle of community violence perpetuates itself.

QUALITY OF THE PARENTS' RELATIONSHIP

The quality of the couple's relationship before the baby's arrival is a good predictor of the later quality of this relationship and of the quality of the parent-small child relationship.[45] There is often a decline in marital happiness after the arrival of the first child; but this shift in marital satisfaction occurs more often when the couple already had differences prior to the birth (Cowan et al., 1991). When parents have a good marriage, the mother-small child relationship is warmer and the mother is more nurturant toward her baby.[46] Actually, fathering may be affected even more than mothering by the quality of the marriage (Goldberg and Easterbrook, 1984). Babies and small children whose parents get along well exhibit fewer behavioral difficulties than those whose parents are in a stressful, conflictual marital situation (Belsky and Isabella, 1988).[47] There are several complementary explanations for these results, but before we examine them, it is important to mention that these results may not apply in cultures where fathers and mothers, men and women, live largely separate lives, and where the definition of the marital relationship may not include affection, companionship, and even discussions concerning the children. It may, instead, revolve around patriarchal authority. We do not know what effect, if any, the marital relationship may have on child development or on parent-infant interactions in these types of societies.

Now, in our society, how do we explain this correlation between a happy marital relationship and warm parenting? The more frequently discussed explanations or mediating processes are strictly environmental. They inform us that a supportive marriage provides a context that is personally rewarding and that allows for the utilization of energies to good ends, such as child care. The supported and loved mother lives in a warm environment that translates into a close and attentive relationship with one's child (Belsky, 1984). In contrast, when marital conflict exists, parents are stressed, feel unappreciated, and may be less able to transfer loving feelings to their child. Child-rearing may be disrupted,[48] and parents may agree less with each other in terms of child care (Lamb, Hwang, and Brody, 1989). Moreover, the difficulties these mothers encounter with their partner may drain them so much that they are often inconsistent in their reactions to their child's demands and misbehavior (Easterbrook and

Emde, 1988). On the other hand, there are mothers in unhappy marriages who maintain a wonderful relationship with their baby. The pleasure that the mother derives from her interaction with her child can compensate for her marital problems (Brody, Pillegrini, and Sigel, 1986).

A second explanation for the positive effect of a good marriage on the parent-child relationship is closely related to the first one. A warm marriage provides family circumstances that are peaceful and secure, and allows room for the exploration of caring relationships and for the development of a secure and better regulated child. In contrast, an openly conflictual marriage produces a family environment that is less secure and can be downright disharmonious: It can be filled with recriminations, sharp verbal exchanges, disrespect, fear on the part of the most vulnerable spouse,[49] long periods of sulking silence, and even physical violence. This is an environment that contains more stressors than rewards, thus life satisfaction is low. Third, this context can teach children that this is a normal way of living and of resolving conflicts (Grych and Fincham, 1990). Small children who are already predisposed to hyperactivity, nervousness, or aggression may be particularly vulnerable to marital stress and may acquire **dysfunctional** behaviors by observing and modeling their parents' interaction (Burman, John, and Margolin, 1987). Children with a more sedate personality may be unhappy but their development is not otherwise derailed.[50]

The fourth explanation goes one step beyond the usual environmental discussions (Erel and Burman, 1995). This added explanation resides in assumptions about personality and temperament. Let's pursue here the example of a conflictual marriage; such a union may arise because the two parents have problematic personalities, are difficult to get along with, do not like to compromise, or are aggressive.[51] Even if only one of the parents is like this, unless the other one has a submissive personality, the marriage is likely to be unstable. Therefore, if a mother is impatient, irritable, and has little tolerance for frustration, she may exhibit these patterns toward her child as well, and the same holds true for the father. This would explain why, in conflictual marriages, the parent-child relationship is less warm and more erratic *and* why the babies and children in these families experience more adjustment difficulties, anxiety, and behavioral problems. Such children live not only in conflictual familial circumstances, but with parents who are difficult to be with in terms of their interpersonal styles. The reverse linkage takes place in a peaceful marriage.

A fifth and complementary explanation flows from the above. It resides in genetic and environmental considerations (Reiss, 1995). Parents who are more aggressive by nature, have little tolerance for frustration, are impatient, not easy to get along with, and consequently have a conflictual marriage, may well pass at least some of these unfortunate traits via genetic inheritance to their children (Plomin, 1994b; Rowe, 1994). The result is that some of these babies may themselves be more fussy and irritable, and may later become more oppositional, hyperactive, and aggressive than children who are born to parents who are warm, patient, cooperative, and who consequently have a stable relationship. Babies who are irritable and not easily comforted will grate on a parent's nerves, especially when the parent is also irritable and when marital conflict is frequent. This situation will lead to a less positive relationship, in addition to reinforcing the baby's predisposition–thus there is an interaction between the child's personality, the parent's personality, and the low quality of the marriage. As the baby grows into a small child and is by disposition overly active, and perhaps defiant and aggressive, he or she will interact with similarly disposed parents who will adopt an erratic and rejecting pattern of child-rearing. Moreover, they will provide the example of a tumultuous relationship, which, in turn, may contribute to exacerbate the child's negative innate tendencies.[52]

What one sees here is that the behavioral manifestations of parental genetic characteristics become part of the children's environment, both as child-rearing styles and as marital styles. In turn, not only do children inherit some of these genes, but, when they are negative, their own behavioral manifestations of these inherited traits elicit a negative reaction from parents and this reaction then becomes part of the children's environment. In turn, these two genetically created environments interact with each other and result in parent-child relationships of lower quality as well as more negative child outcomes or adjustment (Reiss, 1995). Therefore, behavior genetics theories complement and mesh with environmental and interactional perspectives, one of the topics of the following chapter.

CONCLUSION

The parent-infant relationship and early development take place within a context that is both internal to the parents and infants–in this case their respective personalities–and external to them. In families where there are two parents, the environment initially consists of the parents' relationship. It is also influenced by the age of the mother, especially when she is still a child herself. This proximal environment is in turn influenced by various other environmental factors, as well as by the economic situation both of the family and of the neighborhood.

In the parent-child relationship, there is a constant interaction between the personalities involved, the relationships they create, and the environment that supports or stresses them. Personalities and environments create relationships, child-rearing practices, and child development. Infants are not pieces of clay that parents mold, but they are born with characteristics to which parents respond. Parents and infants cocreate their relationship and child outcomes, although infants simply act and react without the ability to make decisions or plan. They are social actors but are not responsible for the reactions they unwittingly elicit. This lack of conscious intent, however, does not make infants less effective nor less active as tiny social actors.

ENDNOTES

1. Belsky and Rovine, 1990. See Featherman, Spenner, and Tsunematsu (1988) for the frequency of change in father's social class when children are between 0 and 6 years of age. See Duncan (1988) for income change.

2. Certain topics that are currently salient in the small child literature are not discussed in this chapter. The most obvious omission is the issue of attachment for which an enormous literature exists. The following publications are suggested: Ainsworth, 1973, 1979; Bowlby, 1969, 1973, 1980; Bretherton and Waters, 1985; Parkes, Stevenson-Hinde, and Marris, 1991; Seifer et al., 1996. All child development (normal and abnormal) journals carry articles on this issue: *Child Development, Journal of Abnormal Child Psychology, Infant Behavior and Development, Journal of Clinical Child Psychology,* and *Journal of Child Psychology and Psychiatry* are the primary ones.

3. A few suggested references are Collins and Gunnar, 1990; Pervin, 1990; Peterson, 1992; Strelau, 1987; Thomas and Chess, 1989; Watson and Clark, 1992. See references in Chapter 4.

4. For a discussion of the neurochemistry of personality, see Davidson, 1992; Kagan, 1994; Pope and Katz, 1994; Zuckerman, 1995.

5. For a good introduction to genetics within the context of child development, see Berk, 1994.

6. The same applies to menarche: see Meyer, Eaves, Heath, and Martin, 1991, although psychological factors may also have an impact: Graber, Brooks-Gunn, and Warren, 1995.

7. These are the first signs of what is called parental attributions or belief systems. See Bugental and Shennum, 1984; Kochanska, 1990; Sigel (Ed.), 1985.

8. This is studied in Chapter 3.

9. We include here legal marriages, cohabitation, homosexual or heterosexual unions, and parents who live separately.

10. **Goodness of fit**: Chess and Thomas, 1984.

11. Belsky, Fish, and Isabella, 1991; Lytton, 1977, 1980.

12. Chess and Thomas, 1984.

13. van IJzendoorn et al., 1992.

14. Kochanska, 1993.

15. See, also, Kochanska, 1995. This element becomes important for Chapter 11 in terms of conduct disorders.

16. The variable of immigrant status, for instance, will undoubtedly become more salient in future research as both the U.S. and Canada host large refugee and immigrant populations, some illegal. In addition, more and more of these arrivals belong to visible minorities, and some are very poor.

17. Lamb and Teti, 1991; van IJzerdoorn et al., 1992.

18. Congressional Budget Office, 1990.

19. The majority of children born out of wedlock are born to women 20 and older. Adolescent mothers account for 30 percent of such births (*Footnotes*, 1995, 23, pp. 1 and 6).

20. Roosa and Vaughn, 1984.

21. This may be especially so for younger than older small children: Nitz, Ketterlinus, and Brandt, 1995.

22. Ketterlinus, Henderson, and Lamb, 1991.

23. For a review of the literature on some sequelae to very low birth weight, see Zelkowitz et al., 1995.

24. Eggebeen, Crockett, and Hawkins, 1990.

25. For a review, see SmithBattle, 1996.

26. For an exception, see Elster and Lamb, 1986.

27. Seymore et al., 1990; Parke and Neville, 1987.

28. Danziger and Radin, 1990.

29. See books edited by Bozett and Hanson, 1991; McAdoo, H. P., 1988; Also, McAdoo, J. L., 1988; Taylor, Chatters, Tucker, and Lewis, 1990; Tucker and Taylor, 1989, among others.

30. Duncan, Smeeding, and Rodgers, 1991.

31. Schuerman and Kobrin, 1986; Taylor and Covington, 1988.

32. Ambert, in press.

33. U.S. Bureau of the Census, 1993a.

34. Statistics to this effect are detailed in Chapter 9.

35. Two issues of the *American Journal of Orthopsychiatry* contain several articles on homelessness (July and October, 1995).

36. Toro et al., 1995; Toro and Wall, 1991.

37. Bruce, Takeuchi, and Leaf, 1991; Kessler et al., 1994.

38. Duncan, Brooks-Gunn, and Klebanov, 1994.

39. Evans, Hygge, and Bullinger, 1995.

40. Elder et al., 1992; Patterson et al., 1992; Zill and Coiro, 1992, among others.

41. Smith and Thomson, 1987.

42. See Garbarino et al., 1992; Marans and Cohen, 1993; Osofsky et al., 1993; Reiss et al., eds., 1993.

43. Lorion and Saltzman, 1993.

44. Ibid.

45. Belsky, Lang, and Rovine, 1985; Fleming et al., 1988; Lewis, Owen, and Cox, 1988.

46. Belsky, Fish, and Isabella, 1991; Cowan, Cowan, and Kerig, 1992; Gable, Belsky, and Crnic, 1992.

47. This observation may hold more for boys than girls–Reid and Crisafulli, 1990.

48. Fauber et al., 1990.

49. Generally the wife, but some husbands also fill this role.

50. See the section on resilient children in the next chapter.

51. Or, yet, they may be too different: Gable, Crnic, and Belsky, 1994.

52. Plomin et al., 1989.

Chapter 2

The Relationship Between Parents and School-Age Children

As children age, they gain access to new environments that contribute to their individual development and modify their relationship with their parents. With the advent of maternal employment on a nearly universal scale in most Western societies, children come into contact with external agents of socialization at a younger age than children of the 1950s and 1960s. External influences render the parent-child relationship less exclusive, less intense than it was when the child was younger, more limited to after-school home situations, and during weekends and holidays.

This chapter focuses on the expansion of the child's world and how this may affect the dynamics of family interactions and child development.[1] Day care is introduced, but not discussed at any length because it is not a universal feature in children's lives. The school system is mentioned only briefly because it is a key focus of Chapter 7. Another important, determining environment that school-age children and their parents encounter is the neighborhood, and this topic is integrated within several chapters, including this one. The other external influence encountered very early in children's lives is the mass media, to which a substantial section is devoted. Then in order to continue building our theoretical model, chapter by chapter, the interactional perspective, already broached in the previous chapter, is presented in greater depth. A section on resilient children adds further dimensions to this perspective, and it is complemented by a discussion on the impact of gender on the parent-child relationship.

THE ROLE OF DAY CARE

While most children remain home with grandmothers, neighbors, nannies, or baby-sitters, others are cared for by a woman who baby-sits a few children at her home to earn additional income. A good number of other children enter an institutional day care which closely resembles a mini-school system. Preschool and kindergarten are becoming widespread and also serve as day care. A substantial proportion of small children have several day care arrangements: 35 percent have more than one care provider (Folk and Yi, 1994). Hence, by the time children reach school age, they often have extensive experience with caretakers, teachers, and peers.

When the quality of day care and preschool is high, children's outcomes are comparable to those of children reared by their mothers (Clarke-Stewart, 1987a).[2] In contrast, poor quality day care of the warehousing type prevents children from fulfilling their potential, exacerbates negative child dispositions, and may strain parent-child relationships (Phillips et al., 1987). It also seems that children who experience low-quality day care in their *first* year are more at risk of developing problems than other children (Howes, 1990).[3] Bronfenbrenner (1990) questions the benefits to small children of being shifted from one place to the next several times a day. At the very least, such a hectic pace may not be suitable to small children who are already fussy.

In very deprived neighborhoods, quality day programs, such as Head Start, can compensate for the limitations and stressors of the home and neighborhood environment. This is found to be particularly so among black children who are very disadvantaged (Lee, Brooks-Gunn, and Schnur, 1988).[4] One of the founders of Head Start, Edward Zigler (1995), recommends that children at risk be reached before they are three or four years of age.[5] Day care can also help parents acquire skills by offering support, direct training, or simply by providing competent caretaking role models. Howes (1990) reports that attachment to a qualified day care worker can compensate for an insecure relationship with a parent. Unfortunately, the fact remains that an astonishing majority of children who are in day programs receive care that does not meet standards for optimal development (Galinsky et al., 1994).[6]

THE IMPACT OF SCHOOL

Formal schooling is certainly the most potent new context that young children encounter. It transforms their developmental path, and it affects the parent-child relationship; unfortunately, the research is very sparse on the latter point. School-age children generally acquire a larger social network as well as "roaming" territory. Their social and cultural world expands and becomes more diversified and here begins the importance of the **nonshared environment,** that is, the environment that children do not share with other family members. They come into contact with people who may be very different from their parents in terms of lifestyle, social status, values, and beliefs, especially if they attend a school located outside their neighborhood or in a nearby town. School bussing for desegregation purposes, for instance, may represent the first opportunity that children have to be with people of another racial or ethnic group, or another social class, and with people who may have different ways of interacting. These new experiences not only impact on the child but they presumably have an effect on parents as well as on parent-child interactions.

Thus, the fabric that constitutes the parent-child relationship at that age is woven with threads of more varied colors and texture than was the case in early childhood. School acts as both day care and educational institution and thus gives more personal freedom to parents and children. School also imposes a routine on parents and children. There are school hours, a school season and vacation periods, books, uniforms or clothes that the child wants to wear to be in style, and teachers who send report cards–teachers whom a parent may want to meet or avoid.

While school-age children are granted more autonomy by their parents than younger children, they also encounter new restrictions resulting from this greater autonomy. Parents may begin to voice admonitions concerning certain peers and even impose restrictions. They may also be concerned about school work, and may begin to monitor their children's whereabouts more carefully in terms of the immediate neighborhood. This monitoring becomes especially salient when neighborhoods and schools are deemed unsafe and constitute what could be called a negative social capital for the family (Coleman, 1988). In such cases, parents may have to keep children at home more than either parents or offspring would want (Furstenberg, 1993). Tensions can arise, especially when overcrowding exists.

MASS MEDIA

The third context explored in this chapter is the role that the mass media, particularly television, plays in the parent-child relationship as well as in child development. In the midst of many others, there are two main research themes concerning television and children: the effect of television violence on the development of aggressiveness, and the effect of television viewing on school performance. Before discussing these, it is important to mention that there is little research in this domain that has much bearing on the parent-child relationship at any age level.

Television Violence

The average child witnesses 8,000 murders on television by the end of elementary school (Waters, 1993). The first studies in the 1960s and even the 1970s established that there were **correlations** between television violence and aggressive behavior in school-age children. That is, the more violence children watched, the more aggressive were their behaviors on average (Liebert and Sprafkin, 1988). But a correlation does not mean causality. For a while, it was believed that aggressive boys selected programs that were more violent, an explanation that is certainly valid to some extent,[7] just as peaceful people are often repelled by violence and therefore will not choose to watch it (Friedrich-Cofer and Huston, 1986).

In the 1980s, researchers began to harvest the results of **longitudinal studies** and found that young adults tended to act more aggressively when they had watched more violence as eight-year-olds. In fact, the correlation between aggressiveness and the viewing of violence on television was even stronger than it had been at age eight. Boys who had *not* been aggressive at age eight but had watched more television violence had become more aggressive young adults than a similar group of nonaggressive boys who had watched fewer episodes of violence (Huesmann et al., 1984). Such results indicate that it is not only a predilection for aggressiveness that leads children to select television violence but that this violence also leads to aggressiveness. A second follow-up of the same sample showed that the effect persisted into adulthood. By age 30, men who had watched more television violence as children had been convicted of more serious crimes, were more likely to treat their children harshly, and were more aggressive when drunk than men who had watched fewer violent programs as youngsters.

In an intriguing study, Joy, Kimball, and Zabrack (1986) compared three Canadian towns, one of which did not receive television transmissions until 1974. They tested the children before and two years after the introduction of television. The children in the town that had received television two years earlier showed a much higher increase in aggressiveness than the young in the other two towns. In addition they exhibited a sharp increase in sex-role stereotyping (Kimball, 1986).[8]

Television violence may "produce" aggressiveness in a proportion of children, and later on adults, via several possible routes. First, violence may teach children that conflict can be resolved only with verbal or physical aggressiveness. Second, it may lead them to develop a lower threshold for frustration, so that they tolerate irritants less easily and react to them more explosively. Third, television violence may desensitize children and adults as to the severity of its consequences, so that even killing can appear routine.

Whatever the explanation, the consequences may be even more detrimental for minority group children who live in distressed neighborhoods. In a large study of eighth graders across the United States, Muller and Kerbow (1993) found that, during weekdays, African American parents restricted television less than other groups, including Asian Americans and whites.

Television and School Achievement

The second aspect of television viewing that has been extensively studied is its effect on school achievement (Fine, Mortimer, and Roberts, 1990). Studies indicate that children who watch more television have poorer grades at school (Corteen and Williams, 1986). Several explanations have been provided that are probably complementary. The first is that children who spend a great deal of time in front of the television set have less time to read as well as to do homework. Another is that, in contrast to reading, television viewing is a more passive leisure activity (Larson and Richards, 1994:35). Moreover, it may lower a child's attention span because its content is segmented, short, and punctuated by ads. None of these factors are conducive to doing well in school. In contrast, educational programs for small children such as Sesame Street encourage learning and reading (Huston and Wright, 1994).

Hence, what is detrimental to school achievement may be the low quality of television content and the manner in which programs are structured. Programs that merely aim to entertain may actually shorten children's attention span for classroom material. In examining the content of stand-up comedians' jokes from the 1960s to the present, one notes that the length of their jokes has decreased so that one-liners are now standard as opposed to longer monologues thirty years ago. Older comedians attribute this evolution of their style to a lowered attention span among their audience.

Effect on the Parent-Child Relationship

Even with all the evidence in, there were ideological factors among researchers and policymakers that prevented them from pointing the finger at television as a contributor to the development of aggressiveness. One is our society's idolatry of freedom of speech: Once it is accepted that television violence may be damaging in terms of human development, the next logical step is to censure it to some extent; however, liberal ideologies of both free speech and free market competition would not condone this, even though several attempts, influenced by a more conservative political ideology, are currently underway. Second, researchers of early studies were convinced that aggressiveness begins "at home," that is via parents' example and treatment of children. Such a belief indeed precludes searching for alternative explanations and policies.

Whenever experts give conferences on these issues, they unavoidably remind the public that parents have to exercise control over what programs children view, and that they should discuss potentially detrimental contents with children. The entertainment industry follows suit and squarely places the entire responsibility on parents' shoulders.[9] How this responsibility affects parents and their relationship with their children is not addressed. At least one observational study has shown that in a supermarket (a public place), 65 percent of all parents' denials for food advertised on television instantly resulted in parent-child conflict or arguments (Atkin, 1978). One can then wonder what takes place in the privacy of the home when parents attempt to curtail television viewing. It is true that many parents use television as a baby-sitter after school and during weekends, even though most are concerned about what their children view. Monitoring television is especially important for children who have emotional or intellectual problems that make it difficult for them to differentiate fantasy from reality (Sprafkin, Gadow, and Abelman, 1992). Perhaps the best approach is to limit television viewing from the time children are very small; when they reach school, they will be used to this restriction. At that point, rational explanations by parents would be helpful. Maccoby (1984) has emphasized that it is easier to adopt an authoritative parenting style early in a child's life rather than later.

Another gap in the literature on the effect of media is pointed out by Abelman and Pettey (1989): parental attributes, such as child-rearing practices, are used as a mediator variable for the correlation between children's antisocial behavior and the viewing of violence. In contrast, Abelman and Pettey utilize children's attributes, such as IQ, and find that they affect to some extent *parents'* behaviors concerning their children's television viewing. Moreover, it would be interesting to find out if children who watch a great many violent episodes are less compliant at home, and if they are more oppositional and aggressive toward their parents than other children. Generally, children's aggressiveness is observed among their peers or is reported by teachers, but is not researched in relation *to* parents. The study of the effect of television violence in this respect would add important dimensions to research on family dynamics.

THE INTERACTIONAL PERSPECTIVE

Above all else, this chapter highlights the large gap that exists in the research literature on the effect of external influences, such as day care, the school system, and television, on the parent-child relationship. The emphasis of the literature is placed on the role that parents play or should play toward monitoring children's viewing habits, for instance. While this is a reasonable focus, it is far from a dynamic one and it is also unidirectional. In the introduction to this book, it was stated that conceptualizations of child development have been heavily influenced by theories emphasizing the role that parents play in children's development. Until recently, children were seen as the product of their parents' child-rearing practices and behaviors (Ambert, 1992). It is consequently unavoidable that teachers and researchers would adopt this line of thinking in regard to schools or the media. In the school environment, the parents' role is believed to have a large impact on children's achievement. Consequently, the way in which the schools affect parents and parent-child interactions is largely ignored. Moreover, how school-age children can impact the parent-child relationship is a question that used to fall completely outside the purview of developmental theories. The same line of reasoning applies to television: Parents are given the burden of responsibility. *No question is asked about the impact of television on their ability to parent.*

In contrast, another theoretical and empirical literature has emerged that examines the effect of children on parents,[10] particularly on marital happiness,[11] which has been hypothesized to vary depending on the child's temperament (Belsky, 1981).[12] An additional step has led to the development of theories positing that parents and children affect each other reciprocally (Buss, 1981).[13] This perspective has been introduced in the previous chapter with the recognition that what eventually creates a child's outcomes resides in the interaction between that child's traits and behaviors and the parents' approach or reaction to the child (Lytton, 1990) within particular contexts (Lerner, 1982; Lerner and Kauffman, 1985). In this sense, children contribute to their development.[14]

It follows that, while there are parents who tend to be punitive and distant, they will be more so toward a child who is moody and irritable, and less so toward a quiet youngster (Rutter and Quinton, 1984)–and again more so in the presence of serious stressors such as divorce, poverty, and unemployment (Webster-Stratton, 1990). Parental irritability may then increase child moodiness and contribute to the development of additional problems, hence the interaction between parent and child effects (Lee and Bates, 1985). In addition, it can be assumed that parents who do not have extreme and rigid personalities will be more likely to adopt inductive methods of control toward children who are easy, intellectually receptive, and prosocial than toward more difficult children (Ambert, 1995). In turn, warm parental control contributes to a higher level of school and peer success in these cooperative children (Ladd, 1992). In this circular process, "individuals are creating their own interpersonal environment at the same time that they are being shaped by this environment" (Maccoby and Jacklin, 1983:83).

Parents and children influence each other, whether negatively or positively (Downey and Coyne, 1990),[15] and, consequently, when the mutual reinforcement is maladaptive, negative child outcomes are more likely to follow.[16] This perspective is widely accepted at the theoretical level. However, empirical research still emphasizes the effect that parenting practices have on child outcomes, disregarding the role played by children themselves (Russell and Russell, 1992).[17] *There is therefore a substantial gap between theory and empirical application*, in part because of the difficulties inherent in designs that examine reciprocal effect,[18] although there are several exceptions.[19]

The interactional perspective can be taken one step further. For instance, Greenberger and O'Neil (1990) report that when parents perceive that their children are more difficult, they experience a higher level of strain in terms of their roles as workers and as parents. Perhaps as a result, such parents, especially mothers, feel more depressed. These authors point out that children who are difficult or are perceived to be difficult make parents' lives more unpleasant. "Further, parents are likely to internalize responsibility for their child's behavior" (1990:632). Greenberger and O'Neil also believe that there is probably another interactive effect in that parents who perceive their children as difficult are not only adversely affected outside their family lives, such as in their work, but in turn, problems in other aspects of their lives may lead them to view their children as more difficult. At that point, child difficultness becomes an additional burden less easily tolerated by an already stressed parent. On the other side of the equation, "the easy-to-rear child can compensate for limited personal resources on the part of the parent in maintaining parental effectiveness" (Belsky and Vondra, 1989:188).

In summary, the interactional perspective emphasizes the interrelatedness between various factors that affect human development as well as relationships. It is a dynamic that views parents and children as active social actors, reacting to and affecting each other while also reacting to and acting upon their environment (Lerner and Busch-Rossnagel, 1981; Magnusson, 1990). In this text, a greater emphasis is placed on genetic influence in conjunction with the environment than do interactional perspectives in general, although there are exceptions.[20]

RESILIENT CHILDREN

The literature on resilient children extends into the interactional perspective and also links with behavior genetics. Although there have not been many studies on this topic, the few that exist clearly indicate that a good number of children do well in the face of adversities such as war, family violence, abuse, poverty, and divorce (Garmezy, 1983; Garmezy and Masten, 1994). These children possess certain personal resources that help them cope and protect them from stressors: cognitive competence, an easy temperament, the ability to form at least one sustaining relationship, and self-esteem.[21] A positive self-concept has also been included in this list of protective factors.[22] Dubow and Tisak (1989) show that children with high problem-solving skills are less likely to develop behavior problems as a reaction to stressors.[23] Children who are very competent intellectually cope better in conflictual homes than less skilled children (Rutter, 1979). One study reports that intellectual ability protects teenage mothers' children against academic problems, but not against behavior problems.[24] High self-esteem, however, imparts resilience against both risks. Other research has linked high achievement to lower levels of anxiety (Zigler and Glick, 1986). Such children, however, may have other vulnerabilities (Freeman, 1995). Compared with less well-endowed siblings, resilient children weather family stressors more adequately,[25] This is not to say, however, that such children would not have been happier and would not have developed more optimally had their environment been less stressful (Luthar, 1991). A good environment obviously benefits even resilient children.[26]

Infants who have difficult personality characteristics, and are at risk rather than resilient, react more stressfully to noise, overcrowding, and later on to the birth of a sibling (Dunn, Kendrick, and McNamee, 1981).[27] Older children with a difficult temperament are more vulnerable to stress (Elder, Caspi, and Nguyen, 1994). Traits that are not valued in our society, such as shyness,[28] may also serve a protective function against the development of behavioral problems in criminogenic areas or families.[29] As Barber (1992:75) points out, some personality characteristics "could be a protective or a risk factor depending on the environment it is coupled with." Adolescents' ability to plan for the future as opposed to impulsiveness may lead to the pursuit of education and the delay of reproduction,[30] hence again opening rather than closing opportunities into adulthood.

Resilient children create for themselves an environment that allows them to function adequately, protects them, and offers them compensations. This is referred to by geneticists as the **active genotype-environment correlation**, whereby individuals choose opportunities to reinforce their dispositions. *But opportunities have to exist,* however minimal they may be, again indicating the importance of the environment in interaction with personality. In fact, some authors extend the concept of resilience to include social resources that act as protective factors.[31] But as Hetherington (1991) has pointed out, resilient children are more able to seek and utilize support and resources in times of stress. We therefore retain only the *personal* resources element or characteristics as markers of resilience (Robins et al., 1996). Otherwise, environmental variables become confounding variables and dilute the importance of personality factors.

GENDER OF CHILD AND PARENT

One key element in people's lives is how society constitutes gender. The variable of gender and some of the ideologies that surround it is a topic that underlines several points throughout the chapters of this book. Gender is an element of the parent-child relationship that has lifelong implications in that parents relate to their offspring on the basis of the children's gender; fathers do so more than mothers. Moreover, as we see in some chapters (such as 12 and 13), children also react differently to fathers and mothers. Therefore, gender roles are at the root of many parent-child interactions.

To begin with, it is still a fact in our society that couples prefer having a son for their firstborn child (Krishnan, 1987). This gender preference often continues over the life time of the child, though it may be expressed in subtle forms, usually by fathers. Lamb, Pleck, and Levine (1987) note that fathers play more with sons and supervise their activities more than those of daughters. They talk more to sons and take them on outings more frequently (Marsiglio, 1991). When fathers have sons, they are more involved with their children in general. In fact, when there is a son in the family, even a girl benefits because girls receive more attention from their father when they have a brother than when they have no brother.[32]

One indirect consequence of this greater involvement of fathers in families that have sons is that wives are happier with their husbands,[33] and get more help from them. Consequently, these families are more stable than families with only daughters, even when the marriage is unhappy (Heaton and Albrecht, 1991). This latter finding may also explain why there is a greater proportion of divorced couples with only daughters than with only sons (Morgan, Lye, and Condran, 1988). Noncustodial fathers who have sons stay in contact with their children more than fathers who have daughters only. We do not know, however, if sons born to never-married mothers have more contact and receive more attention from their fathers than daughters. It is a reasonable assumption that they do. If this were the case, such a father-son relationship might act as a buffer in deprived neighborhoods. Or if the father is an inappropriate role model, he can constitute an additional element of risk for the son.

In spite of this preference on the part of fathers for sons, sons report that they are closer to their mothers than to their fathers (Noller, 1994). They also confide in mothers more, as do daughters.[34] This preference for mothers is pursued into adulthood.[35] In great part, this stems from the fact that mothers spend more time than fathers on child care and continue to be more involved in the basics of children's daily lives when they reach adolescence (Larson and Richards, 1994). Therefore, mothers are recipients both of more love and confidence, and, as is seen in Chapter 12, of more aversive behaviors from their children (Buhrmester et al., 1992). Adolescent sons are particularly conflictual toward their mothers. In fact, the presence of the father diminishes conflict between mothers and sons (Gjerde, 1986). Hyperactive sons, for instance, tend to be more negative and less compliant with mothers than fathers.[36]

CONCLUSION

External influences penetrate more deeply into family life as children age and come into contact with a wider social environment. School-age children have to navigate a more complex world than the one that sheltered them even the previous year. In turn, this means that parents also have to adapt to their children's expanded contacts with the world and their growing cognitive abilities and autonomy. The parent-child relationship evolves accordingly. In this chapter, we have emphasized that this relationship becomes more complex and even more difficult because, among other reasons, parents are expected to play the main role regarding the monitoring of their children's television viewing. However, given a reduction in television channels, greater ease of monitoring, and more educational programs, the parent-child relationship could actually be enhanced by this medium.

The interactional perspective continues to help us understand how parents and children affect each other, and how children cocreate the environment in which they live. Moreover, children who are resilient are better able to withstand adversity. Very little is known about the process whereby resilient children compared with more vulnerable ones negotiate the greater complexities and adversities of their expanding social and geographic world.

School-age children's newly developed cognitive and social skills allow them to pursue greater autonomy while at the same time still seeking close contact with their parents. These skills also allow them to develop various coping mechanisms and use them more effectively in order to maximize what they can get from their environment, including their parents. The primary school years serve as a bridge between early childhood and adolescence in terms of the parent-child relationship and human development. Patterns of behavior and of interaction are developed that often herald the adolescent years to come.

ENDNOTES

1. Books of particular interest on a child's social world, as well as the child's role and interpretation of his or her world are, from several theoretical perspectives, the following collections edited by: Belle, 1989; Lloyd and Duveen, 1990; Prout and James, 1990; Richards, 1974; Richards and Light, 1986; Wertsch, 1984.

2. But there still are a great many contradictions in the research. For example, see Howes and Stewart, 1987; Phillips, McCartney, Scarr, and Howes, 1987, versus Haskins, 1985.

3. For a review, see Belsky, 1990.

4. For a review, see Sylva, 1994.

5. Zigler and Styfco, 1993.

6. Extensive references to the impact of day care on child development can be found in the following journals: *Child Development, Early Childhood Development and Care, Families in Society: The Journal of Contemporary Human Services, Journal of Children in Contemporary Society, Journal of Marriage and the Family,* and *Young Children.*

7. There are indications that the extent to which children watch television may be related partly to genetic predispositions: Plomin, Corley, DeFries, and Fulker, 1990.

8. Another Canadian study comparing a town with no television, one with a single channel, and one with four channels found that high school students' community and sports activities declined most in the community with four channels: Williams and Handford, 1986.

9. Some help is available in Canada and forthcoming in the U.S. with a "V" chip inserted in television sets to allow parents to block out offensive programs.

10. Ambert, 1995; Bell, 1968; Bell and Harper, 1977.

11. Belsky, 1984.

12. Stoneman, Brody, and Burke, 1989; Wilkie and Ames, 1986; also, Umberson, 1989.

13. Ambert, 1992, 1995.

14. Tinsley and Parke, 1983.

15. Plomin, 1994b; Scarr, 1994.

16. Sanders, Dadds, and Bor, 1989; Thurber and Snow, 1990.

17. See Peterson and Rollins, 1987.

18. McGurk, 1992.

19. For example, Anderson, Lytton, and Romney, 1986; Barkley, Karlsson, Pollard, and Murphy, 1985; Brunk and Henggeler, 1984; Patterson, Bank, and Stoolmiller, 1990; Simons, Whitbeck, Beaman, and Conger, 1994.

20. Lerner, 1978, 1991.

21. Anthony and Cohler, eds., 1987; Masten, 1989; Radke-Yarrow and Sherman, 1993; Rutter, 1985; Werner and Smith, 1982. For a review, see Luthar and Zigler, 1991.

22. Compas, 1987; Garmezy, 1983; Werner, 1985, 1990.

23. Losel and Bliesener, 1990.

24. Dubow and Luster, 1990.

25. Rutter, 1979, 1987.

26. Rutter, 1987; Werner and Smith, 1992.

27. Langmeier and Matejcek, 1975; Wachs, 1987.

28. Kagan, 1994.

29. Farrington et al., 1988; McCord, 1988.

30. Clarke and Clarke, 1992; Rutter, 1989.

31. Moen and Erickson, 1995; Schaefer and Moos, 1992.

32. Harris and Morgan, 1991.

33. Barnett and Baruch, 1987.

34. Collins and Russell, 1991.

35. Rossi and Rossi, 1990:279.

36. Tallmadge and Barkley, 1983.

Chapter 3

The Parent-Adolescent Relationship

There is a great deal of scientific and lay interest in adolescence, in part because it is the bridge between childhood and adulthood, and therefore an important life stage.[1] Under the influence of psychoanalytically oriented theorists such as Blos (1979) and Anna Freud (1969), adolescence has been, until fairly recently, considered to be a naturally stormy and stressful period during which children disengage themselves from parents. As if to support this popular view, a percentage of adolescents do cause a great deal of problems for parents, society, and themselves. They consequently receive media coverage and attention from professionals. In contrast, well-functioning adolescents do not receive much publicity. It is not surprising that adolescent-related problems loom large in the concerns of the public and professionals alike.

In this chapter, after a brief introduction to what adolescence is and is not, the focus is on parenting practices, both as one aspect of the parent-adolescent relationship and as determinants of outcomes or, if you prefer, as influences on how adolescents turn out to be. Parent-adolescent conflict, parental influence, and the necessity to make adolescents accountable for their actions are then discussed. Additional material on the teen years is presented throughout Chapters 5 to 15. In order to emphasize depth rather than breadth, several topics germane to the study of adolescents have been omitted: Among these are dating and sexual activity, homosexuality,[2] drug use, and educational aspirations. Moreover, the much discussed issues of autonomy and independence have been left aside.

THE NATURE OF ADOLESCENCE

Adolescence is referred to as the period between ages 12 and 18 or 19. The beginning of adolescence is generally determined by the onset of puberty, that is, the development of primary and secondary sexual characteristics in males and females. These developments are underlined by hormonal changes. The end of adolescence, however, is socially determined, and takes place earlier for females than males in most societies. Everywhere in the world there is a stage of biological puberty, although the age of onset varies depending on life conditions, such as nutrition. A poor diet, for instance, is likely to delay the onset of menarche. However, what is important to underscore is that this period of physiological puberty does not give rise to an identical psychological puberty throughout the world (Schlegel and Barry, 1991). The "storm and stress" **ideology** concerning adolescence does not apply universally, but is still a widely held belief (Holmbeck and Hill, 1988). Margaret Mead (1928), the famed anthropologist, was the first to document the fact that the problematic type of adolescence frequently encountered in North America, and which is becoming more common in most Western countries, does not exist in all societies of the world. At that time, her research was going against the grain of prevailing ideologies. But in the last two decades, most qualified anthropologists, sociologists, and psychologists have reached the same conclusion. "Teenagehood" is a historical phenomenon (Modell and Goodman, 1990). The historians Kett (1977) and Demos (1971) have placed the invention of adolescence as a social category between 1890 and 1920–after most youngsters were pushed out of the labor market and into the school system, separated from the adult world which they had been part of until then (Sebald, 1992).

As emphasized by Steinberg (1990), it is important to distinguish between the fact that our society often presents a perturbing context for adolescents and the supposition that adolescence is in itself "naturally"– thus necessarily–a period that is difficult, stormy, and in opposition to the adult world. We do not minimize the depth of the crisis that afflicts a good number of adolescents, but we also recognize that this crisis is in great part created by the type of environment that has evolved in North America and in other English-speaking countries–not by the nature of adolescence in general. In the United States, Montemayor (1986) estimates that over one-third of adolescents pass through difficult times. However, it should be noted that a good proportion of these teenagers are experiencing problems that already afflicted them in childhood (Steinberg, 1990). One cannot therefore blame adolescence for all the problems encountered by adolescents.[3] Many of these youth will remain problematic as adults: They are problematic *persons* rather than problematic adolescents.

Nevertheless, most clinicians and many researchers, as well as the majority of teachers and laypersons, still cling to the notion that it is "natural" to be rebellious, to have a messy room, and so on, during adolescence. Many medical doctors even tell adolescents that it is "normal" to have secrets from one's parents. And the good doctor should, of course, be told of these secrets. (This professional expropriation of parental authority is discussed in Chapter 8.) These beliefs in the naturalness of adolescent problems are dangerous because they often prevent those teenagers who are truly perturbed from receiving much needed help (Offord, Ostrow, and Howard, 1987).[4] Moreover, these ideas prevent society from making adolescents accountable for their actions and placing maturity demands on them. These beliefs also force parents to accept and suffer painful and useless rebelliousness, and prevent them from making adolescents responsible for their participation in family dynamics.

Adolescence, as it is defined, is what is called a **social construct**. It is an ideology that meets neither the needs of adolescents nor those of their parents (Ambert, 1994b). This ideology has served the purposes of an industrial capitalist economy by keeping children and women at home so that they would not compete for the smaller number of jobs left after mechanization had taken over. But it is still too early to tell whether it is a useful ideology to the postindustrial economic order of the twenty-first century. During recent decades, industrialization and the opening of new world markets have meant that graduating high schoolers could find jobs in various industries, most particularly the auto industry, without additional postsecondary education. With the advent of computers, while new opportunities have been created, skilled and trained personnel have been the main beneficiaries of this technology. The recent restructuring of the economy, in what is known as "downsizing," has also meant additional job cuts at all levels. Consequently, higher education is now even more necessary and, as we see in the next chapter, adolescence, when it is characterized by financial dependence on parents, is extending far beyond age 18.

PARENTING PRACTICES AND PATTERNS

Parenting practices are one of the cornerstones of the parent-adolescent as well as the parent-child relationship.[5] This topic occupies a large segment of researchers, both in child and adolescent development. The purpose of this literature is to link proper ways of parenting to positive child outcomes. It rests on the assumption that the child's family environment determines his or her development. Although others had preceded her, Baumrind was the early initiator of a more sophisticated formulation of this aspect of the parent-child/adolescent relationship and of all those studies that correlate parenting styles with outcomes in youngsters. Three styles were first determined: authoritative, authoritarian, and permissive.[6]

Parents who are authoritative combine both warmth and respect for their children's individuality with monitoring of their activities and whereabouts. Such parents explain to their children the reasons behind their demands; their method is inductive. Once they have explained the reasons and the consequences, they follow through with enforcement of the rules. Authoritative parents are firm. This child-rearing style is one that is high both in warmth and monitoring—two variables that have been correlated with successful child and adolescent outcome in all types of family structures in North America and other countries (Steinberg and Darling, 1994). Of all parenting patterns, the authoritative one correlates the most with good adjustment both in children and adolescents on all dimensions of development (Steinberg et al., 1992).

Parents who are authoritarian rather than authoritative are particularly controlling, although some may also be quite warm. What predominates is the dimension of control and arbitrariness. Parents tell their children what to do and may punish severely and indiscriminately. Others are mainly restrictive (Kuczynski and Kochanska, 1995). Still others are erratic in terms of control: They threaten, then punish one day, but fail to follow through the next day. This type of discipline is not as effective because children resent it and can take advantage of its inconsistencies. However, while it is not so effective for European-American adolescents, it is more acceptable in other cultural contexts (Hong, 1989); restrictive control may even be useful in certain milieux that are particularly criminogenic or disadvantaged (Baumrind, 1972).

For its part, permissive parenting involves a very low level of control, lack of supervision or monitoring, and little parental involvement in making maturity demands on children or adolescents. It can be combined with either a high level of warmth and acceptance or with disinterest and even rejection. Low parental control and rejection is a combination that has been consistently related to a host of negative outcomes, including delinquency and drug use (Baumrind, 1991b). They are the opposite of support and control or monitoring (Patterson, 1992).[7] Subsequent to Baumrind's identification of permissive child-rearing, another style of parenting was added: uninvolved parents (Maccoby and Martin, 1983). Such parents are both permissive and indifferent or permissive and rejecting. For one reason or another, they prefer to have as little as possible to do with their children in terms of providing them with structure. The result is that children are both unsupervised and may feel that they are unloved, which may well be so in extreme cases. Such parents fail to set rules concerning school, behavior at home, or activities with peers. Their adolescents tolerate frustration poorly, are more likely than others to be underachievers, and to become delinquent; they lack emotional control and long-term goals as well as purpose in life (Baumrind, 1991b; Lamborn et al., 1991). At the extreme, such parents are called neglectful.[8]

Bronfenbrenner (1985) indicates that parental permissiveness has more negative consequences than authoritarianism in times when there is cultural and social instability.[9] Baumrind (1991a:114) pursues this line of reasoning by pointing out that "in a context of social instability, caregivers are required to sustain a higher level of supervision than would be needed in a period of stability." In a decade such as the one we live in, there are more dangers that confront adolescents than was the case 30 years ago. Consequently, "premature emancipation is perhaps a greater threat to mature identity formation than delayed separation from family attachments" (Baumrind, 1991a:115).

ORIGINS OF PARENTING PRACTICES

Returning to the discussion on genetics and the environment, combined with the interactional perspective initiated in the previous chapters, parenting styles and adolescent outcomes can be examined from a vantage point that is not yet widely used in sociology and psychology. First, it should be recalled that the statistical correlations that have been established between the various parenting styles and child/adolescent outcomes are not overwhelmingly high and leave plenty of room for explanations that provide a different causality path. In the literature, parenting style is the environmental variable that "causes" the child and adolescent outcomes. Although researchers generally accept the caveat that correlations do not imply causality, the fact remains that the results are generally interpreted causally, as reflected in the use of words such as "effects" and "predictors" of child outcomes with reference to parenting activities. Three possible influences on parenting styles will be examined. *They are complementary rather than mutually exclusive*, and flow from the theoretical perspectives used in this book.[10]

Parental Adaptation to Children

First, there is the obvious possibility that many parents adapt their child-rearing practices to fit their children's behaviors and personalities.[11] There are several examples of this process of adaptation in the research literature on children but not on adolescence, although the study by Simons et al. (1990) on parents' perceptions of how difficult their adolescents are follows this line of reasoning. For instance, when hyperactive children are successfully treated with the drug Ritalin, their hyperactivity diminishes substantially, and mothers modify their parenting style accordingly and become less controlling (Tarver-Behring and Barkley, 1985).[12] In another study, mothers of normal and difficult-oppositional children were paired in an experimental situation with a difficult child (not their own) and then with a normal child (not their own). Both types of mothers exhibited more controlling and intrusive behavior with the oppositional child than with the cooperative one (Brunk and Hengeller, 1984).[13]

There is therefore some evidence that average parents adapt their parenting practices to their children's behaviors, thus supporting the interactional perspective (Corter et al., 1992). And there is every reason to believe that parents also adapt to their adolescents' personalities and demand for independence. But one caveat is necessary here: Parents who are overly stressed, or have a rigid personality, or suffer from emotional problems, may not be able to adjust to their changing adolescents or they may treat them inappropriately.[14] For instance, parents who hold extreme values of success may resort to destructive parenting practices (Simons et al., 1990).

Another way of looking at this is that adolescents contribute to the development of their parents' child-rearing style. For instance, children and adolescents can influence their parents to become coercive or rejecting,[15] even if they do so unconsciously (Patterson, 1986). Adolescents may disobey, talk back, threaten to run away, fail to return home, and may be disrespectful. These behaviors can lead parents to become more forceful. If they attain a higher level of compliance and a certain degree of peace at home when they are authoritarian or just controlling, then they may retain this more forceful approach. Others may simply avoid contradicting their youngsters, who will then be the recipients of a permissive parenting style. Examining this path of behavior more carefully, it becomes obvious that it has been initiated by the adolescents, perhaps even long ago while they were children. Moreover, adolescents who are cooperative may produce an effect on the scores for authoritativeness received by parents (Lewis, 1981). From this perspective, it can be said that *adolescents coproduce the parental child-rearing practices of which they are the beneficiaries or the victims* (Patterson, 1986), as well as the scores that their parents receive on measures of child-rearing practices.[16]

Adolescents can turn off positive parental gestures just as adults can turn off positive spousal behaviors. Indeed, Simons et al. (1994:359) point out that "rebellious, antisocial children often punish parental efforts to monitor and discipline while reinforcing parental withdrawal and deviance." Even normal adolescents do this occasionally. Patterson, Reid, and Dishion (1992:11) observe that it is difficult to monitor the whereabouts of an adolescent who is extremely coercive. Patterson (1982) even discusses the possibility that some children or adolescents may be genetically predisposed to be less responsive to social reinforcers such as praise or punishment; this predisposition would understandably make it difficult to raise them properly.

One could also ask if inductive methods, generally used with the authoritative parenting style, which are believed to be the most appropriate generally, are equally effective for all adolescents. For instance, adolescents who are less skilled intellectually may not benefit from inductive methods because these appeal to a person's ability to reason and to grasp an explanation. A youngster who is less skilled intellectually or who is oppositional may benefit more from a simple, direct order followed by an appropriate reward than a couple of explanatory paragraphs. This might also apply to children who suffer from an attention deficit disorder, as well as those with certain emotional problems. In fact, the literature indicates that schizophrenics become confused when overly stimulated (see Lefley, 1987). It may be that *gentle* authoritarianism could be more appropriate in these instances as it requires less independence and reasoning on the part of individuals who already are at a deficit intellectually or psychologically. This would have important intervention ramifications for professionals. Curtner-Smith and MacKinnon-Lewis (1994) also cite some literature indicating that a certain level of authoritarianism may act as a deterrent in environments that expose youth to deviance and violence.[17] Moreover, it is possible that certain types of children, perhaps as they get older, resent any type of control. Thus they perceive even inductive methods as being highly coercive.[18]

One can argue that, for parents, there are greater *personal* rewards in the use of warm and inductive methods of control than in the use of coercive ones, especially for educated parents, for whom the inductive style may come more naturally. Coercive methods restrict a parent's lifestyle, are stressful, tiring, and for some may even be health-threatening. In contrast, inductive methods are more adult-like, more stimulating, more peaceful.[19] These possibilities can lead to the hypothesis that, *given the opportunity* and the appropriate personality and cultural context, *parents choose inductive methods*. By and large, it is the children themselves who provide the opportunity, depending on their characteristics and their behavior. Environmental factors such as peer influence and a parent's stressful life situation are also important determinants. This section does not preclude the possibility that many parents simply adopt a style because of their own personalities.[20]

Genetic Influences on Parenting Styles

This possibility returns to the behavior genetics model which states that, in biological families, adolescents resemble their parents on some traits. As mentioned in Chapter 1, parents who adopt a peaceful, warm, supportive, and yet monitoring style may do so because they are predisposed to such behaviors (Simons, Beaman, Conger, and Chao, 1993). At the same time, their adolescents may be cooperative and well adjusted, not *just* because of the constructive parenting behaviors, but because they also share some of these traits with their parents—what will be discussed as the **passive genotype-environment correlation** in Chapter 14. These traits are in part caused by genes, and the same genes influence the traits that lead the parents to adopt authoritative practices. In turn, these traits are reinforced by the home atmosphere created by the parenting style, to which both parents and adolescents contribute.

A wide range of adult personality configurations can lead to authoritative parenting. In other words, different types of genetically influenced configurations allow for the development of such a style of parenting. By the same token, another range of personality configurations makes it impossible for adults to become authoritative parents. Consider a man who is easily frustrated, impatient, and impulsive. Such a man, because of his personality, is more likely to become an authoritarian and even harsh, rejecting parent rather than an authoritative one. In turn there is a good chance that his children will show some of these genetically influenced traits and will trigger bouts of impulsive parenting in him, especially when he is under stress. But if one of his children has an easy personality (inherited from the mother, perhaps), this child may trigger fewer bouts of impulsive parenting, and may be called a resilient child (previous chapter). Such an adolescent would have a better relationship with the father than would his more impatient and reactive siblings.

Environmental Influences

An important causal mechanism in terms of child-rearing practices resides in environmentally induced stressors, particularly poverty, unemployment, marital conflict, divorce, and social isolation. Granted that some of these factors are at times related to genetic influences; nevertheless, research indicates that they tend to disrupt parental practices,[21] and make parents less responsive to adolescents' needs (Lempers, Clark-Lempers, and Simons, 1989). For instance, studies show that fathers' warmth decreases and irritability increases following unemployment (Elder, Caspi, and Nguyen, 1994). Other research indicates that stress experienced by mothers leads to a more erratic, punishing, disciplinary relationship with their children.[22] Lenton (1990:173) suggests that harsher disciplinary practices are explained by insufficient income, education, and unemployment, among other factors: "in families suffering such privations there is more stress; because there are fewer resources to help them cope; and because parents may also experience an erosion of their authority." Work overload and work stressors may also affect parenting patterns (Galambos et al., 1995).

One should consider Steinberg and associates' suggestion that authoritarianism may be more acceptable in certain cultural contexts than in others: "What may be experienced by adolescents as parental intrusiveness in some cultural groups may be experienced as concern in others" (Steinberg, Dornbusch, and Brown, 1992:729). Bronfenbrenner's (1988) person-process-context theory is particularly relevant in this respect because it indicates that one condition–in this case, parenting styles–may affect different groups, such as boys compared with girls[23] or Asian Americans compared to European Americans, in different ways.[24]

PARENT-ADOLESCENT CONFLICT

Parent-adolescent conflict is a topic that is important to consider if only because much literature is devoted to it (Smetana, 1995). Yet, much remains to be considered in this domain, perhaps from a more diverse set of perspectives.[25] Research indicates that parent-adolescent conflict generally pertains to daily routine events rather than key value issues (Smetana, 1989). In other words, there does not seem to be too much conflict, although both parents and adolescents report more of it now than in earlier years (Collins and Russell, 1991). It has been argued elsewhere that the low rates of conflictual relations reported by both adolescents and especially parents in North America appear paradoxical in view of the great number of problematic child and adolescent behaviors such as self-reported delinquency, official delinquency, violence, drug use, precocious sexual activity, unplanned teen pregnancies, as well as emotional and learning problems (Ambert, 1995). Surely, parents cannot be happy about these. Even if their own children are not involved, these activities may lend a bitter taste to many parent-adolescent interactions because parents may fear that their children will follow the example of other youth. In addition, the recent unfavorable employment situation of young adults often forces a prolonged dependency on parents, well beyond the wishes of youth and parents. It is difficult to reconcile these potentially conflict-producing facts with a low level of tension between adolescents and parents.[26]

One explanation, as Barber (1994:384) suggests, is that "the absence of conflict over controversial topics such as sex and drugs [. . .] most likely means that parents and adolescents do not discuss these issues, rather than they have no differences in attitudes about them."[27] It is also possible that a distinction between overt and covert conflicts might shed some light on this situation (Collins, 1990). Overt conflict would occur when arguments or fights take place. This may perhaps be the type of conflict measured by studies. But *covert* conflict in which parents are silently angered or disappointed and do not dare or do not want to express such feelings may be more prevalent, yet not measured, *thus leading to an underestimation of parent-adolescent conflict, or, at the very least, of parental frustration.*

Another explanation, provided by Demo (1992:115), is that parents and adolescents "spend very little time together, often not more than one hour per day of direct interaction." In fact, both boys and girls begin participating less in family activities early in adolescence (Hill et al., 1985a,b). While parents' and adolescents' reports on time spent together are somewhat discrepant,[28] they spend only a few minutes each day *talking* (Youniss and Smollar, 1985). There may be a wide variety of situations that adolescents experience and parents never know about, thus reducing the potential for conflict. It is at least logical that, when adolescents' behaviors are at odds with parental wishes, they try to carry on as much of their lives as possible without their parents' knowledge. Moreover, parents are busier than previous cohorts of adults used to be, are generally employed, and many work even longer hours than just a decade ago to make ends meet (Schor, 1991). High rates of divorce and other problems such as alcoholism, spousal abuse, and mental illness mean that many parents are so preoccupied by their own personal difficulties that they overlook their children's. These factors diminish parenting availability and monitoring, and henceforth reduce parent-adolescent friction.

Montemayor and Hanson (1985) as well as Larson and Richards (1994) report that adolescents experience less conflict with their fathers than their mothers partly because mothers interact more with them concerning the basics of their daily lives. The household division of labor based on gender roles places mothers at a disadvantage over fathers in this respect. In this same vein, Collins (1990) reviews studies illustrating that when mothers interrupt their adolescents during a discussion, the youngsters subsequently interrupt her even more, but do not do so for fathers. Yet, all studies indicate that adolescents are also closer to their mothers than their fathers (Noller, 1994).

Rueter and Conger (1995:446) point out that parent-adolescent conflict has more negative results in families that are less warm and supportive. They add that "from early to middle adolescence, parents and children in families with an established pattern of warm and supportive interactions [. . .] reported fewer and fewer disagreements with one another." The contrary takes place among less flexible, critical, and coercive families.[29] It is believed by some researchers that disputes within a supportive family context contribute to strengthen the parent-adolescent relationship (Anderson and Sabatelli, 1990). However, parent-adolescent conflict is related to adolescent drug use in research by Brook, Whiteman, and Finch (1993) and to school underachievement in research by Robin, Koepke, and Moye (1990). We cannot presume the direction of causality in these results.

Pasley and Gecas (1984) found that 62 percent of the mothers and 64 percent of the fathers in their study perceived adolescence as the most difficult and stressful stage of parenting. This may be particularly so for a first-born adolescent.[30] Gecas and Seff (1990:943) concluded that for "the parents of adolescents, therefore, adolescence may indeed be a time of storm and stress, at least in modern times." It is also certainly the most financially demanding period for parents (Oppenheimer, 1982).

At the high school level, one interesting area that may have an impact on the quality of parent-adolescent conflict or harmony is suggested by statistics indicating that a large proportion of adolescents hold a part-time job. So far, most studies have examined adolescent part-time work in terms of school achievement and personal development (see Fine, Mortimer, and Roberts, 1990).[31] For our purposes here, other interesting lines of research involve adolescent employment and the quality of relationship with parents (Greenberger and Steinberg, 1986). One could hypothesize that there is a correlation between the numbers of hours worked and the quantity and quality of contact with parents. Also, Steinberg, Fegley, and Dornbusch (1993) found in a longitudinal study that high schoolers who worked over 20 hours[32] weekly had, even before they began working, more permissive parents than others who worked fewer hours.

Such results indicate that the link between number of hours employed and certain parenting styles should be explored further. Adolescents who work more hours may be home for shorter periods of time. This could lead to low parental control (Steinberg and Dornbusch, 1991). In addition, both they and their parents may reason that adolescents should be allowed to do what they want because they earn their way in terms of discretionary spending.[33] Finally, the *types* of work adolescents engage in and the *contexts* of this work have not been sufficiently examined in terms of their possible impact on the parent-adolescent relationship and adolescent outcome.

The *reasons* for adolescents' part-time employment may also have an impact on or stem from family relationships. For instance, there may be a difference in family atmosphere between adolescents who save for their college education or help their parents provide for the family compared with those who spend all their money on unnecessary items.[34] The latter case would be particularly relevant in situations where parents are relatively poor and deprive themselves of necessities while their adolescents indulge in expensive consumer activities. One would also expect to find more parent-adolescent conflict when employment hours are correlated negatively with grades. Indeed, parents may have difficulty convincing their teenagers that their first duty is to their studies.

THE HISTORY OF PARENTAL INFLUENCE

An issue that is rarely addressed is the likelihood that parents influence their adolescents differently according to prevailing sociohistorical conditions (Rossi and Rossi, 1990). In other words, *there are periods when it is easier for parents to influence their youngsters and others when it is far more difficult to do so.* This could be the case for two reasons. First, social change ushers in new influences on adolescents' lives and diminishes other influences. Fifty years ago, there was no television, but that medium has long since been considered to be a prime agent of socialization. In contrast, religion was then a more powerful influence than it is now throughout all regions and social classes. Therefore, certain adolescent outcomes may be more or less strongly affected by parents than was the case 50 or even 20 years ago, because of the presence or absence, strength of weakness, of a variety of other influences.

Second, as our society changes, it places a premium on certain specific outcomes (Alwin, 1986).[35] For instance, mainstream Anglophone culture[36] currently values self-esteem,[37] educational achievement (to the detriment of learning, perhaps), and autonomy.[38] While these outcomes may be affected by parents, they are also mediated by peers and school, as well as by partly innate factors such as cognitive ability and hyperactivity. A few decades ago, more importance was give in child-rearing to politeness, obedience, conformity, or patriotism (Alwin, 1990). Parents were probably more influential in these respects because these outcomes require direct teaching or example more than is the case for outcomes that are more personality driven such as self-esteem and independence. Thus, how these formerly valued outcomes develop and who influences them may differ compared to the development of more recently emphasized outcomes. Hence, we can say that the impact of parents on adolescent development is historically and ecologically grounded, thus changing with the societal contexts (Bronfenbrenner, 1989).[39]

As Gecas and Seff (1990) remind us, we need to have recourse to a more historically oriented and value grounded (Miller, 1993) perspective in the methods we utilize and the conclusions we draw from our studies. This would allow us to be conscious of the outcomes we choose to study and those we neglect, and to search beyond parents for causes. For instance, when studying the influence of television on youngsters, researchers have overwhelmingly emphasized its impact or lack thereof on acts of violence.[40] Yet television may influence adolescent *values*–a topic that is more difficult to grasp methodologically, although this is not a valid excuse to largely ignore it. Television may well affect self-esteem, for that matter, as teenagers probably find it difficult to compare themselves favorably to their idols who are invariably rich, attractive, popular, and well-developed physically while remaining slim.

Further, the study of the linkage between adolescent development and parental behaviors generally fails to consider the prior history of the parent-child interaction and family dynamics (Steinberg, 1990:257; Wharf, 1994). In most research, adolescent outcomes are segmented from child outcomes when, in reality, a life course perspective should be utilized to illuminate the trajectories across these life stages. The question remains: What are the childhood dynamics that have contributed to adolescent development (Bronfenbrenner, 1988:41)? It can also be noted that studies of adolescent outcomes fail to consider the influence of siblings,[41] and this, in turn, has strong implications for clinical practice.[42] Siblings are considered in Chapter 5.

CONCLUSION

This chapter concludes with the suggestion that the parent-adolescent relationship might be facilitated if adolescents in general were made to take responsibility for their behaviors rather than depend on their parents. At the very least, adolescents would not suffer from this approach and parents' tasks would be facilitated. By giving adolescents more accountability for their actions, parents would have fewer opportunities to have recourse to coercive methods of control. Adolescents who take responsibility–for instance, by contributing to the household functioning (Call, Mortimer, and Shanahan, 1995)–may not need to be controlled because they are willing agents. Similarly, children and adolescents, even young adults, who have learned to respect proper rules of interaction as well as to value learning would allow teachers more time for substantive teaching because the latter would spend less time admonishing and controlling their classes.[43]

At another level, it would be more appropriate in clinical practice to focus on adolescents themselves, as well as their peers, rather than their parents. One reason for this is that peers are important influences at that age level (Sabatelli and Anderson, 1991). Another is that adolescents' insight is greater than that of small children. So is their will–for, as discussed earlier, adolescents can consciously evade, refuse, or discourage parental attempts to socialize them. Hence adolescents might benefit from an intervention strategy that helps *them acquire skills that would lead to a greater cooperation in their own upbringing*. Stahler, DuCette, and Povich (1995) present a clinical intervention program that assigns responsibility to adolescents as well as parents. It is important to redress this imbalance, especially prominent in clinical writings, where parents are blamed for all the ills affecting their adolescents and are held responsible for all their misbehaviors–even when the misbehavior results from disobedience. Parents have to be empowered and greater maturity demands should be placed on adolescents as they pass from one age level to another and as their abilities grow or have the potential to grow.

Indeed, our society may have evolved too many loopholes allowing children and adolescents to grow up without learning to resolve interpersonal irritations other than by swearing or resorting to physical violence, recently including the use of weapons. It may be that too many youngsters are no longer adequately taught how to accept reasonable rules, control their temper, tolerate low-level frustration, and delay gratification (Webster, 1993). Such issues need to be addressed, not only within the family, but within the child's larger environment, including the audiovisual media. A concern as a researcher is that if we do not redress these trends quickly, those adolescents who are volatile and aggressive (and their numbers are growing) will increase the number of tomorrow's negligent and abusive parents, with all the attendant devastating consequences with which we are already familiar.[44]

ENDNOTES

1. There is a vast literature on adolescence and several journals focus specifically on this topic. For example, *Journal of Adolescence, Journal of Early Adolescence, Journal of Adolescence Research, Journal of Research on Adolescence, Journal of Youth and Adolescence*. In addition, the *Journal of Marriage and the Family*, and *Family Relations* regularly publish articles on adolescence.

2. We note a special issue of *Developmental Psychology* on sexual orientation: Jan. 1995.

3. Rutter et al., 1976.

4. Garbarino, 1989:687.

5. For a distinction between the concepts of parenting style and practices, see Darling and Steinberg, 1993.

6. Baumrind, 1967, Baumrind and Black, 1967.

7. See Crouter (1994) for correlations between monitoring of boys in dual-earner families and positive outcomes.

8. For a further refining of parenting patterns into seven types, see Baumrind, 1991b.

9. See also Noller and Callan, 1991.

10. Parental attributions as an influence on child-rearing practices are acknowledged but not discussed. Within our perspective, they could be attached to either or both explanations provided in the text. On parental attributions, see Bugental and Shennum, 1984; Dix and Lachman, 1990; Geller and Johnson, 1995; MacKinnon-Lewis and Lamb, 1992, among others.

11. We do not know if fathers and mothers differ in this as well as in other respects discussed in these sections (Starrels, 1994).

12. Barkley et al., 1985.

13. See Chapter 11 for additional examples of studies on parental adaptation to children.

14. See Elder and Caspi, 1988; Lempers, Clark-Lempers, and Simons, 1989; Radke-Yarrow, Richters, and Wilson, 1988.

15. See also Belsky, Robins, and Gamble, 1984.

16. We see more on this in Chapter 12.

17. Lamborn et al., 1991; Steinberg, Dornbusch, and Brown, 1992.

18. See Amato, 1990.

19. See Henry and Peterson (1995) on a related issue.

20. There may be some support for this in Steinberg et al.'s findings, 1994.

21. Ge et al., 1994.

22. Conger, Patterson, and Ge, 1995; Webster-Stratton, 1990.

23. Cowan et al., 1991. Moreover, the parent's gender may also be a key variable in interaction with the child's gender.

24. Bronfenbrenner and Crouter, 1983.

25. Laursen and Collins, 1994.

26. For a perhaps more realistic study, see Larson and Richards, 1994. This naturalistic study shows higher levels of daily tension than questionnaire surveys do.

27. Gehring et al., 1990.

28. Larson and Richards, 1994.

29. Hill, 1993; Paikoff and Brooks-Gunn, 1991.

30. Small, Eastman, and Cornelius, 1988.

31. See Mortimer, Shanahan, and Ryu, 1994.

32. The cutoff point above which academic problems arise in the United States; it may be lower in Canada because of homework requirements. One of the risks involved in a demanding part-time job is that homework suffers–and time spent on homework relates to educational attainment: Luster and McAdoo, 1996.

33. *Newsweek*, November 16, 1992.

34. This question is being explored by Shanahan, Elder, and Burchinal, in press; see also Elder, Foster, and Ardelt, 1994.

35. Demos, 1971; Modell and Goodman, 1990.

36. Many immigrant groups emphasize other characteristics, such as conformity: Okagaki and Sternberg, 1993.

37. Perhaps not a good thing when carried to excess. See Baumeister, Smart, and Boden, 1996.

38. Lesthaeghe and Surkyn, 1988. See also two interesting studies arriving at different results on the role of adolescent autonomy in outcomes depending on the context of the parent-child relationship: Fuhrman and Holmbeck, 1995; Lamborn and Steinberg, 1993.

39. Bronfenbrenner, Kessel, Kessen, and White, 1986; Elder, Modell, and Parke, 1993a:3 and 1993b:243; Gergen, 1973.

40. See Chapter 2.

41. Bryant, 1989.

42. Pelletier-Stiefel et al., 1986.

43. See Wentzel, 1991.

44. See Chapter 10.

Chapter 4

The Relationship Between Parents and Adult Children

As children reach adulthood, parental responsibility declines and, in our society, parental authority generally disappears. Children become functionally independent, establish a residence, and earn their livelihood separately. The parent-adult child relationship continues but unfolds along different lines for each party, and becomes more reciprocal (Wintre, Yoffe, and Crowley, 1995).[1] Similarly, the parenting role is maintained but within a changing context (Seltzer and Ryff, 1994).[2] This chapter completes the life span approach that is the focus of the first part of this volume. It begins with a demographic perspective on young adulthood, and follows with an overview of the parent-young adult relationship. It then inquires into the continuity of the relationship over time. One of the underlying factors for this continuity may be personality stability, and this is the topic of a subsequent section. The chapter then moves on to middle-aged children and to the help that elderly parents receive from and give to their adult children. Elder abuse by adult children is also discussed.

CHANGING YOUNG ADULTHOOD: A DEMOGRAPHIC PERSPECTIVE

The timing of the passage into adulthood, or full adulthood, may be changing (Hogan, 1980). Adolescence now extends into the early part of adulthood for a portion of the population: As a *social* stage, it starts earlier and finishes later than it did 50 years ago. While adolescence as a social construct was the invention of the dawn of this century, young adulthood is the creation of the closing of the twentieth century. Because of the increasingly prolonged education that is required to make a decent living in Western societies, young adults, aged 19 to 23 and even 25, often remain financially dependent on their parents. While parents have to give freedom to their adolescents, regarding sexuality for instance, earlier than before, they have to remain active in a *supportive* role, both morally and financially, for a far longer period than was the case previously in this century. This duality of freedom and dependence can result in a conflict-generating situation, both for young adults and their parents. Until now, families and researchers have accepted the problematic aspect of this situation for youth, but have failed to appreciate the fact that more and more parents are looking forward to acquiring *their* independence—from their grown children!

In 1990, 74 percent of 18- and 19-year-old young Americans lived at home with their parents, as did 40 percent of the 20 to 24 age bracket, and 16 percent of those between 25 and 29.[3] Note the large drop-off after age 19. College students who are away from home, but have not actually left home "for good," are included as no longer living with their parents (Buck and Scott, 1993). Therefore, during holidays at least, a much greater proportion of young Americans live with their parents and remain financially dependent on them. In Canada in 1991, among the unmarried, 44 percent of men and 33 percent of women between 25 and 29 lived with their parents (Boyd and Norris, 1995); this compares with only 20 percent ten years ago. Statistics Canada also informs us that in 1991, 672,495 adult children over 25 lived with their parents compared with only 414,000 in 1987, or a 62 percent increase. Therefore, in a substantial number of families, the parent-young adult relationship is marked by coresidence, at least for a period of time[4] and, when young adults leave home, they increasingly make a transition to independent living rather than to marriage: The age at first marriage is later than it used to be just a decade ago.

Why do young adults stay home longer and marry later? First, we have seen that youth remain in the educational system longer. Second, between 1979 and 1989, the development of the service economy and the shrinking of the manufacturing base has resulted in an increase in part-time and low-paying jobs for young people, while full-time wages have declined in comparative value.[5] The result is that from 1979 to 1989, the proportion of males aged 18 to 24 who worked full-time in low-paying jobs jumped from 18 percent to 35 percent and the proportion for women jumped from 29 percent to 43 percent. This situation is even more acute for racial minorities, especially those living in inner cities (Bowman, 1990; Zinn, 1992). A similar development occurred in Canada. For example, in Quebec, it is estimated that 60 percent of young people between the ages of 15 and 24 who live alone are poor (Lazure, 1990). A third reason for the lengthening dependence of young adults may be related to the finding that in the United States, high school seniors endorsed more consumerist values in 1986 than in 1977 (Crimmins, Easterlin, and Saito, 1991). What were considered luxuries in the previous cohorts have become necessities for current ones. Consequently, the earnings required to reach such heightened material expectations come later, and, in the meantime young adults can afford them only when they remain with their parents.[6] Shehan and Dwyer (1989) also report that males between the ages of 18 to 21, more than females, think that it is their "right" to receive financial help from their parents. As Hareven (1994:448) points out, while in the late nineteenth century children remained at home to help the aging parents or the widowed mother, now "young adult children reside with their parents in order to meet their own needs." In fact, 20 to 29-year-old young adults are the age group of grown children most likely to receive parental support (Cooney and Uhlenberg, 1992).

THE PARENT-YOUNG ADULT RELATIONSHIP

In the recent past, parents, and particularly mothers, suffered from the "empty-nest syndrome." That is, after their children had gone, parents were lonely, did not know what to do with their free time, and sharply felt the pain of the loss of their parental role. Researchers even used to find that this empty-nest stage led to depression for mothers who were losing their primary, "natural" role in life, that of motherhood. Needless to say, feminism and the burgeoning participation of women in the labor force have cast a shadow on the validity of this perspective for current times (Gee and Kimball, 1987). Parents generally look forward to seeing their young adults settle down with a good job and later on with a family of their own (Clemens and Axelson, 1985). There are strong indications that adult children's departure is related to an improvement in the parents' marital relationship.[7] Other parents look forward to becoming grandparents because it generally is an easier role to play. Goldscheider and Goldscheider (1993a) suggest that parents' expectations are that they would like to live alone.

Still, myths die hard: According to a study, college students usually believe that their parents will be very lonely without them (Shehan and Dwyer, 1989). These students focus on problems that coresidence has for *them* rather than for their parents. Avery, Goldscheider, and Speare (1992) find that when parents' income is high, children delay their departure until their mid-twenties: The parental income helps them through both their college education and first job. At that point, parents' income can again be useful in helping them leave and establish themselves. For instance, parents can provide the down payment for a house or a business. Therefore, parental resources are used to prevent both premature and delayed departure. The same phenomenon is observed in Canada.[8] Goldscheider and Goldscheider (1993b) conclude that parental expectations are very important determinants of the timing of departure. In some cases, parents of young adults who are overly dependent may feel that it is their right and even their duty to force their children out so they can learn to fend for themselves and finally leave the parents alone. Obviously, in many instances, reality lags behind parental expectations.

It has become increasingly expensive to put children through college so that the financial burden has grown considerably and may follow parents into their own retirement. In Canada, tuition fees are considerably lower than in the United States, and a greater proportion of urban students attend college in their hometown.[9] The data are inconsistent and even contradictory when it comes to evaluating parental satisfaction with coresidence (Umberson, 1992). Parental stress is higher when the children are financially dependent, and lower when the interaction is positive and there is little conflict (Aquilino and Supple, 1991). There may also be differences by social class and race in terms of adults' satisfaction with parenting. There are indications that black mothers perceive their children to be less supportive than do white mothers (Umberson, 1992), possibly a question of income and resources differentials between the two racial groups.

As young adults age, their relationship with both parents is still an important variable for their psychological well-being (Barnett, Marshall, and Pleck, 1992). Even a good relationship with a stepfather counts (Amato, 1994). As they marry and enter full-time employment, the parental relationship becomes less salient for their well-being. There are gender differences in the sense that females continue to feel more connected to their parents than males (Frank, Laman, and Avery, 1988). Adult roles, then, are key elements in young people's personal identity and well-being.[10] Shehan and Dwyer (1989) identify four types of autonomy or independence that adult children reach: functional autonomy, attitudinal independence, emotional independence, and conflictual independence. The latter refers to the absence of excessive resentment or guilt in the relationship with one's parents (Hoffman, 1984). Children attain these various types of autonomy at different times and to diverse degrees. In our society, adults who are dysfunctional may never attain any of these forms of independence.

There are unfortunate young persons who are or become emotionally disturbed or who have a disability that forces them to remain under parental care or at least under the parents' roof. They fail to reach the independence we expect with the passage into adulthood. In terms of the life course, they are "off time" and will remain so. Parental expectations of maturity are shattered (Hagestad, 1986). These children cannot emancipate themselves from their parents or hold a job successfully. They may be unable to form intimate relationships with others and even to make friendships. The result is that their parents have to fulfill many roles for them. In other cases, these young persons live in a group home or by themselves but parents remain their main lifeline. Parents, especially as they age, may not only find their predicament difficult to bear, however devoted they may be, but worrisome. Some are concerned that their child is unhappy, or is being taken advantage of by unscrupulous persons; others have to live with the ever-present threat of the adult child's suicide or dangerous behavior. But, above all, the question that such parents ask themselves is: "What will happen to him [or her] when we get really old and after we die? Who will be responsible for him?"

The parent-young adult relationship is affected in subtle ways by the aging of parents. It is one thing to be 25 and have parents in their forties or early fifties who are healthy, busy, lead a full life, and can often help financially. It is quite another matter to be 25 when parents are 65 or 75. At that point, parents are retired, have more leisure time, may travel more, and may have moved into a smaller dwelling; many may be unable to help as much financially as younger parents, and others may already be ailing. Poor health sets the stage for a relationship where the young adult has to become helpful to the parents. This in turn may hasten the maturation process for the young person. While there are many studies on the relationship between elderly parents and their middle-aged children, as will be seen later on, there is a scarcity of research on the relationship between *young* adults and their aged parents or even stepparents. One can only presume that this latter type of research will become more salient as larger numbers of young adults come from families where a remarriage has taken place and where children were born at later parental ages.

Indeed, while child dependence lasts into young adulthood, parenthood increasingly occurs later in life. Not only do adults delay marriage and childbearing, but many divorce and have their first child or additional children in a remarriage. It is therefore not uncommon, for men particularly, to be taking early retirement at 55 or 60 and be the parent of a college-bound youngster. Only 20 years ago, retiring adults were already grandparents. Of course, this delayed situation occurs mainly in the upper-middle class rather than the working class where youngsters enter the workforce and start their families earlier than their more financially advantaged counterparts. In fact, among the more disadvantaged, childbearing begins even earlier, so that it is not uncommon for a woman to become a grandmother at age 30 (Burton and Bengtson, 1985). Therefore, while for the majority of our society various social stages are extending, for the less advantaged, and particularly for disadvantaged women, social stages are collapsing and people fill roles such as early motherhood and grand-motherhood before they are ready for them.

CONTINUITY IN THE PARENT-CHILD RELATIONSHIP

"Over time the roles of parents and child change, but they are never divorced from the history of the relationship" (Mancini, 1989:3). The relationship between parents and their young adult children is generally more harmonious than it was in adolescence (Thornton, Orbuch, and Axinn, 1995). However, very conflictual and/or distant relationships in late adolescence are likely to lead to a similarly unpleasant pattern between the ages of 19 and 30. In other words, looking at it **prospectively**, we can generally predict the quality of the parent-child relationship in young adulthood from the quality of the relationship in late adolescence.

There are two factors that explain this continuity of the adult relation-ship with that of late adolescence. First, the fluctuations that take place in parent-child interactions in early adolescence gradually disappear by late adolescence. When the early adolescent parent-child relationship was good, it survives that period and even improves in late adolescence, at a time when peer pressure diminishes, youngsters' personalities begin to stabi-lize, and parents are more willing to grant autonomy to their maturing children. Therefore, when children reach young adulthood, they generally have completed whatever stage of turbulence they might have encoun-tered, and they settle back to a harmonious parent-child relationship, as they had in childhood—what Rossi and Rossi refer to as the "sleeper effect" (1990:21). A second factor in the continuity of the quality of the parent-child relationship resides in the personalities involved. Because personalities guide patterns of interaction and are relatively stable after young adulthood, the personalities of parents and children add continuity to the relationship they developed earlier. Adult children and parents who have a history of severe conflict are not likely to change much in this respect, for it is possible that one or both parties are persons who are difficult to live with. It does occur, however, that departure from home and consequent reduced contact contribute to a lessening of conflict between the two generations: Parents no longer control some aspects of their chil-dren's behaviors, and the mature responsibilities taken on by young adults, especially marriage and parenthood, give them more in common with their parents (Baruch and Barrett, 1983). Until then, parents and children led lives separated by dissimilar roles. As these roles become similar, a greater mutual understanding between the two generations is possible.

THE ROLE OF PERSONALITY STABILITY

This section pursues the issue of personality stability and change as it impacts on the relationship between young adults and their parents.[11] Some schools of thought, such as psychoanalysis, propose that personality is set for life in the first two to five years of a child's existence and is mainly the result of parental child-rearing practices. Another school of thought sees a great deal of continuity in personality over the life course, but mainly from adolescence onward.[12] Others believe that we keep changing or at least have the potential to change until we die,[13] although the *range* of potential development may be genetically determined for most traits and abilities (Scarr and Carter-Saltzman, 1979).[14] Hence, the debate concerning stability versus change continues, both in terms of personality and behavior.[15] The discussion here only skims the surface of these issues as much as they are necessary for the purpose at hand. These issues are in turn related to the assumptions about human nature that theorists hold (Hjelle and Ziegler, 1992).

Studies indicate stability in some traits over time in a child's life, even through adulthood,[16] in such traits as shyness, aggressiveness and extraversion, and particularly traits that are extreme (Caspi and Silva, 1995). For most traits, stability is fairly high over a few years, for example when infants are studied at age one and then studied again two years later. But there is less continuity between ages one and seven because more years have elapsed. During these years, the child has passed from infancy to school age. In other words, much has happened to the child. In addition, the child has matured, thus allowing for the emergence of new coping mechanisms and for the obsolescence of old ones. But, still, the child will exhibit *some* continuity of personality, particularly in abilities such as intelligence, and temperamental qualities such as extraversion, activity level, shyness, and aggressiveness. This continuity often lasts into adulthood (Caspi, Bem, and Elder, 1989). Moreover, *some of these traits bring consequences for individuals and these consequences* or chains of events, as will be seen in Chapter 14, may strengthen these traits so that they become entrenched. For instance, there are studies on "dispositional optimism"[17] indicating that optimistic people have recourse to more adaptive coping methods and are more skillful at obtaining social support than others (Scheier, Weintraub, and Carver, 1986). One can immediately see that such people will be more successful and this success will in turn contribute to the maintenance of their optimistic disposition.

For other characteristics, if the child is again tested in adolescence and in young adulthood, the correlations between the most recent scores and these distant points from infancy and school age become smaller and there appears to be far less continuity. However, correlations between mid-adolescence and late adolescence become more substantial and so do those between late adolescence and young adulthood (McCrae and Costa, 1990). But, still, a measure of change takes place. Indications are that around age 30 in our society, people stabilize and have acquired all of their personality traits.[18] One would therefore expect that the relationship between parents and their adult children stabilizes when their child is between 25 and 32 years of age, or earlier in the case of individuals who have matured sooner. The quality of the parent-child relationship depends on the child's personality quite as much as on the parents' personalities. The relationship fluctuates over time to the extent that the child's personality and life situation keep changing, while, in comparison, parents' personalities are already stable, although their life situation continues to evolve.

One may ask why it is that personality changes so much from birth to young adulthood if it is in part genetically determined. First of all, genetically determined traits vary as to the age at which they are originally expressed. Also genes may actually trigger change, as in the case of those influencing the onset of puberty. Moreover, there are characteristics that are more environmentally induced and these are more likely to change. But, as mentioned earlier, certain temperamental qualities are more durable than others and these are also more genetically linked (Caspi and Silva, 1995).[19]

THE PARENT-MIDDLE-AGE CHILD RELATIONSHIP

This text adopts a life span perspective, even though the research we refer to is not generally longitudinal. One key aspect of such a perspective is that, by definition, it brings attention to the development of the relationship over time as *both* parents and adult children age (Hagestad, 1984). In order to truly study development, longitudinal designs have to be implemented. But studies focusing on the same sets of parents *and* children over time in order to follow their relationship are rare. In social terms, young adulthood lasts until the mid-forties at the very least, at which point we reach middle age. Old age begins at 65 because this is how it is defined in governmental statistics. The gerontology literature seems to have concentrated on the relationship of elderly parents with middle-aged children and has neglected adult children in their thirties and early forties and their parents, who may be anywhere from their late forties to their nineties.

Parents in their fifties and early sixties may still engage in many activities with their adult children and even their grandchildren. As a consequence, they have more opportunities to develop a peer-like or social relationship with their children. Moreover, since these parents are still employed, they may have reached the peak of their earning ability and may be in a position to help their children and grandchildren financially, whether directly or indirectly. Whatever their age, a majority of adults and their parents report having a good relationship and, when geographic distances are not too large, seeing each other fairly regularly (Connidis, 1989). Generally, the affection that exists between parents and adult children is the chief motivation in continued contact and exchange with parents (Rossi and Rossi, 1990). Lawton, Silverstein, and Bengtson (1994:65) point out that "the more parents and children see each other, the greater affection they will have for each other, and vice versa." This reciprocity of effect docs not apply to fathers, however. Lawton and colleagues concluded that "the motivations for interaction between adult children and their mothers and fathers are different."

Studies tend to present demographic characteristics to explain the quality of parent-child relationships: gender of parent and child, marital status, socioeconomic status, geographic distance, and parents' health status. To fit the interactional context of this book, more refined studies are needed that look at children's and parents' personality characteristics that could affect the relationship. Also to be considered is the matter of goodness of fit or congruence *between* the personalities. Is the parent-adult child relationship closer and warmer when the two have similar or complementary personalities? What if they are similar on traits that are not conducive to harmony, such as restlessness, aggressivity, and disagreeableness? What happens when the personalities are different but not complementary? Here one could think of poised, warm, and peaceful parents whose daughter may be irritable and verbally combative. Do these personality configurations produce a similar result whether the child is a son or a daughter? In other words, parents may have more difficulty getting along with a restless son than with a restless daughter, or the reverse. Or children can have more difficulty getting along with an intrusive mother than an intrusive father, or the reverse. These questions remain to be tested empirically.

In addition to personality, values, attitudes, and lifestyle must be considered. Although these are certainly influenced to a great extent by personality, they are also affected by **cohort** experiences revolving around peers, media, schooling, and other sociohistorical circumstances that may not overlap between the generations. Alternatively, it could be hypothesized that as adult children mature, their values will become more similar to those of their parents because they will have lived through similar experiences, such as getting married, having children, and undertaking work responsibilities (Rossi and Rossi, 1990). But it could as well be that the cultural and social environment of the child cohort is so different from that of the parent cohort that the two sets of values differ greatly. When children most closely resemble their parents in terms of values and beliefs, they also have a better relationship with them. In fact, Aldous, Klaus, and Klein (1985) find that adult children with shared interests and values are favored by parents.

Additional research questions come to mind concerning the parent-adult child relationship. For instance, when there is a sharp distinction in professional standing, and therefore income, between father and adult child or mother and child, is the relationship affected and in which direction? Here families could be studied that have experienced several degrees of **social mobility**—for example, when a child or several children have far surpassed their parents' status, or, the reverse, when a child or all siblings have drifted downward socially.[20] Do these families become fractured by social mobility or does the generation with the most favorable position help the other? One can predict that there will be differences among ethnic groups in this respect.

Another interesting situation presents itself with interracial marriage (Kouri and Laswell, 1993).[21] Does it affect the parent-adult child relationship? Are contacts established between the two sets of racially different in-laws (Rosenblatt, Karis, and Powell, 1995)? Does exchange between the two generations differ from exchange when parents are of the same race? Is there a difference in the relationship of the parents with the son or daughter-in-law who is of another race compared with a same-race relationship? The importance of studying the impact of interracial marriages on family dynamics stems from the fact that we still live in a fairly segregated and racist society (Reddy, 1994).[22]

EXCHANGE WITH AGING PARENTS

Pillemer and Suitor (1991b) pointedly remark that the research on the relationship between adult children and their aging parents resembles the unidirectional parental causality model of the traditional child development literature: The focus in gerontology is on the impact, often negative, *on* children of caring for elderly parents (Silliman and Sternberg, 1988). It may be seen in the following sections, however, that there are other equally important aspects of the aged parent-child relationship that can be researched.

Adult Children as Caregivers

As parents age, each year a number of them fall prey to either illnesses from which they recover or illnesses that will stay with them, or are chronic, such as arthritis or heart disease. Other parents experience problems such as osteoporosis or poor eyesight that can reduce their activity level and their mobility. Still others become frail or can no longer walk far without help. Others become mentally incompetent. Therefore, each year the relationship between many aging parents and at least some of their children is altered in some respects because of these fluctuations in parents' health. Adult children become the key instrumental and social support resources for their elderly parents (Eggebeen and Hogan, 1990). Some children begin to take full responsibility for their care, either in person or by supervising tasks that they have delegated to paid caretakers or even retirement homes (Chappel, Strain, and Blandford, 1986). If the parent's handicaps are physical only, the parent-child relationship may continue to include most of its previous elements.

When parents fall prey to mental disabilities such as senility and Alzheimer's disease, the relationship is totally altered. The parent becomes the child and the child becomes the parent. This is when the burden of caring is greatest because the responsibilities multiply for the child, while meaningful verbal exchanges diminish until even recognition disappears. For the parent, the world, including his or her own children, fades little by little until it has entirely evaporated; this deterioration is very distressing for everyone involved. Children actually lose the parent long before biological death arrives. There is a fairly substantial literature focusing on the stress experienced by adult children, especially daughters, as a result of their role as caretakers of aged and disabled parents (Gerstel and Gallagher, 1993). However interesting, this topic is somewhat out of the purview of this book,[23] but we should nevertheless mention that there is also some research that shows the positive side of caring for one's elderly parents (Gottlieb, 1989).

Studies unanimously find that daughters are far more likely to become their elderly parents' caretakers or helpers than sons.[24] In fact, Spitze and Logan (1991) point out that the key to receiving help resides in having one daughter. This is because women are generally assigned nurturant roles in our society and learn to be responsible for the well-being of others from the time they are young (Montgomery, 1992). Consequently, parents may also expect more help from their daughters than their sons–although the reverse occurs in many other societies such as China or Japan. When a son does have the responsibility for his parents, his wife often assumes this duty or, at the very least, contributes to it. Other studies find that sons provide help mainly in the domains of transportation and finances; when parents become more needy in terms of personal care, sons frequently abdicate their role (Montgomery and Kamo, 1989). Cicirelli (1983) reports that divorced children give less help than married or single children and that they tend to overlook some of their parents' needs, and feel less obligated to help them, perhaps because many are burdened by their own problems or have too many other responsibilities. But Spitze et al. (1994) find that divorced daughters continue to help their parents and also receive more help from them for babysitting than married daughters. Other studies report that unmarried children assist their parents less than married ones.[25] However, White and Peterson (1995) report no difference in help by children's marital status. Obviously, more research needs to be done to resolve contradictions between findings. Ideally, such research should take into account social class, which has not frequently been included.

Gender is a factor not only in who gives care, but in who receives it. As their health deteriorates, widowed mothers receive more help than widowed fathers from their children.[26] Silverstein, Parrott, and Bengtson (1995) report that affection is a stronger motivator for help to older mothers while expectation of an inheritance is more frequently a factor for assistance to fathers, although this is more the case among sons than daughters. But Rossi and Rossi (1990) do not find that subjective sentiment much affects obligations. Several **restrospective** studies show that a primary factor in middle-aged children's current feelings toward their parents is how the quality of the parent-child relationship is recalled to have been when the adults were children (Rossi and Rossi, 1990). This recollection also affects their willingness to help their parents.[27]

When one sibling is more or less forced to take on the main role in the care of elderly parents, the potential for sibling conflict arises. First, this sibling may resent the fact that she does everything. Second, the others may disagree with the decisions she makes,[28] especially when these involve financial outlays that may subsequently reduce their inheritance. Third, sibling rivalry or conflict may already have existed to some extent before, and it may in fact be this prior conflict that had led one of the children to finally take primary responsibility.

White elderly adults who are childless are not unhappier or in poorer health than those who have living children. However, having children, especially if they reside nearby, may be a more important factor in the life satisfaction of older black adults (Taylor and Chatters, 1991). But seniors of both races receive more help when they have children.[29] What seems to count for the well-being of the elderly is not whether they have children but the quality of the relationship between them and their children.[30] Silverstein and Bengtson (1991) find that a warm relationship with adult children may increase parental longevity after widowhood.

Elderly parents are happier when they give more than they receive, and they accept help more readily when they can contribute something in return.[31] In fact, when parents require a great deal of support from their children, they are less satisfied with the relationship (Chappell, 1985). In part, this can be explained by the fact that contact with the child is necessitated by the parent's needs rather than by the child's desire to see the parent or by the spontaneity of a visit just to chat. When the entire family, and not just the parents, have always valued reciprocity, elders may be satisfied that their earlier parental efforts were appreciated and they may not be negatively affected if they are unable to reciprocate in their later years.[32] Lee, Netzer, and Coward (1995) find that older parents who receive more help are more depressed. As they point out, American elders value their independence,[33] and dependence on children may be troublesome. But they also suggest the possibility of reversed causality, where children respond to their parents' depression by helping them more. It is not surprising, therefore, that when older parents are in better health, they report a more positive relationship with their children.

Aging Parents as a Source of Help

However, the truth remains that older parents, especially when they are still in reasonably good health–and most are–provide a great deal of assistance to their adult children (Aldous, 1987). In addition, many elderly parents still have adult children living with them: In a 1988 U.S. survey, 29 percent of adults aged 25 to 65 who had never married and 13 percent of those who were divorced lived with their parents.[34] The greater the number of children, the more likely elder parents are to have one who resides with them because of need (Spitze and Logan, 1991). Some adult children have never left home while others have returned to it (Aquilino, 1991). Parents over 65 who have a coresident child (and 13 to 15 percent do according to Aquilino, 1990) usually receive relatively little in terms of household or financial help from that child.[35] Da Vanzo and Goldscheider (1990) show that male children, whether single or married, are more likely to return home than female children; moreover, males are found to do 20 percent less housework than females when they live with their parents.[36] *Hence, coresidence is more likely to benefit the adult child than the parents.*[37] As parents age, they often do not or cannot disengage from the joys and problems experienced by their adult children. Pillemer and Suitor (1991a) report that 26 percent of senior parents mention that at least one of their children is experiencing serious physical or mental health problems or a high level of stress. These children's problems correlate significantly with depression in the older parents, and some studies report that older parents who have to help their children a lot feel more depressed (Mutran and Reitzes, 1984). In addition, when children have problems, they may receive advice that is not wanted (Greenberg and Becker, 1988). One can see that, at the very least, the potential for intergenerational conflict is high,[38] even when these adult children exhibit a dependency syndrome (Bornstein, 1995).

This promising line of research leads to the following question: What kinds of parents and adult children continue to experience a warm relationship despite the fact that children need substantial parental help? If we follow the line of reasoning developed in the context of behavior genetics (Chapters 10 and 14), we can advance the theory that a certain proportion of parents of perturbed, troubled, or distressed and unsuccessful adults will themselves be problematic persons: They were problematic persons as younger adults, therefore less competent parents, and, in addition, their children might have inherited genetic disadvantages from them. Hence, it is to be expected that a segment of distressed or difficult adults have parents who are or were similar to them. Research on such a theme would contribute to perspectives on adult development and behavior genetics, as well as personality theories.

ELDER ABUSE BY CHILDREN

One sad aspect of the relationship between seniors and their children is the phenomenon of elder abuse. The focus here is only on abuse of elderly parents by their children. Spousal abuse, and abuse by other relatives, servants, caretakers, and nursing staff is omitted. Until now, the emphasis on elder abuse has focused on dependent elderly and their caretakers; the related hypothesis is that the frustrated caretaker lashes out at the frail dependent parent (Steinmetz, 1988). There are indications, however, that the elderly are often abused by a dependent relative who lives with them, even if the elderly themselves are self-sufficient (Wolf and Pillemer, 1989). In that case, it generally is the adult child who depends on the parent financially or for shelter because he or she is unemployed, may be mentally delayed, physically incompetent, or emotionally disturbed.[39] Indeed, after discharge from hospital care, 85 percent of unmarried adult children who are mentally ill are sheltered by their aged parents (Greenburg, Siltzer, and Greenlay, 1993).[40] Hence, Pillemer (1985) believes that we may have placed too much emphasis on the dependence of the elderly as a source of abuse and that we should refocus our attention to include those elderly who have a dependent and physically stronger spouse or child living with them.

If is difficult to know whether adult daughters abuse their elderly parents more than sons do. As stated previously, daughters are more frequent caretakers, therefore they have more opportunities to do so and also more frustration to vent. On the other hand, more sons live with their elderly parents because they are dependent. In addition, males are more aggressive than females and may not be as emotionally attached to their parents as adult females, as noted earlier. These factors could contribute to more parental abuse by sons. Complicating the issue is the existence of covert forms of abuse, such as siphoning off revenues or controlling the house that belongs to the aged parents (Korbin, Anetzberger, and Austin, 1995).

Abuse of elderly parents is a relatively easy act to commit and can have even less social visibility than abuse of school-age children. Consequently, it is possible that today's abused elderly parents are less likely to report the abuse than a maltreated adolescent. Moreover, an abused child can grow up to denounce the parents whereas the elderly parent will carry the secret to his or her grave. There is little research on elder abuse among various ethnic and racial groups (Griffin, 1994).[41] Comparisons between such groups is important in view of the fact that black seniors take children and grandchildren in their homes more than whites (Mitchell and Register, 1984).[42] One can also point out that we know relatively little of the context of elder abuse, and the role that noninvolved siblings might play. Models of child abuse by parents have been used to try to explain the intergenerational transmission of violence in case of elder abuse. There is debate as to whether this approach is valid.[43] The topic of child abuse and its transmission is discussed in Chapter 10.

CONCLUSION

As economic conditions change, young adults postpone marriage and childbearing and remain home with their parents longer in order to pursue their education and establish themselves financially. The "empty nest" syndrome of earlier decades is replaced by a "cluttered nest" or "revolving door" family. In a sense, some aspects of the adolescent-parent relationship are pursued into adulthood, against the expectations of both generations.

At the other extreme of the life course continuum, new cohorts of elderly parents will have fewer children on whom they can rely for affection and instrumental help, compared with parents in the past, who usually had larger families. At the same time, adult children often divorce and remarry, perhaps bringing stepgrandchildren, so that intergenerational linkages are becoming more complex. The quality of these relationships is less predictable because they may be more transient than others.

While these structural changes take place in the lives of adult children and their elderly parents, the same economic conditions that clutter the nest in young adulthood may eventually make dependency of the elderly on adult children unavoidable. Indeed, with high governmental debt load, there are questions as to the ability of the State to aid seniors in the near future, and the willingness of politicians to care both for very young and very old citizens. It is not possible to predict how these potential economic changes will affect the parent-adult child relationship, if at all. But, at the practical level, one may suggest that familial solidarity may need to be reinforced in order to protect society's most vulnerable members. A sense of family solidarity is built throughout the life course. Fractured families, even families linked only by expectations of obligation without mutuality of feelings, may place their members at a disadvantage socially, emotionally, and economically.

One important element highlighted by this chapter is that research on the parent-adult child relationship is far less advanced than that on the parent-child relationship in childhood.[44] It is relevant to conclude Part I by adding that the dynamics of the parent-child relationship and of some aspects of child development change with cohort replacement. It follows that many of the results presented in these four chapters as well as the subsequent ones will no longer be valid in 10 to 20 years as the socioeconomic contexts evolve. This also means that the applicability of theories has to be retested over time.

ENDNOTES

1. Youniss, 1980.
2. Lancaster et al., 1987.
3. U.S. Bureau of the Census, 1992b.
4. Goldscheider, Thornton, and Young-DeMarco, 1993.
5. U.S. Bureau of the Census, 1992c.
6. White, 1994.
7. See Suitor and Pillemer, 1991, for review.
8. *Toronto Star*, June 30, 1995.
9. *Maclean*'s, November 20, 1995.

10. Roberts and Bengtson, 1993.

11. References on personality were suggested in Chapter 1. In addition, see the following: *Child Development, Developmental Psychology, European Journal of Personality, Journal of Personality, Journal of Personality and Social Psychology, Journal of Research in Personality,* and *Journal of Social and Personal Relationships.* For discussions of the concept of stability in personality, see Alwin, 1995; Caspi and Bem, 1990; Kagan, Reznick and Snidman, 1989; Costa and McCrae, 1992; Nesselroade, 1990, among others.

12. Stein, Newcomb, and Bentler, 1986; Jessor, Donovan, and Costa, 1991.

13. Clausen, 1986; Lerner, 1987.

14. Baltes and Baltes, 1980; Kendall, Lerner, and Craighead, 1984.

15. For a review, see Sampson and Laub, 1992.

16. Funder, Block, and Block, 1983.

17. Scheier and Carver, 1985.

18. Stability is greater when people are married to a person similar to them: Caspi, Elder, and Herbener, 1990.

19. Moskowitz and Schwartzman, 1989.

20. The Rossis (1990:299) comment that "occupational success and social mobility may be attained at the expense of embeddedness in family life and intimate ties between the generations."

21. Also, Johnson and Warren, 1994; Kalmijn, 1993; Tucker and Mitchell-Kernan, 1990.

22. Dilworth-Anderson, Burton, and Johnson, 1993.

23. See Loomis and Booth, 1995. A multiplicity of articles on the subject and related topics can be found in journals such as *American Journal of Aging, Canadian Journal on Aging, Canadian Journal of Public Health, International Journal of Aging and Human Development, Journal of Aging Studies, Journal of the American Geriatric Society, Journal of Applied Gerontology, Journal of Gerontological Nursing, Journal of Gerontology: Social Sciences, Journal of Gerontological Social Work, Journal of Marriage and the Family, Research of Aging,* and *The Gerontologist.*

24. Abel, 1991; Silverstein, Parrott, and Bengtson, 1995.

25. Hogan, Eggebeen, and Clogg, 1993.

26. Lawton, Silverstein, and Bengtson, 1994.

27. Whitbeck, Simons, and Conger, 1991; Whitbeck, Hoyt, and Huck, 1994. See Chapter 5.

28. Strawbridge and Wallhagen, 1991.

29. Chatters, Taylor, and Neighbors, 1989.

30. Kingston, Hirshorn, and Cornman, 1986.

31. Dwyer, Lee, and Jankowski, 1994; Marks, 1995.

32. Walker, Pratt, and Oppy, 1992.

33. Lee, 1985.

34. White and Peterson, 1995.

35. Grigsby, 1989.

36. Goldscheider and Waite, 1991.

37. Speare and Avery, 1993; Ward, Logan, and Spitze, 1992.

38. Pillemer and Suitor, 1991b.

39. Bristowe and Collins, 1989; Speare and Avery, 1993.

40. See, also, Jennings, 1987.

41. However, an entire issue of the *Journal of Elder Abuse & Neglect* is devoted to international and cross-cultural perspectives (1995, 6, nos 3/4).

42. See also, Freedman, 1991.

43. For a review and conflicting data, see Korbin, Anetzberger, and Austin, 1995.

44. See Mancini and Blieszner, 1989.

PART II:
THE CONTEXTS OF DEVELOPMENT AND OF THE PARENT-CHILD RELATIONSHIP

Chapter 5

The Parent-Child-Sibling Context

With this chapter, Part II begins the focus on some of the various contexts in which child development and the parent-child relationship are embedded. Part II, consisting of five chapters, further develops the interactional perspective and combines it with an ecological approach: These chapters discuss how parents and children react to each other according to various aspects of their environment. Some of the contexts studied are personal or proximal, while others are cultural and structural or distal. They are siblings, peers, the school, professionals, and family structure. The neighborhood is a key context that is integrated throughout several chapters. Part II begins with siblings because they constitute the most proximal and ever-present context for the parent-child relationship. Siblings are also a salient aspect of children's social lives within the family, at times as important as parents.

One unfortunate gap in the developmental literature and in the research on the parent-child relationship is that children are generally studied as if they are always alone at home with their parents, especially their mother, even when they have at least one sibling (Bryant and DeMorris, 1992; Stocker, 1994). In the United States, 80 percent of children have one sibling or more, although this percentage varies by ethnic group and by region (Hernandez, 1993). For instance, in Canada, a smaller proportion of children have brothers and sisters in the provinces of Quebec and British Columbia where fertility rates are lower and where families with only one child are more frequent.

From the parents' point of view, life is quite different depending on the number of children they have, on their spacing, gender, and age, as well as the quality of the sibling relationship. With one child, only four interactional permutations are possible: mother-father, mother-child, father-child, parents-child. If a sibling is added, eleven permutations result: mother-father, child-child, mother-child A, father-child A, mother-child B, father-child B, parents-child A, parents-child B, parents-children, mother-children, and father-children. The addition of only one more child multiplies possible interactions and changes family dynamics (Lasko, 1954).

This chapter looks at parent-child interactions as they are affected by the presence of the other siblings. In particular, discussion concerns what happens to family dynamics with the arrival of the second-born child. Next, the sibling relationship and its impact on the parent-child dyad both during childhood and adulthood are examined. Also discussed is the effect on the child of its parents' relationship with the older or younger sibling. The question is posed: Do parents treat their children similarly? What is the effect on the child of differential parental treatment? Further, the role that siblings can play when one of them has special needs is explored. Finally, the chapter inquires into the interface between sibling and peer contexts, particularly in terms of impact on parents' ability to socialize their offspring.

THE YOUNGER SIBLING'S ARRIVAL

With the arrival of the second child, parents cannot establish a one-on-one relationship with the new baby as had been the case with the older child. Neither can they pursue this exclusive relationship with the first-born, a factor that may become salient in this child's life experience if he or she feels a loss of status as well as affection (Lasko, 1954). Many studies show that parents give more attention to younger rather than older children (Stocker, Dunn, and Plomin, 1989). The older child may then suffer from a variety of problems of adjustment, including anxiety, clinging behavior, bed-wetting, and even aggressiveness (Gottlieb and Mendelson, 1990). Dunn (1994) points out that small children who are not malleable and are intense react less well to the baby's arrival; they may even protest when the mother pays attention to the infant. An additional complication with the arrival of each baby is that parents have less time for each child individually, although they may actually spend more time interacting with their children altogether. However, additional infants may benefit from the experience that parents have acquired with their earlier-born children.

During the newborn's first months, the infant's schedule is quite different from that of the older child, especially if the latter is already at school. With five years or more of spacing between the two children, the parent-first born relationship may continue to be exclusive during a portion of the day as the baby sleeps. With this much spacing, each is in a way an "only" child, and little competition may take place, especially if the older one likes to play at surrogate parenting. One can contemplate both pleasurable and conflictual concerns for parents who may be happy with the harmony between the siblings, but may find that the older child plays parent too seriously or "spoils" the baby.

There is little research on the differences between parent-child relationships and developmental outcome in families with widely spaced children compared with those where children are more closely spaced. However, one study by Teti, Gibbs, and Bond (1989) finds that much older siblings are more intellectually and socially stimulating for children than siblings closer to them in age. Smaller children tend to look up to their older siblings (Buhrmester and Furman, 1990). Does the older child mature sooner as a result? The answer so far is: possibly (Paulkus and Shaffer, 1981). Does the younger child learn faster because several older persons invest time in him or her? Or does this child rebel at having "one more mother"? Obviously, much remains to be studied. In terms of number of children, there is agreement in the research literature that large sib groups generally do not do as well at school, on average, as children from small families (Blake, 1989). A large sib group dilutes the quality of the home environment (Menaghan and Parcel, 1991).[1] However, there is no indication that adult children from large families are less attached to their parents and vice versa (Spitze and Logan, 1991). But this matter has yet to be studied during childhood and adolescence.

The parent-child relationship is much affected by the needs, personality, and the reactions of the other sibling. Just as the parent-child relationship is bidirectional, as seen in the previous chapters, the addition of a sibling multiplies the directions of effect. If a sibling is ill, the relationship between parent and healthy child may be limited in terms of time. When one child has a demanding and reactive personality, parents may have to give more attention to him or her, to the detriment of the time they can devote to the other sibling. When one child is difficult, the parental relationship may become more controlling and strained with that child, but we do not know how it affects the parents' relationship with a better behaved child in the same family. In one study, it is shown that at the birth of a sibling, little girls who have enjoyed a close relationship with their mother tend to develop a more hostile attitude toward the new sibling (Dunn and Kendrick, 1982). In contrast, girls who have had a more conflictual relationship with their mother are more likely to develop a friendly relationship with the sibling. Both jealousy and compensatory mechanisms are at play in this study.

CHILD AND ADOLESCENT SIBLING RELATIONSHIPS

Sibling relationships are largely determined by children's characteristics, their similarities and differences in personality, the parents' behavior toward them, and the siblings' perception of such. On the basis of these four factors, one can expect a large degree of stability in the sibling relationship given that these elements are reasonably stable through childhood.

When one child has an intense or unadaptable personality, sibling interactions are more conflictual (Boer, 1990; McCoy, Brody, and Stoneman, 1994). High-activity siblings have a more antagonistic relationship.[2] Munn and Dunn (1988) report that brothers and sisters whose personalities are compatible or complementary are more likely to experience a better relationship than those who are very different temperamentally. Overall, when a sibling is aggressive, the other tends to follow suit, so that siblings are important agents of socialization to each other in this respect,[3] and probably in many others that have yet to be researched (Rowe, 1983b).

Older siblings tend to be fairly consistent over time in their behavior toward their younger brother or sister; aggressiveness or friendliness persists. This means that some children spend their entire childhood with a friendly and supportive sibling while others are in a relationship that is hostile, disparaging, and even physically aggressive (Dunn et al., 1994). The impact on child development is substantial,[4] although we do not know if it is more or less salient than that of parental effect. At the very least, the sibling effect will depend on each child's vulnerabilities or, conversely, his or her resilience. It is indeed possible *that negative effects that have been attributed to parents* or their child-rearing practices, such as harsh treatment, *are actually the result of a child being harshly treated by both siblings and parents.* Such a possibility makes sense from the perspective of behavior genetics alone: Intolerant and irritable parents may produce some offspring who are like them and may jointly have a negative impact on the sibling who may be different at the outset. Such a possibility also makes sense in terms of behavior modeling. Younger siblings show less stability of behavior than older ones, perhaps because the reactions of the older sibling are more important to them and they may accordingly adapt their style of interaction in order to gain his or her attention and goodwill. Overall, older children tend to be more domineering while younger ones are forced to be more compliant (Berndt and Bulleit, 1985). It is perhaps not surprising that, in terms of development, Dunn et al. (1994) suggest that the older child has a stronger effect on the younger than vice versa (see also Abramovitch, Pepler, and Corter, 1982). However, older siblings tend to be more helpful and to initiate prosocial behaviors, perhaps because parents emphasize helpfulness toward the younger ones. As children reach adolescence, their relationship generally becomes more even and, in some cases, more distant and egalitarian.[5] East and Rook (1992) note that young adolescents who have a good relationship with siblings are less anxious. Overall, adolescents have more interpersonal conflicts with their siblings than with their parents, whereas they have more conflicts with parents about rules (Montemayor and Hanson, 1985).

There is an association between the quality of children's relationships with their parents and with their siblings. Children who enjoy warm interactions with their mother tend to have a warm and nurturing relationship with their siblings (Teti and Ablard, 1989): A matter of temperamental similarity between parents and children may be involved in some of these cases. In addition, the parental example may have a constructive effect. It may reinforce positive predispositions and offset negative ones. It is also important to look at the impact of the sibling interactions on the parent-child relationship. When brothers and sisters do not get along, especially when they are close in age, are parental feelings toward either child affected? Do parents initiate fewer activities as a family group because of the constant bickering? Do they distance themselves from the children? Does the quarreling limit parents' contact with relatives or friends?

An interesting aspect of the sibling group is that they do not perceive their relationship similarly. Dunn and McGuire (1994:120) mention that only 23 percent of the siblings studied reported a degree of closeness similar to that expressed by their brother or sister. Such results indicate that parents may have to mediate between siblings who misinterpret each other's feelings and intentions and/or who are not positively reciprocal. One would expect, however, that such differences in closeness might diminish with age as communication skills develop. But perhaps not: Instead, a pattern may be set for life, especially when differential parental treatment is perceived. Studies have generally focused on two siblings, so that information about larger sib groups is lacking but could add much to our understanding of human development and family dynamics.

ADULT SIBLING RELATIONSHIPS

As children reach adulthood, the sibling relationship in industrialized societies, particularly those of Western cultures, becomes discretionary. Continuing the relationship is a matter of choice, and it is secondary to the spousal and parent-child relationships. Cicirelli (1994:16) points out that adult sibling interactions "do not have a major effect on family functioning or adaptation to the larger society." In contrast, in other societies, continuation of the sibling relationship into adulthood is normative and is of fundamental importance in the family's integration into society at large.

Among adults, proximity increases both contact and conflict.[6] Moreover, sibling relationships are closer between sisters than between brothers (Cicirelli, 1995). Although both genders tend to have recourse to siblings as friends as they age,[7] close bonds between sisters are more important for their morale in old age than are such bonds between brothers (Cicirelli, 1989). Sisters also provide more help to each other, as well as to other family members, than do brothers; this pattern is more obvious in some ethnic groups than others (Johnson, 1985). Relationships with sisters are also salient for their brothers' morale. Cicirelli (1989) reports that elderly brothers who have more sisters feel happier and more secure (Gold, 1989). This, again, probably stems from the nurturing role to which women are socialized (Baines, Evans, and Neysmith, 1991). Unfortunately, sisters may not benefit equally from fraternal support. For both genders, ties with siblings are particularly important after widowhood and in periods of crisis (Cicirelli, Coward, and Dwyer, 1992). Contact with half and step-siblings in adulthood is more frequent when there are no full siblings (White and Riedmann, 1992).

The elderly parent-adult child relationship was discussed in the previous chapter (Cicirelli, 1991). We already know that daughters are closer to their aging parents and help them more than do brothers, and that parents who have daughters receive more assistance than those who have only sons (Abel, 1991). We also saw that sibling conflict can arise when it is felt that the others do not carry their fair share of caring for parents. But little is known about the emotional quality of the elderly parent-adult child relationship as it may be affected by different *characteristics of the adult sib group and its structure*. The emphasis in the parent-adult child literature is on *one* child, such as the daughter who helps, the child who has divorced, or the one who is dependent. Research disregards other siblings and how the parent-adult child interactions are affected by the sibling system (see Matthews and Sprey, 1989).

DIFFERENTIAL PARENTAL TREATMENT

Parents treat children differently, depending on the child's age, and are generally aware of doing so. The younger child is favored by both parents (McHale et al., 1995) in some circumstances, but the older one is favored in other matters (Baskett, 1985). In fact, Dunn and Plomin (1990) found that a majority of the British and American mothers they interviewed admitted loving one child more than the other, and the preference generally was for the younger one. Both younger and older children were also aware of this differential treatment, a topic which will be discussed later.[8]

However, it appears that mothers treat their children similarly at a given age—at least in the UK and North America, and within relatively small sib groups and spacing. It is not known to what extent the following results apply in the case of larger families and other situations, although, four decades ago, Lasko (1954) studied families with three children and did so within a naturalistic context. More recently, in a long-term research, Dunn, Plomin, and Daniels (1986) reported high correlations between a mother's treatment of the older child at age two and her subsequent treatment of the younger child at the same age.

The fact that the correlations are not perfect between the maternal treatments of the children at the same age deserves further attention and can be explained in at least two ways. First, mothers adapt their behavior to each child's individuality. In a study of language patterns between mothers and siblings at 21 months, McCartney et al. (1991) found both maternal consistency and adaptability to the child's verbal ability over time. This means that mothers tend to treat their children similarly at a given level of child maturity, although they are not as consistent toward the same child while he or she is growing up. The Dunn, Plomin, and Daniels (1986) study also included adopted siblings: Mothers were more consistent toward biological than adoptive siblings on different measures and displayed more attentiveness to their adoptive children (Rende et al., 1992). In the case of greater consistency toward biological siblings, mothers may have been reacting to genetic similarities on certain dimensions. However, the consistency was far from perfect, again reminding us that biological siblings are also different from each other.

Second, the imperfect correlation between the treatment of two children at the same age could also stem from the fact that the latter-born child enters the family system at a different point in the family's development (Hoffman, 1991:193). The mother may be busier or more tired when the younger child is two than she was when the older one was the same age some years earlier. This difference in treatment could also be explained by any other factor that may have changed in the child's and mother's lives and environment. For instance, when child B reaches two, the parents may have separated and the mother may be under more (or less) stress than she was when child A was two. Her higher or lower level of stress could affect her parenting vis-à-vis the younger child.

Information is not available in terms of parenting consistency for adolescence and later ages, but the Colorado Adoption Project or CAP, among others, will eventually yield such data. As children grow older, it is quite possible that parents treat them differently, a process called de-identification by Schachter (1982). Children may contribute to this process as they try to differentiate themselves from their siblings in order to assert their own individuality (Schachter and Stone, 1987). There are early indications in data collected by this author that parents treat sons and daughters increasingly differently as they get older.[9] Hetherington and Camara (1984) have even found that parents are more likely to fight in the presence of sons than daughters. In autobiographies submitted annually as a class project, women students repeatedly complained that their older brother was given much more freedom than they had been given at the same age. In some ethnic groups, a slightly older brother, or even a younger one, chaperoned a sister whenever she went out. Causing even more resentment for these girls was the fact that they had to do more housework, age for age, than their brother, and some even had to clean up after him. The more males are valued in a culture, the greater the difference in the content of the parent-child relationship across genders and the greater the difference in parental treatment.[10] However, due to lack of research, it is not known how parents who have more than two or three children behave in terms of differential treatment nor what the impact is.[11] One could well hypothesize that in large families, parents have less time to react to each child's individuality and accordingly treat their offspring more similarly than do parents with fewer children.

DEVELOPMENTAL IMPACT
OF DIFFERENTIAL TREATMENT

There are actually several types of differential treatment: when parents concurrently treat two siblings differently, when they treat two or more children differently than one child, and when they treat children differently at the same age. (To this could be added the child's perception of differential treatment.)[12] Several studies have discovered a developmental advantage for the sibling who receives the most favorable treatment at a current stage. Daniels (1987) reports that the sibling who enjoys more paternal affection develops more ambitious educational and vocational goals–although the direction of causality cannot be established. Children who are more controlled by their mother or perceive receiving less affection than their siblings are more likely to be anxious or depressed.[13] These children also tend to be more difficult. But it is possible that a difficult child may require parents to become more controlling (Dunn and Stocker, 1989)–otherwise, one would perhaps expect the same parents to be controlling toward all their children. Moreover, it may be that it is the perception of differences rather than the actual differential treatment that causes the problems (see Reiss et al., 1995).

Several other studies, including maternal reports and researchers' observations, indicate that mothers treat children differently in terms of affection, control, and responsiveness,[14] generally resulting in higher levels of conflict and negativism between siblings,[15] and even between mother and child (McHale and Gamble, 1989). The results of differential treatment may extend into adulthood and may be reflected in the siblings' later relationships (Baker and Daniels, 1990). When parents are more affectionate toward one child or more controlling toward another, sibling relationships may be more conflictual. The less favored offspring tends to express resentment toward the more favored one (Boer, Goedhart, and Treffers, 1992). This resentment may be the result of jealousy or, alternatively, the result of the more difficult personality of the less favored child, who behaves less pleasantly toward siblings and parents alike. Clark and Barber (1994) report that adolescents who perceive that their father is more interested in their siblings score lower on self-esteem but only when they live with both parents. In a divorced family, adolescents may be in a better position to rationalize the relative lack of paternal interest because they rarely see the father. In an intact family, the daily presence of the father may make this perceived lack of interest more ubiquitous and painful to bear.

McHale et al. (1995) went one step farther and grouped families depending on whether both parents were congruent in displaying more affection for one same child, or incongruent (each parent preferring a different child). Congruent parents predominated. Incongruence was related to marital distress. Maritally distressed parents at times form a coalition with one child (Reiss et al., 1994), while parents who get along may tend to agree on which child needs more support. Thus, it is important to study *both* parents' differential treatment and in the context of other variables, such as marital happiness, number, and spacing of offspring. It may also be that differential treatment has a more negative impact in a poor quality environment, or in a more privileged environment, or still, in families that have children of only one sex or of both. Moreover, *differential treatment may impact according to parental personality, relative parental power within the family, and overall level of parenting involvement.* One can hypothesize that a weak parent may not have the same impact as one who is psychologically stronger. It is also possible that children may seek attention more from a parent who is socially prominent than from a parent who has a lower profile. These matters have yet to be examined.

ADDITIONAL RESEARCH QUESTIONS

As seen in earlier chapters, the impact of parents' behavior on their children's personality and outcomes has been greatly exaggerated. Therefore, it is essential not to err in believing that whether parents treat their children differentially or not is necessarily going to have a huge impact. What probably counts in terms of effect on the child is the *child's inter-*

pretation of the differential treatment. Some of the above-mentioned studies used children's reports, hence perceptions. If children find it unfair that their sibling is better treated, then they are likely to suffer. But if they find the differential treatment justified (because the sibling is disabled, for example), or do not perceive it, then the differential treatment will not have any *subjective* impact, although it may still have an objective impact that is not perceived by the less favored child. Moreover, there are certainly instances when a child perceives a difference when none exists and the perception, however erroneous, produces a negative effect. But researchers generally do not verify whether youngsters' reports are unsubstantiated or accurate (Simons, Robertson, and Downs, 1989), although Dunn and McGuire (1994) inform us that there is "little or no agreement between the two children within a family about the differential impact."

The few studies that exist on this topic indicate that *perception* of differential treatment continues to be important for adolescents and for adult children, both in how they relate to their parents and how they relate to each other later on in life (Baker and Daniels, 1990). It has been mentioned that children who perceive that they are treated less favorably often have lower self-esteem and are more anxious and insecure. It seems plausible that the perception of differential treatment lowers children's self-esteem and creates anxiety. But there are two additional and complementary explanations. First, parents may feel closer to children who have sound self-esteem and who are self-confident; they therefore treat them with greater affection. Moreover, a pre-existing deficient self-esteem may be *compounded* by differential treatment. Second, children who are anxious and have deficient self-esteem may *perceive* more difference than actually exists. Again, this perception could contribute to further raise their level of anxiety. There are indications that both processes are at work,[16] although one or the other may play a greater role in certain families than in others.

One salient gap in the research is the lack of studies on parenting styles involving siblings rather than just one "target" child (but see Lasko, 1954). Consequently, it would perhaps be more appropriate to talk in terms of parenting behaviors toward *one* child rather than in terms of parenting *style*—the latter term implies that parenting behaviors originate strictly from parents' personalities and do not vary between children. In Chapter 3, it was seen that the causality of parenting styles has several complementary explanations. What researchers need to investigate is how parenting and the parent-child relationship are affected when a sibling is either a difficult child, a developmentally nonnormative one, or one who is disabled. Is there a compensation mechanism that takes place so that parents have a warmer relationship with one child in order to make up for the frustration or burden engendered by the other? Or is it possible that when a sibling is difficult and creates tension for the parents, they may react by being controlling and less warm toward all children, even when the others are easy? The literature mentioned in the first two chapters leads to the belief that even irritable parents treat a pleasant child better than the others, or at least are less aggressive toward this child. Therefore, the research on differential parental treatment needs to be expanded not only to cover more variables, but also in order to better study parenting patterns in terms of their etiology as well as their impact.

HELPFUL SIBLING RELATIONSHIPS

LeClere and Kowalewski's (1994) results from a large sample of children aged 5 to 17 indicate that 17 percent live with at least one sibling or parent who suffers from a disability. When a parent is disabled or there is more than one handicapped person in the family, nondisabled children tend to have more behavioral problems, especially those who were already vulnerable. There is a large literature documenting the potential disadvantage to children who have disabled or chronically ill siblings (Breslau, Weitzman, and Messenger, 1981).[17] A limited literature also focuses on the helping role of siblings (Hunt, 1973), providing evidence that they can be important in the well-being of a physically, emotionally, or mentally challenged brother or sister (Vandereycken and Van Vreckem, 1992).

When the disabled sibling is aggressive toward the helping child or adolescent, the latter tends to be less well adjusted emotionally (McHale and Gamble, 1989). Sourkes (1987) points out that parents can play an important role in this respect by explaining the source of the negative behavior to the helping child. As seen in the previous chapter, parents usually have to shoulder the responsibility of caring for, or coordinating the care for a disabled adult child. A cooperative sibling can greatly lessen the parental burden, and we can assume that parents will have particularly warm feelings for that helpful adult child. Siblings can replace aging parents in the care of brothers or sisters, especially after the death of parents.[18] Horwitz (1994) suggests that therapists should encourage adults who are mentally ill to develop reciprocal relationships with their siblings, given that people are more willing to help a sibling who also helps them. This sibling relationship could contribute to elevate elderly parents' feelings of well-being, as they may worry less about the future of the handicapped child. They may also experience less stress due to the daily care they have to provide to the dependent adult child. It is possible that siblings involved in the care of a disabled adult might be able to prevent the abuse of their elderly parents by the dependent sibling.

Brothers and sisters, especially older ones who function well, can act as a buffer for their younger siblings at times of marital conflict or divorce, or in the event of a parent's illness or emotional problems (Sandler, 1980). The literature, however, indicates that a conflictual parental relationship is more likely to lead to, or be accompanied by, greater sibling conflict,[19] even after divorce (MacKinnon, 1989)–probably because of a combination of genetics, behavior modeling, and stress. Hetherington (1988) finds that the presence of a stepfather is often accompanied by diffident sibling interactions. However, the spacing between children has not been considered in these studies: Such sibling conflicts may occur only when there is little age difference among them. Jenkins and Smith (1990) report that supportive sibling interactions may reduce the number of problems that children experience when they are exposed to parental conflict. Giving and receiving comfort is beneficial.[20] Siblings can also be helpful to adolescent mothers, another topic that is not sufficiently documented because the focus of research has been on the assistance provided by parents.[21]

THE IMPACT OF SIBLINGS' SHARED FRIENDS

In the study of child development, children's networks are separated into compartments: parents, peers, siblings, and teachers. It would be important to seek a more integrative approach, because children's various relationships may exhibit common features. Another perspective advances that children's relationships contain some unique and even complementary features (Pepler and Slaby, 1994:44). In fact, Furman and Robbins (1985) suggest that children's diverse relationships serve different functions.

There appears to be some continuity but by no means great overlap in the quality of a child's interactions with both siblings and peers (Kramer and Gottman, 1992).[22] With regard to parents and peers, children who are rejected by their peers but benefit from supportive interactions with their mother are better adjusted than those whose relationship with their mother is not warm.[23] Stocker (1994) shows that there is both independence and correlation in the quality of the diverse relationships. But she also finds that there is a compensatory mechanism taking place in the sense that children who have at least one warm relationship, either with their mother or close friends, have better outcomes than children who have neither, and outcomes similar to those who have a warm relationship with both.

When siblings are adolescents, and more so when they reach adulthood, similarity of characteristics seems to increase friendliness and contact, as well as the sharing of friends (Lykken et al., 1990). In turn, it is likely that frequency of positive contact contributes to an increased resemblance between siblings over the long term, especially in areas of ideas, values, and leisure activities (Bouchard et al., 1990). As discussed in an earlier chapter, while siblings share at least parts of the same familial environment, it is the environment that they do not share, as well as their genes, that contribute to dissimilarities (Daniels and Plomin, 1985). Peers are an important element of this nonshared environment: Siblings generally do not have the same peers, especially so when there is a large age difference between them. However, when siblings get along well, are close in age, and have peers in common, a greater portion of their environment is shared. In turn, this extended shared environment may increase sibling similarities on certain characteristics.

Rowe, Woulbroun, and Gulley (1994) indicate that nearly half of the brother pairs and 35 percent of the sister pairs they studied have friends in common. It would be beneficial to know how the parent-child relationship is facilitated or disrupted when siblings are similar and share a peer network. One would expect that the sharing of a prosocial peer group by siblings would greatly facilitate parental duties as well as parent-child relationships (Steinberg and Darling, 1994). This network would become a form of social capital to both parents and children.[24] It should lower the necessity to control and monitor, tasks that most parents find difficult and that children often resist. Prosocial peers are also more likely to have authoritative parents; when a group of peers have similarly oriented parents, the burden of supervision is lessened for each individual set of parents, given that they all participate to some degree in the monitoring process (Fletcher et al., 1995; Furstenberg and Hughes, 1995).

However, when siblings who are already predisposed to deviance share a delinquent or drug-oriented peer group, this increases the chance that they will commit delinquent acts (Rowe, 1986; Rowe et al., 1989). Consequently, one can presume that the parent-child relationship will be tense and often devoid of mutually rewarding features, as we see in the chapter on delinquency. Parents of such children must monitor them more and set more limits on their activities and their whereabouts. This level of supervision may go beyond many parents' abilities. Siblings with delinquent peers will in turn rebel more in response to monitoring, and will also be more able to circumvent parental supervision. Adolescent girls who have a sexually active or childbearing adolescent sister, as well as similarly oriented peers, are more likely to be sexually active themselves (East, Felice, and Morgan, 1993). Such sets of sisters are probably more difficult to monitor, particularly in contexts that allow them independence from parents. It is also possible that parents' inability to monitor, in addition to the examples they may have provided of such risk-taking behaviors, have contributed to this situation.

CONCLUSION

Very little is known about the parent-child-sibling interface. This gap in our knowledge is the result of research strategies that have largely focused on mother-child dyads, to the exclusion of both fathers and siblings. In most families, not only does the parent-child relationship evolve within the context of the presence of at least one other child, *but there develop as well several parent-child relationships within each family.* It is particularly important to study parenting practices and child-rearing styles within the context of the various siblings' personalities and behaviors.

Children help produce the home environment that contributes to their and their fellow siblings' development. In some families where one or more siblings is particularly gifted or, conversely, especially difficult, *the environment created by these children may have a greater impact on each child than the environment created by parents.* As will be seen in Chapter 12, antisocial children often rule the home. This is more likely to occur when parents have a quiet and unassuming personality, or have problems that make them less available to their children, or suffer from stressors that impair their parenting skills. The addition of a cohesive antisocial peer group shared by siblings would heighten the negative impact of children on their own development and that of their siblings and peers (Hartup, 1996). Obviously, the topic of this chapter leaves much room for investigation for future researchers, especially when combined with a behavior genetics perspective as described in Chapter 14.

ENDNOTES

1. This is consistent with Blake's (1989) findings in terms of achievement, even after controlling for social class. See also Menaghan and Parcel, 1991; Powell and Steelman, 1993.

2. Mash and Johnson, 1983a; Stoneman and Brody, 1993.

3. Patterson, 1984, 1986.

4. Dunn, Slomkowski, Beardsall, and Rende, 1994.

5. Furman and Buhrmester, 1992.

6. Lee, Mancini, and Maxwell, 1990.

7. Cicirelli, 1980; Connidis, 1989.

8. Dunn and McGuire, 1994.

9. Huston, 1985.

10. For achievement expectations, see Eccles and Hoffman, 1984.

11. Schachter and Stone, 1987.

12. Rowe (1987) indicates that there may be genetic influences on siblings' perceptions of the treatment they receive from their parents.

13. Dunn, Stocker, and Plomin, 1990; McHale and Pawletko, 1992.

14. Brody, Stoneman, and Burke, 1987.

15. Brody et al., 1992.

16. Dunn and McGuire, 1994.

17. Additional references on this negative effect on siblings and on parents can be found in McKeever, 1992, and in *Children's Health Care, Clinical Child Psychology, International Journal of Disability, Journal of Advanced Nursing, Journal of the American Academy of Child Psychiatry, Journal of Clinical Child Psychology, Journal of Chronic Diseases, Journal of Learning Disabilities, Pediatrics, Psychiatry, Psychological Medicine, Social Casework,* and *Social Science and Medicine.*

18. Horwitz, 1993.

19. Jenkins, 1992.

20. Jenkins, Smith, and Graham, 1989.

21. Nitz, Ketterlinus, and Brandt, 1995. There is also some literature on older siblings as teachers: Azmitia and Hesser, 1993; Cooper and St. John, 1990.

22. Stocker and Dunn, 1990.

23. Patterson, Cohn, and Kao, 1989.

24. J. Coleman, 1988.

Chapter 6

The Parent-Child-Peer Context

This chapter pursues the interface between children, their peers, and parents already broached in the previous chapter. Indeed, the role that peers play in the parent-child relationship is another key dimension that is rarely taken into consideration. Yet, this lack of research coexists with a prolific literature on peers, peer groups, and their socialization role, as well as peer rejection.[1] As seen in Chapter 2, children are exposed to peers earlier than was the case 20 years ago because of the popularity of day care, preschool, and kindergarten. Therefore, peers enter not only the child's life, but also that of parents, earlier than before. As the child ages, more time is spent with peers in leisure activities that do not take place at home and are therefore largely out of the parental context (Larson and Richards, 1994). A study done in Quebec showed that adolescents in 1980 returned home two hours later on weekend evenings and spent fewer hours with their families than adolescents did in 1960 (Claes, 1990). For adolescents at least, familial time is decreasing and is replaced by time spent with peers as well as by part-time work,[2] mainly to defray the cost of peer-related lifestyles.

Most of the theories and data on the peer group context are based on white samples. Very little is known of the functioning and the role of peers among black, Latino, and Asian youngsters, and thus of the interface of peers with the parent-child relationship for these groups.[3] There have been a few studies of interracial friendships, but since the majority of friendships are intraracial, such research does not shed much light on the topic at hand (McKenry et al., 1989). It will also be important for future research to study the parent-child-peer context in terms of social class and quality of neighborhood (Kupersmidt et al., 1995).

In the present chapter, we begin with a critique of the literature on the role that peers play in child/adolescent behavior as well as in development. The cultural context of peer groups is then presented. The role of parents as facilitators of their child's peer interactions is investigated, and the results of a study on peer abuse are reviewed. Next, the impact of peers on the parent-child relationship and the concerns that parents may have about their children's peers are explored. Finally, the parent, peer, and neighborhood interface is presented.

PEERS AND THE ACQUISITION OF SOCIAL SKILLS: A CRITIQUE

Peers are considered to be important agents of socialization (Corsaro and Eder, 1990).[4] Researchers emphasize the point that, while children's relationships with adults are hierarchical, those with peers are egalitarian—even though there is a stratification system among peers.[5] Peers constitute an excellent context within which a child can learn to adapt to a variety of situations and to develop social skills (Youniss, McLellan, and Strouse, 1994). While one cannot subscribe to the notion that socialization by peers is inherently negative, necessarily deficient compared with socialization by adults, or always in opposition to the adult world, two cautionary remarks about the optimistic perspective on the role of peers in children's development can be offered. First, practically all normal children go to school with peers: Consequently, we have no control group of average children reared entirely with adults to see how their development compares. It is quite possible that children and adolescents living in an all-adult context would develop as well in terms of social skills, and perhaps better in other domains, than children growing up with peers. In Europe, particularly in past centuries, children of the rich merchant class and of the nobility were often tutored at home. They met peers of their social class within an adult context, that is, as part of family outings, celebrations, and other gatherings. Since no data exists on children raised without peers, it may be somewhat premature to assert that peers are all-important in the development of social competence. Moreover, there is some literature indicating that there is a degree of continuity from childhood to adolescence in children's ability to form and maintain friendships, as well as to experience difficulties in relationships (Collins and Repinski, 1994).[6] This continuity implies that children's personalities are an important element in this respect,[7] perhaps more than the availability of peers and the social skills they learn from them (see Rubin et al., 1995). Peers have different meanings for boys and girls; girls form more intimate relationships (Buhrmester and Furman, 1987).[8] Therefore, the necessity of peers may differ by gender, characteristics of children, and type of parent-child interaction. It also certainly varies by culture.

Second, it is relevant to note that "too much of a good thing" may be detrimental on some levels. For instance, small children who spend a great deal of time interacting with peers in day care and little with adults do not function as well intellectually or socially as children who spend more time with adults (Clarke-Stewart, 1987b).[9] This may mean that, in order to develop optimally, small children need more quality time spent with adult caretakers who can provide them with intellectual stimulation and also proactively teach them social skills. Therefore, at least for small children, adult caretakers or companions may be more important than peers in some developmental domains.

Nevertheless, Harris's theory of group socialization (1995) is relevant in the sense that peers are potent agents of socialization in late childhood and adolescence. Group norms, group acceptance, and fear of social ostracism are salient in children's lives (Ambert, 1994a). But this does not mean that they are a necessity. Harris (1995:474) also points out that as youngsters mature, "the consequences of being different are not so serious." Group influence may have less impact on adolescents approaching adulthood. It has been suggested that, at least in mass market economies, peer groups act as levellers in terms of lifestyle: They contribute to making youngsters more similar on some dimensions, and this leveling effect often proceeds downward to the lowest common denominator. In contrast, parents generally push their children toward loftier goals. When this is the case, peers are a direct source of **cross-pressure** on child and adolescent socialization.

Another critique of the perspective that peer contact is a necessary ingredient in child socialization is the well-known fact that peers often influence each other negatively (Hartup, 1996). To begin with, a majority of delinquent acts are committed with peers (Warr, 1993). Moreover, as we see in the next chapter, good parenting practices can produce little effect when a child lives in a neighborhood and attends schools where peers are focused on delinquent gangs and related activities and are prone to devalue anything that has to do with school achievement or learning. Therefore, peers can be a negative influence on a child's development, especially when that child is already at risk because of his or her own predispositions. If this same child also lives in a fairly dysfunctional family, one has a recipe for school failure and perhaps even a lasting career in crime (Farrington et al., 1988).[10]

YOUTH CULTURES

Societies have nearly always had distinctions between age groups.[11] This type of generational stratification even existed in antiquity. Throughout the centuries in the Western world, beginning with Plato's *Republic* and continuing on through Shakespeare and to the present, much ink has been used to express adults' laments concerning youth groups.[12] Hence, generational cleavage is certainly not a new phenomenon. But what differentiates contemporary postindustrial societies from others in this respect is the drastic separation that exists between the lives of children and adolescents and those of adults. This is due to the fact that youngsters are no longer integrated into the world of work and are segregated in institutions such as day care and schools (Engelbert, 1994).

Another important aspect of contemporary adolescent and even preadolescent peer groups is that peer activities are largely influenced by the media, and thus are at least in part under the control of large international corporations that target youngsters as a consumer market. Contemporary adolescents and even preadolescents partake of a variety of subcultures that differ from youth subcultures of past centuries and even recent decades in at least five ways: (1) The subcultures' main goals are recreational and consumer-oriented; (2) they are characterized by commodities produced by adults for the teenage market for economic profit (Schlegel and Barry, 1991:204); (3) these subcultures, based on a global economy as opposed to a regional one, are becoming international in scope (Youniss and Smollar, 1989); (4) although volatile, temporary, and mediated to some event by gender,[13] class, and ethnicity,[14] these adolescent subcultures are more cohesive and less fragmented for each individual child than are the adult subcultures for each individual parent (Small and Eastman, 1991); (5) although youth subcultures have historically been viewed as a source of intergenerational conflict, current youth subcultures may now have more impact in opposition to parents' values and beliefs precisely because of the preceding four factors (LeMasters and DeFrain, 1989:11). This changing configuration of Western adolescence is spreading to other societies via mass markets and media, where it can also be presumed to affect the parent-child relationship, perhaps more dramatically so than in the West where these changes have at least had some precedents in past decades.

Baethge (1989:33) argues that, as our economic system prolongs education and postpones full-time employment,[15] youth receive an increasingly "consumerist socialization." This situation may contribute to an increase in parental responsibilities. First, parents in large part subsidize a socialization that benefits a profit-oriented economy. Second, it is particularly in areas of consumption and leisure that adolescents are more peer-oriented (Meeus, 1989).[16] Since consumerism now affects more aspects of people's lives than in the recent past,[17] one may logically wonder whether this more intense and longer consumerist socialization[18] may not contribute to rendering parents less influential, yet more burdened.

PARENTS' ROLE
IN CHILDREN'S PEER INTERACTIONS

The quality of children's peers has, not unsurprisingly, become a salient parental preoccupation.[19] Not only are today's parents concerned about peers, but they also have less control than in the past over whom their child associates with after a certain age. More of same-sex peer interactions, especially among boys, takes place outside the home than was the case in the recent past. When children attend schools outside their neighborhood, or have a car, or live in an area where gangs rule, parents are fairly helpless in monitoring what takes place and with whom their child or adolescent associates. This situation afflicts minority-group families even more.

As a result of the traditional emphasis placed on parents, much research has been devoted to discovering their effect on children's competence with peers. This research has proceeded along two lines (Youngblade and Belsky, 1995). First are what may be termed direct pathways, that is, activities that parents pursue to enhance their children's relationships (Ladd, 1992). For their part, indirect pathways include parenting styles, as well as how these styles affect children's problem-solving skills, which then influence their peer relations (Hart, Ladd, and Burleson, 1990).[20] This section focuses on the direct pathways because the combined interactional and genetics perspective on parenting practices presented in Chapter 3 cast doubt on some of the cause-effect explanations concerning parenting practices, and this would apply to the topic at hand. While it is true that children can learn skills "within the family that can be transferred or generalized to the peer group" (Ladd, 1992:5),[21] the genetics perspective suggests that some of these skills may be partly hereditary, while the interactional perspective suggests that children can also learn skills and dysfunctional behaviors from peers that can impact on the family, especially during adolescence.

When the child is small or of elementary school age, parents can play a direct role in the development of his or her friendships. Ladd and Coleman (1993)[22] have pointed out that parents can influence their children's opportunities to meet peers, as well as their peer interactions, in four ways. First, according to their own characteristics such as income, education, and personality traits, parents choose the neighborhood in which they raise their children. They tend to do so on the basis of the quality of its environment in terms of schools and families whose lifestyle may resemble theirs. In this way, parents design their child's social environment. One has to point out here that some parents do this by default: They have no choice in the matter, because of poverty, for instance (Smith and Thomson, 1987). In fact, a majority of disadvantaged mothers who live in neighborhoods that are run down and have a high delinquency rate would want nothing more than to move elsewhere in order to give their children better life opportunities. When houses are closely spaced and when neighborhoods are not divided by commercial areas, highways, or railroads, children have better access to playmates (Medrich et al., 1982). But in dangerous neighborhoods, even when overcrowding exists, parents tend to restrain their children's mobility. This means that children may not even be able to play outside or bring friends home (Cochran and Riley, 1988).

Parents influence their children's opportunities for friendships in a second way, as "mediators," by bringing their children to meet others in environments that might facilitate peer interaction with suitable companions (Ladd and Coleman, 1993). Parents can organize parties, outings, attend clubs, and enroll their children in various camps and classes. A third type of influence occurs when parents act as "supervisors" or teachers. This role consists of monitoring children's relations and teaching them skills that will carry over into their peer relationships. This parental role is more relevant to pre-school children. Finally, as children grow older, parents become "consultants." That is, they give advice and offer a sympathetic ear when their youngsters want to talk about their friendships or about other peers (Laird et al., 1994). Parents can also indirectly influence the quality of the peers their adolescents befriend via the child-rearing practices they use (Brown et al., 1993). Authoritative parenting has been related to adolescents' choosing a more prosocial peer group (Steinberg et al., 1995), although the causality pathway may also involve genetics. In ethnically mixed schools, "minority youngsters find their choices of peer groups exceedingly restricted," because adolescents usually stay within their own ethnic group, and this considerably reduces the range of potential choice (Steinberg et al., 1995:448).

A STUDY OF PEER ABUSE

There is mounting evidence that a small but nevertheless increasing segment of children and youth are cruel, destructive, and even violent toward each other (Munthe, 1989). Such examples are mentioned in the newscasts on a daily basis. Unfortunately, there are abusers among the ranks of children and adolescents: their victims are other children their age or slightly younger. This situation casts a contextual shadow on theories emphasizing the advantages of having a peer group; obviously, these advantages are far from universal. In research on students' written recollections of their childhood, this author unexpectedly found many accounts of abuse committed by students' peers when they were younger (Ambert,

1994a). For many of the students, the impact of the peer group went beyond transitory unhappiness. In examining only the 0 to 14 age bracket, 17 percent (in 1974) and 27 percent (in 1989) of the students recalled negative peer treatment described as having had detrimental and lasting consequences for them; that is, these experiences had affected them for several years, often up to the present time. Were the calculations for the 15 to 18 age bracket included, the percentage would increase to 37 percent for the 1989 cohort.[23]

In contrast, only 13 percent (1974) and 9 percent (1989) of the students described negative parental treatment (and attitudes) that had had a lasting detrimental impact. Even if these negative peer experiences were still a minority phenomenon, there is far more negative treatment by peers than by parents in these autobiographies—and this is even more obvious for the 1989 than the 1974 cohort. This result, corroborated by other research-ers,[24] is startling considering the often single-minded focus of child-wel-fare professionals on parents while neglecting what is perhaps becoming the most salient source of psychological misery among youth—peer con-flict and maltreatment (Ambert, 1994a). In these autobiographies, one reads accounts of students who had been happy and well adjusted, but quite rapidly began deteriorating psychologically, sometimes to the point of becoming physically ill and incompetent in school, after experiences such as being rejected by peers, excluded, talked about, racially discrimi-nated against, laughed at, bullied, sexually harassed, taunted, chased, or beaten. Even school work was often disrupted as a result.[25]

Child and adolescent abuse at home has been estimated at around 3 percent, slightly more or less depending on the study.[26] In contrast, extrapolations from the data collected by this author project a much higher prevalence of peer abuse (see Besag, 1989). Thus, a conservative estimate might be that a minimum of 20 percent of all children will be abused by peers during their young lives—and we are not speaking here of normal transitory conflicts, disagreements, and teasing (Eder, 1991). Moreover, recent surveys reported in the news media, both in Canada and the United States, present much higher estimates. Observed cases of bullying in Toronto elementary schools are higher than those that are self-reported (Pepler et al., 1994). In view of these estimates, however tentative, it is unfortunate that peer abuse is not yet a prominent research topic,[27] and is not included in theories and classifications of *child* abuse. Sexual harass-ment, mainly by boys toward girls, is a particularly pernicious form of abuse (Stein, 1995).[28] It generally goes undetected, may even be approved of by boys' parents, and some girls may be led to believe that it is flatter-ing or simply the normal price one has to pay for popularity.

The data also add a new dimension to theories positing that children acquire social competence and cooperativeness through interaction with age-mates. Although resolution of *normal* peer conflict is useful (Corsaro and Rizzo, 1990),[29] findings regarding peer abuse actually suggest that in many instances the results of conflict are destructive (Roland and Munthe, 1989). In fact, through abusive experiences with age-mates, each child victim sees his or her competence as a social actor placed in question by the abuse; his or her self-esteem is shattered, and his or her fundamental right to a safe environment is violated. Olweus (1994) correctly writes in terms of the violation of a child's democratic rights.[30] One can argue that the topic of peer group socialization requires further theoretical and empirical scrutiny in light of the diversity of rapidly changing social contexts[31]—especially those involving youth gangs (Jankowski, 1991; Sampson and Laub, 1993).

THE EFFECT OF PEERS
ON THE PARENT-CHILD RELATIONSHIP

As already observed in this chapter, children's peers affect their relationship with their parents and also affect parents, whether directly or indirectly. The student autobiographies highlight the extent to which children and adolescents bring home the stress experienced via their peers and the extent to which this stress spills over[32] into their interactions with their parents (Ladd, 1992).[33] There is some literature illustrating how parents who are stressed at work bring this tension home with a consequent negative effect on their parenting role (Small and Riley, 1990). Related results indicate that a mother's dissatisfaction with her employment can have a detrimental impact on her children (e.g., Spitze, 1988).[34] It is at least logical to expect that children's stress away from home may have a detrimental impact on family interactions. In view of the results described above, more research should be devoted to the influence on parents and on the parent-child relationship of children's stress (or happiness) resulting from problems (or successes) with their peers.[35] Moreover, very little is known about the differences between boys and girls in terms of how they may affect their parents as a result of the extra-familial situations they experience. The literature on children in peer groups substantiates the necessity for inquiries based on gender (Maccoby, 1996; Thorne, 1993).

It can be presumed that the greater the similarity between parents' values and those of their children's peers, the lower the level of parent-child conflict. Youngsters whose parents approve of their peers, and particularly of their close friends, will get along better with their parents.[36] Not only do they have more to talk about together, but parents may need to exert less direct control over them. The peer and parent effects are syner-gistic (Steinberg et al., 1995). Moreover, it is likely that these peers will, in turn, "approve" of the parents; this situation will reinforce both the con-nection between child and peers as well as the relationship between par-ents and child. In contrast, when parents disapprove of their children's friends, especially during adolescence, a great deal of tension may exist if parents voice their concerns. Whether they express concern or not, parents will be negatively affected by the situation. They will worry about peers' detrimental influence and may try, often unsuccessfully, to counterbalance it by sending the youngster away to camp, or enrolling him or her in lessons and sports activities. Parents may spend much effort, money, and time in order to provide alternatives to what they perceive to be a negative peer group. Unfortunately, not every parent benefits from such resources; *this means that disadvantaged parents are less able to counteract negative peer pressures than middle-class parents.*

Peers also influence parents through the support (intended or other-wise) that children receive from peers to go against parental teachings, rules, and wishes. What parent has not heard the following? "But all the others are going." This may be the complaint of a 14-year-old girl who wants to go to a nightclub. "I'm going to look like a loser leaving at 11:00 when everyone gets to stay until 1:00 and 2:00 a.m." may be the objection of another girl who has just received permission to attend a party. A 15-year-old boy whose father is inquiring about parental supervision at a house party may inform him: "Of course his parents aren't going to be there! Parents *always* leave for parties." And so on. "Everybody is doing it" and "everybody has one" are powerful messages handed to parents.

Thus, each parenting couple and, more and more, each single mother has to face what is presented as a consensus, as a rule, among youngsters. Parents are made to feel that, if they do not conform, they will do a grave injustice and deprive the child. This alleged consensus among youngsters allows them to speak with great authority to their parents who are gener-ally more isolated than their children when it comes to tactical and moral support. As we have pointed out earlier, adolescent subcultures are much more cohesive and less fragmented for each child than are adult subcul-tures for each individual parent. In reality, there is no such thing as a parental subculture, and this constitutes a disequilibrium that is detrimen-tal to the parents' role (Small and Eastman, 1991). Along these lines, Stein-berg et al. (1995:453) find that, when adolescents' peers have authoritative parents, the latter contribute to positive developmental outcomes above and beyond their own parents' authoritativeness. "We believe that this may be due in part to the higher level of shared social control provided by a network of authoritative parents."

Many parents, especially more educated ones, make it a point of knowing their children's peers' parents (Muller and Kerbow, 1993). Parent networks can fulfill several functions both for parents and their children and, when they are school based, can contribute to a better socialization process,[37] norms that are more closely adhered to, and better-informed parents. It is, however, far more difficult for parents of adolescents than for parents of young children to know their children's peers' parents—at a time when such contacts would be the most helpful.

PARENTAL CONCERNS ABOUT PEERS

From a parent's point of view, a peer group or specific peers may be a source of concern for at least four reasons. First, some children are mistreated and even abused by their age-mates, while others are rejected. For instance, girls who show greater peer conformity are more vulnerable to unwanted sexual contacts (Small and Kerns, 1993). Parents may see the traumas inflicted upon their children and suffer acutely along with them; if they themselves have been rejected as children, they may relive with unpleasant intensity their child's predicament. However, these traumatized children often do not let their parents know the magnitude of their pain so that when the stress they experience suddenly spills over into family life, parents do not understand the source of these outbursts. Some of these children may become dependent and needy, while others may take their frustration out on their parents and strive for premature independence.

When they are aware of it,[38] parents certainly suffer with children who do well in school but are labelled "nerds" or "brainiacs" or accused of "acting white" by their peers. These students, in order to avoid such negative labels, may attempt a variety of strategies, such as clowning and trying to hide their intellectual interests (Kinney, 1993). Junior high school years are particularly painful in this respect, but students often regain a positive sense of self in a more diverse high school, as reported in the longitudinal observational study by Kinney (1993). It is unknown whether these rejected adolescents draw closer to their parents in an attempt to recapture from them a sense of normalcy and acceptance, or if they draw away from them in a futile gesture to establish an identity that has greater peer acceptability.[39]

Other parents who are achievement oriented may be concerned when their child's friends fail at school, skip classes, or entertain low expectations for the future. Black parents may experience this concern to a greater extent than other parents (Steinberg et al., 1995). Here as well, parents may try to counterbalance this effect or at the very least neutralize it. But such peer groups, especially when embedded in a context of poverty, do indeed contravene parental influence, especially in terms of school achievement. This may occur even more frequently among African Americans whose peers often accuse others of "acting white" when they do well in school (Boykin, 1986; Ogbu, 1987). Similar tactics are used among Native American youth (Henry and Pepper, 1990). Therefore, parents, and perhaps especially minority parents, may be worried about the long-term consequences for their youngsters of the values they inherit from their peer culture. Steinberg and Brown (1989–reported in Steinberg et al., 1995) have indeed found that adolescents who have academically-oriented peers do better than others, and this effect is over and above family contribution.

Then there are those peers who gravitate toward drugs, alcohol, or even delinquency (Elliott, Huizinga, and Ageton, 1985). These generally are of grave concern to parents—when they are aware of their existence—and can sour the parent-child relationship to the point where the youth may leave home prematurely. Drug use lowers an adolescent's interest in school and sports activities, and encourages narcissistic attitudes and behaviors; it may also lead to addiction. With addiction, dropping out of school generally follows, and delinquency may evolve to support the habit. Thus, another category of peers that concerns parents are delinquent peers—those who have already been arrested or have committed crimes but have not yet been caught.[40]

THE INTERFACE BETWEEN PARENTS AND THE PEER-SIBLING DYNAMICS

As an extension to the previous chapter, it is important to point out that parent-child-peer dynamics will differ for one-child families compared with multi-children families. In addition, the dynamics will differ depending on any existing overlap among the siblings in terms of their peer groups. And, finally, the spacing between the children will also make a difference. These hypotheses have yet to be studied and therefore research results are not available to present. It is consequently important to develop a few research ideas on these topics.

Generally, the parent-child relationship is more intense when there is only one child. Parents devote more time to him or her because there is no competition for their attention from other offspring. Without siblings as companions, the "only" child may value peers more than a child who has a sibling who is close in age. That only child may therefore be even more peer oriented than a child with brothers or sisters; or the child can be less peer oriented if he or she has been successfully integrated into parental activities and networks. Nevertheless, it is reasonable to assume that these parents will pay a closer attention to their only child's peers.

In families of two or more closely-spaced children whose peer groups overlap, the parent-children relationship will be more pleasant when the parents approve of peers. It can also be assumed that if one child has a negative peer group while the others associate with prosocial peers, parents may find some compensation in the latter situation and experience less stress than if both children had a negative peer group. If several siblings share a detrimental peer group, these adolescents can form a coalition and parents may have a very difficult time fulfilling their socialization duties. Several of this author's students from families with three or more closely spaced adolescents have commented, in class discussions, on how difficult it was for their parents to impose a curfew, monitor their activities and whereabouts, filter out negative peers, and even to make sure that no additional teenager was sleeping over, hidden by one of the siblings. They also described situations where youngsters would "cover" for each other so that one of them could "sneak out" behind their parents' back. Parents themselves have reported having the feeling of living "in a cage," or in a "zoo," and that they were "behind bars" while their children and assorted peers were running the house. Such a peer-oriented group of siblings may have a strictly passing relationship with their parents whom they talk to only when they need something; parents are largely irrelevant to their lives. It would be interesting to follow the long-term consequences of this situation for the parent-child relationship as both children and parents age.

PARENTS, PEERS, AND NEIGHBORHOODS

One important context of the parent-child relationship is the quality of the neighborhood in which families live. **Indicators** of neighborhood quality are: the proportion of low-income or high-income families, percentage of families below the poverty level, the proportion of single-parent families, racial or ethnic concentration, crime and victimization rates, quality of housing, high mobility, and presence of community resources such as recreation centers and health services (Wilson, 1987).

Children who live in distressed neighborhoods, by these standards, have only meager resources and are exposed to few positive role models (Crane, 1991); they may also be influenced by deviant and aggressive peers (Gibbs et al., 1988). The flight of the working and middle classes from inner-city communities has meant a diminishing availability of positive role models, a loss of connections and networks, as well as a lack of collective social control over youth groups (Ellwood, 1988). For instance, a study of inner-city high schools found that too many male students owned guns: 22 percent of the nondelinquent students and 83 percent of the delinquents possessed a gun. Eighteen percent of students still in school were drug dealers and the majority of these owned a gun: 75 percent actually carried guns with them (Sheley and Wright, 1993). Parents who raise children in such neighborhoods have to be able to supervise them carefully, shelter them from aggressive and deviant peers, and provide them with alternative resources and leisure activities (Furstenberg, 1993). But, by definition, these neighborhoods contain large proportions of impoverished single-parent families who suffer from a multiplicity of stressors and are often the least able to supervise their children (McLyod and Wilson, 1991). Indeed, several studies have established that adolescents in mother-headed families are more susceptible to peer influence than those living with two parents.[41] This may well be due to the fact that single mothers have fewer resources that would allow them to counteract peer influence.

This combination of a low-quality neighborhood, a stressful family situation, and little supervision amidst delinquent peers constitutes a recipe for risk in children.[42] In fact, Kupersmidt and Coie (1990) have found that such conditions, along with peer rejection, predict behavior problems. Kupersmidt et al. (1995) compared high-risk children living in relatively low **socioeconomic** areas to high-risk children living in more affluent **SES** neighborhoods. They found that better neighborhoods served as a protection against the development of aggression in high-risk children. Indeed, in these neighborhoods, children were less likely to associate with deviant peers, and, therefore, low parental supervision did not have as detrimental an impact. Children could more easily bring friends home or play at friends' houses, hence they spent less time in unsupervised settings.[43]

When families are poor but function well, living in a safe neighborhood enhances the parent-child relationship in that parents can relax their level of supervision and thus avoid conflict with their children. Such conflicts often arise in dangerous neighborhoods where parents have to shelter their children (Wilson, 1987). Furstenberg (1993:243) appropriately writes of the "supermotivation" that such parents need in order to protect their children and create opportunities for them. In contrast, parents in middle-class neighborhoods, while their children are not totally immune to delinquent peers, do not have to invest so heavily in protecting and providing opportunities for them, as many of these opportunities are built into the environment.

CONCLUSION

Peers are salient in children's lives, and consequently form a primary context in which the parent-child relationship evolves. And, as discussed, peers may even be more important than parents for the development of some child and adolescent outcomes.

But this peer context is itself situated in a media-propelled culture and in neighborhoods of diverse quality and levels of danger. In distressed neighborhoods, there is a general lack of supervision and values are frequently deviant; the result is that little positive collective socialization occurs (Brooks-Gunn, 1995). The entire socialization burden is placed on parents who may themselves be quite deprived on several levels.

The research that has been conducted so far points to very different experiences in daily living for parents and children according to the quality of the neighborhood, and, consequently, the quality of the peer group environment. This topic, initiated in Chapters 3 and 5, as well as this, is pursued in several subsequent chapters. The peer-media interface has not been addressed because, regrettably, there is not enough literature pertaining directly to this topic.

ENDNOTES

1. Literature on these topics can be found in the following journals: *Child Development, Developmental Psychology, Journal of Early Adolescence*, and *Journal of Social and Personal Relationships*. See also Berndt and Ladd, 1989; Feldman and Elliott, Eds., 1990.
2. Greenberger and Steinberg, 1986.
3. Giordano, Cernkovich, and DeMaris, 1993.
4. Corsaro and Rizzo, 1990; Goodwin and Goodwin, 1988.
5. See Asher, 1990; Eder, 1985.
6. Patterson, DeBaryshe, and Ramsey, 1989; Rubin, LeMare, and Lollis, 1990.
7. Jensen-Campbell, Graziano, and Hair, 1996.
8. Diaz and Berndt, 1982. This gender difference continues into adulthood. See Larson and Richards, 1994:31; Weiss, 1990.
9. Phillips, McCartney, and Scarr, 1987.
10. Several studies look at "bullies" and at victims' personalities: Farrington, 1993; Olweus, 1994; Perry, Kusel, and Perry, 1988; Pulkinen and Tremblay, 1992.
11. This discussion closely follows Ambert, 1994b.
12. This section is not intended to address peer *groups* or "crowds," such as "jocks," "populars," or "greasers." On peer groups, see Brown, 1990. It is also important to keep in mind that *children's* cultures exist long before adolescence: Corsaro and Eder, 1990; Mandell, 1986.
13. Nava, 1992.

14. Chisholm et al., 1990.

15. Galland, 1991.

16. Youniss and Smollar, 1985.

17. Zinneker, 1990.

18. See also Bozon, 1990.

19. These parental concerns are substantiated in the literature: Agnew, 1991; Warr, 1993.

20. Pettit et al., 1991.

21. Putallaz, 1987.

22. Ladd, Le Sieur, and Profilet, 1993.

23. For the 1974 cohort of students, data pertaining to the 15 to 18 age bracket were not gathered.

24. Larson and Richards, 1994:99-101.

25. Asher and Coie, eds., 1990; Reid, 1985.

26. Burcky, Reuterman, and Kopsky, 1988; Finkelhor and Dziuba-Leatherman, 1994; Garbarino and Plantz, 1986; O'Keeffe, Brockopp, and Chew, 1986; Strauss and Gelles, 1990.

27. Roland and Munthe, 1989.

28. See also Bird, Stith, and Schladale, 1991; Small and Kerns, 1993.

29. Goodwin and Goodwin, 1988; see also the volume by Berndt and Ladd, 1989.

30. Olweus, 1994.

31. On the latter, see Feldman and Elliott, 1990.

32. See Repetti, 1987: the concept of spillover refers to the transfer of mood or stress from one setting to another. Repetti (1993) is referred to in Parke et al., 1994:139.

33. See also Belsky, Lerner, and Spanier, 1984:80.

34. See also Orthner, 1990; Paulson, Koman, and Hill, 1990.

35. Larson and Richards, 1994:132.

36. For reasons of parsimony, no distinction is made in this text between peers in general and friends. Such a distinction is important, and might be even more so for females than for males.

37. Coleman and Hoffer, 1987.

38. Parents are not generally made aware of peer abuse, as children may feel humiliated or embarrassed to talk about it (O'Moore, 1989). Moreover, children are frequently shrugged off by parents and teachers when they complain about their peers (Stephenson and Smith, 1989).

39. See Gore and Aseltine, 1995.

40. The topic of delinquency is discussed in Chapter 13.

41. Dornbusch et al., 1985; Steinberg, 1987.

42. Goodyear, Kolvin, and Gatzanis, 1987.

43. Patterson et al., 1991.

Chapter 7

The Parent-Child-School Context

When universal schooling was first introduced in the last century, a great proportion of parents resisted, although for a variety of reasons. Working-class parents objected to losing their children as wage earners and workers, a factor that was most important in farm communities. Matters were difficult for families whose children had contributed greatly to the domestic economy (Hareven, 1989). For their part, middle-class parents were concerned about the loss of moral control over their children, which had until then been a family prerogative and function. However, middle-class parents more easily accepted universal schooling because they were able to control the educational system, a situation that more or less continues to this day. Thus, the stratification system that we discuss in this chapter is not a new phenomenon. Some inequalities existed from the outset; others have appeared more recently, especially in inner-city neighborhoods, forced by new economic realities.

Schools constitute a key agent of socialization in children's lives. They also serve the function of reproducing the economic ideologies and structure of the societies in which they are embedded.[1] The school context involves several overlapping environments: The environment composed of the teaching personnel has the steadiest influence on children, parents, and their relationship. The peer group, the topic of the previous chapter, is an environment that overlaps greatly and may be even more influential. There is also the matter, at times controversial, of the curriculum.

In this chapter, after introducing the overall relationship between schools and families, we turn to the role that early school plays in child development and in the continuation of the parent-child relationship. Family routine and organization is then related to children's school achievement. The role of teachers is considered, as are the links between parental involvement in their children's education and family resources. The effect of the school system on minority children and their families is examined. In a following section, schools are situated in the context of specific neighborhood characteristics. A few comments on the curriculum are then presented. The goals of this chapter are limited to selected issues that focus on the parent-child-school interface.

SCHOOLS AND FAMILIES

Both sociology and psychology have subdisciplines specializing in the educational system: sociology of education and educational psychology. Neither of these two areas focuses much attention on the effect of schools on the parent-child relationship. There is a prolific literature on the impact that schools have on the educational achievement of children and adolescents. There is also some research on schools as tools for interracial integration and the lowering of discrimination and prejudice. Programs to retain adolescent mothers in high school, to prevent early pregnancies and sexually transmitted diseases, to feed malnourished children, to deter peer violence, to teach children to avoid sexual abuse and to report it, as well as programs addressing many other issues, have been researched and some have been evaluated in terms of the success of their goals (Halcombe, Wolery, and Katzenmeyer, 1995).[2] Therefore, there is some information on how these programs affect targeted youngsters, but not on how they impact on the parent-child relationship—except in those programs geared to teenage mothers where they are taught parenting skills that, it is hoped, will contribute to a healthy mother-infant bond.

As one can see by this enumeration of the educational system's nonacademic functions, schools are now concerned with a wide range of areas that touch children's lives. Consequently, the educational system should, in theory, enhance the parent-child relationship and help parents fulfill their facilitating role in child development. But it is not known if the parent-school interface is necessarily beneficial to the family, and, if it is, in which respects. It is certain that early schooling takes children out of their homes and away from parental influence at a very young age. Some children, perhaps most, gain from this situation and this, in turn, should benefit parents as well as family relationships. But some families will profit more than others. Overall, there is a gap in the literature in terms of the impact of social institutions on the family via their children. As Parke (1994:219) points out, "It seems that when adults are the family members that are involved in extra-familial settings, the direction of influence flows from outside contexts, back to the family. When children are involved in outside activities (e.g., schools, peers, etc.) it is assumed that the family influences their adaptation in these contexts."[3] The bias stems largely from the traditional perspective that sees children as the product of their parents' child-rearing activities. Such a paradigm leaves little room for the consideration of other influences on children that could in turn impact on family functioning. Children are rarely portrayed as representing their families in external contexts or as utilizing these contexts, consciously or not, to impact on the parent-child functioning.

EARLY SCHOOL

When the last child has begun kindergarten, this is generally the time that stay-at-home mothers choose to reenter the workforce. For many, this is an overdue transition, although it is often done for financial reasons. Work-related satisfactions raise the quality of the mother-child relationship for many women who now enjoy quality time with their small children rather than isolation at home with them.[4] However, the heavy workload and poor employment conditions also produce stressors that may strain the relationship (Menaghan and Parcel, 1990). When one parent stays at home, kindergarten may signify too early an intrusion on their right to educate their small children as they see fit, and too early an interruption in the flow of the parent-child relationship. When kindergarten is nearly universal, reluctant parents may feel that they have to enroll their children in the program for fear that they will be at a disadvantage compared with other children.

Most parents, however, are proud of this new milestone in their children's life, although they may feel nostalgic about the realization that it signifies the end of early childhood. With kindergarten, parents often introduce new responsibilities or privileges to their young children, who may have to start getting dressed entirely by themselves for the first time, eat lunch at school, go to new friends' homes, receive an allowance, and so on. Kindergarten often serves as a signal to parents and children that a new measure of independent living has to be introduced into children's lives. Small children are malleable, and they have so much to learn in so short a period of time. Hence, kindergarten and early primary schoolteachers play an important role in their lives and consequently in parents' lives as well, especially so for mothers. Kindergarten teachers are particularly salient in setting the tone of children's later adjustment to school.[5]

FAMILY ROUTINE AND ORGANIZATION

Children are more successful at school and better adjusted to its requirements when family life is similar to school life in many of its organizational features (Hansen, 1986). Families that have a routine and a schedule, where children eat breakfast, where rules are followed, and where educational activities are encouraged, help their children become integrated more easily into the educational system (Rumberger et al., 1990). In contrast, for families that have no routine, where everyone gets up at any time, does not dress until later or not at all, eats whenever hungry, watches unlimited amounts of television, goes to bed at all hours, and where books are largely absent, daily life is a world apart from the school routine and even goals. Hence, children from these families may have more difficulty fitting in at school as well as more trouble learning, because the two lifestyles may actually clash. If these children have an easy temperament, are cooperative, and are at least of average intelligence, they will likely overcome this lack of congruence between family and school and adjust. Such children may in turn bring some organization into their family life, generally unwittingly, or they may insist on arriving at school on time and hence consciously set about changing family patterns. At that point, the child may open a window of opportunity for the family, especially when parents have low educational levels and are chronically unemployed.

These changes may enhance the parent-child relationship and bring children closer to their parents as they seek their help and request that stories be read to them. At that point, parents who are very poor readers, as are many high-school dropouts,[6] may begin reading more easily as they use their children's first grade books, for instance. But, when children are less intelligent or have temperamental difficulties, the child-school fit is usually poor; such children are likely to be unable to integrate themselves into this alien world. This may be especially so if their parents cannot help them with their lessons; these parents may have felt equally alienated by this world when they were themselves small. These children immediately come to teachers' attention, and we have the beginning of what can be a long and ongoing struggle between parents and teachers, or at least tension between the two. That tension may spill into the parent-child relationship as parents may feel blamed and are perhaps overwhelmed by the school's requirements and the difficulties their children appear to be creating. Scarr (1985) posits that children who come from a disadvantaged family, but are intelligent and "spunky," are more likely to be noticed in a positive way and encouraged by teachers than are their less personable counterparts from a similar background.

SCHOOL PERSONNEL

The family-school fit may increase, probably enhancing both the children's and parents' well-being, when the following happen: The school's personnel is sensitive to the existence of a variety of family types and levels of functioning, as well as methods of communicating; the personnel is trained and willing to help; and parents are receptive to this help. It may be especially important to improve the child-school fit for sensitive children: The more sensitive a child is, the more easily that he or she can be affected detrimentally by the school experience; such youngsters have a low threshold for frustration and may negatively interpret teachers' neutral gestures. They may return home distressed; at that point, if their distress is diffuse rather than specific, and if they fail or are unable to explain its source to their parents, they may negatively affect family dynamics, at least for a while upon their daily return home. Yet, as pointed out for peers in the previous chapter, there is very little research on the impact on this type of spillover effect that school personnel, as a source of stressors, have on the parent-child relationship. Teachers emphasize that parents have to cooperate with the school toward the goal of child adjustment and achievement. Generally, little thought is given by school personnel to how they impact family dynamics, a factor we discuss more extensively later on.

Competent and empathic school personnel may impact positively or minimally on family dynamics. Their effect is minimal or simply reinforcing when problems do not arise and there is a great deal of similarity between home and school values and routines. Their impact is positive when problems exist, and a supportive and cooperative relationship is established with parents. In contrast, unskilled school personnel unavoidably impact negatively on children and their parents. The evidence indicates that this is a more frequent occurrence in schools that have a large proportion of minority students (Bridges, 1992). It can be predicted that when teachers are not skilled, competent parents will be frustrated and outraged, and may have to put in a great deal of time and energy to remedy the situation and to help their children. Parents who are less skilled and knowledgeable may instead feel helpless, confused, and humiliated, and may not be in a position to contribute anything. As a result of difficulties encountered with the school system, parents may become more supportive of their children, or more critical and restrictive, depending on the extent of the perceived loss of responsibility, as well as on parenting styles and the personalities of both parents and children. Consequently, the parent-child relationship may become more strained, or it may become closer.

The research so far has focused on the positive or negative impact on children of entire schools compared with more or less effective ones; not surprisingly the results indicate that good schools generally benefit children (Mortimore, 1991).[7] There is a new trend in research that looks at differences between classrooms within the same school (McNamara, 1988). Such a focus would place greater attention on teachers, whose expectations affect children's achievement,[8] and whose skills correlate with children's learning (Brophy, 1988). Eccles and Midgley (1990) find that junior high school is a particularly difficult period, and that students' experiences with their teachers are too often negative.[9]

PARENTAL INVOLVEMENT AND RESOURCES

Parental involvement in schooling is related to children's achievement (Dornbusch et al., 1987),[10] and is consequently a key concern in research (Epstein, 1987). It is also a concern of teachers who expect parents to support them and to prepare children for school. Education manuals emphasize the "partnership" that exists between teachers and parents. This is particularly important for minority children (Berger, 1991). Yet, partnership implies equality and this is generally not what teachers seek. They do not want parents to question their professional qualifications and classroom behaviors—especially when these are not up to par. Neither do they like parental interference in the curriculum. White, Taylor, and Moss (1992) criticize the types of parental involvement evoked by educators as being of little benefit when parents are simply used as backup staff. They suggest that more attention should be devoted to programs that provide assistance to parents and family members. Moreover, as Kerbow and Bernhardt (1993) point out, the traditional concept of parental involvement implies that it depends solely on parents' motivation. In practice, there are several elements that either encourage or prevent parents from being involved, as will be seen later on in this section.[11]

Lareau (1989), an educational sociologist, has written an interesting book illustrating how parents are unequal vis-à-vis schools, teachers, and curriculum. Building on Coleman's (1988) theory of resources, she emphasizes the gap between educated and advantaged upper-middle-class parents and a much less educated, more disadvantaged group of working-class parents, many of whom were unemployed at the time of her study. This research demonstrates how parents' social class position equips them with an unequal set of resources that can impact differentially on children's school performance,[12] and especially on parents' ability to be involved in their children's education. Slavin (1994a:114) points out that, in this context, "The life of a middle-class family in the United States or Canada is probably more like that of a middle-class family in Italy, Ireland, or Israel than it is like that of a poor family living a mile away."

According to James Coleman (1988), there are three types of resources (which he calls capital) that a family provides to its children: financial capital, human capital (parents' intelligence and education), and social capital, which refers to the quality of the parent-child relationship, as well as to the quality and quantity of the relations that parents and children maintain within their community. Each of these resources is important in different ways, and the resources that parents benefit from may not necessarily be those reaching their children. For instance, Muller (1995) reports that when maternal employment (which provides financial resources) deprives the child of adequate supervision (social capital), the child does less well in mathematics at school (human capital). However, when maternal employment is linked with supervision and involvement, the child receives the full benefit of resources available to his or her mother. Consequently, the child's academic achievement benefits[13] and, as seen in earlier chapters, so do other types of child outcomes.

Upper-middle-class parents, who, in Lareau's sample, are well-educated executives or professionals, have the competence to help their children when they have learning problems. Such parents also feel self-confident with teachers, and do not hesitate to request changes that could benefit their children, or to question teachers' decision. In their own social networks, they have access to professionals, such as other teachers, psychologists, and tutors, whom they can consult on school matters. These parents are also more aware of school requirements (Astone and McLanahan, 1991).[14] Moreover, they are better equipped to meet teachers' requests because they have more material resources at their disposal (Zill and Nord, 1994). These resources allow them to provide their children with educational materials, computers, tutors, art or music lessons, and perhaps summer camps, and to pay for babysitting if they need to have a conference with the teacher (Stevenson and Stigler, 1992). Lareau also mentions that these advantaged parents often bring work home from the office, and this work allows their children to have at least some idea of their employment activities. In contrast, less advantaged parents are used to the separation of work and home, and they apply this separation to school and home as well. They see teachers as professionals who are more competent than they are, and they do not question their decisions.

Comparatively disadvantaged parents value education as highly as do their wealthier counterparts; in fact, Muller and Kerbow (1993) report that minority parents have higher expectations than white parents for postsecondary education. The problem resides in that disadvantaged parents generally lack the skills to help their children when they have school problems (Gibson and Ogbu, 1991). Moreover, they often feel intimidated by teachers, and it is a well-known fact that parents of lower-class origins attend parent-teacher conferences far less frequently. Often, lack of day care or babysitting prevents them from meeting with teachers. Also, working-class parents may not have the benefit of a flexible work schedule that would allow them to participate in school activities, such as volunteering, that would give their children an advantage *within* the system–an "inside track."

Several researchers have emphasized the difference that exists between children of diverse social classes in terms of summer holiday activities. Upper-middle-class children benefit from summer activities that are compatible with school routine, while disadvantaged children often spend their summers in pursuits that increase their distance from what is required for school performance (Heyns, 1988). Not surprisingly, research indicates that these children lose a few points on the IQ scale, as well as on tests of mathematical ability during vacations; a knowledge vacuum is created and they have more difficulty than advantaged children in readapting themselves to school work once classes resume (Entwisle and Alexander, 1992).

The parent-child relationship will be more tense when children do not do well in school, or as well as expected by parents. Lareau (1989) presents circumstances where parents make demands which children rebuff, leading some parents to back off and others to use different strategies. When children are not particularly rebellious, they can react to poor grades and parental pressure with internalized distress and become overly anxious. Some develop **psychosomatic symptoms**. In turn, these reactions affect parents and the relationship in an interactive cycle. Lareau believes that the upper-middle-class parent-child relationship is more prone to this problem than is the case among the less educated and advantaged social classes. Among the former, family life and school are viewed as interdependent; among the latter, as pointed out earlier, schooling is seen as separate from family life. Therefore, the consequences in one domain, the school, are less likely to affect the other, that is, the family.

Moreover, less educated parents who want to help their children often meet resistance if the youngsters lack confidence in their parents' competence. Lareau (1989:109) gives the following description provided by a mother who lives in a disadvantaged area:

> My kid will come home and I will sit down and help him do homework. [And he says], "My teacher didn't do it that way, you are doing it *wrong*, Mom!" When you get to that point, [you say], "Forget it! Do it at school!"

In a chapter on the parent-child school context, it is important to refer to a fairly substantial literature in sociology, in part initiated by Kohn (1969), which shows that parental values concerning their children's socialization vary depending on their class situation, and more specifically their occupation (Kohn, Slomczynski, and Schoenbach, 1986). These parental values are related to the quality of the home environment and to the way in which they interact with their children (Menaghan, 1994). Parents' occupational changes are related to changes in child-rearing values (Kohn and Schooler, 1983). Also, in turn, as we have seen, parents' social class is related to children's educational achievement. Menaghan and Parcel (1995) demonstrate that single mothers who are employed in high-wage jobs provide their children with a home environment compatible to that provided in similar two-parent families. In contrast, single mothers who have low-wage jobs or are unemployed experience a reduction of the quality of life they can provide their children. Again, this literature points to resources as being a key determinant in the parent-child relationship and child development. To some extent, the more advantaged parents are in terms of resources, the better they are able to provide an environment that is congruent with the school system. On a historical note, it is interesting to recall that earlier studies focused on the *father's* work and related social position; it is only recently that the *mother's* social position has been taken into consideration in this respect. Moreover, current research no longer emphasizes the detrimental effect of maternal employment, as used to be the case from the 1940s through the 1970s.

MINORITY FAMILIES

In a nutshell, there are important social class differences that advantage one group of parents and their children and disadvantage other groups. There is a middle-class home-school fit that does not exist to the same extent for less advantaged families. This is more obvious when these families also are members of a minority that is visible, either because of race or because of language differences. Such parents and their children may be doubly disadvantaged: Not only are they poorer on average but cultural and structural differences may make it difficult to understand teachers' requirements and help their children. In an interesting ethnographic study, Heath (1981) illustrates how different (but not inferior) the method of question-and-answer played out in working-class African American families is from that of "known-answer" questions used by middle-class families and teachers. This difference creates misunderstanding between the two groups. In other words, the style of conversation at home, especially among minority groups and lower-class families, may conflict with the one utilized in school and hamper children's achievement (Mehan, 1992).

When schools do not have personnel from their ethnic or racial group, parents may feel that the school is a foreboding, alien world. They may be afraid to talk to teachers and may not understand their vocabulary. Unless they form an organized group, such parents are unable to influence the system so that it can assist their children. They usually value school highly because they see it as the door to future opportunities for their children. But there is a gap between their values and their ability to implement them in compliance with a system that is so different from their life at home.[15] Kerbow and Bernhardt (1993) indicate that 42 percent of Hispanics attend schools where more than 50 percent of the students are also Hispanic. Similarly, over half of blacks attend schools populated largely by blacks, and 60 percent of white students attend schools were 90 percent or more of students are white. Schools with "very high concentrations of African-American and Hispanic students show significantly higher levels" of parental participation in meetings with teachers and parent-teacher organizations compared with other schools (Kerbow and Bernhardt, 1993:126). Although these minority schools are overwhelmingly disadvantaged materially and educationally, parents have a higher rate of involvement than white and Asian parents whose children are enrolled at more advantaged schools–although Asian parents are often involved in other forms of educational activities with their children.

One barrier to school achievement for minority students, both in the United States and Canada, is that black and Mexican-American peers often accuse same-race students who achieve academically of "acting white." No doubt many black students who receive encouragement at home are hindered by their peers (Steinberg et al., 1995). This phenomenon had already been noted by Holt (1972), who called it "cultural inversion." This means that black children regard a behavior as *not* black because they see it as characteristic of whites. It is rather intriguing that this occurs both in Canada and the United States where the two black populations generally have different immediate origins, with a great proportion of black Canadians having recently immigrated from Caribbean countries. Black parents have high expectations in terms of school achievement. Both in Toronto and Montreal, some of these parents temporarily return their adolescents to their country of origin (e.g., Jamaica or Barbados) to complete high school when they realize the inadequacy of their children's new environment and the negative impact of the peer group. But too many parents see their dreams for a better future shattered as their youngsters are caught between the minority-group culture that predominates at these age levels and the inability of the school system to outweigh this influence. How do these parents express their frustration to their children? Can they do so? Here again, a wide field of inquiry is suggested for future researchers.

During classroom discussions in my course on the parent-child relationship, immigrant students of all races are more likely than Canadian-born students to mention that parents are frequently perceived by their children, and particularly their adolescents, to know less than their children because they are ignorant of the American or Canadian "way of doing things." This type of inverted intergenerational superiority can prevent adolescents from benefiting from their parents' help with school work. Most children and parents talk about school and future educational plans (Muller and Kerbow, 1993); it is reasonable to assume, however, that such conversations are facilitated when there are good communication lines within the family, and parents' competence is not questioned by children. However, the high academic expectations of Asian parents, particularly in terms of grades,[16] may carry both benefits and disadvantages for the parent-child relationship.

While studies on education do recognize these differences related to social class and race/ethnicity/culture membership, there is little research that inquires into the impact of these differences on the family and on the parent-child relationship. Basically, researchers are once again too busy focusing on the impact that such families have on children's educational achievement. This perspective is short-sighted because, when schools have a negative impact on families, their children will be less advantaged, and the cycle of failure and frustration will be perpetuated. In theory, the school has the opportunity to impact positively on family life, especially if teachers recast their role as helpers to parents rather than seeing parents as potential facilitators or impediments to their own role. When children do well at school, this is one concern that parents do not have and one less source of potential conflict or strain between parents and children. Generally, school achievement enhances the child's self-esteem and parents' pride and sense of accomplishment. This situation has a positive effect on the parent-child relationship and may also contribute to marital harmony. The latter, in turn, is an important factor in children's ability to do well at school.

SCHOOLS AND NEIGHBORHOODS

Schools can be considered a neighborhood resource, while the neighborhood may be either a resource or a liability to schools. There is some relatively recent research pointing to the influence of the quality of the neighborhood on child development and on outcomes such as school achievement. Jencks and Mayer (1990) provide a taxonomy of the theories explaining neighborhood effect. In this section, some of the key results of existing research are briefly surveyed. The main focus of these studies is on disadvantaged inner-city American neighborhoods,[17] a topic of concern because of the concentration of joblessness and poverty that continues to grow there (Gramlich, Laren, and Sealand, 1992; Kasarda, 1990).

Although there are some differences in the findings depending on the samples and the year the studies were carried out, research generally indicates negative effects on adolescent outcomes as a result of living in neighborhoods with a large concentration of unemployment or low-skilled jobs (Brooks-Gunn et al., 1993).[18] The results are still too tentative to indicate whether African American males or females (Rosenbaum et al., 1993) or other ethnic/racial groups are more affected, as well as whether it is the concentration of poor or of affluent neighbors which is the important variable (Duncan, 1994).

Disadvantaged parents living in poorer neighborhoods generally encounter greater difficulties with their children's behavior and school adaptation due to the neighborhood's negative influence. Such parents may have to give up monitoring children if they want to maintain a warm relationship with their independent and often delinquent offspring who associate with other at-risk adolescents. These parents would definitely benefit from institutional support, and so would their youngsters. Teachers make more frequent requests for involvement from parents among the less advantaged classes,[19] perhaps because their children need more help: In fact, when children's grades are low, parents have more contact with the school (Muller and Kerbow, 1993). These requests and contacts are likely to place a strain on parents, especially if they do not find the teachers friendly.

Another important aspect of the social stratification system is that low-income students have a less positive school experience than do higher-income ones. Their school performance is, on average, lower,[20] and several possible explanations for this disadvantage have been discussed. Brantlinger (1993) has compared the responses of well-to-do versus disadvantaged high school students and found that the latter reported more acting-out problems and felt more ostracized and rejected (Elias, 1989).

It is necessary to know how these results hold depending on the quality of the neighborhood in which the school is situated. Fine (1991) has also addressed the matter of the inferior school environment that is presented to low-income students which is conducive to their eventual decision to drop out. Other studies find that low-income students are more often ignored by teachers (Good et al., 1987), are more frequently punished (Marotto, 1986), and are disproportionately encountered in low-ability groups and special education classes.[21] Kellam (1994) reports that low-ability classrooms in one study had rates of aggression of 60 percent or more compared to 5 percent in higher-ability classrooms. Obviously, students who are economically disadvantaged are not treated as well by the school system and, if the interactional perspective of this book is followed, we would probably find that those who are more prosocial and gifted are likely to persevere despite this disadvantage. But, overall, it is important for future studies to investigate what impact these students' unpleasant school experiences have on their relationships and functioning within the family system, *and how this impact is related to neighborhood quality.*

CURRICULUM

What is officially taught in schools, particularly via textbooks and teachers' handbooks,[22] and what is unofficially taught are two salient preoccupations of very diverse groups of parents. The unofficial curriculum may be the result of conscious intent on the part of teachers or it may exist at the unconscious level. What goes in the written curriculum is far easier to analyze and detect than what is casually said in class, what behaviors are tolerated, promoted, or punished, and what ideologies are passed on or are not considered (Beane, 1990). How the class is structured and what sort of relationships are encouraged–cooperative or competitive– are also part of this hidden curriculum (Stevens and Slavin, 1995).

For some parents, the curriculum or the "hidden agenda" are too sexist. For others, they are racist, go against God's words, are anti-Christian, promote violence or consumerism or materialism, are pro- or anti-war, or anti-national–and this list could be expanded.[23] In view of the fact that American children trail behind most industrialized nations in test results,[24] for a majority of parents, the *quality* of the educational system is a huge problem. They are concerned about what and how much children learn in terms of the three basic skills of reading, writing, and arithmetic, as well as history, languages, and sciences. Many parents are also concerned about bilingual education: Some ethnic parents wish their children to learn both English and their native language, such as Spanish. Others are against such curricula on the basis that the predominant language of the United States and Canada is English and immigrants should become integrated.

One particularly interesting experiment in restructuring the curriculum takes place in cooperative schools where children of all abilities are mixed together, help each other, and where parental participation is encouraged (Slavin, 1994b). Such a system may benefit both gifted and delayed students (Johnson and Johnson, 1989), provided teachers are well trained (Gallagher, 1991). It also benefits teachers (Stevens and Slavin, 1995), may help prevent traditional divisions between boys an girls (Thorne, 1993), and facilitates the parent-child relationship. This latter benefit, not surprisingly, has not been as well documented as the others. But one can easily suggest that, when special-needs children achieve better and are placed in an environment where they make more friends, both children and parents will be happier. Another school experiment in Baltimore, Success for All, involves a team that assists families on a variety of levels (Madden et al., 1993). Learning that is connected to process, as well as to content, and is also connected to the child's environment, including the family, is advocated by many (Morrison, 1994). Separate all-male classes for African American boys are also currently being assessed (Hudley, 1995). Hence, these various developments interest educational researchers, but should be equally important to researchers of the family.

CONCLUSION

Peers, schools, and neighborhoods are three contexts that generally overlap. Therefore, their effect on the parent-child relationship and on child development interact and often augment each other, whether negatively or positively. This is why living in urban ghettos or poor, isolated rural areas is so detrimental to families and their children. In some cases, the introduction of a "magnet" school in a deprived neighborhood produces advantages in terms of peers and curricula, and acts as a buffer against the social and physical deterioration of the neighborhood. School bussing may also serve a protective function and provide children, who would otherwise be walled in a world of poverty without escape, with windows to other options.

The topics of religious and private schools, as well as private boarding schools, have not been discussed. Although such schools are attended by relatively few children, they nevertheless constitute interesting laboratories in which researchers might study the parent-child relationship. What is particularly interesting about such schools is that they are *selected* by parents, presumably because they promote a philosophy of education, a lifestyle and values that are seen as closer to those of parents than what is offered by a neighborhood school (Fasick, 1984). While *the parent-school fit may be high, the student-school fit is not automatic nor assured,* and this could lead to family difficulties.

What this chapter indicates above all is that research on the effect of the schools needs to be expanded to cover many child outcomes other than achievement. The existential experience of children should be a prime focus of research, as should be the impact of schools on the family and on parent-child relations.

ENDNOTES

1. E.g., see Bowles and Gintis, 1976.

2. For additional references on schools, and schools and children, as well as schools and parents, see *American Educational Research Journal, American Journal of Education, Anthropology and Education Quarterly, California Journal of Educational Research, Educational Review, Early Childhood Research Quarterly, Harvard Educational Review, Journal of Educational Psychology, Oxford Review of Education, Review of Educational Research, Review of Research in Education, Sociology of Education*; also, *Black Issues in Higher Education, American Educational Research Association, Journal of Teacher Education, Journal of Education, Equity and Leadership, Phi Delta Kappan, Language Arts, Journal of Educational Issues of Language Minority Students*, and *Action in Teacher Education*.

3. This point rejoins the remark by Pillemer and Suitor (1991b) reported in Chapter 4 concerning older parents' effect on their adult children.

4. Moreover, a good marital and parental relationship can act as a buffer in stressful employment situations (Barnett, 1994).

5. Ensminger and Slusarcick, 1992; Pianta, Steinberg, and Rollins, 1995.

6. Venezky, Kaestle, and Sum, 1987.

7. Mortimore et al., 1988; Sylva, 1994.

8. Blatchford et al., 1989.

9. Larson and Richards, 1991.

10. Fehrman, Keith, and Reimer, 1987.

11. Hoover-Dempsey, Bassler, and Brissie, 1987.

12. Stevenson and Baker, 1987.

13. Muller, 1993.

14. Baker and Stevenson, 1986.

15. Kagan et al., 1985.

16. Kao, 1995; Sue and Okazaki, 1990.

17. Wilson, 1991a, and 1991b.

18. Dornbusch, Ritter, and Steinberg, 1991.

19. Hoover-Dempsey, Bassler, and Brissie, 1987.

20. Mullis et al., 1991.

21. Gartner and Lipsky, 1987; Mitman and Lash, 1988.

22. Britton, Woodward, and Binkley, 1993.

23. See a general perspective in McLaren, 1995.

24. Stevenson and Stigler, 1992.

Chapter 8

The Parent-Child-Professional Context

PROFESSIONAL AUTHORITY OVER PARENTS

One important context for the parent-child relationship consists of the various professionals who define what good parenting is and what normal child adjustment should be. Since approximately the middle of the last century, a variety of professionals have socially constructed the boundaries of parental propriety. At first, various religious leaders, and what has been called the **child-saving industry**, have brought their moral stamp to parenting. They were followed by physicians, who also took it upon themselves to reform parents. The parenting role became "medicalized," and parents were admonished to follow proper rules of hygiene in accordance with the morality and the knowledge of the day.

The interlude between the two World Wars saw the appearance of psychologists and psychiatrists whose **hegemony** continues to this day, more recently aided by lawyers. Social workers have long been important members of these helping professions (Gordon, 1988), but their standards and decisions are generally determined by the more powerful professions of psychiatry, psychology, medicine, and law. In tandem with the emergence of this series of experts, the last century and early twentieth century saw the emergence of what became a lucrative commercial enterprise: books intended to teach parents how to take care of their children.

We live in a century where expert knowledge is given preeminence. The lay public, especially the less educated segment, has gradually lost power over a variety of areas of life that have fallen under the aegis of science and the professions. Thus, people have become dependent on various experts, not only for knowledge, but for their rights, their health, the education of their children, and, more recently, the quality of their sexual and conjugal life, and even the definition of what constitutes happiness.

Professionals have become highly valued by various state agencies. They are regularly consulted in matters that pertain to the family, over and above parents, and contribute to the enactment of laws and policies in this domain. Those laws and policies in turn further the interests and the power of the professions. "The manufacture of modern social problems is an industry in which professionals play major roles" (Sullivan, 1992:5). Experts are now so prominent in the definition and the treatment of various problems that many thinkers are asking themselves whose best interest is being served, that of children and their parents or that of the professionals who define and oversee that "best interest?" Nelson (1984) illustrates how alcoholism, considered a sin or a crime earlier on in this century, is now defined as a disease. "Many behaviors with significantly aggressive or violent components have been similarly 'medicalized.' In addition to child abuse, examples include alcoholism, drug abuse, hyperkinesis, and to a lesser degree rape and domestic violence" (Nelson, 1984:17). This situation has been searingly discussed and thoroughly documented in an article titled, "The professional response to child sexual abuse: Whose interests are served?" (Fincham et al., 1994).

Professionals "police" the care parents give their children (Donzelot, 1979), assign blame to parents when youngsters develop problems, and treat children; they may even treat *parents* when children suffer from emotional problems and physical ailments. Parents can no longer be just parents: They have to adhere to a set of professional norms and expectations.[1] Moreover, children and especially adolescents have also been schooled to accept these sanitized versions of their parents' role–which place the onus of child outcome on parents and deprive youngsters of the assumption of responsibility for their own behaviors.

Professionals can therefore either facilitate or complicate parents' lives as well as the parent-child relationship. They can contribute to child and adolescent development or they can unwittingly hinder it. The reasons behind these contradictory effects are explained below. It is also important to note that there are several movements among the helping professions and family scientists that critically study their own impact and constructions of reality (Paré, 1995). There is a growing awareness of cultural biases in determinations of therapeutic interventions (Gergen, 1985, 1992). There is greater recognition that clinicians and family scientists should receive more extensive training in cultural diversity (Ganong, Coleman, and Demo, 1995; Yutrzenka, 1995); such programs have already increased in number (Hills and Stozier, 1992). There is also a renewed consciousness to the effect that some ethnic groups have recourse to certain types of treatment facilities over others,[2] with recommendations that facilities adapt to their culturally different clientele (Dilworth-Anderson, Burton, and Turner, 1993). In addition, there is a growing awareness that some problems, such as hyperactivity or depression, are partly genetic in nature, and it is therefore unlikely that purely environmental interventions will be successful (Bronfenbrenner and Ceci, 1993); unfortunately this topic has yet to be addressed systematically (Plomin, 1995). Finally, experts have criticized the tradition of parent blaming, and, for instance, urge greater compassion for parents of the emotionally disturbed (Hatfield and Lefley, 1987).

This chapter first examines how professionals (doctors, lawyers, psychiatrists, and psychologists) can facilitate or burden parents' lives. We begin with the history of the "schizophrenogenic" mother to illustrate one detrimental effect of professional hegemony. This hegemony is then discussed in terms of the pitfalls that can lead experts to overlook the best interest of the child and parents. Parent effectiveness training is examined as a constructive as well as a potentially problematic method of intervention. We conclude by inquiring into the role, positive and negative, that researchers such as psychologists and sociologists play in the lives of those who participate in their research.

THE "SCHIZOPHRENOGENIC" MOTHER

In the 1950s and 1960s, the "schizophrenogenic" mother was the buzz word in research and clinical work on children and adults with schizophrenia. This fashion began with the publication in 1948 of an article by psychoanalyst Freida Fromm-Reichmann. She defined the schizophrenogenic mother as one who, by her behavior and faulty mode of communication, *caused* her child to become schizophrenic. Given that psychoanalysis had already emphasized the negative role that mothers can play in the child's development, the ground was fertile to receive a theory that placed blame solely on mothers (Parker, 1982). Consequently, a battalion of clinically oriented researchers began studying schizophrenics' families and family interactions, focusing on mothers and their "double bind" mode of communication (Bateson et al., 1958). Unavoidably, the results of their research showed that in comparison to mothers of normal children, schizophrenics' mothers suffered from a variety of personal problems and shortcomings. Hence the conclusion was drawn that these mothers caused schizophrenia.

Although the conclusion was unwarranted, this result was not surprising—for several reasons. First, studies of adopted children, as well as of identical and fraternal twins reared apart and separately, indicate a fairly high degree of heritability for schizophrenia, as discussed in Chapter 11

(Gottesman, 1991). It is therefore reasonable to assume that a certain number of schizophrenics' mothers are also either schizophrenic themselves or suffer from emotional problems that can be genetically linked to schizophrenia. Consequently, the causality is a genetic one and not one stemming from faulty child-rearing practices per se. Second, it is likely that a certain number of schizophrenics' fathers, who, by the way, were rarely implicated by these researchers, are schizophrenic and could transmit this genetic propensity to their children. In this scenario, the mother would experience stress from the simultaneous presence of a disturbed spouse and child, therefore, her own behaviors might be affected negatively.

The third explanation resides in just that point: It is difficult for a mother to care for and live with a schizophrenic child. Hence, the causality may well be reversed. The mother's life becomes stressful because of the child, rather than the child being "caused" to be schizophrenic by the mother. For instance, the researcher Beels (1974) has noticed that parents of schizophrenics exhibited better reasoning skills when he met them separately. Thus, how professionals perceive parents may depend in large part on the circumstances under which they meet them. A fourth explanation was provided by the psychiatrist Terkelsen (1983) who has shown that some of the research carried out on families of schizophrenics took place in the artificial environment of a laboratory and within an accusatory atmosphere. These circumstances contributed to making parents feel blamed and ill at ease. They reacted with stress and at times with uncharacteristic aberrant behaviors and styles of communication. Unfortunately, researchers were not studying the effect of *their* own research methods on the hapless parents; the latter's atypical behaviors were seen as a cause of child abnormality rather than as a detrimental result of biased research.

A last explanation is based on the fact that mothers who have a schizophrenic child must *adapt* to him or her, and must learn to communicate with the child according to his mode of thinking and behaving, especially when he is in an acute phase (Liem, 1974). Therefore, the communication pattern of mothers of schizophrenics may be "disturbed" when they are in the presence of their child. Many studies have since shown how adults adapt to children; this is particularly obvious in those instances where children are hyperactive or delayed.[3]

This example of the "schizophrenogenic" mother serves to illustrate how research and professional fashions of an era can burden parents with useless blame and guilt. This notion of the schizophrenogenic mother was unsupported by all but the most superficial and biased evidence (Hirsch and Leff, 1975). It was abandoned in the mid-seventies, but not before it had inflicted much pain on these already-burdened women (Torrey, 1983). Unfortunately, the myth is perpetuated to this day because there are still clinicians, especially in private practice, who believe it and continue to "treat" mothers in order to cure their children![4] This section should not conclude without mentioning that autism was once believed to be created by a "cold" mother, and that homosexuality was until recently attributed in clinical circles to a domineering mother and an ineffectual father. In the meantime, we have learned that both autism and homosexuality, like schizophrenia, are in great part genetic.[5] In the case of homosexuality, this assumed pattern of accusatory causality stemmed from a clinical ideology that defined or constructed homosexuality as pathological in nature, therefore subject to clinical intervention.

PROFESSIONAL HEGEMONY

How can professionals, with the best of intentions, be detrimental to parents' well-being and the parent-child relationship? Individuals who belong to the helping professions are victim to three pitfalls that can unintentionally corrupt their good intentions and contribute to professional hegemony.

The first pitfall was illustrated above in the example of the schizophreno-genic mother: Researchers and professionals, just like everyone else, form ideas to explain what is wrong with people and hold values about what should be done (Smith et al., 1991). In the case of experts, their ideologies are assumed to be guided by scientific principles, a factor that bestows upon them a great deal of credibility and power. For instance, there are therapists who attempt to change their clients' lives in ways that are not desired. There is also some research indicating that clients whose values become more similar to those of the therapist are judged to have improved more (Beutler, Machado, and Neufeldt, 1994). Hence, normality comes to be defined along a set of professionals' values. Moreover, clinicians and other helping experts often do not test the validity of their ideas, and fail to do research to verify if their treatment or social policies are bearing fruit.

The second pitfall resides in the professional and scientific hierarchy: Experts possess knowledge not available to laypersons. This knowledge becomes power and it is used to impose ideas, theories, interventions, and social policies. While many are well guided and sound, others produce results that are far from being in the best interest of the target population, which has little to say in the matter (McElroy, 1987). For instance, while many clinicians seriously consider parents' point of view in the treatment or rehabilitation of children and adolescents with problems, others prefer to keep parents at arms' length, with detrimental results (Spaniol et al., 1987).

A third pitfall stems from the fact that once a professional group is established, there is a tendency to institutionalize a structure that promotes the group's expansion and its visibility. One consequence is a vested interest in ensuring that members of one's professional association are heard as experts on key social issues, and have as much power as possible in the definition of what a problem is and how it should be remedied. Hence, subspecializations emerge; agencies, clinicians, and legal experts who specialize in child sexual abuse are one recent example.

The British sociologist, David Oldman (1994:45), points out that "the growth of child protection work must be explained by changes in the adult labour market," rather than "in any recent change in the conditions of childhood itself." As Maddock (1993:116) put it, "Wittingly or unwittingly, mental health care professionals have given the message to the public that they need help for a wide array of disorders, and the public has responded by demanding higher quality professional services." Moreover, there is often competition between the new mental health experts and this may result in interventions that are incompatible with each other (Cummings, 1986). While some new problems, such as youthful drug addiction, require special training, it is difficult to tell to what extent "professional expertise" is more useful than parental training and empowerment. Professionals have, however, been able to prevent some child abuse and neglect by disturbed or uncaring parents. Unfortunately, it is perhaps also true that this achievement has occurred at the expense of the moral authority of caring and conscientious parents.

PARENT BLAMING

What too frequently happens with expert opinion on children and adolescents is that parents are marginalized, disempowered, and their role is consequently substantially reduced (Castle, 1986). The result is that conscientious parents can no longer be as effective as previous generations were because they have lost much of the moral authority that belonged to them in the past. Parents are placed in a dilemma. On the one hand, they may be told to "mind their business" when their child has problems and comes to the attention of various experts. But then they are often blamed for the problems. In fieldwork, this author has discovered that many adolescents find this marginalization and blame of parents a convenient excuse for avoiding any accountability for their actions and for continuing to pursue potentially self-destructive behaviors.

"Professionals under siege sometimes begin to fall back on their perception of parents to justify their desire to excuse themselves from their inability to respond to parents' concerns" Rubin and Quinn-Curan (1983:79). These authors point out that when society cannot meet a parental request for services, the assumption is that there is something wrong with the parents. As they write, "seeing the parents as 'the problem' assumes that the parents are emotionally disturbed" (p. 73). This rationalization preempts the need for an examination of **systemic** failures. Terkelsen (1993:191) points out the unfortunate consequence of such ideas: "When either therapist or family harbor the belief that schizophrenia is caused by personal experience with family members, therapeutic misalliance is bound to follow." He came to this conclusion after having first misinterpreted the patients' parents' words. He describes how he "listened to the parents talk about life with the ill person, abstracting from their reports those interactional phenomena that I thought suggestive of parental pathology" (p. 192). He finally came to realize that abnormal patterns of family interaction were interpreted in terms of parental causality.

Burden is a useful concept to apply to families where one member has emotional problems. One person's poor social performance often becomes another's burden; it is consequently important for clinicians to map out familial burdens (Gubman and Tessler, 1987). While professionals as well as the workforce in mental hospitals and in social agencies have chosen to care for the emotionally ill as their career, the patients' families have made no such choice. They have no alternative. Moreover, the family's potential to contribute to the treatment of its mentally ill members is usually not actualized: The family is simply given a custodial role (Hatfield, 1987). As Falloon and Pederson (1985:156) point out, "In this capacity, they are often denied access to information concerning the nature of the patient's illness and guidelines on its management." However, caution must be taken so that an increased role for the family, especially the parents, would not increase their burden. Falloon and Pederson (1985) show that an effective family management program on the part of the therapeutic community substantially reduces parental stress. In contrast, a program focusing intensively on the patients does not relieve family burden. Moreover, professional and agency intrusion means that parents' personal and family lives are closely scrutinized and "their family's boundaries will need to become highly permeable" (Rubin and Quinn-Curan, 1983:89).

THE EFFECTIVENESS
OF THERAPEUTIC INTERVENTIONS

Greater success for therapeutic intervention with children and adolescents has been found in research rather than in clinical settings.[6] As Suin (1993) pointedly remarks, too many clinicians, once installed in their practice, simply ignore literature that could inform them of new techniques and diagnostic improvements. And, we might add, that would keep them within the boundaries of sound and ethical practice. Weisz, Weiss et al. (1995b) summarized, via meta-analysis, the results of a variety of psychotherapeutic interventions with children and adolescents that were carried out mainly within a research setting where the therapist is closely monitored. Overall, the results show that about 75 percent of the children were functioning better after treatment than a comparative control group of children.[7] However, in attempts to replicate such results on therapy carried out in regular practice, with little monitoring of clinicians and a more heterogeneous set of interventions, they found that outcomes ranged from detrimental to only minimally successful. And these were clinical interventions for which a control group existed. *In reality, very few clinicians use a control group or do research to measure the effectiveness of their interventions* (Kendall and Stoutham-Gerow, 1995). This omission is especially important in view of the fact that non-research clinicians treat youngsters who are more disturbed, and who come from more dysfunctional environments, than do therapists who practice in a research setting (Weisz, Donenberg et al., 1995).

There are indications, supported in the Weisz, Donenberg et al. study (1995), that behaviorally focused interventions have a higher rate of success than other therapeutic programs (Piercy and Sprenkle, 1990). Such treatments have been more extensively evaluated than others, perhaps because research clinicians utilize them more. It is not known, however, which features of their approach–that is, "targeting specific problems, use of explicit reinforcers, and direct teaching of coping skills" (Weiss and Weisz, 1995:320)–are the most effective. As in any other type of intervention, a therapist's interpersonal skills constitute an important element in treatment success (Kottler, 1991).

PARENT EFFECTIVENESS TRAINING

One type of behavioral intervention that has been researched involves training parents to modify their children's behaviors. Parents are now at the front line of therapeutic interventions directed at redressing or alleviating their children's behavior problems,[8] with a good measure of success with young children, but less so with violent adolescent offenders (Henggeler, 1989).[9] Conduct disorders and opposition, generally occurring together, are situations that particularly involve parents because most researchers find a combination of difficultness in children and lack of parenting skills at the base of these problems (Patterson, 1984). What Patterson and his colleagues describe as a cycle of coercion sets in when parents are ill equipped to deal with problematic episodes and use inappropriate techniques such as permissiveness, giving in to tantrums or opposition, or harsh and erratic punishment. Children become rapidly more adept at coercing their parents into acquiescing; this parental retreat in turn encourages children to further escalate their negative behavioral repertoire. Studies also find that parents who are under severe stressors, such as marital disruption, social isolation, and poverty are more likely to exercise inefficient child-rearing practices. It has already been seen that both neighborhoods and peers can also play a negative role in children's outcomes. (The etiology of behavior problems is discussed in Chapters 12 and 13.) Moreover, one has to consider that factors that cause the initiation of a behavior or an emotional disorder may not be the same as those that maintain it. Inefficient parenting may play a role at one stage (maintenance) but not at the other (causality).

Whatever the etiology, a variety of parent effectiveness training programs have shown a good measure of success in breaking the cycle of coercion,[10] at least in the short term (Bank et al., 1991). What happens in the long run is not generally studied.[11] Spitzer, Webster-Stratton, and Hollinsworth (1991) have documented the stages that parents enrolled in such a program go through, from admitting that their three- to eight-year-old child has severe behavior problems about which they feel helpless, ashamed, and even angry. As the chain of training sessions moves on, parents learn new coping skills and more appropriate methods of discipline, and, as they regain a certain level of control, the children's coercive episodes diminish in numbers and severity. Parents feel great relief, as if a terrible burden had been lifted from their shoulders. They learn to utilize their support system more efficiently, and are also encouraged to lower their expectations and to be more realistic concerning their children's behaviors and personalities (Kazdin et al., 1985).

Spitzer, Webster-Stratton, and Hollinsworth (1991) also documented how, at one phase or another of the training cycle, a majority of the parents "resisted" the process, and setbacks occurred. As these authors (1991:426) explain it, this resistance occurs because parents maintain unrealistic expectations and hope that success will come rapidly. They underestimate "the commitment and energy needed" and they are frustrated over "having to deal continually with children who are aversive and nonreinforcing despite their best efforts." The authors sympathetically describe some of the pitfalls and frustrations that parents encounter during the weeks of the training process as they implement new techniques and use rewards and punishments more efficiently (Lochman et al., 1984). A few are listed here to illustrate the magnitude of the difficulties facing such parents.

First, they blame themselves, evaluate themselves negatively, and believe that they are the cause of their children's problems. They feel isolated because they cannot discuss their situation with others, such as relatives and teachers, who might blame or reject them. They learn that their children have a chronic problem that will require continuous monitoring (Spitzer, Webster-Stratton, and Hollinsworth, 1991:422). Parents may also experience unanticipated setbacks as siblings who have been easy become difficult in order to benefit from the problematic child's reward system, "thus taxing the already depleted resources and energy of these parents" (p. 420). There are also instances when a boyfriend or a grandmother who lives with the family, but does not participate in the training program, creates a conflictual situation by using inappropriate techniques or contradicting the mother. Many parents feel that the time and patience they must invest in the child are excessive. In other instances children who are particularly resistant use the reward system to find yet another way of controlling their parents: Some "children refused to do anything without a reward" (p. 423).

This litany of problems encountered by well-intentioned parents of young children is only magnified for parents of older children whose behavior is more entrenched and even potentially dangerous. Adolescents have additional means with which to confront their parents if they so wish: truancy from school, running away from home, breaking their curfew, being verbally or physically threatening, and using assaultative behavior. Appropriate reward systems can be nearly impossible to establish because such youngsters may prefer rewards from the streets to those from their parents. It is at that stage, one often leading to delinquency, that many parents become desperate; many then turn to a parent support group (Chapter 13).

This section illustrates that, because parents have to be involved in intervention programs aimed at helping their children, professionals wield a great deal of power over them, and their compliance is necessary if they are not to be judged "resistant." As discussed earlier, the success of the intervention, as assessed by the experts themselves, lies largely in parents' own resocialization progress: Parents who accept the professionals' views are considered the most successful. But not all parents will be reeducated, either because of their own personality problems, their lack of resources (transportation, babysitting, and money), and their right to disagree when they find the regime objectionable or the therapists unpleasant. Disturbed or poor parents are the most likely to drop out of such programs. Moreover, there is often a great deal of disagreement between professionals and families about goals and the causality of a child's problems. It is also possible that some parents are mistreated by less skilled or less scrupulous "therapists" who may be largely unregulated, self-employed, and often self-trained (Hatfield and Lefley, 1987). In addition, Patterson and colleagues report that parent psychopathology, poverty, and marital conflict disrupt the rehabilitation process and its outcomes.[12] Community-based intervention and education programs may be more efficient at reaching a greater number of parents and at a lower cost than therapy (Cunningham, Bremmer, and Boyle, 1995). Indeed, one of the main problems facing clinical types of intervention is that they do not attract and do not serve a large enough clientele (Zahner et al., 1992).

RESEARCHING PARENTS AND CHILDREN

Researchers can also become a part of the professional context of the parent-child relationship. However, aside from participating in the collection of census data, few families actually become subjects of research. Because studies often focus on negative child outcomes, parents who are problematic, or have special-needs children, or are undergoing difficult transitions are probably more frequently researched than the average population. Few researchers return to ask respondents how they felt about the questionnaire, the interviews, or even the videotapes to which they contributed time. One such recent study by Russell et al. (1995) found that a small group of respondents and families had experienced strong negative emotions as a result of their participation in a research project, although the majority felt either no change in their life as a result or felt that the change had been positive.

Although research is often beneficial to the persons studied, one can hypothesize that the more intrusive it is in parents' and children's lives, the less certain one can be of the participants' positive reaction, unless the direct purpose is to *immediately* help the families in question. By intrusive, one means, in particular, methods that include several members of a family in a proposed discussion of *personal* topics, especially when videotaped. The closer these sessions are to family therapy, the greater the likelihood of creating unanticipated problems.[13] The more family members are involved together in such a task, the more likely someone is to divulge something that will hurt at least one other member, possibly because the speaker feels that the research context grants total freedom of expression. The hurt feelings will linger on. In other cases, a member may suddenly disclose something that the others did not know and the abrupt revelation could have a devastating effect. Examples of such negative results from research are the impact on children of being openly discussed by their parents, the pain felt by parents upon hearing their children blame them, the revelations of spouses concerning negative feelings they harbor about each other, and stepparents discovering that they are not wanted in the family. Yet there is practically no examination of these research-created dangers or risk factors.

One could also argue that even questionnaires given to children and adolescents should be carefully scrutinized from an ethical perspective, because, if not properly designed *to balance the positive and the negative*, they could influence vulnerable adolescents to interpret the questions to mean that their parents' child-rearing approaches are detrimental, even though this may *not* be the case. In other words, even questionnaires–and especially interviews–can be suggestive, either because of their slanted wording or because a suggestible child reacts negatively.[14]

CONCLUSION

Although relatively few parents consult professionals directly, the latter still constitute a key *cultural* context in the parent-child relationship because of their power to *define* what good parenting is. This power is accompanied by the prerogative to blame and even punish parents. The latter case can be illustrated by the possibility of having one's child unjustifiably taken away.

There are categories of parents who are more vulnerable than others to professional control. Aside from parents whose children have obvious problems requiring help, the following are also particularly defenseless: parents who themselves have problems (Chapter 10), impoverished single mothers, perhaps minority group single mothers, and all those who are most likely to come to the attention of welfare agencies and other intervention institutions. Middle-class parents who make it a point of following the latest trends in the popular "how-to raise your child" literature may be particularly receptive to and hence affected by the opinions they encounter. Parental vulnerability and control by experts may produce good results or questionable ones. What is important to remember in the final analysis is that parents have been disempowered and have been "professionalized." One of the results of this situation is that they may be less effective at parenting. This point is further discussed in the concluding chapter.

ENDNOTES

1. In general, they have been internalized more easily by middle-class than lower-class parents.

2. Vessey and Howard, 1993.

3. Such studies are mentioned in Chapters 3 and 11. Buckhault, Rutherford, and Goldberg, 1978.

4. On a related issue, see Kazdin, 1991.

5. For autism, see Rutter, Bailey, Bolton, and Le Couteur, 1993. For homosexuality, see Bailey and Pillard, 1991; Bailey et al., 1993; Golombok and Tasker, 1996.

6. Kazdin et al., 1990; Weisz, Donenberg, et al., 1995; Weisz, Weiss, et al., 1995.

7. Weisz and Weiss, 1993; Weisz, Weiss, et al., 1995.

8. Kazdin et al., 1987.

9. Other forms of therapy, such as Aggression Replacement Therapy, and various forms of training for problem solving (Tate, Reppucci, and Mulvey, 1995), may be more useful with violent adolescents given that they often suffer from cognitive deficits: Lochman and Dodge, 1994. See also Mulvey, Arthur, and Reppucci, 1993; Yoshikawa, 1994.

10. Webster-Stratton, Hollinsworth, and Kolpacoff, 1989.

11. But see Weisz, Donenberg, et al., 1995. Weisz, Weiss, et al., 1995.

12. Patterson and Chamberlain, 1994; Stoolmiller et al., 1993.

13. See Krauss and Slavinsky (1982) on the potentially negative effects of family therapy.

14. On a related topic, see volume edited by Doris, 1991.

Chapter 9

The Family Structure As Context: Divorce, Single Parenting, and Remarriage

DEMOGRAPHIC INTRODUCTION

Forty-four percent of American marriages end in divorce and so do 30 percent of Canadian marriages. In the United States, about 44 percent of children born between 1970 and 1984 will live in a single-parent family before age 16 (Bumpass, 1984); it is expected that this rate will reach 60 percent for the more recent cohort born since 1985. In 1991, 25 percent of American children and 17 percent of Canadian children under 18 lived with a single parent:[1] 60 percent of children living with a single mother had separated or divorced parents and 35 percent had a never-married mother.[2] These statistics contrast sharply with those pertaining to the 1970s at which time 73 percent of children living with a single mother had separated or divorced parents and only 7 percent had a never-married mother.[3] The rate of nonmarital births is 67 percent among African American women and 17 percent among white women.[4] Marriage rates have gone down more for African American women than for other women,[5] probably because of a decline in the proportion of young black men who hold well-paying jobs that would allow them to support a family (Wilson, 1987).

Poverty rates provide an economic context for these statistics on single-parent families. In Canada, in 1991, 18 percent of all children lived in poverty, compared with 65.8 percent of children in single-mother families (Vanier Institute of the Family, 1994).[6] In 1993, 23 percent of all American children were poor; however, 10.5 percent of all non-Latino white children were poor, compared with 35 percent of those in single-mother families. For children of Puerto Rican descent, 41 percent lived in poverty, compared with 68 percent of those in single-mother families.[7] Among

Mexican-American children, 31.5 percent of the total were poor versus 55 percent in single-mother families. Among black children, 38 percent were poor compared with 57 percent in single-mother families (Lichter and Lansdale, 1995:349). In 1989, the median income for a black family headed by a mother was $11,630, but it was $30,650 for a black two-parent family (U.S. Bureau of the Census, 1990).

In 1989, in the United States, only 7 percent of two-parent families had incomes below the poverty level, and 17 percent had marginal incomes; in comparison, 18 percent of father-only families were poor while another 21 percent were marginal.[8] In contrast, 43 percent of mother-headed families were poor, and another 26 percent were marginal—and we know that mother-headed families constitute the majority of single-parent families (Meyer and Garasky, 1993).[9] Moreover, the increase in the proportion of children born to never-married mothers has important implications in terms of well-being because *never-married mothers are much poorer than divorced and widowed mothers*, and they stay on welfare longer, both in Canada (Dandurand, 1994) and the United States (Ellwood, 1989). Many are adolescent, which usually reinforces disadvantages. Never-married mothers may also be more socially isolated than ever-married mothers, even among African Americans,[10] especially when they live in areas of concentrated poverty.

In terms of divorce, a longitudinal study of data constructed from Canadian tax files by Finnie (1993) demonstrates that, in the first year after divorce, women's family income falls by about 50 percent while men's declines by 25 percent.[11] When income-to-need ratios are utilized, that is, when the figures are adjusted for family size, women's income drops by 40 percent while men's increases slightly. Women's poverty rate rises from .16 pre-divorce to .43 post-divorce. Even three years after divorce, women's income remains far below what it had been during marriage and far below their ex-husband's current income. Similar results hold for the United States (Duncan and Hoffman, 1985). These statistics indicate a direct causal relationship of divorce to poverty; they do not, however, preclude the fact that many families experiencing a divorce were already poor. This may be particularly so for minority families (Bane, 1986). Although approximately 70 percent of divorced women remarry (Norton and Moorman, 1987), another concern is that children have a nearly 50 percent chance of having at least one of their parents divorce again before they are 18 (Furstenberg and Cherlin, 1991:14). It is not known how repeated divorce affects the family's economic situation.

The remainder of this chapter is divided along the developmental lines of Chapters 1 through 4, that is, largely following a life course sequence.

Within each age group, the effects of divorce, remarriage, and single parenting on children are examined. The impact that marriages and divorces of varying quality have is then discussed. Before proceeding with these sections, the implications of differences in child outcome by family structure are critically investigated.[12]

DIFFERENCES IN OUTCOMES
AND THEIR IMPLICATIONS

In a nutshell, children from divorced and single-parent families[13] on the average suffer more from behavioral and psychiatric problems, lower self-esteem, and higher levels of anxiety than children from two-parent families (Burgoyne, Ormrod, and Richards, 1987).[14] These adolescents have particularly high delinquency rates (Le Blanc and Fréchette, 1989).[15] They generally do less well academically.[16] As adults, they are more likely to divorce (Thornton, 1991) and become single-parents themselves (McLanahan and Bumpass, 1988), to reach lower occupational levels (Zill, Morrison, and Coiro, 1993), to experience a somewhat lower level of well-being (Amato and Keith, 1991), and later on to have their life expectancy reduced (Friedman et al., 1995).[17] Daughters of never-married mothers have a higher rate of single motherhood (Burton, 1990).[18] These results have been replicated in several Western societies, even in countries with little poverty such as Finland (Aro and Palosaari, 1991).[19] Many of these differences remain in stepfamilies (Dawson, 1991).[20]

Although all studies are unanimous on the point that children from divorced and single-parent families score lower on most measures of positive outcomes, the differences between their outcomes and those of children from two-parent families are generally far from substantial (Demo, 1993). This means that a great proportion of these youngsters do as well as others who live with both parents. It also means that many do *better*.

Family Processes

The processes that lead to negative outcomes can exist in any type of family structure, whether single- or two-parent (McFarlane, Bellissimo, and Norman, 1995). They are, however, more likely to occur in the former (Rossi and Rossi, 1990). Detrimental processes include parental conflict, spousal abuse, stress caused by poverty, and social isolation.[21] These conditions may contribute to a disruption of parenting practices, or may be accompanied by inadequate parenting, such as erratic behaviors and lack of monitoring, which in turn impact negatively both on the parent-child relationships and on children, particularly those whose personalities already place them at risk or who associate with peers who are not prosocial. Bank et al. (1993) suggest that boys who had no adjustment problems before divorce are likely to recover more quickly than those who were already maladjusted.

The divorce itself leads to a series of changes, including the resumption of dating by the custodial parent (Seltzer, 1994). Additionally, with parental separation, the family income drops, children often lose their home,[22] and may have to move to a less affluent neighborhood and adjust to a new school with peers who may also be less prosocial than their former peers (Silbereisen, Walper, and Albrecht, 1990). Moreover, the single parent may become depressed or even seriously disturbed following separation, and the parent-child relationship then further suffers. In other words, parental separation brings a host of concurrent changes into a child's life and these, in turn, create what have been called irritants or daily hassles that have been correlated to problematic child outcomes (Dubois et al., 1992).[23]

Another process relates to monitoring. Children of single mothers are less supervised than those in stepfamilies and in two-parent families, especially when mothers are employed full-time. Mulkey, Crain, and Harrington (1992) show that, after controlling for income and parental education, the variable that best explains the small difference left in test scores and grades between children from single-parent and two-parent homes is students' misbehaviors, perhaps the result of a lack of supervision. Nevertheless, in general, once parental involvement and supervision are controlled for, the effect of family structure still lingers on, albeit less strongly so (Lee, 1993).

Other researchers find that it is not the single-parent status itself that lowers women's parenting skills, but probably the consequences of divorce. However, they note that single mothers experience more stress than married mothers and it may be this stress that impacts negatively on child outcomes. This stress may also contribute to lower monitoring of and involvement with children, factors that are important in preventing juvenile delinquency, particularly in disadvantaged neighborhoods (Sampson, 1985). Children who live in very conflicted two-parent families are unhappier and perform worse in many instances than those of divorced families in which parents are nonconflictual and the custodial parent is well adjusted. This also applies to young adult offspring.[24] *Family processes are therefore probably as important as structure; however, the one-parent family structure can more easily lead to disrupted family processes.* Thus, even when income and social class are controlled for, the association between single parenting and negative child outcome still remains (McLanahan, Astone, and Marks, 1991).

Genetic and Environmental Influences

It is possible that only a relatively small group of extremely dysfunctional single-parent families "produce" very negative parent-child relations and child outcomes. If this hypothesis were correct, the net result would be that these families would reduce the *averages* for all children in single-parent families. Dysfunctional parents tend to trigger painful transitions in their own lives, including divorce and unmarried parenthood, and by elimination are less likely to be found in two-parent families.[25] Following the behavior genetics perspective, it can be assumed that many of these dysfunctional parents pass on genes predisposing their children to negative outcomes, subject them to poor child-rearing practices before and after divorce, and create a stressful environment (Patterson and Capaldi, 1991).[26] These parents' vulnerabilities may prevent post-divorce adjustment.[27] It is also possible that such extreme parents tend to mate assortatively to other problematic individuals;[28] this **assortative mating** or homogamy would naturally increase, if not necessarily double, their children's genetic risk; it would certainly exacerbate conflict and family dysfunction both before and after divorce (Capaldi and Patterson, 1991).

To pursue this line of reasoning, it can be argued that there may be a link between dysfunctional parenting practices, low level of marital functioning, and the unavailability of resources in a family. Adults who are incompetent parents compared with others who are competent may also be dysfunctional spouses as well as dysfunctional workers and citizens (see Simons, Beaman, et al., 1993). Incompetent parents may fail to take advantage of resources available to them or may prevent the creation of such resources: They often have a poor employment record or are chronically unemployed. They therefore become cocreators of their detrimental family environment, with negative consequences for their children, especially the less resilient ones. In contrast, skilled individuals create and utilize resources for themselves, their spouses, and even ex-spouses and children (Patterson and Capaldi, 1991), and contribute to positive child outcomes–provided that their children's own characteristics are within the normative range.

To this list of correlated disadvantages, poverty should be added, along with living in a neighborhood with a high concentration of similarly deprived families. These disadvantaged adults' own parents and siblings are probably less able to help them financially or may be as disorganized as they are. Such constellations of outcomes or "chains of events" (see

Chapter 14) are also encountered in two-parent families, but, it is argued, less often. When they are encountered, the results are the same as those for single-parent families (see McLanahan and Booth, 1989:573). Children from families that are dysfunctional on multiple dimensions are consequently vulnerable to stressors, to becoming difficult, not doing well in school, and dropping out; they often turn to delinquency, and stand a good chance of transmitting the cycle of disadvantage to their own children. However, a proportion of the offspring who are born with an adaptable temperament and good intellectual abilities will escape. They are referred to as resilient children in Chapter 2.

YOUNG CHILDREN

Small children who live in never-married single-parent families were often born to a very young, uneducated, and inexperienced mother. A very young mother may not be able to give her small children the care and attention they need because of her immaturity and her consequently unrealistic expectations (Baranowski, Schilmoeller, and Higgins, 1990). It was seen in Chapter 1 that adolescent mothers on average empathize less with the needs of their little ones and often do not respond adequately to them. Their parenting practices may fluctuate between total adoration and harsh punishment at the slightest provocation. They generally take less pleasure in caring for their infants than older mothers (Culp et al., 1991). The small children in turn are often weary, defensive, withdrawn, and uncertain of what to expect. If they happen to have a difficult temperament, they may soon become oppositional, demanding, or even aggressive, and the mother-child relationship evolves into a stressful one.

After a conjugal separation or divorce, the quality of the relationship between parent and small child depends a great deal on how easy the children are and on how distressed the custodial parent is. Moreover, when conjugal conflict persists, as it often does, it impacts negatively on the functioning of the newly formed single-parent unit, disrupts a mother's parenting skills, and casts a negative shadow on her perceptions of her children's behaviors.[29] Hetherington, Cox, and Cox (1982) report that conflicted custodial mothers often become impatient, punitive, erratic, nervous, and tense, even with their toddlers. In addition, they have less time for them and may be less sensitive to their needs. Small children are perturbed by this changed relationship with their mother, especially if they have a less adaptable personality. In addition, they are too young to understand the situation. Some come to believe that the loss of their father is their fault (Jenkins and Smith, 1993).

However, small children adapt better to remarriage and, consequently, are more likely to benefit from a warm stepparent-child relationship than older children (Clingempeel, Brand, and Segal, 1987).[30] At the very least, small children have not yet been contaminated by negative stereotypes of stepparents, and especially stepmothers (Ganong and Coleman, 1983).[31] Several authors suggest that if stepparents were to have legal rights and duties, their role might acquire greater legitimacy (Fine and Fine, 1992).[32]

SCHOOL-AGE CHILDREN

School-age children face very much the same situation as young children; although their cognitive level increases, and they may feel less guilt, they are nevertheless quite affected by the parental breakup. The difficulties they encounter contribute to behavior problems, especially among boys (Hetherington et al., 1992). The mother-son relationship may remain conflictual two to three years after divorce because many of these boys continue to be less compliant and more aggressive than boys from two-parent families.[33] Girls express their distress differently: While boys tend to act out, girls tend to internalize their distress (Doherty and Needle, 1991). In two prospective studies, Block, Block, and Gjerde (1986, 1988) in the United States, and Elliott and Richards (1991) in Great Britain report that even long before divorce occurred, boys from families that later divorced already exhibited more problems than girls. In addition, both boys and girls had more problems than children whose parents had remained together.

There is some conflicting evidence that children, and especially adolescents, do better when they live with a same-sex custodial parent, particularly in terms of school and self-esteem (Zill 1988).[34] This may be a question of having an appropriate gender role model, or of parental ability to better understand a same-sex child (Gately and Schwebel, 1991). It may also relate to the fact that mothers have more difficulties with boys than girls; hence, if boys live with their fathers, they may be less conflictual (Peterson and Zill, 1986). However, a large study by Downey and Powell (1993) reports few advantages for boys or girls living with a same-sex parent. Furthermore, a Canadian study, carried out in Montreal, with a sample of economically deprived families, finds that sons are more prone to delinquency when they live in a father-custody home (Le Blanc, McDuff, and Tremblay, 1991).

It may be that, particularly in economically disadvantaged neighborhoods, fathers do not supervise their children enough so that they become at risk for developing antisocial behaviors in the company of similarly oriented peers who are equally unsupervised. It may also be, as suggested by Le Blanc et al. (1991) that these children's mothers were emotionally disturbed or deviant, and that this deviance had led to father custody. If this were the case, the children might have inherited negative predispositions, in addition to having been victims of a more unstable family environment before the divorce. Obviously, which parent is a better custodial parent deserves more research. Crouter et al. (1990) report that generally, mothers monitor children more adequately than fathers. Rather than investigating the gender of parents and children, one might want to study the parent-child fit in terms of personality and needs–an approach that has yet to be tested.[35]

In terms of parental remarriage, school-age children adapt better than adolescents (Anderson and Hetherington, 1989). They are more home-centered and less resistant to rules so that the parent-child relationship is more important to them and so are demonstrations of affection; therefore, they are in a better position to accept a stepparent. However, the closer children are to adolescence, the longer it takes them to adjust to the reconstituted family. Often, a least at the outset, there is a resurgence of problems among boys and girls (Hetherington, Cox, and Cox, 1985).

ADOLESCENTS

There is some evidence that for many children, a parent's remarriage represents a more difficult adjustment than a divorce–perhaps because children are older at the time of the remarriage and have already undergone one painful change in family circumstances.[36] The second transition may represent an untimely cumulation of stressors just as the first set of stressors was receding (McFarlane, Bellissimo, and Norman, 1995).[37] Even after more than two years, many adolescents who originally had difficulty with the remarriage do not show much improvement in adaptation, and do not fare as well as those in two parent-families (Hetherington, Clingempeel et al., 1992). Adapting to a stepparent is a slow process at best (Cherlin and Furstenberg, 1994). Hetherington (1991) emphasizes that teenage boys with a difficult temperament may take longer to adjust to a stepfather than boys who have easier dispositions. Even the less adaptable boys, however, may in the long run realize the benefits of this new relationship and accept the stepfather. This, in turn, may contribute to easing the adolescents' difficulties.

There is also a difference between adolescent boys and girls; while boys often seem to benefit from the presence of a supportive stepfather, girls' problems frequently increase (Brand, Clingempeel, and Bowen-Woodword, 1988).[38] They seem to resent the intruder who "steals" their mother's affection away (Hetherington, 1989). In short, they have more difficulty than boys in adapting to their custodial parent's remarriage (Bray, 1988).[39] "The trauma of their mother's remarriage may be greater for girls than boys and may suppress any possible effects of temperament" (Hetherington, 1991:187). This trauma results from the fact that girls are often closer to their single mothers and give them fewer problems than do boys. Hetherington (1991) reports that two years after the remarriage, girls are still more negative toward their parents than girls in other types of families. While the introduction of a stepmother is initially more difficult than the introduction of a stepfather for adolescents or younger children who see their own mother regularly, girls once again do not adapt as well as boys (Brand et al., 1988). But they may benefit from the arrangement if both mother and stepmother cooperate.[40] It seems that children resent a substitute mother more than a substitute father, probably because mothers are more salient figures in their lives.

Early adolescents may be particularly vulnerable to the transition of a parent's remarriage because it coincides with a biosocial period in their own lives that requires a great deal of adjustment, thus, the addition of a stepparent may be one adjustment too many. Their mother's renewed sexual activity at close proximity may represent a difficulty for early adolescents who are at the stage of discovering their own sexuality. Whitbeck, Simons, and Kao (1994:120) report that maternal dating affects adolescent daughters' attitudes and behaviors. "This implies a need for discussions with adolescents to distinguish between appropriate adult behaviors and choices and those appropriate for young people. The results also suggest that mothers' own dating be combined with careful parental monitoring of adolescents' dating to clarify boundaries and distinctions between adult and adolescent sexual behaviors." In fact, several studies indicate that adolescents from single-parent families engage in sexual activity at a younger age than those from two-parent families. This result remains after several variables have been controlled for, including race and social class (Day, 1992). Not surprisingly, at least one study has found more adjustment problems for children whose mothers had had a greater number of dating partners (Montgomery et al., 1992).[41] There is not enough research on the effect that parental dating and sexual activities outside of marriage have on the parent-adolescent relationship and on the parent's ability to socialize his or her youngster.

Hetherington et al. (1992:197) point out that disruptive and noncompliant early adolescents "may have a larger effect on parenting in remarried families than in nondivorced families, particularly for the stepfather." Both stepfather and mother may be driven to have a more distant relationship with these disruptive teenagers and may be less able to support and monitor them. Giles-Sims and Crosbie-Burnett (1989) hypothesize that adolescents may have too much power in some stepfamilies, and this may contribute to the demise of these remarriages.[42]

For adolescent boys, divorce may be related to various behavioral problems (Needle, Su, and Doherty, 1990). After a divorce, mothers often have great difficulty with their sons as the latter become defiant, disobedient, disrespectful, and even abusive (Hetherington, Clingempeel et al., 1992). They are more so when parental conflict persists and fathers sabotage mothers' attempt to authoritatively monitor their sons. When there is parental conflict, boys who are in regular contact with their nonresidential parent tend to have more problems than boys for whom this contact is limited (Amato and Rezac, 1994). Sons who were already difficult before divorce may become even more out of control as their mother is too distressed to cope with the problems these boys add to her already burdened life (Ambert, 1982, 1984). Adolescents, like children of all ages, suffer the consequences of parental conflict that continues after divorce (Enos and Handal, 1986). Studies correlate parental conflict to children's internalizing and externalizing problems, with the latter occurring more frequently for boys (Kline, Johnston, and Tschann, 1991). "The worst scenario is for divorce to occur *and* for parents to continue to engage in conflict in front of the adolescent" (Forehand et al., 1994:392). These youth feel "caught between parents" (Buchanan, Maccoby, and Dornbusch, 1991).[43]

YOUNG ADULTS

Most of the studies focus on young adults whose parents had divorced when they were children or adolescents. Little exists on the impact of a parental divorce occurring at that age level, and even less research examines these effects on older adults (but see Aquilino, 1994a). Yet, over 20 percent of divorces in 1990 involved couples who had been married for more than 25 years. One can assume that young adult children accept parental divorce more easily, although not necessarily painlessly, because they are less dependent on their family. Moreover, they are more mobile than younger children and can maintain a relationship with the nonresident parent on their own. Custody is not a variable that enters into consideration (Cooney, 1994).

For these same reasons, it is also easier to accept a stepparent given that the latter does not have any authority over them. Young adults' personalities are more stable, so they will be less affected emotionally, unless the divorce was preceded by years of marital conflict. Also, they may have completed their education so that a parental divorce impacts less negatively in economic terms and in their opportunities to build a successful future. On the negative side, parental divorce depresses the parent-child relationship, at least temporarily, and lessens frequency of contact, but only for fathers (Cooney, 1994). This occurs even more so for father-daughter than father-son relationships (Aquilino, 1994b). Divorce also reduces parental help to young adults, more so for sons than daughters. At least one study finds that the later the divorce takes place, the less of an impact it has on the father-children relationship (Bulcroft and Bulcroft, 1991).

Young adults from single-parent families (Aquilino, 1991) as well as those from stepfamilies leave home earlier than children from two-parent families (White and Booth, 1985). They are more likely to cite family conflicts as the reason for leaving home (Kiernan, 1992). In Canada, in 1991, 68 percent of all unmarried children aged 18 to 29 from two-parent families lived with their parents, but only 51 percent did so when parents were separated or divorced. When parents were divorced and neither was remarried, 59 percent lived with a parent, while 56 percent did so when only the father was remarried. The percentage was 47 percent when only the mother was remarried but plummetted to 27 percent when both parents were remarried (Boyd and Norris, 1995).[44]

Hence a mother's remarriage is far more likely to induce nest leaving, partly because most children live with their mother to begin with and continue to do so into early adulthood. For instance, in the same study, when the mother remarries and the father does not, 72 percent of young adults still living at home reside with the father! These figures would seem to indicate that following a parental remarriage, young adults may feel that they are "in the way" or they may simply feel less at home. Indeed, Goldscheider and Goldscheider (1987) report that both stepparents and stepchildren are less likely to expect young adults to live home until marriage than is the case in intact families. White (1994) also finds that adults who grew up in a divorced family report lower solidarity with their parents. She observes that the relationship is also more distant, especially with fathers. However, those adults who grew up in a stepfamily mention closer relationships with their parents than children from a divorced family, although less so when there was a stepmother rather than a stepfather.[45]

In a longitudinal study of young adults who were living with both parents a decade earlier, Booth and Amato (1994) found that when the young adults had earlier given a low score to the quality of their parents' relationship, they were not as close to them ten years later, even when the parents were still married. When a divorce had occurred, it was followed by an added deterioration in the relationship, especially between fathers and children. Sons were less close to both parents, while daughters were much less close to fathers than daughters from families where divorce had not occurred. In a study on a large group of students, Bolgar, Zweig-Frank, and Paris (1995:148) found that when a mother's remarriage had taken place during children's adolescence or younger years, these children were better adjusted as young adults than those whose mother had not remarried. They conclude that the benefits of a *stable* mother's remarriage appear "only later in life as children of divorce explore young adult relationships."

ADULT CHILDREN

Cooney and Uhlenberg (1990) report that one-third of ever-divorced fathers have lost contact with at least one of their adult children; one in ten has virtually no contact with any of the children, a situation not encountered among never-divorced fathers. On the positive side, it seems that as they age, a proportion of fathers are able to reestablish regular contact with children and to see them more often than they did when they were young. These authors also report that educated fathers have more contact with their children, perhaps because they had the resources needed to continue to support them when they were young, and "children may be more motivated to maintain contact with a father who has more resources to offer them" (Cooney and Uhlenberg, 1990:686).

Another vantage point from which to examine the parent-adult relationship in the context of family structure is to turn to parents aged 60 and over who have a divorced child. Approximately half of this cohort of parents with at least one child who married has one or more children who are divorced (White and Peterson, 1995). About 10 percent of parents in their sixties have grandchildren not in the custody of their adult child. Hagestad, Smyer, and Stierman (1984) report that adult children's divorce distresses elderly parents who have to provide financial or child care assistance or, at the very least, a sympathetic ear.[46] Parents of a divorcing son are often unable to see their grandchildren, and this can be a source of distress. Others refuse to see their grandchildren when accompanied by their ex-daughter-in-law and the resulting tension created by the elderly parents probably negatively affects their own well-being.

Differences in the parent-adult child relationship by the sex of the divorced child may exist (Spitze et al., 1994). Divorced daughters with children have more contact with their parents, and also receive more assistance from them than do married daughters. Sons, however, receive more help when they are married, although less than married daughters.

Divorced daughters who have custody receive more babysitting support but they assist their parents no less than daughters who are still married. Because most help comes from daughters, this latter finding assuages fears that an increase in divorce will lower the support received by senior parents.[47] Sons, for their part, help their parents the most when they have never married, and least of all when they are divorced or widowed. However, assistance aside, the overall quality of the relationship does not appear to be diminished by a child's divorce, although the children's stress or unhappiness may have negative effect on parents who are concerned about them (Pillemer and Suitor, 1991a).[48]

TYPES OF MARRIAGES AND DIVORCES

There are several types of conflictual marriages, and each may have different consequences, although research has only recently begun to take this caveat into consideration.[49] To begin with, not all divorces are preceded by parental conflict and open acrimony (Ambert, 1989).[50] One could also be concerned by the potential effect of a marriage where the spouses are covertly conflictual: They avoid each other, avoid confrontations, and express their acrimony or mutual dislike via body language rather than by verbally or physically attacking each other (see Margolin, 1988). This is a simmering conflict, and a palpable tension exists that children can often perceive; the parent-child relationship may either suffer or be strengthened, perhaps by a coalition between children and one parent (Gable, Crnic, and Belsky, 1994). Such coalitions are not, however, beneficial for a secure emotional development (Sroufe and Fleeson, 1988), and one would expect that children in these marriages would not have good outcomes on all levels.[51]

Another type of conflictual marriage that is problematic occurs where open verbal conflict degenerates into shouting matches, door slamming, and even physical violence (Cummings and Davies, 1994a)[52] The level of family stress is high and affects most members (Katz and Gottman, 1994). Depending in part on their coping abilities, children's outcomes will be negatively affected by this type of marital conflict (O'Brian, Margolin, and John, 1995). In fact, children in severely conflictual families are more adversely affected than those living in single-parent families following a divorce.[53] Studies show that the level of negative emotions is a better predictor of marital quality[54] and divorce than the level of positive emotions (Gottman and Levenson, 1988). Activities and time spent together also predict marital stability (Zuo, 1992). Another type of openly conflictual marriage includes parents who are disorganized and dysfunctional in other areas of their lives, such as employment, friendships, and child-rearing. Such multiproblem families have a serious negative impact on all their members; they are also the most likely to be characterized by parents and children sharing some genes predisposing them to negative outcomes.

Unfortunately, when looking at the category of "children of divorce," researchers do not compare those children whose parents' marriage had been quite good[55] with those whose parents' marriage had been overtly or covertly conflictual, or simply devitalized (Shaw and Emery, 1987). One could expect the impact of divorce to be different depending on the quality of the marriage, as confirmed by one study (Amato, Loomis, and Booth, 1995). Moreover, it is likely that the greater the level of conflict during the marriage, the greater its level after divorce (Ambert, 1989), so that children experience a very conflictual family situation both before and after divorce, or a total absence of the noncustodial parent after separation because of the intensity of parents' animosity. Much research indicates that, when parents are in conflict *after* divorce, children's prognosis is less favorable than is the case when parents set aside their own differences and cooperate to raise their children (Maccoby, Depner, and Mnookin, 1990).[56]

CONCLUSION

In our society, single parenting, divorce, and even remarriage correlate with somewhat more negative outcomes for children than does the two-parent family. In addition, families who live at or below the poverty level, *whatever their marital structure*, also correlate with negative child outcomes. Third, these outcome-poverty correlations may be stronger than outcome-family structure correlations. Fourth, the combination of poverty and mother-only families, especially in inner cities, is a potent contributor to very detrimental child outcomes. Fifth, a disproportionate number of single-parent families, especially those headed by mothers, are at or below the poverty level.

The impact of poverty, especially in single-mother headed families, has long-term negative consequences for mothers' and children's social and economic mobility.[57] When controlling for poverty in analyses of single parenting, the correlations with negative child outcomes diminish substantially.[58] Unfortunately, in our society, it is easier to attack family structure than poverty as one of the sources of children's problems. Indeed, poverty is systemic so that substantially reducing it would require a redistribution of resources, an alternative that goes against the ideological grain of capitalism.

ENDNOTES

1. Statistics Canada, 1992; U.S. Bureau of the Census, 1992b:55. In the U.K., the rate is 21 percent: General Household Survey.

2. U.S. Bureau of the Census, 1992b. The percentages are nearly identical in the U.K.: Roberts, 1995.

3. U.S. Bureau of the Census, 1990.

4. U.S. Bureau of the Census, 1993b.

5. Bennett, Bloom, and Craig, 1989.

6. The poverty floor is higher in Canada than in the United States, thus producing comparatively higher poverty rates in Canada than if the U.S. floor was used.

7. See also Lichter and Lansdale, 1995; Miranda, 1991.

8. Hernandez, 1993, concludes that mother-only families contribute to raising the percentage of children living in poverty. However, were the poverty rate of single-mother families no higher than that of two-parent families, children's poverty would diminish (p. 290).

9. Single mothers are more often unemployed than married mothers, have a lower educational level, on average, and fewer own their home. In Canada, while 79 percent of two-parent families own their home, only 30 percent of female-headed families do. Moreover, they tend to own homes that are older and in poorer condition (Lindsay, 1994). Among renters, 15 percent of lone parents have difficulties paying the rent (Lo and Gauthier, 1995).

10. Franklin, Smith, and McMiller, 1995.

11. See Smock, 1994.

12. The literature on the effect of divorce on children, as well as child and adolescent adjustment after divorce, is very extensive. Although a substantial review of this literature is included in the following pages, far more exists. Journals mentioned in the reference section should be consulted for additional studies on these topics.

13. The discussion does not involve child outcome following the death of a parent or the effect of such an event on the relationship of the children with their widowed parent. In previous decades, this topic would have been emphasized over that of divorce because divorce rates were so much lower. Currently, however, 10 percent of children have lost a parent to death by age 25 (Umberson and Chen, 1994), a much lower figure than by divorce. Generally, studies find that, in terms of outcome, children of widowhood resemble children from two-parent families more than they do those from divorced families (Ambert and Saucier, 1984; Tennant, 1988). This may in part be due to the fact that parental conflict may not have existed prior to widowhood; also because the deceased parent is not absent in the same sense that a noncustodial parent is, and because the poverty rate is lower than that of divorced families.

14. Amato, 1995: McLanahan and Sandefur, 1994.

15. Matsueda and Heimer, 1987; Sampson, 1987.

16. Mulkey, Crain, and Harrington, 1992; Thompson, Alexander, and Entwisle, 1988.

17. Schwartz et al., 1995.

18. See Bumpass, Martin, and Sweet, 1991.

19. E.g., for Canada, see Ambert and Saucier, 1984.

20. Hetherington, 1993; Hetherington, Clingempeel et al., 1992; Thomson, McLanahan, and Curtin, 1992.

21. See McLanahan and Sandefur, 1994.

22. At least 55 percent of Canadian women and their children move after separation: Dandurand, 1994:532.

23. Compas et al., 1989; Dubow et al., 1991; Wagner, Compas, and Howell, 1988. These results have led to research on coping strategies developed by children (and their parents) and possible consequences: Causey and Dubow, 1992; Creasey, Mitts, and Catanzaro, 1995; Pryor-Brown and Cowen, 1989.

24. Amato, Loomis, and Booth, 1995.

25. Bank et al., 1993; Simons, Beaman, et al., 1993.

26. Cowan et al., 1991; Lahey et al., 1988a, 1988b; Toch, 1969.

27. Kitson, 1992; Kitson and Morgan, 1990.

28. See discussion by McLeod, 1995; Merikangas, 1982.

29. Webster-Stratton, 1989.

30. For a well-balanced review of the effect of parental remarriage at all age levels, see Coleman and Ganong, 1990.

31. Fluitt and Paradise, 1991.

32. See Duran-Aydintug and Ihinger-Tallman, 1995, for a review and proposals.

33. Wallerstein, Corbin, and Lewis, 1988.

34. Camara and Resnick, 1988.

35. There are no indications that shared custody results in better parent-child relationships. The key variable is again parental conflict, which exists in shared custody as well: See Donnelly and Finkelhor, 1992; Maccoby and Mnookin, 1992.

36. Results of negative child and adolescent outcomes following remarriage apply to both African American and white stepfamilies (Fine et al., 1992).

37. "We found that adolescents' negative states were related to the pileup of transitions and life events they encountered" (Larson and Richards, 1994:86). These results were obtained in two-parent families.

38. And may include sexual abuse by the stepfather.

39. Brand, Clingempeel, and Bowen-Woodward, 1988; Hetherington, 1988; Zaslow, 1989. For an overall review, see Ganong and Coleman, 1994.

40. Research is needed in which both the residing stepmother and the mother are studied. See Ambert, 1989, for relevant dyadic analyses.

41. This study also provides interesting results on the timing of remarriage.

42. Hobart (1988) and Orleans, Palisi, and Cadell (1989) also find that adolescents have some impact on marital adjustment in remarriages.

43. On parental conflict, see Forehand et al., 1988; Grych and Fincham, 1990; Long et al., 1989.

44. Similar results were obtained in a 1984 analysis: Mitchell, Wister, and Burch, 1989.

45. But, see Aquilino, 1994b.

46. Greenberg and Becker, 1988.

47. But see Marks, 1995.

48. These topics have been discussed at greater length in Chapter 4.

49. Howes and Markham, 1989; Katz and Gottman, 1994.

50. Cuber and Harroff (1965:43-65) define five types of marriage which include the conflict-habituated, devitalized, passive-congenial, vital, and total marriage. See also Katz and Gottman (1994) for a review on marital interaction.

51. Christensen and Margolin, 1988; Sabatelli and Anderson, 1991.

52. Also Fincham, 1994. On the intergenerational transmission of domestic violence and conflict, see Carlson, 1990; Smith and Williams, 1992. As well, see the first section in Chapter 10.

53. Hanson, 1993.

54. Larson and Richards, 1994:124.

55. Ambert, 1989.

56. See also Enos and Handal, 1986; Long, Forehand, Fauber, and Brody, 1987.

57. McLanahan and Bumpass, 1988; Scott and Perry, 1990.

58. When parental conflict and parental adjustment are also removed from the equation, much less difference in child outcomes is left that can be explained uniquely by family structure.

PART III:
NEGATIVE PARENTAL
AND CHILDREN OUTCOMES

Chapter 10

Problematic Parents
and Their Children

This chapter begins Part III which includes four chapters focusing on problematic parents and children. In the present chapter, three types of parents are discussed who may place their children at risk in terms of development. Chapters 11 and 12 focus on children who suffer from emotional problems and those who have conduct disorders, respectively. Delinquent adolescents are addressed in Chapter 13. Throughout these chapters, the parent-child relationship and child development are emphasized. Questions of etiology and intergenerational transmission are also examined. Part III further highlights various aspects of the combined interactional, ecological, and behavior genetics perspectives. Consequently, when discussing negative child outcomes in Chapters 11 through 13, these outcomes are also considered as context for future development and for the parent-child relationship.

INTRODUCTION

There are parents who fail at all or some of the key functions they should fulfill toward their children.[1] These parents and the family environment they provide strain relationships and place children at risk in terms of normal development. Most dysfunctional parents are so because of a combination of personal characteristics and contextual stressors, although in many cases, they may have unwittingly created part of their own stressful environment. In turn, this stressful environment contributes to reinforcing the parents' negative traits. Hence, such parents not only inherit stressors but many also create stressors; moreover, they often react inappropriately to them. Along these lines, Patterson and Capaldi (1991) have found that a small group of parents, specifically mothers in their study, are at risk of triggering negative transitions in their lives because they are antisocial. In addition to their own difficult temperament and lack of prosocial behaviors, such mothers exhibit poor child-rearing skills while married and, after separation, their child-rearing is further disrupted.

Another group of parents not discussed herein deserves mention as potentially problematic parents: We will call them "borderline" parents. Their situation stems from the fact that our society is a more dangerous place than it used to be 20 and even ten years ago, particularly in some neighborhoods. It follows that parents may have to be more vigilant and invest more of themselves in their children in order to achieve the same results that parents obtained a decade ago. Consequently, "borderline" parenting, including permissive parenting, that may have been adequate in the past, may no longer suffice. As society's demands increase in complexity, and as options presented to children become more dubious in quality, parenting becomes more complex and difficult. This means that more parents than in the past will barely manage to keep their children safe, healthy, and well adjusted, especially when these children are already at risk because of their own negative characteristics, or because they live in a dangerous neighborhood.

The focus of this chapter is on three categories of parents who receive particular attention in research: abusive parents, alcoholic or drug-dependent parents, and parents who suffer from depression. Little literature exists in terms of the overall parent-child relationship for the first category of parents because the research emphasis is placed on negative child outcomes. In fact, the bulk of the research in these domains focuses on developmental issues.

ABUSIVE PARENTS

Between 1.6 to 2 million children are seriously injured or impaired by abuse or neglect each year in the United States, with perhaps 2,000 resulting deaths.[2] There are several correlates to and outcomes of maltreatment.[3] To begin with, fathers who abuse their wives physically are more likely to abuse their children (McCloskey, Figueredo, and Koss, 1995), and abused mothers use harsh punishment more than nonabused mothers (Strauss and Smith, 1990). Women who have been abused as children have a higher chance of marrying an abusive husband.[4] These factors together mean that child abuse often coexists with spousal abuse and related difficulties.[5] Children of abused mothers have more problems and exhibit less interpersonal sensitivity than others (Rosenberg, 1987). In addition, children who have been or are abused do less well in school, on average (Eckenrode,

Laird, and Doris, 1993), are more frequently delinquent (Sternberg et al., 1993), have more peer-related problems (Howes, 1988), are often more aggressive, perhaps because they tend to attribute hostile intent to others (Dodge, Bates, and Pettit, 1990), and are less reciprocal in their relations with others (Salzinger, Feldman, and Hammer, 1993).[6]

Parents who abuse their children, compared with parents who do not, have been more frequently abused or harshly treated themselves.[7] Abusive parents, especially those who are sexually abusive, lack empathy for their child, and have unrealistic expectations of what the child can do for them (Pianta, Egeland, and Erickson, 1989). In families where a parent abuses a child sexually, parent/child role reversals have been noted, as well as powerful boundaries restricting contact with acquaintances outside of the family (Trepper and Barrett, 1989).

Sequelae and Transmission

Despite these observations, studies that are longitudinal and prospective indicate that most abused children do not grow up to be abusive or criminal, nor do they develop behavioral problems or full-blown psychiatric disorders. Most are constructive members of society, although many remain unhappy. Kaufman and Zigler (1987) have estimated that the transmission rate of family violence is about 30 percent or lower.[8] Many other researchers have emphasized that abuse is not unavoidably transmitted because several factors enter into play,[9] including the meaning that people attach to having been abused (Korbin, 1986). While some abusive families appear to be more at risk of transmitting this pattern than others, the mechanisms through which this occurs are still poorly understood.[10]

In this respect, Simons, Wu, Johnson, and Conger (1995) report that a parent's antisocial orientation may well be one such mediating factor in recurrence of family violence in subsequent generations. Thus, it is possible that abusive *parents who have other antisocial traits* are more likely to transmit various abusive and violent behavior to their children than parents who, except for being abusive, function adequately (Frick et al., 1992). This perspective inquires into family violence in association with other forms of deviance.[11] In a small core of families, it is possible that harsh treatment and physical abuse are transmitted across generations by heredity[12] through aggressiveness or other genetically influenced predispositions. This explanation is plausible in view of the fact that a core of abused children remain aggressive and antisocial into adulthood (Lewis, Mallouh, and Webb, 1989). Moreover, parental stress induced by the child's behavior often precipitates abuse (Pianta, Egeland, and Erickson, 1989). Hence, another pathway to intergenerational transmission of abuse in some families may be the child's conduct disorder, which is responded to inappropriately by the parent, and is pursued in adult relationships.

When dealing with the effects of abuse or the correlation between other severe stressors and an outcome, generally negative, it is important to point out that these effects may not occur at all or they may be activated *at different times* in the lives of different people, depending on the type and persistence of abuse. Some may react quickly but others may have long-delayed reactions, and these reactions may not be the ones we are led to expect. Some forms and degree of severity of abuse may affect personal development, others may affect parenting behaviors, or interpersonal relations, others may be linked to antisocial behavior, and still others may be causally linked to all such negative outcomes. It is equally possible that certain personality deficits have to be present or that a second stressor has to be combined with the first one so that specific negative outcomes can occur. The initial "causative" factor may be mitigated or outweighed by personality variables, resilience, happy circumstances in the person's life, and a general lack of subsequent stressors (Rutter, 1989). Therefore, the path between a variable believed to be causal and its resulting outcome may be circuitous, dependent upon many other factors, and may lead to a nonpredicted outcome. Salzinger, Feldman, and Hammer (1993) pointedly remark that protective factors must be operant for abused children whose outcomes are positive, while risk factors must exist for nonabused children who become problematic.

Sexual Abuse

A perpetrator of sexual abuse can be a parent, particularly a father, but more often it is a stepparent,[13] a mother's boyfriend, a relative, a sibling, or an older peer. Young girls are more often sexually abused intrafamilially and boys are more often abused outside of the family (Kelly, Regan, and Burton, 1991). Radio or television commentators frequently announce a horrid crime and then conclude with a line similar to this one: "The perpetrator had been sexually abused by his stepfather as a child." Such statements convey the message that the sexual abuse suffered ten to 30 years earlier caused the current crime and explains it. Does it? Science does not yet have the answer. What is certain is that sexual abuse may trigger problems in a child who may not otherwise be at risk[14] or it may increase preexisting problems, even later on in life (Mancini, Van Ameringen, and Macmillan, 1995). It can also set some individuals on a life course of further sexual abuse (Simons and Whitbeck, 1991). Moreover, many victims of sexual abuse are traumatized for life.[15]

In the autobiographies written by this author's students it was found that each year, from 15 percent to 25 percent of the women students mentioned at least one case of sexual victimization before age 14. These reports occurred under the rubric of a general question asking students to focus on what had "made you the most unhappy" at various ages. Only a few particularly depraved cases of abuse perpetrated by grandfathers and older relatives seemed to result in the young women becoming dysfunctional at some level, generally in their relationships with men and in the form of anxieties. In other words, the more severe, the longer the abuse, and the closer the familial link, the stronger the negative effects.[16] (There were no reported cases of father-daughter incest.) The majority of the young women were either sad or angry or a mixture of both at the recollection of the sexual abuse but functioned well and at this point seemed to the author to be in no danger of becoming bad parents. The fact that they were university students is in itself proof of a certain level of success in life. By the same token, it is possible that women college students suffer less sexual abuse, especially at home, than women who do not pursue higher education. Or it could be that, among this group, the abuse takes place later in life or is less serious and may be less damaging than if it had occurred early in childhood.

Parents and Communities

Students who reported any type of maltreatment by their parents were in the minority. For the 1974 cohort, only 13.3 percent described negative parental treatment that had a lasting detrimental impact on them. By 1989, although child abuse was then a much more talked about and "disclosed" topic, even fewer students made such reports: 8 percent (Ambert, 1994a). Of course, these could be under-reportings as easily as they could be over-reportings. The autobiographies cover students' lives up to the age of 14. Because the negative parental acts mentioned included others besides abuse, the proportion of students reporting maltreatment is well above the estimate of about 3 percent of children who are abused by parents (Garbarino and Plantz, 1986).[17]

Severe and persistent abuse is more likely to occur in dysfunctional homes, and in homes with frequent partner changes (such as serial marriages or coresidences), severe stressors, or parents who lose control more easily than others.[18] Similarly, child maltreatment in general occurs more often in areas that are characterized by poverty, single-mother families, high population turnover (Coulton et al., 1995), and violence (Cicchetti and Lynch, 1993).[19] Stressors related to poverty are particularly implicated in child abuse (Horowitz and Wolock, 1985). It may be that the intergenerational transmission of abuse is promoted in such environments.[20] Neighborhood distress is itself an important element to consider (Kasarda, 1993), as it increases parental social isolation, which is a contributing variable in abuse and neglect.[21]

Although the focus here has been on sexual and physical abuse, there is growing recognition that child maltreatment as a broader category is a more important issue, because it also comprises children who are neglected (Claussen and Crittenden, 1991). Among neglected children are included those who are unsupervised and largely unprotected by their parents, even in dangerous neighborhoods. Such conditions are intricably linked with conduct disorders (Chapter 12) and delinquency (Chapter 13).

ALCOHOL- AND DRUG-DEPENDENT PARENTS

Children experience a wide variety of relationships with their alcoholic or drug-dependent parents (Whipple, Fitzgerald, and Zucker, 1995). Although a majority of children of alcoholics do well, a greater proportion of such children than of controls exhibit emotional problems and conduct disorders (Rubio-Stipec et al., 1991), and use alcohol or other substances (Chassin et al., 1996). They are at the very least at risk of being unhappy and ashamed of their parents, as well as possibly neglected and abused.[22] When children have two alcoholic parents, they suffer from negative outcomes more often than children who have one alcoholic parent (Earls et al., 1988). Alcoholism may be partly hereditary (McGue, 1993), perhaps especially among males (Jacob, Krahn, and Leonard, 1991). There are also indications that the tendency for drug addiction may be in part genetic (Cadoret et al., 1995a). But how can alcoholism and drug addiction be genetic when we know that they involve behaviors that are dependent upon environmental influences, that is, availability of and exposure to substances?

McGue (1993) surmises that three inherited behavioral precursors contribute to an inclination toward alcoholism, and perhaps other drug addictions as well. One of these precursors is alcohol sensitivity, particularly a strong feeling of relief after alcohol consumption. Another is being aroused by alcohol (becoming more outgoing or aggressive) so that the person feels happier and is then inclined to repeat the experience. Personality or temperament variables such as low impulse control or moodiness as well as biased cognitive patterns may also be contributory variables. Alcoholism has a high **comorbidity** with other psychological problems (Regier et al., 1990), so it is possible that children inherit some of their parents' problems via other genetic pathways. Thus, it may not be the direct propensity to alcoholism that is the inherited factor but other predispositions, that given environmental influence and opportunities, lead to alcoholism.[23] If parents drink too much, this provides an incentive for genetic influences to be activated via modeling.[24]

A proportion of domestic violence is committed under the influence of alcohol. The presence of an alcoholic parent may disrupt family functioning (von Knorring, 1991), may increase the likelihood of divorce (Schulsinger et al., 1986), and may impair proper parenting (Hawkins, Catalano, and Miller, 1992). Children of alcoholics may therefore be affected by parental conflict, violence (Fitzgerald et al., 1993), episodic unemployment and poverty, as well as erratic parenting practices–all consequences of alcoholism that in themselves impact negatively on children.[25] They may also be negatively affected by the suffering of the nonalcoholic parent. Jacob et al. (1991) suggests that children have normal outcomes when alcoholic parents are able to maintain a warm and supervisory relationship with them. Supportive parenting acts as a buffer to preserve children's mental health (Roosa et al., 1993). When parents use drugs or alcohol but are not dependent and maintain a nonpermissive role vis-à-vis their offspring, the latter are less likely to use drugs (McDermott, 1984). However, when parental attitude is favorable to substances, children are more likely to use them.

Drug-addicted parents are more often found among the underclass or among families that have lost everything because of the addiction and have consequently moved downward socioeconomically. Children of drug addicts are at risk of being utterly neglected, especially when it is the mother who is addicted. Moreover, parents who are drug-dependent often resort to criminality to maintain their habit. For women, this may mean prostitution, at times occurring right in the same apartment where their children are. The father is often in jail because of crimes committed to support his habit. At the very least, these children suffer emotional and behavioral deficits (Hawley, Halle, and Drasin, 1995). When they are adolescent, neglect includes lack of supervision and consequent possible drug use by the youth, particularly if peers also use drugs (Fischer and Wampler, 1994:477). Thus, drug abuse by parents may be more detrimental in neighborhoods that have a high concentration of both poverty and delinquency (Kandel and Davies, 1996). If the parent is unmarried and was young at the child's birth, the adolescent may be interacting with a parent who is immature and functions more like a deviant peer than a parent. Dunlap (1992:181) points out that these children "inherit a lifestyle that swiftly forecloses alternative opportunities." Surprising as it may be, many of these adolescents manage to "get out" and survive quite well. But the price paid in terms of emotional adjustment and unfair obligations at such an early age has yet to be documented. Finally, one should certainly emphasize that the use of and dealing in drugs by older siblings and young uncles also has an unfortunate effect on youngsters–a culture of drugs may permeate the family.

PARENTS WHO SUFFER FROM DEPRESSION

Emotional or psychiatric problems, at times called mental illness, involve disturbances in the way people feel, think, and relate to the external world.[26] Among the most severe, or psychoses, are schizophrenia and manic depression. Depression takes two forms. The most serious, manic or bipolar depression, involves a loss of contact with reality and shifts over time from a depressed state to a highly excited (manic) state, or the predominance of such a state. In the manic phase, the persons are hyperactive, elated, at times loud and aggressive, and may need to be sedated because they could be dangerous to themselves or to others. In the depressed mode, the persons may lose contact with reality, feel hopeless, helpless, alone, and have suicidal ideation. Unipolar or simple depression contains the same elements, such as hopelessness, as the depressed mode in bipolar depression, but does not generally involve a cognitive break with reality. Of the two, simple depression is the one that is the most susceptible to environmental stressors. People may be depressed, off and on, for most of their lives; others may suffer only one episode and live normally thereafter. Obviously, the effect on children will vary accordingly.

Etiology

By comparing **concordance rates** for severe depression for identical and fraternal twins, Gershon et al. (1977) discovered that when one identical twin suffers from the disturbance, there is a nearly 70 percent chance that the other twin also does. In contrast, among fraternal twins, the concordance rate is about 13 percent. These rates indicate a strong genetic element. Therefore, a child with a chronically depressed parent may already be at risk because of genetic predispositions. However, the mechanisms that initiate a mental illness are not necessarily the same as those that maintain it. Patterson and Forgatch (1990) have studied the processes that help maintain depression after it has appeared in single mothers. They assessed a group of mothers three times over a period of 12 months. They found that when a single mother who has been depressed before is symptom free at the beginning of the study, there is a 28 percent chance that she will be depressed a year later. In comparison, when she is depressed at the start of the study, she has a 59 percent chance of remaining so to the end of the year.

Patterson and Forgatch (1990) note that the high level of stressors and the loss of social support incurred by single mothers contribute to the *initiation* of the depressive state.[27] But some of these women are obviously more vulnerable than others in the *maintenance* of their depressive mood. They propose that mothers who are more irritable and sad may incur further losses of social support as friends distance themselves and as children react by becoming more difficult and diffident (Mangelsdorf et al., 1990). Mothers who are what they call "socially incompetent" and somewhat socially and legally deviant have more problems with discipline and have more confrontations with their sons than other mothers. Their stressors consequently continue to mount (Hammen, 1992b), and this situation increases their irritability as well as their social isolation, and contributes to a continuation of their depression.

Crook, Raskin, and Eliot (1981) show that depressed adults who see themselves as worthless often originate from families where parents were less accepting, and more detached, hostile, and rejecting. There could be a concern here that clinically depressed adults' recollections are simply a reflection of their current unhappy state of mind. Indeed, states of mind are known to affect recollections (Halverson, 1988).[28] Fortunately, the researchers had interviewed respondents' siblings, relatives, and long-time friends, who confirmed the respondents' perception. It is therefore possible that one of the many sources that lead adults to experience depression resides in a rejecting home atmosphere in childhood. But it is also possible that these adults' parents were themselves clinically depressed when they were raising their children—hence the combination of genetic and environmental influences on children. This would explain both the parents' rejecting behavior and their adult children's depression and feelings of worthlessness.

There exists a large literature on depression, not in parents in general and not in fathers (Downey and Coyne, 1990), but in mothers, and on the effect that the presence of a depressed mother has on children (Cummings and Davies, 1994b). On the whole, the correlations between maternal depression and negative child outcomes and difficulties in the parent-child relationship are not high, but they are consistently present (Downey and Coyne, 1990). It is quite difficult to know what the correlations mean because too many variables are overlooked that could be important and could affect the child even more than maternal depression. More studies should focus on the processes and mechanisms involved in this statistical relationship.[29] Poverty is one key variable (Teti, Gelfard, and Pompa, 1990). In addition, children and mothers both could have problems because of marital conflict; we already know that parental conflict is one process that is detrimental to children's well-being at all age levels (Caplan et al., 1989). In such a case, there would be no direct cause and effect between maternal depression and child problems because both would be created by a third variable, marital conflict (Fergusson, Horwood, and Lynskey, 1995).

The Dynamics Between Etiology and Effects

Parents who suffer from serious emotional problems place their children at a double disadvantage. First, these children are at greater genetic risk for depression (Mullan and Murray, 1989). Second, they have a higher probability of suffering from an abnormal familial environment created by their parents' illness,[30] perhaps in part via detrimental parenting styles (Susman et al., 1985). Moreover, spousal depression increases the chance of marital disharmony. In turn, the latter could impact negatively on children,[31] and particularly on children who are already at risk because of their own temperament (Graham, Rutter, and George, 1973). A mother's depression is related to lower levels of overt aggression in a family where the parents have a good marriage but higher levels where the parents are maritally distressed.[32] Hops et al. (1987) show that when the marital relationship is satisfactory, husbands of depressed mothers give more caring affection to their children than husbands in families with an unhappy marriage. These studies again underscore the importance of taking the marital relationship into consideration in the research of parental depression and child outcome.

Rates of depressive symptomatology increase with age, and even more so among girls.[33] Hops, Sherman, and Biglan (1990) propose that the impact of maternal depression on children depends on their age.[34] A genetically linked vulnerability to depression may increase with age; hence, during adolescence, especially for girls, interaction with a depressed mother may reinforce genetic predispositions more than at younger or older ages.[35] In contrast, boys may be more affected in the direction of developing behavior disorders, and the latter may or may not be accompanied by depressed mood.

Infants who are cared for by a depressed mother may receive inconsistent or rejecting messages so that, not knowing what to expect, they can become avoidant of contact, and may look sad and depressed. Some of these children may grow up feeling insecure, perhaps uncertain of the mother's attachment. If they already have negative predispositions and do not benefit from a supportive relationship with another close adult, such as the father, they are at risk for developing a variety of problems (Hammen, 1988, 1992a). Children who live with depressed persons are exposed to a certain type of body language that they may learn and adopt (Cummings and Cicchetti, 1990). They may simply follow the model of "acting depressed." This learned behavioral configuration may lead them to be socially inept; consequently, other children and teachers may not readily accept them or understand them. Social isolation could result, along with the loss of important opportunities in life, including employment.

Several studies remark on seriously depressed mothers' lack of child-rearing skills (Zahn-Waxler et al., 1990), while others find no disturbance in the mother-child relationship (see Mowbray et al., 1995, for a review). The literature generally reports a great deal of concordance between maternal depression and negative behaviors among children and adolescents.[36] Difficult child behaviors probably exacerbate maternal depression, with a further disturbance in parenting activities (Mash and Johnson, 1990). Patterson and Dishion (1988) report that maternal depression does not seem to be related to discipline problems in *two*-parent families. Radke-Yarrow (1990) finds that depressed mothers tend to avoid confrontation with their children, so that when children are not compliant, they can continue to be so because no one sets limits. When mothers are severely depressed, daughters are far less compliant than girls with nondepressed mothers. The research methods utilized by Radke-Yarrow's team are particularly interesting because they involve naturalistic observation of families temporarily living in a specifically designed apartment. Some of her key findings are as follows (1990:180):

- Depressed mothers spend more time exhibiting negative moods— 27 percent versus 12 percent of the minutes that were **coded** during the first day for depressed and nondepressed mothers respectively.
- When the interaction between child and mother is high on negative emotion, this negativism tends to be replicated between siblings when they are left alone.
- Mothers and two- to three-year-old children observed together as a dyad tend to be **concordant** in negative emotionality in 60 percent of the cases.

She concludes that these small children are not only subjected to their mothers' negativism but also learn to feel and display patterns of negative emotions. It could also be added that at least a few of these small children may themselves be genetically predisposed to depression so that they more easily "absorb" the negativism: They are more vulnerable or attuned to it. Nevertheless, studies such as those by Cox et al. (1987) and

Stein et al. (1991) indicate that depression does not unavoidably alter family patterns. Many children function quite well (Williams and Carmichael, 1985), perhaps because they are more resilient,[37] have parents who are caring, and/or benefit from other positive advantages present in their environment.

Methodological Complications

There are several difficulties inherent in research designs imputing causality between maternal depression and children's negative outcomes. For one, *depressive motherhood is a very heterogeneous phenomenon* and should not be treated as if all such mothers are identical (Rutter, 1990a). A particularly worthwhile aspect of the Radke-Yarrow (1990) study is that it differentiates between types of depressed mothers. A group of depressed mothers tends to express more sadness and anxiety, a second is more apathetic, while a third shows mixed symptoms, including unpredictable displays of anger and irritability. Not surprisingly perhaps, there are differences among the behaviors of these mothers' children.

A second methodological complication resides in the *timing* and the *duration* of maternal depression. It is generally not known how long the respondent's depression has lasted prior to the time a study is carried out. Presumably, a longer depression has more time to remold the parent-child relationship into a less flexible and more dysfunctional pattern of interaction, and the more likely the children are to be negatively affected. When a mother's depression is her first and is the result of specific stressors, does the mother-child relationship recover after depression abates? If the child has been negatively affected, can the damage be reversed? The child's age when the depression is diagnosed is also a third important factor: Because behaviors change over time, those behaviors that are well established before the mother becomes depressed may not be affected. Fourth, reactive depressions have a lower genetic component; hence the child is less at risk at the genetic level with only a brief episode of maternal depression that is triggered by a personal loss or other stressor.

A fifth methodological complication resides in the role that fathers play, particularly given the fact that few studies examine depression in fathers. One exception, among a few others, is a research by Keller et al. (1986), who report that only mothers' depression is statistically related to children's problems. If such results were replicated in other studies of a longitudinal nature, they might imply that mothers' depression is indeed more consequential for children, probably because they have more contact with mothers than with fathers. However, at the genetic level, a father's depression is probably as hereditary as a mother's.

Another problem resides in the factor of comorbidity, whereby a good proportion of psychiatric patients, perhaps as many as 60 percent, concurrently suffer from a second disorder or have done so in the past (Robins, Locke, and Regier, 1991). Consequently, children of seriously emotionally disturbed parents may inherit a broad spectrum of negative predispositions, and this could explain in part why they suffer from a variety of negative outcomes other than depression. However, not all of these predispositions may become actualized. Adversities in the parent-child relationship, in part created by comorbidity rather than by depression per se, may be the trigger that results in a negative child outcome. Comorbidity complicates, but does not invalidate, the applicability of the genetic model.

Finally, it is pertinent to remark overall, that discussions and studies on the effect of maternal depression on children generally fail to consider two key points: the child's own predispositions for becoming problematic and the effect of a difficult child as a trigger to reactive maternal depression or as a variable in its persistence.[38] Were such methodological problems resolved, they would shed much light on the *mechanisms* through which a depressive mother might affect her child. An interactional interpretation of the data probably goes like this: While there are depressed mothers who affect their children negatively, the extent of this impact depends on a variety of other circumstances. Moreover, the structure of the mother-child interaction is such that certain children with negative behaviors create stress for their mother who reacts depressively; in turn, children may become more difficult or dysfunctional.[39]

FUTURE PROBLEMATIC PARENTS

An increase in the sheer number of problematic parents may be cautiously predicted as the current cohorts of preadolescents and adolescents grow up and have children. This possibility is based, neither on an expected increase in serious mental illness, nor on a decline in the quality of the gene pool, but on the following current social conditions.

1. As will be seen in Chapter 13, there has been an increase in the rate of violent crimes committed by youth and especially by children below age 12. More youngsters are aggressive and impulsive; these characteristics are fairly stable over time and predict adult criminality, erratic employment, and harsh parenting (Farrington, 1991), even in females (Huesmann et al., 1984). Young people who are impulsive enter sexual relations prematurely and early reproductive activities are often followed by larger family size. Violent young

men will likely be harsh, negligent, or absent parents, and will constitute our future population of problematic fathers who provide poor role models for their children, cannot educate them, and possibly abuse or abandon them. Delinquent girls not infrequently grow up into unsupportive and even malfunctioning mothers (Lewis et al., 1991). Pepler and Slaby (1994:49) suggest that antisocial girls "may express their aggressive tendencies within the confines of the family and close relationships," and this could include their small children in addition to their own parents and siblings.

2. A larger number of very young girls, some as young as 12, have babies than before. When these girls are impulsive, have little support, have dysfunctional parents of their own, and low maternal skills, they risk becoming problematic mothers.

3. Child poverty has increased.[40] Children who now live in environments that are dangerous, stressful, and overcrowded have lower chances of becoming adults who can parent adequately. When people who face these disadvantages form a certain percentage of a neighborhood and constitute the majority of their children's extended family system, they have few ways out of poverty–and few options for their own children. They become parents who are problematic, not because of their own genetic characteristics or ill will, but because of a deprived environment. The environment creates these disadvantaged children, hence generates a greater supply of future problematic parents.

4. The general social climate is not necessarily worse but it does contain some serious risk elements for the children who will be tomorrow's parents (Eron, Gentry, and Schlegel, 1994). These include television violence, job instability, parental divorce and redivorce, weapons, and drugs. In addition, the dominance of technology and technocrats may lead to helplessness in some segments of the population. The unfolding sociopolitical environment is more unpredictable, gives less self-empowerment, is less welfare oriented, and more dangerous and violent. This more hazardous environment is less predictable and safe for children to navigate than past environments and it requires more parental support and vigilance. Yet there are no indications that parents can now offer more because they are already stretched to the limit. Indications are that they are offering less than needed, especially when they live in urban pockets of poverty.

These conditions taken together may lead to an upsurge of parents who will either abdicate or will not be able to increase their caring investment because they have too many other demands placed on them. For instance, there are conflicts between trying to be a good parent and trying to find yet another job or yet another spouse. There are contradictions between being a good parent and working from 7 a.m. to 10 p.m. (Hareven, 1994:439). These are common examples of a multitude of contemporary preoccupations that compete with each other in terms of time and energy, and may lead to child neglect.

CONCLUSION

Parents who have psychiatric problems, are abusive, and/or are behaviorally deviant create stressful situations in their lives (Depue and Monroe, 1986), including transitions such as divorce, unplanned single parenthood, unemployment, and accidents, as well as loss of social support. In turn, stressors complicate these parents' lives, defeat them, make them irritable, and cause poorer health. They often react to their children more unpredictably and may be easily irritated by noncompliant behavior. Others who are not abusive but simply depressed avoid confrontations with increasingly difficult children so that the latter are rewarded for their antisocial behavior. Moreover, these children may have inherited detrimental predispositions, and these are then triggered by the stressful environment produced by their disturbed parents.

Once again, multiple and interactive causality is found in terms of explaining a deteriorated parent-child relationship, as well as negative child development. It is also necessary to attend to several possibly concurrent variables, including a certain degree of genetic heritability, comorbidity, parents with difficult temperaments, and stressors that increase their level of distress and disrupt what parenting skills they have, especially in terms of monitoring and support (Patterson and Capaldi, 1991). This environment in turn affects children who are already vulnerable; it reinforces negative predispositions and contributes to antisocial or unhealthy behavior patterns—the focus of the following chapters.

ENDNOTES

1. See a description of five family functions in Radke-Yarrow, 1990:175.
2. Office of Disease Prevention and Health Promotion, 1991. We are not entering the very complex issues surrounding the validity of children's reports nor the validity of the techniques utilized to elicit reports of sexual abuse. See Fincham et al., 1994; Koocher et al., 1995.
3. Journals to consult on child abuse that mainly focus on the family are: *American Journal of Disease of Children, American Journal of Orthopsychiatry,*

Child Abuse and Neglect, Journal of Family Violence, Journal of Interpersonal Violence, Pediatrics, Social Work and Human Sexuality, and *Violence and Victims.* Additional references in Boney-McCoy and Finkelhor, 1995; Briere, 1992; Sedlak, 1991; Finkelhor and Dziuba-Leatherman, 1994; Williams and Finkelhor, 1995.

4. Downs et al., 1992; Simons, Johnson, et al., 1993.

5. Salzinger, Feldman, and Hammer, 1993. There is some evidence that individuals who commit domestic violence have more contact with the police for a variety of other behaviors (Sherman et al., 1991).

6. Salzinger et al., 1991; Salzinger, Feldman, and Hammer, 1993.

7. Simons, Whitbeck, Conger, and Wu, 1991; Egeland, Jacobvitz, and Papatola, 1987.

8. Widom, 1990.

9. Egeland, Jacobvitz, and Sroufe, 1988; Kaufman and Zigler, 1987; Widom, 1989.

10. Korbin, Anetzberger, and Austin, 1995.

11. Hotalling, Strauss, and Lincoln, 1990.

12. DiLalla and Gottesman, 1991.

13. Daly and Wilson, 1994.

14. Smith and Bentovim, 1994.

15. Scott, 1992; Saunders et al., 1992.

16. Kendall-Tackett, Williams, and Finkelhor, 1993.

17. A 1986 estimate is used to correspond with the time period studied.

18. For further reading on child sexual abuse, see Faller, 1990; Gomez-Schwartz, Horowitz, and Cardarelli, 1990; Kendall-Tackett, Williams, and Finkelhor, 1993.

19. See also Garbarino et al., 1992.

20. Community factors have been understudied in this respect; Garbarino and Kostelny, 1992.

21. But see Thompson and Wilcox, 1995.

22. On parental alcoholism or alcoholism in general, see journals such as *Alcohol and Alcoholism, Alcohol Health and Research World, Drugs and Society, Journal of Abnormal Psychology, Journal of Consulting and Clinical Psychology,* and *Journal of Studies on Alcohol.*

23. Concerning the role of personality, see Rogusch, Chassin, and Sher, 1990.

24. Children born to mothers who are alcoholic or drug dependent during pregnancy are also at risk of suffering from various developmental problems. This outcome arises because the fetus has been affected by the drugs at a critical time (fetal alcohol syndrome). However, evidence is still too fragmentary, especially for crack cocaine, to be discussed at length here.

25. Wampler et al., 1993.

26. Journals to consult on depression and schizophrenia are: *Acta Psychiatrica Scandinavica, American Journal of Orthopsychiatry, American Journal of Psychiatry, American Journal of Public Health, Archives of General Psychiatry, Australian and New Zealand Journal of Psychiatry, British Journal of Psychiatry,*

Canadian Psychiatric Association Journal, Canadian Journal of Psychiatry, Clinical Social Work Journal, Comprehensive Therapy, General Hospital Psychiatry, Health and Social Work, Hospital and Community Psychiatry, Issues in Mental Health Nursing, Journal of Abnormal Psychology, Journal of Clinical Psychology, Journal of Consulting and Clinical Psychology, Journal of Nervous and Mental Diseases, Journal of Personality Disorders, Journal of Psychiatry in Medicine, Journal of Psychosocial Nursing, Psychological Medicine, Psychosomatics, and *Schizophrenia Bulletin.*

27. Consult Monroe and Simons, 1991, for diathesis-stress theories, and Coyne and Whiffen, 1995, for personality-diathesis theories. These theories are integrated in this text, but the concepts are not used.

28. "We need to assess what constructs separate people who are relatively accurate about family issues from those who are not or who systematically distort their recall in different ways" (Halverson, 1988:442).

29. Dodge, 1990a; Coyne, Downey, and Boergers, 1992.

30. Wachs, 1993:382.

31. Shaw and Emery, 1987.

32. Biglan et al., 1985.

33. Rutter, 1986.

34. Goodman et al., 1993.

35. Weissman et al. (1987) provide indirect support for this hypothesis.

36. Several studies indicate that depressed mothers are not reliable judges of their children's problems and behaviors. But this is also questioned (McCloskey, Figueredo, and Koss, 1995; Richters and Pellegrini, 1989). For a refutation and a review of this literature, see Tarullo et al., 1995.

37. Garmezy and Masten, 1991; see Chapter 2.

38. Downey and Coyne, 1990; Forehand, McCombs, and Brody, 1987; Larson and Richards, 1994.

39. In relation to this point, see Webster-Stratton, 1990.

40. See Ambert, in press.

Chapter 11

Children with Severe
Emotional Problems

The discussion now turns to the parent-child relationship in two instances of negative child outcomes: children and especially adolescents who suffer from depression or schizophrenia.[1] This topic leads to an inquiry into the etiology of severe emotional problems, or psychoses. In so doing, the information presented in the previous chapter is completed, and additional methodological issues are addressed. Next, the impact of children's emotional problems on the parent-child relationship is discussed,[2] as well as the effect that external agents, such as professionals and relatives, exert on this relationship and on parental burden.

ORIGINS OF EMOTIONAL PROBLEMS

As indicated in the previous chapter, there is solid evidence that psychotic emotional problems, such as manic depression and schizophrenia, run in families, not necessarily because of vertical cultural transmission or child-rearing practices, but mainly because of genes. However, a cautionary note is necessary here: The majority of people suffering from either schizophrenia or depression (or autism, for that matter) come from families where neither parent is afflicted with the disease. Such an observation may indicate that most mental illnesses are **polygenetic**, and hence require a particular genetic configuration that is not that easily transmitted in its entirety. But, for each individual, the fact remains that the greater the **genetic loading** for an emotional problem, "the less environmental stress is required to produce developmental deviations" (Wachs, 1992:119). In other words, the stronger the abnormal genetic predisposition, the more likely it is that people develop their illness spontaneously, "whereas other patients in whom there is a smaller and unspecific constitutional predisposition develop their illness as a result of obvious stress" (McGuffin and Katz, 1993:187).[3] Therefore, even in a normal family with loving parents, a person with a strong genetic predisposition will become schizophrenic or manic depressive (McGuffin et al., 1994).[4] Others who have a lesser predisposition may need very detrimental living conditions or high levels of stress to become so severely disturbed.

SCHIZOPHRENIA

Schizophrenia is now called a disease of the brain that brings deviant and dysfunctional behaviors (Lefley, 1987). It is characterized by various degrees of distancing or withdrawal from reality as it is perceived by others. Interpersonal difficulties are also present. The more severe forms involve hallucinations (hearing voices and seeing things), loss of contact with one's bodily needs and external reality, inability to care for oneself, delusions, rigid bodily mannerisms, and inability to initiate or maintain relationships. Untreated adults who are chronic schizophrenics stand out in a crowd. They constitute a substantial proportion of the older street people, wandering about because they have no place to go that they can adapt to now that they have been deinstitutionalized. They are true social isolates, shrouded in their delusions, clothed in maladorous rags, and shunned by all. Schizophrenia in pre-adolescents is extremely rare. When it does occur, it resembles the adult description. Psychotic problems are often difficult to diagnose in childhood because they contribute to delay cognitive development, and this makes it a complex task to differentiate psychoses from cognitive disabilities.

Because schizophrenia is such a serious illness, one would expect schizophrenics to "produce" severe disorders in their children. Yet this is not necessarily the case. In order to ground this discussion, we first have to refer to other etiological facts. Schizophrenia and its precursors tend to appear quite early in life, particularly in males (Burke et al., 1990). Because it is such a debilitating illness, male schizophrenics only infrequently marry and have children (Saugstad, 1989). This selection process contributes to reducing the prevalence of the disease in the population to about 1 percent. However, a majority of schizophrenic women still marry, although at a lower rate than other women (National Institute of Mental Health, 1986). Currently, women who suffer from one of the serious mental illnesses are nearly as likely to have children as other women (Apfel and Handel, 1993), and as many as 60 percent of their pregnancies may be unplanned (Forcier, 1990).

There are two main reasons for this difference in the marriage and reproductive rates between schizophrenic men and women. First, the disorder appears a few years later in the lives of females, and this allows women to marry and/or to bear children before noticeable symptoms appear. Second, a woman who suffers from a mild case of schizophrenia may still be considered functional enough to marry, especially if she is attractive, because her social role as a woman and homemaker may shelter her from becoming dysfunctional in other spheres of life where she would be noticed as such. In contrast, a man may not be able to escape attention so easily because he is less likely to be sheltered from scrutiny by his gender role.

The *lifetime* risk for schizophrenia in the general population is 1 percent, but it increases markedly when close relatives are afflicted by the illness (Tsuang, Gilbertson, and Faraone 1991).[5] For instance, the siblings of a schizophrenic have anywhere from a 2 to 9 percent chance of also becoming schizophrenic.[6] **Monozygotic twins** have a 17 to 60 percent concordance. Children with either one or two schizophrenic parents respectively have a 7 to 13 percent risk and a 40 to 50 percent risk (Gottesman, 1991). Other studies have gone one step further: They have compared the *adult offspring* of older monozygotic twins who are discordant on schizophrenia.[7] These studies have found that the risk of morbidity for the *non*schizophrenic identical twin's children equals that of the schizophrenic twin's children (about 17 percent): These two sets of cousins are actually siblings genetically because one of their two parents share 100 percent of their genes. In contrast, when twins are **dizygotic**, and hence share perhaps less than 50 percent of their genes, the offspring of the normal twin have a 2 percent chance of being schizophrenic (Gottesman and Bertelsen, 1989). There are indications that childhood-onset schizophrenia may have a higher genetic loading than that originating later in life (J. Asarnow, 1994). For instance, preliminary analyses by R. S. Asarnow[8] indicate a high rate of schizophrenia among family members of children with early-onset schizophrenia (Pulver et al., 1990). Studies of twins with an early onset find concordance rates of up to 88 percent for monozygotic twins and 23 percent for dizygotic twins (Kallman and Roth, 1956).

Heston had already shown in 1966 that children of schizophrenic mothers who are adopted away from the biological family still retained a 13 percent risk of developing schizophrenia as adults even though their adoptive family environment was nonschizophrenogenic. If genes played no role, such children would have a 1 percent **morbidity** risk (Kety et al., 1968). Gottesman (1991) has summarized the results of four studies of children where both parents had been schizophrenic: About 50 percent of the offspring became schizophrenic, 25 percent had other psychiatric problems, and 25 percent were unaffected. These statistics are startling if we consider that despite a very high familial loading and the risks associated with living in a household burdened by double schizophrenia, one fourth of the children were unscathed. Other studies also support the fact that life with a schizophrenic parent does not unavoidably lead to the same outcome among children. However, the more severe the parental illness and the more numerous the psychosocial disadvantages the child encounters, the greater the possibility that the child will develop a negative outcome.[9] Gottesman (1991) estimates that schizophrenics' offspring who are not reared by their parents have a decrease of about 37 percent in their risk of morbidity. If raised by their schizophrenic mother, they have an increase in risk of about 59 percent.[10]

Therefore, when children are already vulnerable because of a genetic predisposition, living with a disturbed parent increases morbidity above and beyond their initial predisposition. However, one can presume that, when the other parent is stable and has a supportive relationship with them, the children will be far less vulnerable. Offspring with no immediate observable familial loading who are adopted by parents who later become schizophrenic also suffer from an increased morbidity but not of a great magnitude. Hence, while a poor familial environment by itself rarely results in a serious emotional problem of a psychotic nature, a strong genetic predisposition is more likely to. Moreover, the two combined increase the chances of morbidity.[11]

The family environment plays an important role in the guise of stressors caused by poverty, a disadvantaged neighborhood, or dysfunctional parents who lack or have poor parenting skills, and are mentally ill or antisocial. Schizophrenic parents, or other emotionally disturbed parents for that matter, present an environmental risk: The parents' symptoms may interfere with proper parenting, impair the quality of the parent-child relationship, and result in stressful family transitions such as unemployment, poverty, serious marital discord, divorce, and institutionalization (Rutter and Quinton, 1987).

DEPRESSION

Prevalence and Etiology

The lifetime risk for depression, including simple depression, may be as high as 10 to 30 percent, depending on the definition (Kendler et al., 1992). Serious depression usually occurs later in life and does not generally prevent people from marrying as is the case for schizophrenia (Gottesman, 1991) and autism (Rutter, 1991b). Thus, depression is genetically reproduced on a larger scale than the other two conditions (Jones and Szatmari, 1988). Moreover, depression is more dependent upon environmental stressors than is schizophrenia so that, during difficult social and cultural transitions, its lifetime prevalence may rise accordingly, even though the gene pool remains constant (Nigg and Goldsmith, 1994:349).[12]

Manic depression or bipolar depression is partly hereditary (Harrington et al., 1993), but the varying definitions of what constitutes depression or the number of symptoms included change estimates of heritability (McGuffin, Katz, and Rutherford, 1991).[13] Bipolar depression, like schizophrenia, is very rare before puberty and even during adolescence. The concordance rate for manic depression among adult monozygotic twins is about 67 to 69 percent compared with 13 to 20 percent in fraternal twins.[14] It seems that relatives of bipolar or manic depressives are at a greater risk both for bipolar and unipolar depression. As with schizophrenia, an early age of onset for depression is related to a higher familial or genetic loading; when parents' depression began early in life, their children are at a higher risk than those of parents whose illness started later (Weissman et al., 1987). Where depression occurs *without* obvious precipitants, there is a greater chance that other relatives are also affected or will be affected by the disease—not because it is contagious but because the absence of observable causal stressors implies that the problem is more largely genetic than when causal factors are present.

For unipolar disorder, which includes only depressive symptoms, the genetic influence is more modest and leaves "greater room for working environmental effects" (McGuffin and Katz, 1993:219).[15] Symptoms of unipolar depression in children include sadness, irritability, poor concentration, loss of interest in usual activities, fatigue, self-pity, as well as thoughts of death or suicide. Contrary to bipolar depression, the unipolar type is common among children, although it may be infrequently diagnosed because of comorbidity with other problems (Angold, 1993; Mesquita and Gilliam, 1993).

McGuffin and Katz (1993) review some literature indicating that when stressors act as precipitants, the familial loading is generally lower. As pointed out earlier, strong stressors require less genetic predisposition in order to cause depression, often called *reactive* depression; thus, it is only reasonable that family members who are not affected by these stressors in a similar way should not become depressed. However, these points are still in dispute. For instance, Bebbington, Tennant, and Hurry (1991) report equal familial risk with or without preceding stressors. What they find is that "threatening life events" or stressors tend to be more common among relatives of depressed persons compared with relatives of nondepressed persons (42 percent versus 7 percent). This could imply that when a family has a given loading for depression, more of its members are victims both of serious stressors and of depression, in part because the stressors in turn trigger depression. Thus, *the genetic vulnerability that runs in a family may actually lead to behaviors and situations that create stressors*–these family members would be the opposite of resilient persons described in Chapter 2. Familial continuity for depression is explained both by genes and by environmental stressors to which family members may be more vulnerable[16] and may even help to create.[17] Kendler et al. (1992) also believe that one of the reasons a higher genetic loading for depression exists in hospitalized patients is because depression is well known in the family; therefore, when a member becomes ill, he or she is more likely to receive professional help, and consequently to appear in studies of mental illness, than in families in which depression does not exist. One could also add that hospitalized depression is a more serious illness; hence it may carry a higher genetic loading to begin with.

Depression increases during adolescence (McGee et al., 1992). Moreover, girls and women tend to be overrepresented among depressed persons. However, for younger children, boys are overrepresented in some studies,[18] while the rates are equal in others.[19] Follow-up studies into young adulthood indicate that around 75 percent of those who were schizophrenic during adolescence still have related problems, while about 40 percent of those who suffered from bipolar depression continue to have related difficulties (Cawthron et al., 1994).

Environmental Stressors

For *any* psychiatric disorder, unless there is a high genetic loading, cumulative disadvantage or multiple stressors seem to contribute substantially to morbidity, especially for nonpsychotic illnesses such as reactive depression (Sameroff and Seifer, 1990). Several studies indicate that the *number* of risk factors increases the chance that a child suffers negative outcomes in general. Marital discord, poverty, overcrowding, and poor parenting are some of the main stressors that, if they occur jointly, place children at great risk, both for psychiatric problems and conduct disorders (Garmezy and Masten, 1994). But some of these environmental difficulties, particularly parental marital conflict,[20] that have been related to children's emotional problems, may in part be explained by a genetic link in two ways. First, parents may contribute to the creation of the familial stressors because of their own negative traits. Second, conflictual parents who are also antisocial may beget genetically at-risk children for whom parents' marital malfunctioning triggers and exacerbates negative predispositions.

Other environmental adversities are child specific rather than family specific. One can think here of a transition to a new school, the loss of a familiar peer group, peer rejection or abuse, a violent peer culture, poor school performance, and a teacher's maltreatment. Often, these adversities are specific to one child in a family and do not affect the other siblings (Beardsall and Dunn, 1992). Thus, children who experience concurrent stressors in several domains of their lives,[21] that is, in their family, peer group, and school situation, are at a particularly elevated risk for the development of emotional problems such as depression, even with little genetic predisposition, as well as for the development of conduct disorders, as we see in the following chapter.

Methodological Considerations

In models using a combined genetic and environmental causality, estimates of the risk for developing schizophrenia or depression vary from study to study. This variability results from several factors. One factor pertains to the *age of the parents and the children at the time of the study.* In the case of schizophrenia, the age of onset is anywhere between late childhood and 50 years of age, although it generally begins late in adolescence or in early adulthood, while manic depression and unipolar depression may have a more delayed age of onset. Therefore, when comparing parents with children on one emotional problem, the lifetime risk can be evaluated more accurately when the parents are older than when they are younger. In order to evaluate heritability, one has to have originally studied both parents *and* children who become or did not become schizophrenic, for example, or bring in corrections for age (Nigg and Goldsmith, 1994:350).

But let's assume, *for heuristic purposes,* that statistical corrections for age are not brought in. If researchers match school-age children or even adolescents with parents, the research design is flawed for the following reasons:

1. Children's emotional problems may have an etiology that differs from that of adults' problems and be related to a different genetic and environmental configuration. To eliminate this possibility, children's rate would have to be compared with the prevalence of parents' emotional problems *when parents were themselves children.*
2. Childhood emotional problems do not necessarily lead to adult emotional problems, although schizophrenia in adolescence and childhood tends to persist more than does depression.[22] Thus, we may find that most parents of such children do not have the same emotional problem but perhaps they had it when *they* were children.

3. Concomitantly, childhood problems may lead to *other* adult emotional problems. Once again, we may find that children who have one emotional problem tend to have parents with a different illness, in part because of comorbidity. However, had the parents been tested as children, we might have found that they *then* also suffered from the same problem as their children.

It follows that children and adolescents who are emotionally disturbed *and* have emotionally disturbed parents often do not suffer from the exact same illness as their parents. Either they will eventually develop a problem similar to that of their parents, or they may have inherited a broad spectrum predisposition that makes them vulnerable to a variety of emotional problems. Or their illness may be strictly caused by the environment and is likely to disappear as matters improve or as they are old enough to live away from the familial stressors.

It is perhaps more valid to compare parents to *adult* children and, preferably, compare deceased parents' medical or psychiatric record to those of their elderly children's, at a time when whatever problems the children could have developed have actualized, except for senility and Alzheimer's disease. Thus, all problems will have been accounted for, both for parents and children, and the concordance rate between the two will be more accurate.

But we also have to return to the cautionary statement offered at the outset of this chapter. It follows that genetic transmission can occur via parents who are *carriers* but are not themselves afflicted. In some cases, parents can transmit a psychiatric illness to their children from their own disturbed parents–the children's grandparents. So far, the research literature largely bypasses these discussions, in part because we need further advances in molecular genetics to determine who is a carrier. Moreover, if it is assumed that most emotional problems are polygenetic in nature, it becomes less likely that parents and children share the exact identical gene configuration leading to a specific illness.

EFFECTS ON THE PARENT-CHILD RELATIONSHIP

There is a sound, albeit small, body of literature describing the deleterious effects on parents of having adult children who are psychiatrically ill,[23] especially when the child coresides with the parents,[24] or there is a great deal of contact (Anderson and Lynch, 1984).[25] Thus, emotionally disturbed children can exert a negative influence on the relationship with their parents all the way into the parents' last years of life (Greenberg et al., 1993).

One can expect that the impact of children's emotional problems on the parent-child relationship will differ by social class: Uneducated persons often do not understand emotional problems as well as their more educated contemporaries do (Hollingshead and Redlich, 1958). Mental illness may thus carry a heavier objective burden (such as financial costs), but a lighter subjective burden among members of the lower class. Subjective burden is defined as the "family's perception of duress and oppression caused by the patient's presence in the home" (Arey and Warheit, 1980:16).[26] Another effect of children's emotional problems may be that, when difficulties persist and demands on parents mount, parents may become less interested, less affectionate, and less communicative. As Loeber and Stouthamer-Loeber (1986:54) point out, it is "difficult to love children who make one's life miserable," even though the ill children are not responsible for their actions.

Because it is normal for parents to supervise their children less as they grow older,[27] one can ask what kinds of strains on the relationship result from continued supervision, especially when it is not accepted by the disturbed adult children. Cook (1988) and Cook and Cohler (1986) have well illustrated the high level of stress that parents of young schizophrenic adults experience–feelings of hopelessness and despair. There is still a widely held assumption, especially in private practice, that all emotional disorders are caused by the parents' handling of the child. Consequently, parents may feel needlessly guilty and frustrated, while adult children may turn against a parent whom they erroneously believe to be the source of their problems–a parent who could otherwise be most helpful.

In 1972, Brown et al. found that relatives' negativity toward schizophrenic family members was strongly related to relapse,[28] and that a decrease in the patients' symptoms led to a reduction of negativism in relatives. They added, "the fact that expressed emotion acts as strongly in marital partners as in parents argues for a reactive rather than a causal model" (Brown et al., 1972:255). This concept of reverse causality, which, at the time, was quite revolutionary, is supported by several researchers who argue that parents' negativism may be the result, rather than the cause, of the difficulties encountered because of the child's mental state and consequent aberrant behavior.[29] Moreover, Cook et al. (1990) report that mothers of schizophrenic children try to deescalate negative interaction, as is also often the case with mothers of children with conduct disorders. It is relevant here to recall that mothers of hyperactive children whose symptoms diminished after taking methylphenidate, known as Ritalin, showed corresponding behavioral changes: They became far less controlling as there was a lesser need for monitoring (Schachar et al., 1987).[30] The same maternal changes have occurred in experi-

ments where children were trained to behave in a compliant or in an oppositional manner (Brunk and Henggeler, 1984). Adults interacted more with a
child who had been trained to be responsive.[31] Researchers have established
that the presence of a schizophrenic child in an experimental situation hinders
parents' ability to perform cognitive tasks (Tompson et al., 1990). Goldstein
et al. (1992) do not report any communication disturbance among parents of
adult schizophrenics. Finally, Liem (1974) noted that parents of nonschizoph-
renic children do not differ in their behavior from parents of schizophrenic
children when experimentally paired with a normal and then a schizophrenic
child.[32] These studies taken together indicate that *the emotionally disturbed
do influence others' responses to them and contribute to the disruption of
relationships and child-rearing activities within the family.*

The impact of a child's emotional problems is more serious for the
mother than the father (Cook, 1988; Kazak and Marvin, 1984). Similarly,
the effect of a mentally or physically disabled child is greater on the
mother, especially in terms of workload (Dupont, 1980),[33] and so is the
effect of conduct disorder and delinquency, as we see in the following
chapters. It would therefore be expected that the mother-child relationship
will be far more affected than the father-child relationship. Mothers and
fathers may adopt different styles of communication and of parenting
practices with their emotionally disturbed children. These differences may
become more obvious as the child passes into adolescence and young
adulthood. These gender-related hypotheses remain to be tested.

THE EFFECT OF OTHER PERSONS
ON THE PARENT-CHILD RELATIONSHIP

An important aspect of children's emotional problems and conduct
disorders pertains to the parents' relationship with professionals, especially psychiatrists, psychologists, and clinical caseworkers (Lefley, 1989).
The literature on disabled children well documents how parents are often
led to feel helpless, as well as incompetent, when dealing with various
service delivery personnel (Darling, 1987).[34] It is not difficult to see how
this could be even more so in the case of parents of emotionally disturbed
or disruptive children, especially when the teaching and research literatures
too frequently hold them responsible (Caplan and Hall-McQuorquodale,
1985). Many parents feel that mental health professionals do not have a
realistic view of the patient, whom they often see under very limited and
artificial circumstances. The mother of a schizophrenic adolescent
explained the matter in an interview:

The psychiatrist has not the slightest inkling as to how difficult it is for us to care for Jimmy. Right now he thinks that he is doing better. I mean, he says that because these days Jimmy communicates better and he was able to have a good conversation with him (his psychiatrist). But his behavior isn't any different. He doesn't see it . . . At other times, we beg him to hospitalize him and he only tells us that we exaggerate. Strange thing is that when we think he's doing better he disagrees. That's when he starts digging up a new symptom. You know, it's enough to drive parents to become schizophrenic themselves (Ambert, 1992:119).

A large proportion of children and adolescents who suffer from emotional problems go undiagnosed and are never treated (Boyle and Offord, 1988). They do not appear in clinical statistics and cannot be studied. Many of these children are gifted in some areas and/or are physically attractive, and thus appear unafflicted. Others simply do not live in an environment possessing the resources to diagnose and treat problematic children, or they may live in a neighborhood where instability and deviance are the norm. They would thus blend in with a relatively dysfunctional environment or one that is undemanding in terms of school achievement and encourages unemployment. Therefore, it would be an important research endeavor to locate such a sample of undiagnosed children and compare the parent-child relationship with that of cases where children are in treatment. While the parents of nondiagnosed children do not have to suffer from public disclosure and contact with professionals who are at times unsympathetic, the parents of nondiagnosed children may suffer from confusion, lack of understanding, self-blame, and lack of social support because their child's behavior is inappropriate (either with peers, at school, with parents at home, or with them in public places). If such parents confide to their relatives about their children's problems, they may trigger negative reactions against themselves, especially if the relatives see only the positive or pleasant aspects of the child. Jimmy's mother had this to say on the topic:

When he's better, we take advantage of this to visit his grandparents on both sides, but that's difficult for us because they practically always see a normal Jimmy, so to speak. And when he is normal, well, he is charming. His grandparents *adore* him [he is the only male grandchild] and that's fine but the problem is that they don't want to hear us talk about him when he isn't OK. You should even see the incredulous looks they give us or the long silences over the phone. They think we're crazy. I'm sure they think we're bad parents and let me tell you that this creates a great deal of distance between us. We, my husband and I, are *their* children and they don't believe us. It's a big strain on us, as if we needed one more (Ambert, 1992:121).

Whatever the reasons, parents who have problem children often have fewer contacts with relatives (Cunningham, Benness, and Siegel, 1988). They often feel misunderstood and fear relatives' blame (Terkelsen, 1987).[35] Some of these parents are dysfunctional themselves and may have always maintained a distant relationship with their families. Others, although not affected themselves, have problematic families and their child has inherited the disorder. Other parents have intolerant families, while still others have well-intentioned but intrusive family members.

CONCLUSION

Severe emotional problems do not develop without a genetic predisposition; the stronger the genetic loading or the more severe the illness, the less likely it is that environmental factors enter into the causality path. They may, however, contribute to the persistence of the illness, whether in the form of a poor parent-child relationship or other stressors. It is unavoidable that parents who are stressed by marital conflict, unemployment, poverty, or a large number of closely spaced children will exert a detrimental influence on these children, at the very least in terms of contributing to the continuation and the worsening of the children's symptoms and disorders.

Moreover, because of the fact that some of these parents may share detrimental genes with their offspring, these predispositions may also prevent them from being adequate parents. In turn, the presence of disturbed children constitutes an added stressor in parents' lives, and this stressor becomes part of the children's environment via their parents' reactions. This perspective, proposing an interaction between genetic predispositions, parenting, child disorders, parental reaction, and extra-familial environments is far more complex and textured than simple causal assumptions of poor parenting as the source of children's emotional problems.

ENDNOTES

1. Other problematic child and adolescent outcomes could have been selected. Early onset of sexual involvement and alcohol/drug use and abuse, for instance, have generated a great deal of research found in journals such as *Adolescence, Family Relations, Family Planning Perspective, Journal of Marriage and*

the Family, and *Journal of Youth and Adolescence*. Similarly, there is much literature on autism, developmental delay, attention-deficit disorders, anxiety, and hyperactivity. Clinically oriented journals such as *Family Process, Journal of Abnormal Child Psychology, Journal of Child and Family Therapy*, and *Journal of Clinical and Consulting Psychology* contain relevant articles.

2. For both depression and schizophrenia, definitions applicable to children have given rise to a great deal of discussion: Werry and Taylor, 1994. On ethnic issues pertaining to adolescent mental health, see the volume edited by Stiffman and Davis, 1990.

3. Gottesman, 1991.

4. The role of genes in anxiety disorders, believed to be perhaps the most frequently encountered psychiatric problem (Klein, 1994), is still debated (Thapar and McGuffin, 1995). Autism, which occurs only in 0.3 percent of the population, is considered to be 98 percent genetic (Rutter, 1991b).

5. This risk differs somewhat depending on the types of schizophrenia considered: Nigg and Goldsmith, 1994.

6. The estimates vary with the studies and we return to this methodological problem later on in the text. What is important to recall is that *all* studies show a substantial increase in risk the closer the biological relatedness is.

7. Kringlen and Cramer, 1989.

8. Referred to in J. Arsanow, 1994.

9. Goldstein and Tuma, 1987; Sameroff and Seifer, 1990.

10. Note that this does *not* mean that they have a 59 percent chance of being schizophrenic on average, but a 59 percent *increase* in risk. Their actual risk is probably around 7 to 13 percent or slightly more.

11. See Cadoret et al., 1995a, for similar conclusions in terms of alcoholism and antisocial behavior.

12. For qualifiers, see Kendler, 1995b.

13. Kendler et al., 1992; Winokur, 1995.

14. Bertelsen, Harvald, and Hauge, 1977; Gershon et al., 1977. Several other studies exist. See McGuffin and Murray, 1991; Tsuang, Gilbertson, and Faraoane, 1991.

15. See Bertelsen et al., 1977; Winokur et al., 1995.

16. Goodyear et al., 1993.

17. Plomin and Bergeman, 1991. There are studies that identify personality traits, such as helplessness and low self-esteem, that predate symptoms of depression: Block, Gjerde, and Block, 1991.

18. Kashani et al., 1987.

19. Brooks-Gunn and Petersen, 1991. For a comprehensive review of the factors that lead to this gender difference in adolescence, see Nolen-Hoeksema and Girgus, 1994.

20. Jouriles, Bourg, and Farris, 1991. Jouriles, Farris, and McDonald, 1991; Snyder et al., 1988.

21. What others call cumulation of stressors: Rutter et al., 1995; Sameroff et al., 1987.

22. Asarnow, 1994; Cawthron et al., 1994.

23. Arey and Warheit, 1980; Cook, 1988; Hatfield, 1978; Thompson and Doll, 1982.

24. Arey and Warheit, 1980; Cook, 1988.

25. There is also a sizable literature on the effect of having a mentally delayed, an autistic, and a physically disabled child. As we have also seen in Chapter 4, there is some literature documenting how dependent seniors exert a considerable degree of stress on their adult children and spouses: Eagles et al., 1987; Gilleard, Gilleard, and Whittig, 1992; Gilleard et al., 1984; Robins et al., 1982.

26. See also Gubman and Tessler, 1987.

27. Goldstein, 1984; Patterson and Stouthamer-Loeber, 1984.

28. See also Leff et al., 1982; Vaughn and Leff, 1976.

29. Cook and Cohler, 1986; Hooley, 1987; Kanter, Lamb, and Loeper, 1987; and Seywert, 1984.

30. Barkley, 1981; Tarver-Berhing and Barkley, 1985.

31. For other experiments, see Bates, 1975; Keller and Bell, 1979; Vasta and Copitch, 1981.

32. Mishler and Waxler, 1966; Waxler, 1974.

33. Gath and Gumley, 1986; Pahl and Quine, 1984; Wilkin, 1981.

34. Budoff, 1975, Strickland, 1982; Yoshida et al., 1978.

35. See Chapter 13 for evidence that the same problem arises with delinquent children.

Chapter 12

Children with Behavioral Problems

There is theoretical and empirical overlap between this chapter and the other chapters in Part III. Not only are there children who suffer both from emotional and behavioral problems, but a good proportion of delinquent adolescents have behavior disorders, while others also suffer from emotional problems (Fabrega, Ulrich, and Loeber, 1996). Moreover, there are some common points in the parent-child relationship within these diverse situations, as well as in terms of effects on parents, particularly mothers. Finally, many children with severe behavior problems have parents who are themselves problematic.

This chapter beings with sections on the definition and etiology of behavior problems, as well as on their persistence and desistance. Next comes an examination of how children with behavioral problems contribute to the disruption of parenting skills, as well as how they particularly affect mothers. This is followed by sections presenting environmental factors in the etiology and persistence of conduct disorders, as well as a discussion of correlates and intervention possibilities.

DEFINITION AND ETIOLOGY

The definition of what constitutes behavioral problems or conduct disorders is quite involved (Earls, 1994). The following behaviors are generally included (Herbert, 1987). The first category consists of overtly hostile acts such as fighting, hitting, and name calling; some children are more verbally than physically aggressive. Then there are aversive acts such as fussiness, unwarranted crying, interruptions, sharp and immediate demands that are difficult to meet, disobedience, refusal to comply, and repeated temper tantrums. The hyperactive syndrome is a related entity and is characterized by moving about constantly, short attention span, shifting from one topic to another or one activity to another.[1] Hyperactivity has a high level of comorbidity with other conduct disorders (Taylor et al., 1986); for instance, more than 65 percent of hyperactive children are also aggressive (Barkley et al., 1989). Attention-seeking behaviors fall in any one of the above categories but a child who is so inclined may exhibit a great many episodes of aversive activity. Another category involves dishonesty: lying, cheating, and stealing. But a mere enumeration of the behaviors involved is insufficient to grasp the problem because even normative children occasionally engage in one or several of these acts. Children with conduct disorders exhibit some and even many of these behaviors *regularly*, as a way of life so to speak, and *persistently*. Often, but not always, the pattern begins at an early age.

The etiology of conduct disorders is therefore much more complex than that of severe emotional problems. Although there are genetic influences (Braungart-Rieker et al., 1995), *conduct disorders are more heterogeneous and more culture-specific than emotional problems*. Many contributing elements are at the forefront and, except for extreme cases, there are many pathways leading to similarly negative behavioral outcomes (Lahey et al., 1989). There is a variety of underlying causes depending on the type of behavior studied (McGee and Newcomb, 1992). Moreover, a youngster problematic in some domains may be normative in others (Resnicow, Ross-Gaddy, and Vaughan, 1995). There is much research in psychiatry on what is called "antisocial personality disorder," focusing on early onset and indicating substantial heritability, perhaps even more for females than males.[2] Although generally developed separately, this line of inquiry is related to theories and research on personality functioning and personality types (Block, 1971). Of particular importance here is the construct of ego resiliency (Block and Block, 1980), which correlates with a low level of behavioral problems, and the category of undercontrol, which is linked to impulsiveness and other aspects of behavior problems as herein described. The Big Five personality factors have also served as a basis to help explain children's and adults' behaviors,[3] including externalizing problems and delinquency (Robins et al., 1996).

In a study of adoptees, children at genetic risk for behavior difficulties were far more influenced by a negative adoptive home than children with no known genetic risk (Cadoret et al., 1995b).[4] Longitudinal research in New Zealand indicates that most adolescents who exhibit *several* behavioral problems (early onset of sexual activity, substance use and abuse, police contact, mood disorders) come from seriously disadvantaged and dysfunctional families, even though 13 percent of all children from such backgrounds are problem free (Fergusson, Horwood, and Lynskey, 1994). For children reared in advantaged homes (economically and emotionally), only one out of 400 to 500 becomes a multiproblem adolescent, and 80 percent are totally problem free. Patterson and Stouthamer-Loeber (1984) found that 21 percent of the nondelinquents in their sample were poorly supervised by their parents, compared with 50 percent of the one- and two-time offenders and 73 percent of the repeat offenders. Farrington (1978) reports that aggressive children are also less supervised, while McCord (1982) mentions the same for aggressive and antisocial children.

PERSISTENCE AND DESISTANCE

When a child exhibits either one type of *extreme* behavioral problem, such as aggressiveness or constant temper tantrums, or a *wide* range of conduct disorders in multiple settings (Loeber, 1990), this child is more likely to become both a problematic adolescent and adult, and perhaps even a criminal, than a child who is prosocial (Robins, 1984).[5] In a 22-year follow-up study, Eron and Huesmann (1990) found that the level of aggressiveness at age eight predicted seriousness of crimes and number of convictions by age 30. But persistence does not imply a straight line: The type of problem may change with age. For instance, temper tantrums may be replaced by insubordination to parents in adolescence and, in adult life, by difficulties with employers and marital conflict (Caspi and Moffitt, 1991).[6] It can be inferred that severe conduct disorders that perpetuate themselves throughout the life course, albeit under different guises,[7] are influenced by genes,[8] especially when the environment discourages these behaviors (Dodge, 1990b). This is particularly true for aggressiveness (Ghodsian-Carpey and Baker, 1987). Adult antisocial behavior is far more genetically influenced than the childhood type (Lyons et al., 1995).

Parents whose child exhibits *severe* conduct disorders are often, although by no means always,[9] faced with a lifelong course of adversity, both for their child and perhaps for themselves. The latter topic has yet to be studied. Fortunately, research indicates that, with the passage into adulthood, a substantial proportion of troubled youngsters either outgrow their problems or express them in different but more benign ways (Loeber, 1988). This change often occurs as a result of associating with a prosocial spouse who provides a resocialization experience away from the former lifestyle, or as a result of being involved in a legitimate work environment (Pickles and Rutter, 1991).

Some children develop overt forms of difficult behavior (confrontation, aggressiveness) while others develop covert forms (stealing, vandalism, truancy, drug use). A third group of children develop both types of problems (Loeber et al., 1993). This group appears to be at a higher risk of being eventually arrested for criminal acts. Certain types of problematic behaviors appear quite stable over time, especially aggressiveness.[10] In fact, throughout childhood and early adolescence, conduct disorders are fairly persistent for both boys and girls,[11] and are more persistent than emotional problems (Esser, Schmidt, and Woerner, 1990). *It is possible that serious conduct disorders bring a premature closure in terms of life choices and self-identity,* in part because of the biased cognitions that accompany such disorders, and in part because of the negative peer and adult reactions they evoke. While it is difficult for a child predisposed to aggressiveness and sensation seeking to activate such behaviors in a well-regulated and monitoring family, as this child ages and becomes more independent, he can choose an environment that suits his temperament better: "Partly via his self-selection into a predisposing social environment, his genetically influenced temperament has now reached fuller expression, while the early family environmental influences have attenuated" (Kendler, 1995b:846). However, if the advantages he has gained within his family persist, he may select a prosocial environment that will help direct him toward a more functional mode of behavior.

There are some indications that certain temperamental traits exhibited by small children relate to future strengths or, conversely, to behavioral or emotional problems.[12] The long-term longitudinal studies by Block, Block, and Keyes (1988), as well as those by Chess and Thomas (1984), and other somewhat shorter-term longitudinal studies (Bates et al., 1991; Rende, 1993) have established such correlations. Studies using several follow-ups and multiple informants also find significant correlations between early childhood traits and mid-adolescent outcomes (Caspi et al., 1995). However, these correlations, although significant, are usually fairly modest. This indicates the difficulties involved in measuring the continuity of a trait over time and/or its specific sequelae. It also indicates, as seen in Chapter 4, that unless traits are extreme, there is perhaps more change than continuity over the years. A genetic model would posit that, when traits are not extreme, thus not very genetically based, they need environmental stimuli or influences to be actualized—whether negatively or positively. For instance, intrafamily stressors as well as external stressors pressuring the family elevate a child's risk of developing adjustment problems (Ge, Conger, Lorenz, and Simons, 1994). Stressful family conditions may contribute to parental depression and increase negative mood and irritability, which in turn can lead to a disruption in parenting practices and resultant child/adolescent problems (Conger, Patterson, and Ge. 1995).

Moreover, emotional and behavioral disturbances experienced by a child of eight or ten (Ronka and Pulkinen, 1995) relate 20 years later to a life that is more burdened with chronic stressors and negative events. Rutter et al. (1995:74) find that such individuals are less likely to "show planning in relation to key life transitions," and this inability to plan, which often accompanies behavioral problems, in turn leads to additional negative events. Children who had behavioral problems at age ten were far more likely to enter a first union with a deviant partner, in part because such youngsters had antisocial peers and lived in areas where there was a higher ratio of antisocial persons (Pickles and Rutter, 1991).

DISRUPTION OF PARENTING SKILLS

Research has shown that conflictual interactions between parents and young children occur 3.5 to 15 times an hour (Dix, 1991).[13] Children's voices rise sharply when their mother's attention is not immediately forthcoming. Over 25 years ago, Minton, Kagan, and Levine (1971) found that mothers of two to three-year olds issued a command or a disapproval every third minute. These results demonstrate that even normal children in our society exhibit difficult behaviors; nevertheless, the rate of disruption is higher among problematic children. Hence, Patterson (1982) reports that difficult boys engage in aversive-coercive behaviors with their mothers at the rate of 0.75 per minute, compared with 0.31 for other boys. As children's conduct disorders become more established, not only does the rate of aversive behaviors increase, but so does their severity. Attempts to control these behaviors often result in an escalation of parent-child adversity until the conflicts spill outside the home (Patterson, 1982). In extreme forms of parenting breakdown, the child controls the house.[14] Many mothers of difficult children become desensitized to misbehavior and accept it as normal: They are often less able than mothers of nonproblematic children to distinguish misbehavior from regular behavior.[15]

While adults' inappropriate parenting skills contribute to child's conduct disorder in many families, as the child gains the upper hand, he or she may cause a further disruption of parenting practices, and perhaps even of the marital relationship (Befera and Barkley, 1985). *The child facilitates the disruption of its own environment* "by eliciting maladaptive parental behaviour, or increasing the strain on a marginally good marriage" (Earls, 1994:316). Moreover, there are some stressors specific to children that can affect their behavior as well as their relationship with their parents. Patterson, Bank, and Stoolmiller (1990) call these transitional stressors in that they involve changes such as residential moves, passing from junior to senior high school, and parental divorce. As a result of these stressors, and others related to peers, adolescents may become more irritable toward siblings and parents (Ambert, 1994a). It is at this crucial point that parenting competence is important in order to prevent the perpetuation of a disruptive pattern of behavior among children.

Patterson, Reid, and Dishion (1992) show that, when a child has an extreme antisocial score on personality tests in grade four, parenting practices are much more disrupted when the same child is assessed again in grade six, compared with a child who had been more prosocial in grade four. They hypothesize that, in any environment, the person who is the most coercive has control of the situation (Patterson et al., 1992:44). Families with disruptive children are marked by conflictual mutuality between mother and child (Johnston and Pelham, 1990). While the mother usually prevails with normal children, with difficult boys in particular, it is the child who does. Hence there is a role reversal and the parent-child relationship becomes dysfunctional. Children who are hostile, conflictual, and even aggressive also impair a family's ability to solve problems that are relevant to its good functioning (Forgatch, 1989).[16] In turn, this type of interactional deficit is related to poor adolescent adjustment (McCombs, Forehand, and Smith, 1988).

When the oppositional behavior becomes chronic, parents lose control over family life and over their children (Patterson, 1982). "Some children ultimately 'win' when they perform in such a way as to stop virtually all parental behaviors aimed at changing the misbehavior" (Loeber and Stouthamer-Loeber, 1986:110). Brown et al. (1988:126) add that parents of children who suffer from ADD (attention deficit disorder) score significantly higher on depression than other parents. "ADD children often have a way of disrupting activities, wherever they may be." The authors conclude that "these parents who have emotional difficulties react less well to provocative child behavior, and this reaction may exacerbate the child's behavioral difficulties"–hence, there is circularity of effect between child and parental characteristics.

It can even be hypothesized that when children become too difficult, certain types of parents (more individualistic, perhaps) may choose to distance themselves and ignore the situation. This behavior would serve as a protective mechanism on the part of parents who may have tried everything in their power and for whose children nothing seems to have worked. At some point, they may simply decide to "get on" with their own lives, and let the youngster pick up the pieces. By default they then become permissive and even neglectful parents. There are also upper-middle-class households where both parents are too involved in their careers, and in climbing the social ladder to be concerned with supervision of teenagers, especially when it could give rise to unpleasant scenes. Unfortunately, there are no studies of such parents, nor of related reciprocal parent-child dynamics.

MOTHERS AND DIFFICULT CHILDREN

Mothers have been studied more extensively than fathers in their interactions with children, in part because mothers are more available at home, but also because ideologies posit that mothers are a more salient causative agent in child development. Patterson (1980:10) pertinently remarks that "The role of mother is structured in such a manner as to almost guarantee higher rates of aversive events than does the role of the father." Coercive boys actually *target their mothers rather than their fathers as victims of conflict,* perhaps because mothers "are more likely to reinforce coercive attacks" (Patterson et al., 1992:49). Fathers engage more in play interactions with their children (Lamb, 1983), which allows them to attract less coercive behavior from their conduct-disordered children than the mother, who may be solely responsible for enforcing routines. As a result, fathers may not sympathize with the child's mother when she complains about the behavior, hence increasing the mother's isolation (Wahler and Dumas, 1989). Fathers of difficult children are little different from fathers of normal children in terms of stress reactions (Patterson, 1976). As Patterson 1982:24 remarks, "this leads to the conclusion that the role label most appropriate for fathers might be that of 'guest!'"

At some point in the escalation of parent-child conflict, the mother may become afraid of disciplining or even contradicting the child. Patterson (1982:32-33) also notes that "mothers tend not to provide an aversive antecedent for these chains" of behaviors and desperately try "to avoid/escape from confrontations with a practiced aggressor." In fact, a mother's positive behavior toward a usually disruptive boy may encourage the latter to take advantage of her (Lavigueur, Tremblay, and Saucier, 1995).

With regard to infants, mothers who describe them as difficult at three months (Campbell, 1979) or four months (Kelley, 1976) are less responsive to them, even later on, and more negative when the infants do not behave appropriately. In other words, certain types of mothers become affectively turned off when their infants are temperamentally fussy or nonresponsive. Stevenson-Hinde and Simpson (1982) show that mothers of three-year-olds who are rated as difficult have higher anxiety and irritability levels than other mothers. The authors propose an influence of child's temperament on mother's mood rather than the reverse. Related results for maternal depression are presented by Wolking and De Salis (1982). But we also know that mother and child share some genes so that a difficult child may also happen to have a difficult mother, and hence be at double risk as the more irritable mother helps the child maintain his or her difficult temperament.

Not surprisingly, maternal satisfaction correlates with child compliance (Kochanska, Kuczynski, and Radke-Yarrow, 1989): The mother-child interaction is less conflictual when a child is compliant. The child is therefore more easily socialized, thus providing the mother with greater interpersonal and parental rewards. Mash and Johnson (1983a) note that mothers' interactions with their hyperactive children are more stressful than is the case for interactions between mothers and normative children. One likely effect of difficult child behavior, at least on the mother, is an increasing tendency on her part to issue directives, commands and threats in an effort to reduce the negative behavior (Patterson, 1980). But this is usually to no avail because, although parental reprimands do lower negative child behavior in *normal* children, they do not generally affect the behavior of problem children. Quite the opposite often occurs, and children may simply increase the frequency and severity of their coercive and oppositional episodes.

ENVIRONMENTAL FACTORS
IN CONDUCT DISORDERS

It is imperative to study the development of antisocial behaviors[17] within an ecological perspective that allows for the recognition "that the contexts of development vary for different groups of children" (Tolan, Guerra, and Kendall, 1995:579). Detrimental environments in which families live, especially if the family is already malfunctioning on some levels, place children at greater risk of developing antisocial behavior. While there is much agreement in the literature that poverty increases the likelihood that children will develop conduct disorders,[18] we need studies that concurrently examine different levels of poverty both in the family and the community in which it resides (Guerra et al., 1995). *Low income per se is not necessarily the root cause of deviance* because many categories of people are poor and yet have low deviance rates (Jencks, 1992). However, poor *communities* place disadvantaged families and their already vulnerable children at greater risk because of a lack of health care and educational resources,[19] fewer positive role models in the neighborhood, and lower community participation in the supervision of adolescent groups, among many other detrimental factors.

Guerra et al. (1995:519) note that the effects of economic deprivation are particularly potent for children who enter elementary school in a community with a high level of violence: Their aggressiveness can rise sharply at that young age. Such children are also likely to adopt beliefs favoring aggressiveness. Moreover, they report differences between white, African American, and Hispanic children in how these family and community variables interact to produce conduct disorders: Stress is a more important factor for whites and blacks, while beliefs favoring aggressiveness are more influential for Hispanic children.

Another perspective from which to study the role that environmental factors indirectly play in conduct disorders is suggested by behavior genetics: *The more antisocial children are, the more they tend to choose an environment that maintains and even increases their aggressiveness* (Patterson, 1982). They gravitate toward peers similar to them and they learn to "cut school," therefore segregating themselves from more prosocial role models. And they teach their parents to abandon efforts to socialize them. This is an instance of what is referred to as the active genotype-environment correlation.

CORRELATES AND INTERVENTION

Both field work conducted by this author and casual conversations with approximately 60 parents of difficult adolescents in the past three years have revealed a pattern that deserves further exploration. It consists in the fact that some youngsters who run away, or are grounded, and constantly run afoul of their parents' home rules, often report their parents for physical abuse and, in the case of girls, their fathers for sexual abuse–although no abuse exists. These parents then are investigated by concerned agencies. Generally, matters stop there, but not without having created much stress and disruption in the family. Several cases of falsely reported sexual abuse, however, have had long-lasting consequences for parents and siblings, and are likely to contribute to a long chain of negative events in the life of the accusing adolescent who will be left with little family support, if any at all, from parents who may feel forced to distance themselves for self-protection. Apparently, there are derelict adolescents who become vindictive and try to get back at their parents. Others may rationalize their own comportment by projecting socially unacceptable behaviors and attitudes on to their parents. These projections may fulfill the additional function of convincing the youths that they are justified in running away from such mean parents.

These observations may be related to those made by other researchers who indicate that aggressive children are often biased in how they process information (Dodge and Frame, 1982). *Difficult children may be difficult in part because their perceptions and cognitions are faulty, including the ones they maintain concerning their parents and other authority figures.* In turn, problematic behaviors and their consequences reinforce and even heighten the level of bias in the youngsters' cognitions as they are faced with negative social reactions that they cannot appreciate or accept. Bates (1987:1132) has hypothesized that infants and children who are difficult may learn less about their parents' attitudes and feelings than easier children. They may have an attention bias that orients them to ignore their parents and to focus on other areas of concerns to them, such as delinquent peers. Similar attention biases are observed in adults who suffer from emotional problems (MacLeod, Matthews, and Tata, 1986). Difficult children may be less able or willing than others to learn social cues and to "read" other people, perhaps due to high levels of impulsivity. This deficit may, in turn, contribute to friction between the parents, as well as between child and parents, further reinforcing the negative child behavior (Pepler and Slaby, 1994:35). Moreover, difficult children are less prosocial and *may identify less with their parents.* Intervention and research questions easily suggest themselves in these areas.

As seen in Chapter 8, there have been several successful interventions designed to reduce or prevent a further escalation of conduct disorders in children and adolescents by training the parents of such children in family management practices (Dishion and Andrews, 1995).[20] The degree of long-term success, however, in unknown because follow-up studies have been generally short term. Nevertheless, even a brief reprieve could be sufficient to break the impetus in the developmental sequence that leads to a wider range of problems (Loeber et al., 1993). This reprieve could allow for successes as a result of prosocial behavior and, in turn, success could teach the child that prosocial behaviors "pay." Tremblay et al. (1995) report successes that lasted through mid-adolescence after young boys, who were already disruptive or potentially so, benefited from a two-year program beginning in kindergarten–the program combined a parent-training focus and a school focus.

Dishion and Andrews (1995:545) also included youth focus groups in their interventions. While there were positive changes, there also were negative changes that resulted from the adolescents' exposure to other high-risk peers.[21] In other words, such adolescents reinforce each other's negative behavior when in groups that are not anchored in an immediate prosocial environment. This is why Dishion and Andrews agree that a cost effective strategy, such as suggested by Gottfredson, Gottfredson, and Hybl (1993), focusing on school policies that promote prosocial behavior is most promising.[22] Such policies would create a pervasive prosocial peer environment that would support rather than undermine parents' and teachers' socialization efforts.

CONCLUSION

How emotional problems and conduct disorders develop and persist is a complex question that involves genetic predispositions, parenting practices, and intra- and extra-family environmental factors. These factors, however, are not equally important throughout the entire spectrum of conduct disorders. Moreover, they may not be equally important for male and female children, nor, as emerging documentation suggests, for all cultural groups and social classes. In other words, the factors influencing the emergence and the continuation of, as well as cessation of, conduct disorders are contextual as well as specific to the disorder. Unfortunately parsimony dictated that conduct disorders be discussed here under one generic chapter title. Far more research is needed in these domains, and several questions were raised, implicitly or explicitly, throughout the chapter.

While there is certainly a great deal of comorbidity in this area, it is not clear at all whether youngsters who exhibit a variety of behavior problems do so because (1) they have inherited a broad spectrum of predispositions that tend to cluster genetically; (2) they have inherited a different type of broad spectrum predispositions which instead places them at risk for a nonspecific variety of problems, the nature of which will stem from environmental risks or opportunities; (3) they have inherited one predisposition which, when and if it becomes actualized, may lead to subsequent deficits. For instance, it is possible that the reason why aggressivity and ADD often coexist is that ADD may lead to frustration in many children and in some contexts result in aggressiveness; or (4) because they live in particularly deviant families and environments that provide a strong socialization framework *toward* behavioral problems, even in the absence of any predisposing element.

Environmental risks or opportunities for actualization of genetically influenced traits change with time since societies are far from static. For instance, conduct disorders find a wide range of possibilities for actualization in large and heterogeneous societies such as ours, where social change is rapid, and social control less potent. The following social elements, among others, currently combine to prevent children who may be genetically at risk from getting the dosage of structure, supervision, stability, and calm that they need to grow up without a disorder or series of disorders. These same elements, it can be argued, also prevent the actualization of prosocial tendencies that other children have inherited. They are: access to mass media products and programming of dubious value, less frequent parental presence at home, neighborhoods that no longer are effective communities, hence inadequate adult supervision, lesser importance of religion as a life-structuring element, fewer family rituals, and classrooms that are not sufficiently structured, are replete with distractions, and are not effective, whether for learning or for discipline. To these, we can add constant shuffling of children from home to day care, to school, to the mall, to sports, to the streets after school, and back home.

It may not be surprising, therefore, that the incidence of various forms of conduct disorders (and of delinquency) is by all accounts increasing. *Our society, especially for some groups, may present too many opportunities for the emergence of conduct disorders and too few opportunities for the optimal development of children's abilities and positive or prosocial traits.* Conduct disorders, as well as depression and anxiety, may well be the price parents and children pay for rapid and unplanned social change, and a consequent lack of what James Coleman has called an effective community.

ENDNOTES

1. Research on twins indicates that there is genetic influence for hyperactivity: Goodman and Stevenson, 1989.

2. For a review, see Nigg and Goldsmith, 1994.

3. For a review, see Goldberg, 1993.

4. See also Cadoret, 1985, Cadoret, Cain, and Crowe, 1983; Crowe, 1974. For critiques of the approach used in twin and adoption studies, see Kendler, 1995a.

5. Loeber, 1991; Robins and McEvoy, 1990.

6. Caspi, 1987.

7. This is called heterotypic continuity.

8. Caspi and Bem, 1990.

9. Loeber and Le Blanc, 1990.

10. Farrington, 1978, 1982; Fishbein, 1990; Huesmann et al., 1984; Lefkowitz et al., 1977; Loeber, 1982; Nylander, 1979; Robins and Ratcliffe, 1979.

11. Bates et al., 1991; Hymel et al., 1990.

12. Prior, 1992, for a review.

13. See also Patterson, 1980.

14. Loeber and Stouthamer-Loeber, 1986; Madden and Harbin, 1983.

15. Loeber (1982) reports a similar phenomenon for college students exposed to coercive child behavior: They become less apt to detect coercive behavior in a laboratory setting.

16. McColloch, Gilbert, and Johnson, 1990; Rueter and Conger, 1995.

17. Loeber and Hay, 1994.

18. Patterson, Kupersmidt, and Vaden, 1990.

19. Bronfenbrenner, Moen, and Garbarino, 1984.

20. See also, Patterson, 1984; Patterson, Reid, and Dishion, 1992; Dumas, 1989; Kazdin, 1987; McCord and Tremblay, 1992.

21. See also Elliot, Huizinga, and Ageton, 1985; Dishion, Andrews, and Crosby, 1995.

22. This is known as group resocialization; see Harris, 1995.

Chapter 13

Parents, Adolescents, and Delinquency

Delinquency is a most important topic because we can logically assume that it must have a tremendous impact on families and on the parent-child relationship, especially after a youngster has been arrested. Moreover, when the delinquency degenerates into adult criminality, we again will want to know how it affects the parent-child relationship.[1] The question that is generally asked about parents in delinquency is: What kinds of parents do juvenile delinquents have? What child-rearing practices correlate with delinquency? The research on juvenile delinquency could benefit from interactional and behavior genetics theories (Rowe and Gulley, 1992; Rowe, 1983b, 1986).[2]

Within the perspective of this text, inquiries are made into etiology and the outcome called delinquency is considered as a context within which the parent-adolescent relationship evolves. The chapter begins by presenting typologies of delinquency and follows with a section on causality before moving on to sections on the consequences it has on parents as well as on the adolescent-parent relationship. Preliminary results are then presented of a study we are completing which indicate that the effects of delinquency differ for mothers and fathers. Because no direct research exists on the impact of delinquency on the family, we offer some suggestions for orienting the field in this direction.

ASPECTS AND TYPES OF DELINQUENCY

Official delinquency involves an arrest and therefore an awareness on the part of authorities that a minor has committed a crime. Researchers have access to police statistics for arrests, and these come closer to estimating actual levels of delinquency than court statistics for convictions. Then there is self-reported delinquency, which involves researchers giving questionnaires to adolescents in school, for instance, and asking them to place check marks alongside a list of infractions to indicate which they have committed and if they have been arrested for each. This method is also used in research with delinquents who have been arrested to determine what other infractions they have committed in addition to the known crimes.

Delinquency has not increased recently, but *violent* youth criminality has and so have such crimes committed by children below the age of 12. Violent juvenile delinquency begins at younger ages than in previous decades. We now routinely hear of boys aged six to ten who participate in brutal acts and who carry firearms. Overall, more adolescents commit acts of violence and they more frequently do so with a weapon than ever before. Therefore, juvenile delinquency has become more lethal, attracts more media attention, and spreads feelings of fear and insecurity in the population at large, and particularly among law-abiding children who frequently worry about their own safety at school or in their neighborhood (Sheley and Wright, 1995). Consequently, the phenomenon of violent youth gangs is especially destructive in the ghettos of our cities and has victims beyond those who are directly victimized or aggressed. Another recent development is that girls are becoming more involved in attacks on other children and are participating in gang activities more than in the past. Most juvenile delinquents are arrested only once. Although repeat offenders constitute only a minority of all delinquents, they commit over 60 percent of all recorded offenses (Farrington, 1987). There is a hard core of juvenile delinquents in our social landscape.

There are at least two developmental paths to delinquency. Delinquents who start very young and graduate to more serious crimes are, on the average, different from delinquents who start in mid to late adolescence (Farrington et al., 1988). This is referred to as early-onset versus late-onset delinquency (Simons, Wu, Conger, and Lorenz, 1994). Early-onset delinquents generally exhibit more behavioral problems, are diagnosed more frequently with personality disorders, and often come from a dysfunctional or pathological family. They resemble the children with serious conduct disorders discussed in the previous chapter. Early-onset delinquency is usually accompanied and preceded by conduct disorders[3] that often begin early in life,[4] and frequently lead to adult criminality and other problems if no clinical intervention occurs, especially when the neighborhood is particularly criminogenic (Le Blanc and Fréchette, 1989). Late-onset delinquents also include youngsters who are similar to the above described ones but they tend to function better in many respects, to come from an adequate family, and do not as a rule become recidivists or adult criminals.

Nagin and Land (1993) divide adolescent offenders into three categories: those who do not commit crimes beyond late adolescence, those who are "high-level chronic" offenders, and those labeled "low-level chronic" offenders. The "adolescence-limited" offenders begin their delinquency two years later, on average, and commit far fewer illegal acts than the other two categories. Nagin, Farrington, and Moffitt (1995) pursued this typology and found that high-level chronic offenders also admitted to more criminality that did not come to the attention of the authorities from ages 14 through 32 than the other groups. By age 32, the two types of chronic offenders lived in poorer areas and conditions, and were "social failures." In contrast, "adolescence-limited" offenders had, by definition, no convictions after 21, and, by age 32, their employment pattern was undistinguishable from that of nondelinquents. However, according to their self-reports, many continued to engage in property crime, particularly theft; "they also continued to use illicit drugs, drink heavily, and get into fights" (Nagin, Farrington, and Moffitt, 1995:128).

The authors conclude that adolescence-limited offenders were better able than the other two types of offenders to restrict themselves to forms of deviant activities that did not lead to arrest and consequently did not harm their family relationships. They surmise that a greater proportion of delinquents than believed may continue a deviant career, albeit with a low profile. There is still much that remains to be done to understand the implications of age of onset and continuity of involvement in delinquent and criminal activities.[5] Despite recurrent failure to prevent recidivism among serious juvenile offenders (Weisz et al., 1991), a few programs have had some success and have also contributed to improving family relationships (Borduin et al., 1995). But effective interventions for chronic offenders have to operate on several levels, including parents and peers, and also target short-term goals in order to break the cycle and achieve long-term prevention (Yoshikawa, 1994).

CAUSES OF DELINQUENCY

In terms of etiology, the research has become quite sophisticated in the past two decades, with a diverse and complementary array of theories.[6] The etiological models not only differentiate between types of delinquency, as seen above, but they implicate a multitude of causal variables. Although the familial environment continues to be emphasized in terms of parents' background, their mental states, personality, disciplinary practices, and criminality,[7] other theories focus on peers (Warr and Stafford, 1991), gangs (Sampson and Groves, 1989), siblings (Rowe and Gulley, 1992), opportunities (Grasmick et al., 1993), motivation, beliefs, school performance (Zingraff et al., 1994), maltreatment, and personality (Caspi et al., 1994).[8] A touch of genetics and neurology also appears in the research (Moffitt, Lynam, and Silva, 1994). Other researchers emphasize risk factors in the form of various types of familial deprivation (Kolvin et al., 1988a and b).[9] However, these explanatory models have been tested mainly on males. There is some evidence that, in our society, the etiology of female delinquency may be somewhat different and may implicate a stronger genetic predisposition than for boys,[10] given that there are more social constraints against deviance for females than males.

Delinquents who commit *serious* crimes and are arrested seem to originate predominantly from a background that combines heavy risk factors: poverty, questionable peers, deprived neighborhood, unstable parenting, and low supervision. A disproportionate number of delinquents come from single-parent families, and this finding holds for both black and white, Canadian and American, or even British delinquents (see review by Sampson, 1993). Moreover, serious delinquency originates far more from disadvantaged families than from other families, and this finding has also been replicated in several countries.[11]

One familial factor that researchers emphasize is parental monitoring, which was discussed at great length in several chapters. There is consensus to the effect that poorly supervised youngsters are at a greater risk for juvenile delinquency, as well as for other problems such as illicit drug use, early sexual involvement, and school underachievement (Patterson, Reid, and Dishion, 1992). Inadequate supervision, in turn, occurs more frequently in homes where there is marital conflict, or only one parent, and where one or even both parents are emotionally disturbed, use drugs, or have committed crimes. In such families, the parent-child relationship and parental example may be proximal causes of delinquency. In previous chapters, it was seen that proper monitoring may be particularly important in ghetto neighborhoods that have a high rate of criminality. Although proper parental supervision is emphasized, we surmise that there are *other* salutary processes going on in families that monitor their children. These families are probably better organized, have more stable parents, children with easier temperaments, and spend more time on prosocial parent-child interaction than in other families, whether single- or two-parent families.

In disrupted neighborhoods with a high level of criminality, high mobility or turnover rate, concentration of poverty, and gang supremacy, children do not need a dysfunctional family to become aggressive and delinquent (Sampson, 1993). One would hypothesize that they merely need a weak family structure, such as a single parent, who cannot outweigh the strength of the negative environmental forces (Wilson, 1987). There is some literature supporting this hypothesis.[12] In fact, communities that are able to control teenage groups, especially gangs, have less delinquency (Sampson and Groves, 1989). The classroom and school is included here as part of this community environment.[13] For instance, Kellam (1994:155) reports that "in one class, being aggressive was deviant, whereas in another not being aggressive was deviant." And he is referring here to grade school children. One could perhaps push matters further and suggest that it is the street/classroom/neighborhood context that often makes these children difficult at an early age, thus at high risk for early-onset delinquency, and that their behavior is sufficient to disrupt the functioning of their family, including parenting skills. Or such children may constantly escape from family influence and control by "hanging around" with their older siblings, cousins, and peers in gangs that take on the role of socialization agents very early in their lives (Hogan and Kitagawa, 1985). Children with vulnerable predispositions may succumb more easily in these environments. The family may play no role whatsoever, whether positive or negative, because the environment is too powerful.

Poverty is particularly detrimental in this respect when it exists in high concentration. Studies in fact indicate that violence rises in areas that have seen an increasing concentration of poverty (Taylor and Covington, 1988). Black children who are poor are more affected than similar white children because they live in more disadvantaged areas than do their white counterparts. Sullivan (1989b) found that in the 1980s, 70 percent of New York City's poor blacks lived in neighborhoods with a high concentration of poverty, while 70 percent of poor whites lived in neighborhoods that were not particularly disadvantaged. In other words, poor white children live in "superior ecological niches," and this certainly contributes to lower opportunities for delinquency (Wilson, 1987:59).[14]

PERSONALITY FACTORS

The relationship between family and delinquency is also affected by partly genetically influenced characteristics. If a parent and a child share genes that lead to low impulse control and a difficult temperament, what results is a long chain of events: irritable and erratic parenting practices, a conflictual parent-child relationship, poor supervision, the likelihood that the youngster does not do well in school, that he or she is attracted to peers who are in similar circumstances, and is rejected by peers who are more prosocial. Patterson, Reid, and Dishion (1992) have reviewed five areas of research that point to a certain genetic or innate component to antisocial behavior, and therefore repeated delinquency.[15]

First, many antisocial children are hyporesponsive to punishment. That is, they do not respond to punishment, while prosocial children generally do: They alter their behavior to avoid it. Second, there seems to be an element of hyperresponsiveness to stimuli,[16] such as seeking excitement and thrills, even dangerous ones, which may explain why antisocial children have more accidents than other youngsters (Rydelius, 1988). The fear of being caught, for instance, adds stimulation and therefore may be an *incentive* rather than an impediment. A third factor is what is called hyperresponsiveness to exchanges with authority figures, particularly parents: Such youngsters immediately respond to requests by becoming more difficult, noncompliant, and aggressive. In other words, they seem to derive gratification from *negative* attention. A last factor reviewed by Patterson et al. (1992) is slow electrodermal activity. That is, reactions on the surface of the skin, such as perspiration, are not as easily produced by antisocial persons as by prosocial persons when they are experimentally subjected to stimuli designed to create excitement or fear.

Therefore, while the role of environment seems to predominate,[17] the data indicate that early-onset and persistent delinquents, as well as adult criminals, may be more genetically predisposed than casual offenders or those who are arrested for delinquency only once or twice. Of course, *genetic predispositions will more readily be actualized in environments that offer criminal opportunities and that block access to legitimate achievement.* Some schools and neighborhoods present few temptations for delinquent behavior and may protect their vulnerable children. Moreover, parents who have a warm, supportive and monitoring relationship with their youngsters act as deterrents to juvenile delinquency. Unfortunately, not all parents who are warm and supportive also monitor their children adequately. As soon as the element of supervision is eliminated from the equation, children are at risk, especially if they have an external locus of control or other negative traits that would benefit from supervision. In contrast, children who naturally possess self-control, are reasonably intelligent, and have a well-balanced personality may not need parental supervision beyond a certain age. If the parent-child relationship is warm, these youngsters are multiply protected against delinquency: by their own characteristics, their attachment to their parents, and by a parent-child relationship that suits their parents' temperament and their own.

However, as seen in the previous chapter, not all parents who want to *can* monitor their children. They may try but their youngsters react aversively so that parents feel forced to back off in order to maintain a semblance of peace on the home front. It is worth repeating here that Maccoby (1992a:235) points out the possibility that "the failure of parents to guide adolescents effectively may stem largely from the adolescents' resistance to being socialized rather than from parental incompetence. . . ." Simons et al. (1994:359) add that "rebellious, antisocial children often punish parental efforts to monitor and discipline while reinforcing parental withdrawal and lenience." As mentioned earlier, Patterson (1982) has discussed the possibility that some children may be genetically predisposed to be less responsive to social reinforcers; this predisposition would impair parental efforts to socialize and supervise them, especially in low-quality neighborhoods. This predisposition can also prevent parental sanctions or punishment from having any effect at all.

EFFECTS OF DELINQUENCY ON PARENTS

In the remainder of this chapter, this author relies on her research on the effects of delinquency on parents and on the parent-child relationship. In 1992, interviews were initiated with parents who had conduct-disordered or delinquent adolescents to explore how this situation affected them. Middle-class and well-functioning parents were selected to avoid the potentially confounding effect of poverty, marital conflict, and inadequate parenting. The interviews were in-depth; parents could talk as long as they wished on any given question and this was followed with additional probes tailored to each situation. The sessions lasted from two to four hours at parents' homes or offices. Ten sets of parents were interviewed (two fathers, five mothers, three couples) and all but one were members of two-parent families. Their youngsters ranged from 15 to 22 at the time.

The outpouring of parental suffering was simply overwhelming. The results indicated that the "effect" of delinquency on parents is a deceptively mild term: Parents were actually devastated. Most of them cried repeatedly during the interviews as well as over the phone. Basically, these were parents who had done their best for their children and had given them a lot on all levels. They had never imagined that delinquency would arise in their family and, before their child was arrested, they knew of no other parents in the same predicament. The immediate reaction was similar to that of sudden bereavement: disbelief, followed by self-examination, in which they asked themselves, "Where did *we* go wrong?" They automatically blamed themselves because they, like most parents, had accepted the prevalent belief that parents cause all their children's problems. Moreover, most of the professionals with whom they came into contact, whether police, court, lawyers, clinicians, or teachers, also blamed them, although often indirectly. Some parents started accusing each other as well so that the marital relationship declined at a time when couples would have benefited from mutual support.

A searing psychological pain followed that pervaded their lives to such an extent that these parents were constantly preoccupied and even obsessed with the problem. Most reported doing more poorly at work, eating too much or too little, being edgy, concerned for their other children, and worried about the difficult child. They slept little and were often depressed. One mother, upon being called to the police station in the middle of the night while her husband was absent on a business trip, became so perturbed that she drove their jeep into a tree and destroyed it. One father started drinking, and another began returning home late from work to avoid contact with the difficult and provoking teenager.

This author had in the past done hundreds of interviews with divorcing couples. What was so striking about the parents of delinquents was how much more socially isolated they were compared with the divorcing persons interviewed, most of whom had also been parents. In contrast to delinquency, divorce is a socially accepted phenomenon in our society; there are **rites of passage** that accompany it; there is social and legal recognition of the new marital status. Delinquents' parents have no such social recourse or recognition. They are at first totally isolated socially, have no one with whom they can share their experiences, although some eventually meet other such parents in court, for instance. They feel that they have to hide the situation from most relatives, friends, and neighbors to protect their child, and to protect the family's boundaries. Because there is no institution that takes care of the needs of these parents, they are all alone. The parallel with parents of emotionally disturbed youngsters is quite striking (Hatfield, 1987). Yet while emotional problems are finally being recognized for what they are, that is, diseases of the brain, delinquency is still viewed strictly as a parental failure.

EFFECTS ON THE PARENT-ADOLESCENT RELATIONSHIP

As all but two of the delinquents were returned to their parents' custody, the parent-adolescent relationship became rocky. First, parents no longer trusted the youngster who had lied, disobeyed, betrayed their trust, and behaved in a way that they had never expected from him or her. Parents became more controlling and monitored more closely the youngster's whereabouts; they also began scrutinizing the friends the child went out to meet. As a result, most of these youngsters rebelled, typically accusing their parents of "not trusting me," a maneuver intended to displace their own guilt onto their parents. Half of them resumed disobeying again and seeing their co-offending peers. This string of events led to many parent-adolescent confrontations, with the result that two youngsters ran away; one returned sheepishly, but the other, taking advantage of the clement summer weather, became a "street kid" until rearrested for dealing drugs. Three parents explained that they began hiding some of their expensive possessions for fear that their child or his or her peers might steal from them. They also slept with their wallet under their pillows or next to their beds. One set of parents installed an alarm system to deter their 14-year-old daughter from sneaking out at night through her bedroom window to meet her older boyfriend, who was on probation for credit card fraud and possession of stolen property.

A second study was undertaken from June 1992 through October 1993 with the help of a colleague who is a criminologist at a Young Offenders' Court in Montreal. In brief, her job and that of her colleagues consists of interviewing delinquents and their parents–although often only the mother shows up–to assess the situation before making clinical and legal decisions. With the court's permission, she and her colleagues distributed 132 questionnaires to parents after conducting the official interviews; 88 percent of the questionnaires were returned (Ambert and Gagnon, 1995).

The main statistical findings indicate that a majority of the parents are more stressed, more tired, and less happy since learning of their child's delinquency. Nearly half of them also mention a decline in health. Moreover, a majority report having been ashamed because of their adolescent's behavior, and having been blamed for it by others. A good proportion have had to seek help from police, or teachers, or professionals in order to control their youngster's difficult temperament or disobedience. Most parents report that the adolescent has additional problems, such as school difficulties for boys, association with delinquent peers, disobedience, problematic temperament, being easily influenced by peers, arriving home after curfews and so on. Multiple problems are more common among boys than girls.[18,19]

FATHERS AND MOTHERS

Another key finding of this research, along the lines of the preceding chapter, is that mothers are usually more affected by a child's delinquency than fathers (Ambert and Gagnon, 1995). This result emerged in both the qualitative and quantitative studies mentioned above as well as in a third study described below. In the interviews, fathers even spontaneously offered comments such as the following: "This is much harder on my wife," "Let me add here [turning to his wife] that she finds our daughter's problems much more difficult to live with than I do because she is with her more," and "If you interviewed my wife, I know you'd find her much more upset than I am because we've had some serious disagreements on account of this." Mothers had become more stressed, tired, unhappy, and had more health problems than fathers, although the differences were not large. But there were substantial and statistically significant differences in the number of times they had felt ashamed about their adolescent's behavior, had been blamed, and had experienced problems with people because of the youngster's behavior or attitude. They had sought help far more frequently than had fathers. Moreover, mothers mentioned more problems that afflicted their child than did fathers.[20]

A third study involved observing parents support groups in Fall 1994. The weekly meetings included 35 to 55 parents of conduct-disordered as well as delinquent adolescents. Again, far more mothers participated than fathers. A few couples that had endured quite nicely until then became conflictual, and the conflict was observable during group sessions. In both the United States and Canada, there are networks of such parents' groups and their presence reflects the fact that parents do not find help or sympathy from their regular support network, that is, their relatives, friends, or co-workers. Talking about one's child's problems is often perceived as taboo in this society: It creates embarrassment in the listeners. Parents reported having lost friends in whom they confided because they were perceived to be "losers." One mother explained that admitting that one's child is delinquent is "a death sentence socially. People avoid you after that because they think there's something wrong with you."

What all three studies in this multimethod research highlight is that the relationship between parents and difficult adolescents is usually unpleasant, to put it mildly. It is conflictual and tense; parents feel as if they are "walking on eggshells"; they often try to avoid the youngster because their mere presence is likely to trigger a conflagration. These children are often manipulative, may deny doing anything wrong, even when they are caught with stolen goods in their school bag or throwing them out of the bathroom window.[21] They lie. They frequently blame their parents rather than taking responsibility for their actions. They may talk back, swear, and some assault their parents.

SUGGESTED RESEARCH QUESTIONS AND HYPOTHESES

Parent-delinquent adolescent relationships are not unavoidably strained, however. Although parents in the studies described above were very distressed, delinquents who have no school-related problems generally maintain reasonable family relationships. In our sample, these less problematic youth usually are girls, given that delinquent boys are more likely to experience school difficulties and drop out. Moreover, when the crime committed is a minor one, such as shoplifting, *and* the youngster is otherwise nonproblematic, not only are parents less distressed, but the parent-adolescent relationship is only temporarily disturbed. Therefore, the impression gained by this author, but which needs to be substantiated with other more diverse and larger samples, is that delinquency may not be overly traumatic for parents under the following conditions: When it is not too public, does not lead to extensive contact with the legal system, and is not accompanied by other problems that require parent-teacher interviews, counseling, or other forms of external intervention. Two key variables in parental distress are the social stigma attached to the delinquency and concurrent problems created by the youngster, either at home or at school.

It is suggested that researchers study the evolution of the parent-delinquent adolescent relationship over time. It would be particularly interesting to compare situations where the delinquency desists with situations where it persists: What happens when delinquency leads to adult criminality (Gartner and Piliavin, 1988)? Most adult criminals have been previously delinquent or have shown antisocial or deviant tendencies in childhood (Jessor, Donovan, and Costa, 1991). Do parents of these adult children become undistinguishable from other parents as they get used to their situation? Do they detach themselves from the adult child? Do the stressors wear off or do they cumulate? What are the differences in these respects by social class and quality of neighborhood? What kind of old age do such parents experience? How is their relationship with their other children affected? The delinquent "career" has been well documented. What is lacking is a parallel interest in the career of delinquents' *parents*.

Studies are especially needed that examine the relationship between parents and delinquents and the reciprocal effects they have on each other depending on the type of community the families live in. Hypothetically, this relationship is different in communities that have high levels of criminality, poverty, and absentee fatherhood compared with communities where the levels of criminality and poverty are low, and where families with only one parent are not overrepresented (Reiss, 1986; Sampson, 1993). In criminogenic neighborhoods, what happens to male gang members when they return home to their mother at the end of the day? How do these mothers reconcile their disappointment in the child's behavior with the financial benefits their son may contribute? How do they live with the violent streaks that these boys and young men have exhibited from early childhood? Do these mothers try to protect their younger children from the influence of older delinquent siblings, or do they helplessly acquiesce to a training for delinquency from the older to the younger? What happens in the home when the older boy(s) is jailed, dies, or is wounded?

None of the three studies described in this chapter involved many multiproblem parents. Therefore, it is important to study how parents who are dysfunctional in many domains of life or are too permissive or rejecting react to delinquency. Are they less affected or more so than average parents? Such parents are already highly stressed from other problems, some self-created. It could be expected that parents who are themselves criminal, who abuse drugs, or are disorganized by severe emotional problems may be less affected than others; they may be detached from their environment and less responsive to negative social reinforcers. It is also expected, both because of environmental and genetic reasons, that such parents will "produce" a disproportionate number of early-onset multiple-problem offenders–recidivists who will become adult criminals (Rutter and Giller, 1983).

The situation of delinquents' parents may improve in community-based therapeutic programs using multisystemic therapy (MST) that focus not only on the family,[22] but also on the rest of the delinquents' environment. This ecologically oriented intervention[23] is designed in collaboration with the family, and at the very least may help parents develop a better support system (Borduin et al., 1995; Henggeler, Melton, and Smith, 1992).[24]

CONCLUSION

Compared with other types of problems, it appears that delinquency depends far more on environmental factors than on genetics. For instance, most of the delinquents in our study had committed their crimes in the company of peers. Delinquency is almost always a dyad or a group phenomenon (Warr and Stafford, 1991). However, adult criminality may have a stronger genetic component because it involves a multiplicity of personality defects that persist over time and are genetically linked: low IQ, lack of impulse control, and inability to delay gratification. One would expect, therefore, that early-onset delinquency, compared with the late-onset type, would also be more genetic. This hypothesis is valid because early-onset delinquents tend to have more problems, are less tractable, and come from more dysfunctional families. Others begin at an early age because of the neighborhoods they live in. They are therefore at a double risk: genetic and environmental. Their disturbed, violent, deviant, or simply impulsive parents, especially when both parents show such traits, certainly pass on at least some of these detrimental tendencies to their offspring who are then at risk.

In addition, these parents often provide a very poor environment and may lack in parenting skills; hence, the already susceptible child is "triggered" into delinquency and acting-out problems. Some of these parents may have competent child-rearing practices, but the example they otherwise give, combined with the impulsive, hyperactive, or violent predisposition of their child is sufficient to lead the child astray. Other competent parents are simply overwhelmed by the criminogenic influence of their neighborhood. However, it is important to note that youngsters who have negative traits that are not counterbalanced by salient positive traits may become delinquent even in an excellent family, given the slightest external opportunity. Finally, there are other children with no particular predisposition to delinquency who are simply unable to extricate themselves from the influence of delinquent peers. One would assume that good parents would be especially adversely affected by such an occurrence because they have done nothing that could have led to such an undesirable outcome. We can particularly think of those conscientious parents caught in ghettos of poverty and gangs whose children are totally out of their control and where a culture of violence rules.

ENDNOTES

1. It is worth noting that there is very little research on the lives of children whose fathers or mothers are incarcerated.

2. See also Cloninger et al., 1982; Cadoret, Cain, and Crowe, 1983; Hutchings and Mednick, 1975; Rowe, Rodgers, and Meseck-Buskey, 1992. For adult criminality, see DiLalla and Gottesman, 1989; Mednick et al., 1986.

3. Caspi and Moffit, 1991; Sampson and Laub, 1992.

4. Lewis, Robins, and Rice, 1985.

5. Tolan and Thomas, 1995, for a review.

6. For reference to these theories, an introductory text to criminality and juvenile delinquency is suggested. For theorists themselves, see Agnew and White, 1992; Bursik, 1988; Gottfredson and Hirschi, 1990; Luckenbill and Doyle, 1989; Warr, 1993, to name only a few.

7. Loeber and Stouthamer-Loeber, 1986.

8. Robins et al., 1996.

9. This point is developed at length in Chapter 12.

10. Werner and Smith, 1992.

11. Fergusson, Horwood, and Lynskey, 1994; Wilson and Herrnstein, 1985.

12. Ensminger, Kellam, and Rubin, 1983; Kupersmidt et al., 1995.

13. Werthamer-Larsson, Kellam, and Wheeler, 1991.

14. See Attar, Guerra, and Tolan, 1994; Shakoor and Chalmers, 1991.

15. See also Krueger et al., 1994.

16. Raine, Venables, and Mark, 1990.

17. Plomin, Nitz, and Rowe, 1990.

18. In Canada, adolescent girls are not usually arrested for prostitution or running away. Rather, they are referred to other agencies and do not appear in delinquency statistics. Such girls are probably more problematic than the girls in our sample who were mainly shoplifters.

19. The caseworkers had distributed questionnaires only to reasonably normal and cooperative parents. This might explain why our sample does not contain any of the serious crimes encountered in the district at the time. The base population consisted of 3,184 delinquents during a 15-month period. Of these, five had been accused of murder, two of attempted murder, 35 of sexual aggression and 86 of armed robbery—but none in our sample. This exception aside, the sample is representative of the rest of the delinquent population in that district (Ambert and Gagnon, 1995).

20. In the questionnaire study, in contrast to the interview study of 10 families, the fathers and mothers were not part of a same couple.

21. Delinquent adolescents (Butler, MacKay, and Dickens, 1995), those suffering from behavior problems (Verhulst and van der Ende, 1992), or ADHD (Barkley et al., 1991) compared with nonproblematic ones report far fewer problems than do their mothers, indicating a wide difference in perception between parents and nonnormative children.

22. Nelson and Landsman, 1992.

23. Henggeler and Borduin, 1990.

24. For a review, see Henggeler, Schoenwald, and Pickrel, 1995.

PART IV:
GENETICS AND ENVIRONMENT

Chapter 14

Genetics and Environment

The fourth and last section of this text includes two fundamental chapters.[1] Chapter 14 focuses on behavior genetics and the concluding chapter examines parental contribution to child and adolescent outcomes. Indeed, one of the themes of this book is that parents are influential in terms of their children's development and outcome, but are far less so than people are inclined to believe. Instead, it was seen that other aspects of a child's and an adolescent's environment also have a great impact, particularly the peer group, siblings, school, media, neighborhood, and professionals. Moreover—and this is the focus of this chapter—human beings are organisms with a genetic infrastructure; children are born with their own temperament, predispositions, and potential abilities, and these participate in determining child outcome.

Consequently, behavior genetics is a key perspective in the study of child development, socialization, and the parent-child relationship. It intertwines well with the other main themes of this book, that is, the interactional theory that views parents and children as social actors affecting each other in a circular process (Chapter 2), as well as environmental theories that focus on the context of parent-child interaction (Part II). By now, we have already assimilated quite a few principles of behavior genetics, particularly in Chapters 1, 2, and 10 through 13. This chapter expands on the background already acquired. Only those aspects of behavior genetics that are generally accepted in the field itself are presented, as well as results that have been replicated. Most issues that are controversial have been left aside (Baumrind, 1993; Bronfenbrenner and Ceci, 1994), as these would be superfluously complex for a text designed for an audience without extensive knowledge of genetics.[2] However, several critiques are presented.[3]

This chapter begins with two foundation sections on genetics and the environment as a prelude to examining the reasons for differences among siblings within a family. We then present the research on twins and adoption, sometimes referred to as "natural experiments" in behavior genetics.

The chapter concludes with an examination of the problems inherent to the assessment of genetic similarity between parents and children.

INFLUENCE OF GENETIC FACTORS

Plomin, DeFries, and McClearn, 1990 as well as Belsky (1990) reiterate the fact that the entire research linking parental practices to various child outcomes is clouded by one fundamental limitation (Scarr, 1993). That is, *it confounds genetic and environmental influences*. What is interpreted as cultural transmission[4] can actually be partly genetic (Kendler, 1995a, 1996). In biological families, parenting behaviors and child outcome may have one common factor: The fact that parents and children share genes (Rowe, 1994). These genes in part influence both the parenting behaviors and the children's behaviors; this common factor is referred to as the passive genotype-environment correlation.

Each child inherits 50 percent of its genes *on average* from each of its two parents. This means that biological children are more similar to their parents than they are to other nonrelated adults, and that, as the degree of biological relatedness increases, people share more of their genes. In two biological siblings, each has inherited 50 percent of its genes from the same two parents. It follows that on average, they will be more similar to each other than they will be to the other children in the neighborhood or to an adopted sibling. But unless the two siblings are identical twins, they will be different because the set of genes each has inherited is not identical. For instance, while Pedro may have inherited his mother's IQ and facial features and his father's artistic nature, his sister Maria may have inherited her father's facial features, so that the two may not even look alike physically. In addition, Maria may have inherited her father's average IQ and her mother's optimistic disposition. This is why we insist on including the qualifier "on average," because in some families a child may be different from both siblings and parents. While siblings share the same gene pool, the *combination* of genes inherited by each is what determines the child's own genetic make-up. A child may inherit a gene from the mother that cancels the potential effect of another gene inherited from the father, or instead increases the potency of that gene within a given context. The resulting configuration of personality predispositions may be very different.

Twins who are identical, or monozygotic, share 100 percent of their genetic make-up and are similar to each other, even when they have been adopted into different families at birth (Plomin, 1994a). In contrast, fraternal twins are dizygotic and may share about 50 percent of their genes on average, while half-siblings share about 25 percent of their genes, and adopted siblings and stepsiblings have no genetic similarity except for the usual patterns that are found in homogeneous societies. If, for instance, everyone in a social group has blue eyes, even adopted siblings may share that gene because it is a predominant one in their society. What we have is a descending order of genetic similarity, from monozygotic twins (100 percent), to dizygotic or fraternal twins, siblings, and parents (about 50 percent), to half-siblings (about 25 percent), to adopted siblings–around 0 (Reiss et al., 1994).[5] Moreover, when monozygotic twins have children, these offspring who are social cousins are actually biological siblings.

NATURE AND NURTURE

It is somewhat ironic that while environmentally oriented researchers are generally oblivious to genetic influences and their studies rarely consider genetic variables, many geneticists highlight the environment in their analytic models (Rutter, 1991a; Wachs, 1992). From this viewpoint, it would seem that environmental researchers are lagging behind geneticists (Rowe, 1994).[6] While the nature versus nurture controversy may still be eagerly discussed elsewhere, behavior geneticists have long replaced this futile dichotomy with a perspective emphasizing the interaction between genetics and environment (Wachs, 1983): One cannot exist without the other. Moreover, behavior geneticists point out that the environment is a more important influence than genes on most behaviors (Plomin, 1994b, 1995). Behaviors *per se* are not inherited but influenced (Nigg and Goldsmith, 1994).[7] In addition, much emphasis is placed on personality change (Goldsmith, 1993), on the variability of genetic and environmental influences over time (Cairns, McGuire, and Gariépy, 1993),[8] on prevention and on the complexity of the role of genes. Each personality trait is polygenetic, that is, determined by several genes in combination with the environment. Therefore, any behavior may be influenced by many different genes in interaction with the environment. Moreover, one gene is likely to influence many different kinds of behaviors (this is known as pleiotropy: Zukerman, 1991:90). Basically, some genes seem to operate mainly through their effect on susceptibility to environmental influences (Rutter and Rutter, 1993:18).

Genotype-Environment Correlations

Most personality characteristics can be explained by genes as well as by "correlations" between genetic and environmental factors. These correlations form the cornerstone of the dynamics between genetics and environment: They help explain *how* genes and environment work together to produce outcomes. The three **genotype-environment correlations** are: passive, **reactive**, and active (Plomin, DeFries, and Loehlin, 1977).

The *passive* gene-environment correlation occurs because children and parents share both heredity and environment (Plomin, 1994a:106). When correlations between children's outcome (say, aggression) and parents' child-rearing style (harsh treatment of children, for instance) are found, environmental researchers conclude that the harsh parental treatment has contributed to or even caused the offspring's aggressiveness. While there is some truth to this, the *way* in which this "causality" occurs is actually quite different from explanations provided by a purely environmental conceptualization. It is not only harsh parenting practices that cause children's aggressive behaviors, but the fact that both these practices *and* child aggressivity are in part explained by genes shared by parents and children. Or, as Rowe (1993:187) put it: "More punitive discipline in parents of aggressive children may reflect a cluster of genes manifested as greater emotionality in the parents and physical aggression in a young child." In other words, both parents and children may be genetically predisposed to aggressiveness. In turn, these harsh parental practices become part of the children's environment and trigger their negative predisposition to aggressiveness. Moreover, when parents are predisposed to being harsh and aggressive, stressors such as poverty will exacerbate this negative style of parenting (Patterson and Capaldi, 1991) to further impact detrimentally on the aggressive child's predispositions.[9] The passive genotype-environment correlation occurs only among biologically related persons, and does not take place between parents and adoptive children because they do not share genes.

The other two types of correlations, while also occurring in the family, take place in other contexts as well. The *reactive* genotype-environment correlation refers to the fact that a parent, or sibling, teacher, or peer *reacts* to a child's behaviors, which are in part genetically influenced. For instance, a parent becomes more controlling with a difficult child. Peers who are introduced to a new schoolmate who is shy may not interact with him or her very long or may simply ignore the child. The peers react to the child's shyness, a trait that seems in part heritable.[10] Scarr and McCartney (1983) refer to this as the "evocative" effect: The child evokes a specific reaction. It is important to point out that the evocative effect has been underinvestigated for parents, though not for teachers and peers.

An example of the *active* genotype-environment correlation would be a musically gifted child who asks for music lessons. Or the child may buy records and music sheets and request permission to attend concerts, thus creating an environment that suits him or her (Plomin, 1994a). *Niche picking* occurs when persons select environments that are rewarding to them because they suit their talents or personalities (Scarr and McCartney, 1983). When they design their environment, the term used is *niche building*. What these concepts illustrate is that children coproduce their development,[11] which is also a tenet of the interactional perspective.[12] Children are actively involved in their own development, and in the building of the parent-child relationship, albeit generally unwittingly so. As children age, they can become more consciously active in these endeavors. These genotype-environment correlations allow us to understand that parents are much less responsible for their children's outcome, positive or negative, than we have been led to believe (Barber, 1992). Children and their genetic predispositions weigh heavily in deciding their outcomes.

Another aspect of the relationship between genes and environment is that certain genetic predispositions make parents and children vulnerable both to environmental stressors and environmental advantages. On the negative side, a child with high reactivity and low impulse control may be susceptible to failure in a nonstructured school situation. For such a child, the stimuli contained in an open classroom environment become distractions that cannot be resisted, and are thus risk factors. The two conditions, one genetic and the other environmental, combine to produce a negative outcome labelled school failure.

Chains of Events (Genetically Influenced)

The active genotype-environment correlation can explain *in part* various chains of events in a person's life, a subject already broached in Part III. We have a tendency to think in terms of "accidents." We often say that a person is "accident prone,"[13] that he attracts "bad luck," or that "she is lucky." However, the fact may be that certain persons, because of their genetic configuration supported by the environment, "cause" or initiate entire chains of life events (Rutter and Rutter, 1993). Let's illustrate this point with the example of a child with deficient impulse control,[14] hyperactivity, and verbal aggressiveness. Because he does things on impulse, he has had several "accidents": He has fallen from a tree, has crashed his skateboard against a moving car, and later on, gambled all the money that his parents had put away for his education. As an older adolescent, on an "impulse," he decides to join a group of young men in a bet to see who can drink more and ends up comatose in the hospital; as a result he loses the job he has just found. He comes to be defined by everyone as a "loser," a "bad luck" person. We could continue the scenario into low occupational success,[15] repeated marital failures in spite of the fact that he is also a loving person, and the birth of a defective baby as a result of having joined ranks with an alcoholic woman.[16]

In short, genes or the characteristics they contribute create various paths in the individual's life course. However, cumulative risks are better predictors than a single genetic risk (Luthar, 1993).[17] Does this mean that one's life is preordained by genes? No, *it means that once we accept the influence of genes, we can intervene to change the environments that combine with genes to create negative life courses*, and, hence, prevent these life courses or at least ward off the worst consequences (Sroufe and Rutter, 1984).[18] It would be helpful to be able to identify those persons who are genetically most at risk of suffering from negative environmental impact (Weatherall, 1992), or most at risk for *creating* an environment that is stressful (Kendler, 1991).

Chains of events can be broken by the individual ceasing a habitual behavior, whether this desistance is conscious or simply happens. In the latter case, the individual may have met and married a stable and supportive person, for instance (Rutter, Quinton, and Hill, 1990). This fortuitous event may lead to an increased motivation to be stably employed, thus propelling the individual into a more functional trajectory (Elder, 1985).[19] This is why it is so important to elaborate social policies that allow individuals to adopt a different life course, otherwise negative events, genetic and environmental, cumulate and form a syndrome from which it is difficult to escape.[20]

Chains of Events (Environmentally Influenced)

Similarly, when children are born to an environment of disadvantage, this disadvantage tends to persist, whether it is family conflict or poverty (Sameroff et al., 1987). It persists because of mechanisms similar to those stemming from deleterious genetic predispositions (Sameroff, 1994). Therefore, a negative environment can also create chains of events in a person's life, although a person's own characteristics or resilience may put a brake on the process, provided the environment is not extreme. And, naturally, the same applies to advantages. We have seen that children born to great poverty experience many disadvantages that tend to perpetuate themselves throughout their growth, unless a parent's remarriage or better paying job rescues them. Poverty is often accompanied by poor housing, low-quality schools, and unsupervised peers. Unless a child is particularly resilient, she may fall behind at school, lose interest, drop out, and even become pregnant to finally have the feeling of getting something out of life. Unfortunately, the pregnancy itself may only compound the disadvantage and is one more link in a chain of unfortunate events initiated by a negative environment, along with predisposing characteristics.

In contrast, a child raised in a middle-class environment has greater chances of attending a school that will motivate her to go on. She will get involved in extra-curricular activities that will enhance her already existing advantage–depending on her personality. With her parents' support, her high school success leads to college. The home advantages are accompanied by school and recreational advantages (Rutter and Rutter, 1993). It is as if advantage breeds advantage. Or just as genes "choose" their environment in niche picking and niche building, *environments "beget" other similar environments, and enhance or depress genetic potential as the cycle is perpetuated.* This again provides a reason to interrupt the deleterious environmental cycle and intervene socially to create better conditions for children to grow in–conditions that will prevent the development of negative predispositions and will actualize positive potential (Bronfenbrenner and Ceci, 1994).

DIFFERENCES WITHIN FAMILIES

Another important contribution of behavior genetics is that it emphasizes differences *within* families, while developmentalists generally compare children *between* families.[21] For instance, in studies of the effect of maternal depression on adolescents, researchers select one sample group by choosing as a respondent one adolescent per family that has a depressed mother; this group of adolescents is then compared with another group whose mothers are not depressed. The goal of this exercise is to establish whether depressed mothers have a negative impact on their children. If researchers find that the group of adolescents with depressed mothers has more problems than the group with nondepressed mothers, they may conclude that depressed mothers are problematic for adolescent development. Matters are actually far more complicated. As stated previously, genes can play a role via passive genotype-environment correlations. Hence, geneticists would design their study to ask a different yet complementary set of questions. They would take two adolescent siblings close in age and compare them with each other to see if siblings in homes with a depressed mother tend to be more concordant on depression compared with siblings in homes with a nondepressed mother. They would also consider the personality traits of each child to determine what makes him or her resilient or vulnerable to the depressed environment that some mothers may create. This approach, taken up to a point by Smith and Prior (1995), emphasizes the importance of a positive temperament as a resilience factor.

In a book titled *Separate Lives: Why Are Siblings So Different?* Dunn and Plomin (1990) have accumulated evidence to the effect that siblings are often dissimilar on at least some important personality characteristic and related behaviors. Remember that the children have a shared and a nonshared environment. The *shared environment* is largely the family environment: family structure, social class, age of parents, family routines and events, activities that family members engage in, values emphasized by parents, and so on. The logical outcome of this shared environment is to make siblings more similar (Plomin and McClearn, 1993).[22] If family environment is all important, we should expect that children in a family will be very similar with regard to values that parents teach them and that they will benefit equally from the opportunities parents give them.[23] Yet in spite of a shared environment and shared genes, some siblings are different from each other while others are more similar–although the current emphasis in this type of research is on difference, an orientation that generally does not include those variables for which developmental studies have found similarities, and with which one does not have to agree.[24]

Why are they so different? We have seen that there are some differences as well as similarities in their genetic make-up, and hence their predispositions. But they are also different because of the *nonshared environment* (Reiss, 1993).[25] This concept essentially refers to environmental influences or experiences that differ for each child, and that presumably take place mainly outside of the home environment (Rowe and Plomin, 1981). For our purposes, these can include different peers and school experiences,[26] birth order, a unique relationship with a parent,[27] differential treatment by parents, accidents,[28] *family events that impact more heavily on one child than on the others, or are perceived differentially by siblings,*[29] special relationships with adults other than parents, and different exposure to various media, to name a few examples.

Within an interactional perspective, we can expand upon this concept of the nonshared environment by saying that it also resides in those aspects of the shared environment, such as parental divorce, that *children experience differently* because of their individual personalities (Monahan et al., 1993).[30] Although their parents treat them similarly, one fraternal twin may perceive less parental warmth than the other perceives because he is very sensitive (Baker and Daniels, 1990).[31] In turn, this difference in perception may result in a distancing from parents and a sense of resentment. Let's look at the example of a disadvantaged family with six children: The two siblings who are easygoing and less demanding do not notice that they are poor, do not feel deprived, and make the best out of a bad situation. Two other siblings sharing the same poverty are materialistic, envious, and demanding, and consequently react with stress, behavioral problems, dissatisfaction, and lack of respect for their parents. The last two siblings, while aware of their poverty, are industrious and determined to improve their circumstances. Their differential reaction (active genotype-environment correlation) in turn creates a nonshared environment, that is, one that they do not share with the other four siblings. Or, if we take birth order, older siblings may be given more responsibility than younger ones (Elder, 1974); except for twinship, birth order constitutes an element that is not shared by family members.

But there are several complications that need to be addressed concerning the concepts of shared and nonshared environments (Zuckerman, 1987). The first is *that families are not equally adept at providing an influential environment* and at socializing their dissimilar offspring into adopting a more similar lifestyle (Lykken, 1987). Second, the methods utilized to measure similarities need to be refined and must take observation of behaviors, and not just self-reports, into consideration (Plomin, Chipuer, and Neiderhiser, 1994). It is possible, indeed, that the latter underestimate or overestimate the impact of the shared environment (Coon and Carey, 1989; Hoffman, 1991). A third complication resides in the possibility that the *shared family environment may be differentially important depending on social class* (Rutter and Rutter, 1993). A fourth limitation is that, *in some cultures, there may be little difference between the family environment and that of the rest of society.* This makes the usefulness of this dichotomy less obvious. A fifth limitation is that parental influence is not equally important at all age levels, and some parental examples and teachings may produce an effect only later on in life—*hence shared environment might occasionally have a delayed impact* (Clausen, 1991).[32] Sixth, we have already underscored the fact that we do not know what specifically constitutes the nonshared environment,[33] nor which of its constitutive elements are important (Reiss et al., 1995). The family is multidimensional and, as pointed by Bronfenbrenner (1989), different combinations of family elements may produce different results; for purposes here, *each child may be affected by a somewhat different combination of family variables.* Finally, it can be presumed that siblings will be more similar, for both genetic and environmental reasons, in families *where there is a great deal of similarity between parents*, and where this similarity is echoed in the school system and the neighborhood.

TWIN AND ADOPTION STUDIES

Twin studies present a practical research approach because of the frequency of such births (Little and Thompson, 1988). Designs comparing monozygotic (MZ) and dizygotic (DZ) twins reared apart with twins raised together in their family of birth allow for studies of the role played by genetics, shared environment (generally considered to be familial and parental variables), and nonshared environment.[34] Samples of adopted and unadopted siblings, and even stepsiblings are also used for this purpose. For twins, the research design is expressed in the following schema:

MZ twins together   MZ twins apart   DZ twins together   DZ twins apart

    (1)   (2)   (3)   (4)

Assume that we take the characteristic of extraversion and examine these four groups of twins when they are four years old. If genetics plays no role, and family environment is the main developmental cause, then there should be a large difference between twins reared apart and twins reared together: The latter should be much more similar because their parents essentially teach them the same things. For the same reason, there should be no difference among twins who are reared together, thus MZ and DZ twins should be equally alike in extraversion. Yet, all studies indicate that if we first look at twins reared together (groups 1 and 3), MZ or identical twins are much more similar than DZ twins on those characteristics that have been tested by geneticists. This indicates a role played by genes, because even though the family environment is the same, identical twins are still more similar than fraternal twins.

Then, when we look at different family environments, in this case those in which twins have been raised separately (2 and 4), we would expect no similarity between them if parental influences were all-important. But studies indicate quite the opposite: MZ twins reared apart are far more similar to each other than are DZ twins reared apart. This means that, despite completely different family environments, identical twins still show similarities on some important dimensions of temperament and abilities. Moreover, they also exhibit a substantial similarity in *perceptions* of the (different) homes in which they have been reared (Plomin et al., 1988). There may be "important biological foundations for individual differences in perceptions of family environment" (Hur and Bouchard, 1995:339). This similarity probably stems from the fact that their different sets of parents were reacting similarly to the twins' similar behavior.[35] Rowe's

(1981, 1983a) studies of adolescent twins' current perceptions of their family environment also point to genetic trends. In research on *adult* twins, reared apart and together, assessments of their current family environment show approximately 26 percent heritability (Plomin et al., 1989). However, the studies mentioned above collectively indicate that environmental factors (shared and nonshared) still predominate in perceptions.

When comparing monozygotic twins reared together versus separately, we also find that the ones who were raised together are more similar, and the same holds for fraternal twins. This means that the shared family environment is a factor in personality development, although less important than genes combined with the nonshared environment. But, this result *depends on the characteristics studied; some traits are more genetically influenced than others*, particularly those related to abilities (Scarr and Kidd, 1983). This result also depends on the *age* of the twins because some traits become more or less actualized as a person ages. Moreover, some traits may be more influenced by the shared family environment than others.[36] In order to estimate the effect of the nonshared environment, geneticists use an additive statistical model. In general terms, the part played by genes is added to the part played by shared environment. The balance, calculating for errors, constitutes the effect of the nonshared environment, which is left unspecified as to its nature. Therefore, one of the weaknesses of behavior genetics so far is that *what exactly constitutes the influence of the nonshared environment is unknown* (Reiss et al., 1995). One can agree with the suggestion by Harris (1995) that "unexplained environmental variance" is a more accurate label.

Another interesting research design that warrants repeated mention from a previous chapter is the study of the children of MZ twins. Genetically a MZ twin is as likely to resemble his or her sibling's children as his or her own children. These children are socially considered to be cousins; but, genetically, they are siblings (Price et al., 1982). This type of design has been extended to include not only DZ twins and their children (Perusse et al., 1994) but also the twins' older parents as well as the twins' parenting of their own children in order to test how parenting is perceived through these generations (Kendler, 1996).

It is important to point out that the various twin models can be valid only if the characteristics of individuals who are twins are comparable to those of people who are nontwins, and if parents do not treat MZ twins more alike than DZ twins. In other words, we could easily presume that the fact of being a twin makes twins different from the start, which would introduce a confounding element in research designs. In order to verify this possibility, Loehlin (1992:29) tested twin and nontwin individuals on

131 different personality, attitude, and behavioral variables and found few differences. "The twins appeared on the average to be quite similar in personality to similarly chosen nontwins."[37] Other tests have shown that fraternal twins who are mistakenly taken for identical twins by their parents are less alike than true identical twins (Goodman and Stevenson, 1991).[38] There are additional reasons to keep an open mind concerning both the limitations and the advantages of the twin studies.[39]

It has been found, somewhat to the surprise of researchers, that adoptive children resemble their adoptive parents in terms of personality most when they are small and less so as they become adolescents and then adults (Scarr and McCartney, 1983). This means that adoptive parents do influence children's outcome to some extent.[40] But, as these children begin to make their own choices in life, they become less similar to their adoptive parents, because they make these choices according to their predispositions (the active genotype-environment correlation). Socialization theory would lead us to expect that the longer a child lives with adoptive parents, the more similar to them that child becomes. But this occurs only in early childhood for the characteristics that have been tested (Loehlin, Willerman, and Horn, 1987a). However, it is important to note that on dimensions such as achievement and interests, adoptive parents may continue to have a great deal of influence because of the environment they provide, both inside and outside the family (Grotevant, 1979). In fact, in a study carried out by Fergusson, Lynskey, and Horwood, 1995:613), the authors concluded that the low incidence of behavior problems noted among adolescents in adoptive families stemmed from the advantages of the adoptive family. These advantages, including good child-rearing skills and marital stability, reduced "the risk of disorder that this group might have expected to have experienced had they remained with their original biological families." Similar results and conclusions were reached for intellectual ability and school achievement (Fergusson, Lynsky, and Horwood, 1995:613): Adoptive children had higher achievement scores "than would be expected given their biological parentage but lower scores than would be expected on the basis of the social background and characteristics of their adoptive parents."[41] Studies that compare adopted children with their adoptive parents and their biological parents find greater similarity between children and biological parents on many characteristics, again indicating the importance of genes. Another aspect of adoption studies resides in the comparison of adoptive and biological siblings. While there is generally a greater sibling similarity among biological than adoptive siblings, siblings in general are not very similar, as was seen in Chapter 5.[42]

Although many researchers find the adoption studies more valid than the twin studies, questions are nevertheless raised[43] concerning the extent to which a correlation between the personality trait of adoptive parents and adopted children is an appropriate test of environmental influence. A second question concerns the extent to which dynamics are similar in adoptive, biological, and mixed families (Hoffman, 1985). Finally, the matter of selective placement has to be considered in each study but does not generally present a problem (Rowe, 1994:40).

PROBLEMS IN ASSESSING GENETIC SIMILARITY

As behavior geneticists themselves recognize, their science is still in its infancy. More questions are raised than can be answered. Moreover, there are methodological and theoretical difficulties in assessing genetic similarities or differences between biological relatives, particularly between children and parents. In addition to the ones already discussed, two are presented: first, age differences or over-time changes in temperament and abilities and, second, access to one rather than two parents in making these comparisons.

Changes in Genetic Influence Over the Life Course

When comparing parents and children, or even adolescents, on variables such as IQ, impulsivity, agreeableness, and creativity, among many others, behavior geneticists *are actually comparing two age groups or two very different life stages:*[44] a 10-year-old child with her 40-year-old parents, for instance (Plomin, 1995:54). As Plomin and McClearn (1993:62) point out concerning IQ, "Because the IQ heritability estimate of 51 percent is derived from studies of mostly preadolescents and adolescents, its applicability to other stages of the life span remains an open question." To begin with, a 10-year-old child may not yet have reached his IQ potential, while his 40-year-old parents have.[45] Therefore, it would make more sense to compare the 10-year-old's IQ with the IQ his parents had at the age of 10, obviously a more difficult task. Or, preferably, one could compare his IQ when he reaches 40 to that of his parents when they were at the same age. This matter of age in terms of predicting the heritability of emotional problems was discussed in a preceding chapter.

Scarr and McCartney (1983) have argued that as people age and become independent of the shared familial context, they are more free to select their environment according to their ability so that one can expect the heritability of IQ to increase with age, whether it becomes lower or higher (Bohman and Sigvardsson, 1980). There may be some characteristics that increase in heritability as a person ages, whereas others show less heritability but more environmental influence with age (Slater, 1995). The former seems to be the case for antisocial behavior in adults (Lyons et al., 1995), whereas delinquency in adolescence is largely environmental (DiLalla and Gottesman, 1989). *Stability at some level may not necessarily be an indicator of genetic influence, but an indicator in the stability of the environment* (Baumrind, 1993). Pedersen et al.'s (1982) Swedish study of twins reared apart versus those reared together indicates higher heritabilities for cognitive abilities (the twins were 50 years or older), and McCartney, Harris, and Bernieri (1990) also found an increase in heritability for IQ and a decrease in heritability on most personality characteristics over time. O'Connor et al. (1995) report that genetic influence increases from mid-childhood to adolescence in adolescents' behavior to parents. These results indicate that *as people age, the role played by the environment decreases for some characteristics and increases for others.*

Therefore, it will be important to determine which characteristics are more genetically influenced at certain ages and which are more environmentally influenced at the same ages. This would allow us to better understand the joint and changing relative roles played by genes and environment in human development. In addition, the possibility of differential heritability for boys and girls for certain traits needs to be examined more carefully (Baker, Ho, and Reynolds, 1994; Braungart-Rieker et al., 1995). It will also be important to establish whether present findings are culture-specific, that is, whether they apply only to industrialized societies or are applicable to the rest of the world. This question is particularly relevant for small societies where the shared and the nonshared environment overlap to a great extent.

Finally, we have to consider the point that an ability or a personality trait that is much higher than average in an individual may be more genetically determined, and perhaps less changeable, than one that is close to the average in the population. Very low abilities, such as a subnormal IQ, may be more genetically influenced and less changeable over time. Moreover, as Bronfenbrenner and Ceci (1994) point out, optimal environments contribute to raising heritability on positive traits because they allow for the full actualization of genetic potential. A deprived environment prevents the actualization of positive genetic potential and increases the actualization of negative predispositions.

Comparisons with Only One Parent

Another problem in assessing genetic similarity or difference resides in the fact that when the comparison is made between children and parents, it is often made with only one parent, most frequently the mother. Such an approach would *lower* total parents-child similarities, both genetically and environmentally caused. In terms of environmental influence, both parents contribute to create the home environment in two-parent families, although fathers and mothers have different levels of influence in different families.[46] One would therefore need to *consider the share or contribution of each parent in creating the different facets of the home environment* that affect the child, a very difficult enterprise. When both parents are used, parental scores are generally averaged, which can also be problematic (Plomin, DeFries, and McClearn, 1990).

At the genetic level, the child inherits an average of 50 percent of its genes from each parent. If one correlates children's IQs with those of only fathers *or* mothers, one misses half of the equation. Indeed, *it is possible that some children inherit their IQ more from a father while others more from their mother.* While this complication is not a huge problem in terms of IQ because couples are somewhat similar on this dimension,[47] the same cannot be said for other characteristics (Gruber-Baldini, Schaie, and Willis, 1995). For instance, one child may inherit his mother's IQ and his father's passivity. The other sibling may have inherited the father's IQ and the mother's internal level of control and active orientation. We thus have two very different siblings who, although they share genes from the same parents, have not inherited the same identical genes from each. Yet, in a research design using only one parent, the child's characteristics may be correlated to the parent who resembles the child the least (or the most), depending on the trait. While this matter is not a problem when comparing twins or siblings together, it is a serious problem when comparing biological *parents* and children. This problem is compounded when parents have mated assortatively so that they are similar on some traits. Their children should therefore be more similar on these traits both to their parents and to their siblings than if no such parental homogamy existed. Finally, it is pertinent to mention that children are not always the biological offspring of their presumed biological fathers (Hirsch, McGuire, and Vetta, 1980). Unless blood tests are provided, this vexing reality somewhat leaves in doubt the magnitude of results of studies.

It should also be recalled that the genetic resemblance calculated by the various methods discussed earlier is constituted by actualized genetic potential, that is, observable or reportable resemblance. But the unactualized genetic potential remains unknown (Bronfenbrenner and Ceci, 1993:315).

Comparisons of unactualized traits will have to await advances in molecular genetics.

CONCLUSION

Combining perspectives from behavior genetics with interactional theories contributes a more accurate and detailed description and explanation of developmental processes, both in terms of child development and the parent-child relationship. This more holistic perspective avoids the pitfalls of either genetic or environmental determinism. This approach has important implications for theory, future research designs, a critical examination of existing research, and social intervention.

Parents and children in a biological family share both genes and environment. Many of the results that have been interpreted to mean that certain parenting activities cause certain child problems actually stem from the fact that both parental child-rearing practices and child outcomes are affected by the personalities of both parents and children which are all in part influenced by shared genes. Genes and environments combine to create parenting behaviors as well as child outcomes. For future researchers, the challenge resides in determining genetic configurations related to personality and behavior, in defining and measuring environmental influences more accurately, and in explaining the mechanisms that link the two sets of influences.

Purely environmental research unavoidably explains only a very modest part of the variance in regression analyses. Repeated failures to reach both higher correlations and higher explained variance, regardless of the number of variables included in the models, should lead researchers to look toward new models that may eventually explain phenomena more fully. Such models can be constructed only by combining genetic and environmental variables.

ENDNOTES

1. Hoffman, 1994; Lerner and von Eye, 1992; Gottlieb, 1995. Instructors, depending on class focus, may prefer to assign Chapter 14 earlier on.

2. Readers interested in the finer points of behavior genetics will find several references indicating possibilities for further reading in this and other chapters. A few suggestions are Eaves, Long, and Heath, 1986; Davies and Read, 1991; Falconer, 1989; Neale and Cardon, 1992; Plomin, DeFries and McClearn, 1990; Plomin and Rende, 1991; Plomin and Bergeman, 1991; Loehlin, 1992; Wachs and

Plomin, 1991. Some of the journals are: *Acta Psychiatrica, American Journal of Human Genetics, American Journal of Psychiatry, Archives of General Psychiatry, Behavior Genetics, British Journal of Psychiatry, Development and Psychopathology, Heredity, Human Biology, Journal of Child Psychology and Psychiatry*, and *Nature*.

3. We have also largely left aside presentation of data indicating significant genetic influences on measures of the family environment. See Plomin, Reiss, Hetherington, and Howe, 1994.

4. Cavalli-Sforza and Feldman, 1973.

5. See also, Bouchard et al., 1990; DeFries, Plomin, and Fulker, 1994; for reviews, see Loehlin, 1992; Loehlin and Rowe, 1992.

6. In addition, a subdiscipline of developmental behavior genetics has arisen to address concerns that developmentalists share with behavior geneticists. See Hahn et al., 1990; McGue, Bacon, and Lykken, 1993.

7. For a biochemical perspective, see Zuckerman, 1995.

8. Kendler, 1995a.

9. We have already discussed these interactional pathways in previous chapters.

10. Kagan, Reznick, and Snidman, 1989.

11. Goldsmith, 1989.

12. See Belsky, Gilstrap, and Rovine, 1984; Lerner, 1982; Lerner and Busch-Rossnagel, 1981. For additional references, see Chapter 2.

13. Accidents may have a genetic component, probably created by physiological and personality characteristics such as motor coordination and risk taking. Phillips and Matheny (1993; referred to in Plomin, 1994a) have found correlations of .51 for monozygotic twins in terms of accidents that had happened to them in their first three years, compared with .13 for fraternal twins.

14. Friedman et al. (1995), using the death certificates of the respondents in the longitudinal study initiated by Terman in 1921 (Terman and Oden, 1947) on gifted children, found that those who had been impulsive children had both more often been divorced and had died younger. Adults who had been prudent and conscientious as children had a 30 percent lower likelihood of dying at any year.

15. Caspi, Elder, and Herbener, 1990.

16. Cumulative and interactional continuities: Caspi, Elder, and Bem, 1987.

17. A single risk factor can easily be counterbalanced by the rest of a child's personality.

18. We also know that emotionally disturbed individuals report much stress and that their behavior contributes to increasing this stress; Depue and Monroe, 1986.

19. Sampson and Laub, 1992, 1993.

20. Laub and Sampson, 1993; Magnusson and Bergman, 1990. See, also, Pulkinen and Tremblay, 1992.

21. In this respect, Bronfenbrenner and Crouter (1983) have pointed out that "social addresses," such as divorced families, contain a great deal of *within* address variability that is not tapped by comparisons *across* social addresses. See, also, Wachs, 1992.

22. For a critique, see Hoffman, 1991.

23. For religiosity, see Hayes and Pittelkow, 1993.

24. Monahan et al., 1993.

25. Also, McGuire et al., 1994; Plomin, DeFries, and Fulker, 1988; Rutter, Silberg, and Simonoff, 1993. Loehlin, Willerman, and Horn (1987a) use the perhaps more appropriate term of within-family environmental variation.

26. Plomin and Daniels, 1987.

27. Brody, Stoneman, and McCoy, 1992.

28. Plomin, 1994a:186.

29. McCall, 1987.

30. Lamb, 1987, Wachs, 1987.

31. Dunn, Stocker, and Plomin, 1990.

32. Caspi, Herbener, and Ozer (1992) and Gruber-Baldini, Schaie, and Willis suggest studying the spousal shared environment for adults.

33. Harris, 1995.

34. Some of the authors of twin studies are: in the United States: Eaves, Eysenck, and Martin, 1989; Tellengen et al., 1988; in Australia: Martin and Jardine, 1986; in Finland: Rose et al., 1988; in Sweden: Pedersen et al., 1988.

35. Hur and Bouchard (1995) also point out that this result could be explained by genetic influences on how one recalls one's past.

36. Religion may be one aspect that is more affected by shared experiences: Rose and Kaprio, 1987.

37. See, also, Edwin et al., 1995.

38. See Scarr, 1968; Scarr and Carter-Saltzman, 1979. For other assumptions concerning the twin model, see Morris-Yates et al., 1990.

39. Hoffman, 1991.

40. See the results by Loehlin, Willerman, and Horn (1987a) indicating that adopted *infants'* personalities show some similarities with that of their adoptive rather than biological parents.

41. Also Bohman and Sigvardsson, 1980; but Plomin, DeFries, and Fulker, 1988. See also, Copron and Dwyne, 1989.

42. Lamb, 1987; Scarr, Webber, Weinberg, and Wittig, 1981; Wachs, 1987.

43. Hoffman, 1991:189.

44. This problem is discussed in Chapters 1 and 11.

45. However, Schaie's longitudinal study argues that there exists stability of family similarity over time and age, up to 21 years (1994:309).

46. In most families, the mother is the main parent: Kandel, 1990.

47. Watkins and Meredith, 1981.

Chapter 15

Conclusions: Parental Contributions to Child Development

The previous chapter certainly does not argue that parents should give up and entrust their children's development to genes (Plomin, 1995:61). Indeed, Chapter 14 equally underscores the importance of the environment. It is true that the scientific evidence, when properly weighed, indicates that parents are not as influential nor as powerful in terms of their children's development and future as they are credited for–or as they are blamed for when things go wrong (Barber, 1992; Miller, 1993). But "parental determinism" aside, the evidence also indicates that parents are the cornerstone of young children's well-being and, to some extent, that of most adolescents. Consequently, within the context of the theory and the data presented in the previous chapter, this chapter begins by outlining six important parenting contributions to child outcome and well-being. We then discuss the limitations on parental influence as well as the cultural roadblocks preventing parents from being as effective as they could be. Next an overview is presented of the current social and psychological conditions affecting the quality of life of children and adolescents in our society; it is suggested that a general deterioration in the social environment makes parents even more important for child well-being than before. This text is therefore concluded with suggestions of how to strengthen parental influence and effectiveness.

Before proceeding, an important caveat is mandatory: The theoretical framework utilized in this text probably holds cross-culturally; particular aspects of behavior genetics, however, would benefit from cross-cultural testing. Also, the results of many studies reviewed throughout the text may not be universally applicable; in fact, some are quite specific to the American and Canadian situation or to that of similar societies. The discussion that follows in this chapter henceforth focuses on the North American context, although many of its facets are applicable to other Western societies, as well as to societies that are in the midst of radical and rapid social change toward a global economy and a salience of audiovisual media.

THE PARENTAL CONTRIBUTION

First, parenting is important because not all human characteristics and behaviors are equally affected by genes. Genetic influence may be near zero for some aspects of personality and particularly for behavior. For instance, impulsiveness that appears during childhood but is easily "cured" suggests a less genetically based and more environmentally induced characteristic. One must assume that beliefs, values, religiosity, manners, study and work habits, among others, are greatly influenced by the environment, and particularly by parents. Therefore, the parents' task remains quite formidable.[1]

Second, even those traits that have a high genetic component can be at the very least improved or tempered by proper parental practices and a good extra-familial environment, such as a stable and resourceful neighborhood (Bronfenbrenner and Ceci, 1994). This proposition is important to keep in mind, because many objections are brought to bear on ideological grounds against the science of behavior genetics and against what is erroneously interpreted as insurmountable determinism. Yet, *heredity does not mean irrevocability.*[2] A child who is mildly to moderately hyperactive (which may be innate) can be given opportunities to "vent" a surplus of energy through activities such as karate or gymnastics classes and can be given enough structure to lower the hyperactivity. In contrast, when such children live in a stressful family situation, where parents do not get along, are erratic, too punitive or too permissive, and the house is noisy and overcrowded, the child's hyperactivity may increase, along with other problems. Therefore, such children are likely to achieve more optimal results in a home that is better than average, and not just "good enough," as perhaps implied by Scarr (1992). However, when a characteristic is innate *and extreme*,[3] there is very little that parents can do to change it. These are exceptional cases. Nevertheless, one has to consider that the role of parents does not rest solely on *changing* children.

Therefore, third, even in extreme cases, there is another role that parents can play. As an example, one can think of a child with a very low IQ. While IQ is perhaps the most genetically grounded ability,[4] a very low or a very high IQ may even be more genetically fixed than the average (Brody, 1993).[5] There is little that parents can do to change the child's intellectual deficit. But they can facilitate functioning and they can prevent the child from becoming even more incompetent by teaching him or her basic social skills. Parents may also affect other aspects of the child's life, and, consequently, add to the child's well-being. For instance, they may nurture the child's affective qualities and encourage the development of motor skills when the latter are within normal range. Once again, this indicates that children who are subnormal on one dimension can still benefit from their parents' guidance on others.

Fourth, when children possess partly hereditary traits that are deemed positive in a society, parents can contribute to the enhancement of these traits (Bronfenbrenner, 1994). A child may be musically gifted, but if the parents discourage this talent, the child may not persist and the "gift" will not be utilized. When parents encourage a natural ability and provide compatible resources, that gift will go much further and the child may also be happier and more fulfilled. In turn, this enhancement of an ability may result in a positive impact on other child characteristics such as self-esteem and sociability. It may also counterbalance the potential effect of negative characteristics such as impulsivity or shyness. Thus, parents can contribute to the child achieving balance—of course, they accomplish this within the range of the child's potential, but they nevertheless do contribute.

Fifth, in many cases, parents can prevent a youngster from being negatively influenced by detrimental forces in the external environment such as a delinquent peer group, a poor school system, violent mass media, or neighborhood criminality. But here we have to recall that parents are not all-powerful. Child cooperation is required. Sixth, parents are a great source of social support and, in our society, the main origin of attachment for the children: Without support and attachment children would not fare so well nor be so happy. This may well be parents' foremost contribution to their children. Parents provide a haven that serves as a respite "from the frenzied world of peers and the demands of school" (Larson and Richards, 1994:99).

LIMITATIONS TO PARENTAL INFLUENCE

Having mentioned six reasons why parents are important in their children's development and well-being, we now review five of the main reasons why their influence is also limited, especially in some instances. To begin with, as emphasized in this text, there is the matter of genes: There are inherent abilities and limitations to each personality. These can either be enhanced or improved, as seen, but abilities cannot be created by parents as one would design a dress; nor can limitations be entirely ignored or even eradicated. Hence genes constitute the first limitation to parental influence, whether negatively or positively (Rowe, 1994). In the literature, there is discussion (Baumrind, 1993) and some supportive data to the effect that a viewpoint that emphasizes genetics might discourage parents and lower their motivation to improve their children's negative behavior (Bugental, Blue, and Cruzcosa, 1989). However, such reactions may be due to a lack of understanding of the field and of its results and conclusions, and particularly to a misinterpretation of what is erroneously perceived as determinism. Hence, a better balanced picture, as presented in this text, can eliminate these biased reactions and yet have the advantage of lowering the burden of guilt that parents often carry. A properly interpreted behavior genetics perspective is no more deterministic and discouraging than an environmental one. In fact, it may be more encouraging because it includes both genes and environment.

A second factor that limits parents' influence has also been widely discussed in this text. The interactional perspective proposes that while parents influence children, the effectiveness of this influence depends in great part on how children, and particularly adolescents, perceive and react to their parents' efforts to help them, socialize them, and monitor them. Even a very small child can choose to ignore requests made by parents. *Parents actually need a child's cooperation in order to raise him or her.* So do teachers, as well as clinicians who engage in any form of psychotherapy. True, there are indirect routes that adults can utilize to attempt to defeat children's self-destructive resistance. It is for this reason that parents whose difficult children rule the home can be trained to become more effective. This is what was referred to as parent effectiveness training in Chapter 8. However, children's responses to parents remain a potentially mitigating factor in their authority. A third restriction of parental influence resides in the fact that interventions, such as parent effectiveness training, have several shortcomings: (1) they are too costly to reach and benefit most parents; (2) parents who are highly dysfunctional cannot be trained; and (3) children who are very problematic on many fronts cannot be changed. Interventions are not a panacea for all ills affecting all parents and children.

A fourth limitation to parental influence stems from the fact that children create their environment to some extent; this has been discussed in Chapter 14 under the rubric of an active genotype-environment correlation. Depending on their abilities and deficiencies, children actively choose certain courses of action that reinforce their characteristics. Hence, while very bright children may receive much encouragement from their parents (reactive nature-environment correlation), they alone create, without any help, many facets of their experience. They may teach themselves to read; they may linger over books long after their parents have finished reading to them; they may utilize their imagination to dream up all manner of stories that enliven their world. "Bright children can use the stimulus of an empty room to think about the geometric configuration of its corners" (Plomin, 1994a:157). Children who have an easy temperament may similarly find sources of happiness in minor details of their life, with or without parental help. At the negative end of the spectrum, parents could uselessly exhaust themselves trying to satisfy children who constantly want more, or are dissatisfied with what they have, or have an unhappy streak. Such children have the habit of focusing on what displeases them and what they do not have—even when they have everything else. They are not the type to "count their blessings."

A fifth limitation occurs because parents and children do not live in a closed environment. They are bombarded by a variety of external influences, and these particularly affect vulnerable children. Good child-rearing practices can be defeated by a negative peer-school-neighborhood environment. This can occur even in otherwise good schools if children with behavioral problems seek out the two or three similarly deviant peers present in the entire school. Unknown to parents and staff, such children create a little world of their own, manage to avoid supervision, and often "sneak" out for illegal drug use, shoplifting, and other questionable activities, to the detriment of their school work. In the long run, when this behavior comes to light, some of these youngsters straighten out but others remain deviant.[6] As seen in Chapter 6, children and adolescents bring home their peer group's joys and frustrations, ideas and values, as well as their lifestyles (Harris, 1995). Being like the others is a very important element for American and Canadian youngsters and only the stronger ones are able to resist the lure of peer acceptability. Parents are often rendered useless in the face of such conformity to peer values. Moreover, parents suffer from this spillover of the negative environment into family life, or benefit from it when it is positive (Ambert, 1994a), which may, again, augment or damage their ability to influence their children positively.

CULTURAL AND SOCIAL ROADBLOCKS TO EFFECTIVE PARENTING

The research is very clear on the point that parental support and monitoring are important for youngsters' outcomes. Unfortunately, a growing body of observations indicates that parents do not receive sufficient social support to carry out these functions; this means that, at times, a huge, lonely, and burdensome investment is required on their part. There are several structural and cultural roadblocks that mitigate the ability of parents to assume their full responsibility and that school be considered more closely in terms of policy implications (see Small and Eastman, 1991).[7] Five are examined here, although many more could be added.

The first roadblock stems from a combination of recent demographic changes, especially those changes that are accompanied by poverty:[8] High divorce rates and unsupported childbearing and childrearing have resulted in high levels of single parenting under particularly difficult circumstances (Duncan, 1991). The necessity for many single parents, as well as both parents of many two-parent families,[9] to be employed is another structural barrier to parents' involvement with their children–or perhaps to simply enjoying that involvement. These changes cumulatively mean that parents are too often emotionally distressed, socially isolated, financially disadvantaged, overworked, and have too little time at home, while others are frequently too young and ill-equipped to parent adequately. These circumstances take time[10] and energy away from the parenting role,[11] while some even cause a decline in parenting skills, thus reducing the level of support and monitoring that children and adolescents can receive. Policies aimed at further reducing the financial and social assistance that parents receive are usually ill-conceived (Huston, 1991). Such policies may merely contribute to raising the emotional and financial deficits of the next generation (Kitchen, 1995)–hence raising the future price tag for social problems that politicians are currently trying to rein in at a low financial cost but at the expense of the family.[12]

Moreover, fiscal policies focusing on fighting inflation to the detriment of job creation, especially in already deprived neighborhoods, are particularly dangerous (Conger et al., 1992, 1993). Indeed, neighborhoods with a high concentration of underprivileged families are generally plagued by criminality and juvenile gangs. The escalation of violence in such areas would require much more, not less, intervention (Guerra, Tolan, and Hammond, 1994). Living in such neighborhoods places parents and children at risk (Garbarino, Kostelny, and Dubrow, 1991).[13] As Patterson, Reid, and Dishion (1992:105) point out, such areas "require a very *high* level of parenting skills just to keep their children out of the juvenile court system." They add that "there is no sense in which it is fair for our society to expose these families to such adverse conditions." Poverty and the noxious environment it generally creates is probably one of the most serious roadblocks to effective parenting and to positive child outcomes (McLoyd and Wilson, 1991).

The second roadblock preventing children from receiving parental support and control is less often discussed: It stems from a combination of the effect of individualism and materialism on the family system, whereby individual rights and satisfaction rather than mutual obligations take precedence (Etzioni, 1994; O'Neill, 1993).[14] One simply cannot assume that parents are immune to these trends–nor are their children. It may be logically presumed that this mentality leads some adults to be less willing to make a commitment to adequate parenting when the cost is too high and the reward too low.

The third societal roadblock was mentioned earlier and resides in all the extraneous influences that bear on children and encourage them to prevent their parents from fulfilling their role adequately. These influences or cross-pressures range from detrimental content of television programs to deleterious peer groups, dangerous neighborhoods, and the easy availability of drugs and weapons.

The fourth roadblock stems from a widespread cultural reliance on philosophies of life, outdated scientific theories, and clinical practices that fail to make adolescents accountable, thus blaming parents (Maziade, 1994:71). This situation will persist as long as the view is maintained that children are *tabula rasa* for their parents. Lopsided and ineffective clinical practices and interventions will be pursued as long as theories continue to deprive adolescents of their responsibility vis-à-vis their parents. To compound this difficulty, parents do not enjoy a cultural climate that bestows upon them a sense of personal efficacy and moral authority. As discussed in Chapter 8, professionals have effectively granted themselves the right to define what proper parenting is, thus disempowering parents. In addition, recent State policies whereby parents, particularly mothers, have their welfare checks taxed if their adolescents are truant from school are inappropriate methods in a *society where parental authority is no longer valued or supported*. As a consequence, such policies can be quite ineffective, especially in certain milieux: Such policies unfairly penalize parents and may strain the parent-child relationship.

The last roadblock to be mentioned resides in what Bronfenbrenner (1985:377) pointed to as the "unravelling of the social fabric in which families, schools, and other immediate contexts of development are embedded." For the purposes of our discussion, the result of this unravelling of the social fabric is that parents become more socially isolated. They no longer generally belong to a neighborhood or community with a high consensus of values, an element that would facilitate their task and enhance their moral authority (Coleman and Hoffer, 1987). They do not have any subculture of their own, nor any lobby group.

CHILDREN'S AND ADOLESCENTS'
QUALITY OF LIFE

No modern institution has been able to replace parents or even do better than they: not the schools, not the churches, not the health services, and not welfare agencies. Each of these State or religious institutions takes care of only part of the child, while parents take care of the *entire* child. Parents are vital because the quality of life of adolescents and children has deteriorated in the past decade. This deterioration is the focus of this section, in which youngsters' material, physical, and psychological quality of life is compared from the 1970s to the late 1990s.

Violence rates are high,[15] and statistics indicate that violent delinquency has increased substantially. Aggressive acts committed by children younger than 12 have skyrocketed (see Chapter 13; O'Donnell, 1995). A Harris poll has recently found that 15 percent of children ages 10 to 19 had carried a gun and 4 percent had brought one to school (Scanlan, 1993). Sixteen- to 19-year-olds now have the highest rate of victimization by handguns of any other age group (Federal Bureau of Investigation, 1993). Even teachers are too often assaulted and verbally abused, an indicator of a lower level of restraint and impulse control on the part of youngsters— certainly not because their genes have suddenly deteriorated, but because their culture and environments have (Rowe, 1994:58). There is more peer abuse than in the past: Psychological, physical, and even sexual assaults are common occurrences (see Chapter 6). Moreover, youngsters are tempted by the wide availability of illicit drugs and many become addicted. Alcoholism now begins earlier than in previous decades. More emotional and behavioral problems are detected, and more hyperactivity and learning disabilities are diagnosed; the latter increase, however, may be the result of scientific advances in diagnostic methods rather than an actual surge in these two problems. Adolescents commit suicide more frequently than before (Fuchs and Reklis, 1992). Moreover, functional illiteracy may have increased among the schooled population of youngsters.

Finally, nearly half of all children experience a parental divorce. In addition, there has been a tremendous increase of babies born to very young mothers, many of whom have no child-rearing skills because of their age, and live at or near the poverty level. While living with a single parent is not necessarily a problem, especially when the parent is an adult and is financially self-sufficient, the fact remains that single-parent households are disproportionately poor and vulnerable to a vast array of stressors and risks.

With an increase in child poverty, live opportunities have become restricted because economic disadvantage correlates with living in more deprived neighborhoods, in more dilapidated housing, both rural and urban, and in more polluted and dangerous areas, with less adequate schools, more delinquent peers, lower access to health and cultural resources, a higher death rate, and a host of other deprivations.[16] As seen in the first chapter, disadvantaged children suffer disproportionately from all the ills affecting children and adolescents in general (McLoyd and Wilson, 1991).

Paradoxically enough, this recent deterioration in the quality of life of youngsters occurs at a time of unprecedented material wealth in our society, leaping technological advances, and multiplication of life alternatives and leisure styles. Obviously, material and technological progress do not necessarily connote an improvement in the quality of life at the psychological, social, and cultural levels. Quite the contrary: The indicators described above argue that children and adolescents lead a more "random," risky, difficult, and confusing life than was the case just ten years ago. Such information argues for the necessity of a stronger parental role rather than a weaker one.

STRENGTHENING PARENTAL INFLUENCE

Amidst these somber realities, the question generally asked is "What is happening to the family?" However, political and ideological concerns about the "disappearance" and the weakening of the family are not necessarily pertinent to our discussion. When talking about the "family" or the "loss of its functions," what really is at stake here is parenting. *It is not the family that cares for children in our society, but parents.* Of course, parents are very busy, some are quite preoccupied, others are poor, and many are single. But one could argue that these would be ample reasons to *help* parents rather than emphasize their shortcomings. After all, the main culprit in this rout is generally located outside rather than inside the parenting unit, or, if one prefers, the family. Consequently, the question should rather be "What should be done to help parents in their role?" Several suggestions are offered below. Matters related to discrimination and to the economy, such as those concerning unemployment and poverty, are left aside, both because these have been mentioned frequently throughout the text, and because other researchers have adequately discussed them (see Ambert, in press).

First, parents need an effective *moral* authority in order to fulfill their role in an environment that has become more difficult (Elshtain, 1990). Parents' authority has been eroded, and this loss is related to other weakening aspects of our culture because, in fact, no one is left with great moral authority—neither teachers, clergy, nor elected officials. Parents should be in a position to request that their child respect and follow rules of behavior, secure in the knowledge that they are supported by other institutions in this endeavor. Parental authority has become synonymous with a breach of children's rights in certain quarters, and it can be observed on a daily basis that children take advantage of this obvious lack of support for their parents. A proportion of the calls children place to lines such as "Child Help Line" are from youngsters who complain about parental rules such as curfews, etc. Others want to know how to find a lawyer to sue their parents because they are not allowed to smoke or participate in other desired activities. Such calls are indicators, not only that children are less isolated than in the past (a heartening point), but also that they perceive the erosion of parental authority and the increase in social support they themselves can obtain when complaining (even unjustly) about their parents. Moreover, it is reasonable to suggest that it is those parents who would most need to see their authority valued who are the most likely to be deprived of it and castigated–single mothers and the poor; too often, these two are synonymous.

If we lived in a society where parents were respected and socially supported (by schools, professionals, welfare agencies, and law enforcement personnel), and where children were encouraged from all quarters, including the media, to respect their parents, the family would become a more effective institution–whatever its size and structure. Generally speaking, parent-child relations would be facilitated and child development enhanced. *Within such a context, children would more easily accept and internalize norms of behavior and would be more inclined to cooperate in their upbringing.* (Basically, this echoes some of the implications of James Coleman's functional community [Coleman and Hoffer, 1987].) In contrast, our children are bombarded from the time they are very small by conflicting and discouraging messages concerning parental authority. The cultural climate of certain neighborhoods in particular leads to disobedience, disrespect, and provocation on the part of youngsters. Parental punishment often follows, is frequently ineffective, and even some good-tempered parents react irrationally in the face of such provocation. In worse-case scenarios, abuse ensues, either abuse of the child by parents or abuse of the parents by the child. One provocative thought already alluded to in Chapter 3 is the following: *Is it not possible that by disempowering parents we are facilitating child abuse and neglect rather than preventing it?* If we encourage children to disobey and flaunt their disrespect toward their parents, may this not lead those more temperamental parents and those who feel helpless to resort to abuse in a desperate attempt to control their difficult child?[17]

Faced with often contradictory how-to advice, constrained by a variety of professionals whose blame they fear, and muzzled by a better organized peer group at their doorstep–far better organized than their own social support is–many parents become indecisive, unsure of themselves, and unable to say no. They may be afraid to displease their children. Some fear that their youngsters will run away; at any rate, they frequently threaten to do so. This threat instills a potent and realistic fear in parents of the specter of their youngster ending up as a street kid immersed in drugs and prostitution. Therefore, within this context, many parents find it easier to disengage from the parental role and reduce it to one of being their child's "friend." This role confusion may work well with adolescents who are self-controlled, have an easy personality or are achievement oriented, and benefit from a prosocial peer group. But this type of "egalitarian" relationship, which resembles the permissive parenting style and even has elements of neglect,[18] can be disastrous with children who have less favorable personal characteristics and a deviant peer group.

A new role for teachers, child/adolescent professionals, police, and welfare workers suggests itself. It would consist of encouraging children and adolescents to develop behaviors that are more altruistic and collectivist, or less individualistic and self-centered. Youngsters could be encouraged to turn to their parents for advice and to cooperate with them in their upbringing. Professionals may object to this suggestion with the following: "But if these teenagers feel that no one understands them, what will happen to them?" It can be argued that this concern is exaggerated given that many adolescents themselves place barriers to others "understanding" them. Also, the question is defeatist from the perspective of the parent-child relationship because it implies that only people *other than parents*, preferably professionals, can understand adolescents. *It is an indirect and poorly camouflaged condemnation of parents* that does not escape adolescents' attention. When clinicians, social workers, or youth workers form therapy or support groups of adolescents who have problems, they often forget that the principal ingredient in the recipe should be the psychological reinsertion of the child with the parents (Henry, 1994)–but not at the cost of promoting parental ineffectiveness.

Adolescents have been left out of the adult world by industrialization and mechanization. They have been legislated to stay in school–therefore in a youth-centered environment separated from the realities of the adult world (Quortrup, 1995). They have been transformed, along with older children, from fully contributing members of the household economy to mere dependents. While child labor is to be condemned as exploitative, and paid work is available for adolescents only at low-skill jobs and on a part-time basis, one could begin to think of other ways in which adolescents could contribute both to their society and their family.

CONCLUSION

We give far too much credit to parents when their children do well and far too much blame when their children have problems. But this is a far cry from saying that parents are useless. They are the most important persons in children's lives. This fact is agreed upon both by conservative and liberal policymakers, although often for different ends. Conservatives may want to cut budgets and therefore give parents the entire burden of seriously disturbed, chronically ill, or delinquent youngsters–and traditional theories of parental blame conveniently buttress such policies. Others wish for a return to the "ideal" type of family of the 1950s: two parents, a gainfully employed father, one paycheck, and a mother at home–now a minority type of family.

For their part, libertarians and even liberals insist on more rights for children and on their emancipation from their parents. They want the State to interfere more in family life, police parents more (although not adolescents) and make them more accountable, while at the same time taking away their empowerment, which is then transferred to legal, medical, welfare, and psychiatric State agents. Unfortunately, these various professionals and State agents often have vested interests of their own, as well as "turfs" to protect, which may not be in the best interests of the child. Moreover, they take care of only that part of the child that falls under their expertise (e.g., feet, learning disabilities, delinquency, eyesight, etc.). Only parents take care of the child's entirety. But, in view of the complexity of their responsibilities in our world, parents need moral and instrumental help–not disempowerment.

Research recognizes that parents who have mentally delayed, autistic, and physically challenged children have more responsibilities, more work, and less free time and freedom compared with other parents. Yet, we rarely recognize that this also applies to parents whose children are at a deficit either because of (1) a negative predisposition, such as hyperactivity or aggressivity; (2) a lack of abilities, such as difficulties in thinking linearly, poor reasoning skills, or poor motor coordination; (3) a lack of physical attractiveness; and, finally, (4) an environment (schools, neighborhood) that is disorganized or even criminogenic. Any of these deficits, whether personal or strictly external, places children at risk for poor outcomes and complicates the parent-child relationship. The more of these deficits each child accumulates, the greater the risk and, consequently, the more complex the parental task.

It follows that such children and environments require a *greater parental investment* than do average children living in a high quality environment. Parents have to *compensate* for the deficits, teach alternate coping skills, and protect, monitor, and encourage such children more than other parents. These parents hence *require more personal skills and greater environmental resources or social support* to help their children optimize their potential or even just to prevent them from having highly negative outcomes.

Yet one already sees the unfairness of this situation because these parents are often given less social support than others, especially if they live in a disadvantaged environment. Others, such as parents of difficult children, often *lose* social support when they are blamed for their youngsters' failures. The fact that some of these parents are themselves problematic and dysfunctional only increases their need for support. It is therefore important to recognize that children at risk, as defined herein, require a huge parental investment, one that goes well beyond what is required of the average parent.[19] It is also important to recognize that, today, the investment demanded of all parents is greater than that required of parents some years ago because the social and cultural environment is less supportive of children's needs, and more harmful, complex, and random. We have not evolved an environment that is particularly supportive of parents and their children, and it is essential that we make the multiple efforts needed to do so.

ENDNOTES

1. Edelbrock et al., 1995; Hoffman, 1986.
2. Moreover, the type of behavior genetics used herein has nothing to do with topics such as comparisons between genders or races, as in the untenable argument that there are differences of intelligence between the races.
3. Bradley and Caldwell, 1991.
4. Plomin and Neiderhiser, 1992.
5. We are referring here to a very low IQ that does not have a nonorganic cause such as severe deprivation. Therefore, very low IQs are more likely to be genetic in high-income and optimal family environments than in deprived ones: Bronfenbrenner and Ceci, 1993; Jackson, 1993.
6. In contrast, their parents may be traumatized: Ambert and Gagnon, 1995. See Chapter 13.
7. For Africa, see Killbride and Killbride, 1990.
8. Starrels, Bould, and Nicholas, 1994.
9. The debate over the effect of maternal employment mainly pertains to very small children. Belsky and Eggebeen (1991) find negative implications for exten-

sive and early maternal employment, while Greenstein (1995) finds that the consequences are minimal. Parcel and Menaghan (1994), for their part, locate negative consequences only when mothers are in low-skill jobs—perhaps because the latter are not well paid, thus the day care they can afford may be of poor quality. Moreover, these mothers may be particularly distressed because they subsist near the poverty level. For a critique of the research on day care and maternal employment, see Hochschild, 1989; Silverstein, 1991.

10. The U.S. Bureau of Census has estimated that, between 1960 and 1986, parental time potentially available to children has diminished by ten hours per week for whites and 12 for blacks (Fuchs, 1990).

11. Nock and Kingston, 1988.

12. See Swift, 1990; Zimmerman, 1992.

13. Garbarino, Dubrow, Kostelny, and Pardo, 1992.

14. See book edited by Blankenhorn et al., 1990.

15. Rosenberg, 1991.

16. For instance, researchers have recently found that primary school-age children from poor families score less well on aptitude tests: Entwisle and Alexander, 1995.

17. This question, of course, is not addressed to the abuse of small children and infants.

18. Adolescents are, from some perspectives, often more neglected than are small children (Powers and Eckenrode, 1988).

19. Furstenberg, 1993.

Glossary

active genotype-environment correlation: This term is used by behavior geneticists to refer to situations whereby individuals choose opportunities and environments that reinforce their dispositions.

acute illnesses: Illnesses that consist of one episode that ends by treatment or is self-limited. Examples are the flu or appendicitis. In contrast, a chronic illness persists.

assortative mating: Refers to the theory that people select spouses or mates in a nonrandom fashion. In the case of homogamy, they marry persons who are similar to them on a given characteristic. The characteristic may be physical appearance, IQ, values, one or several personality traits, or even SES. The opposite of homogamy is heterogamy. The opposite of assortative mating is random mating.

child-saving industry: Refers to all the professions and para-professions whose mandate is children's well-being and protection. It is called an "industry" because, except for philanthropists, all these persons derive an income from their services. A similar term is the "hospitality industry" to refer to hotel and tourism employees.

coded: The adjective for coding. Coding consists in attributing numerical values, or a relative value, such as a plus or a minus on a scale, to observations or statements made by people.

cohort: A group of people who were born around the same time and who therefore go through life experiencing similar sociohistorical conditions. For example, people born during the Great Depression form a cohort.

comorbidity: Exists when one disorder or illness is accompanied by another.

concentration ratio: Refers to the proportion of people with a certain characteristic in a neighborhood. The larger the proportion of impoverished families, for instance, the higher the level of concentration for poverty in that neighborhood.

concordance or **concordance rate:** A concept used particularly in comparisons of twins (or of parents with children). It signifies the percentage of occurrences for which both twins have a characteristic that is observable in one of the two twins. For example, we take 100 pairs of monozygotic twins where one twin is known to be schizophrenic and examine the other twin: We may find that 60 also have schizophrenia. The concordance rate for schizophrenia is then 60 percent.

configuration of traits: The form of personality that several traits take when combined.

correlations: Correlations exist between two factors or variables, such as poverty and violence when, as one increases or decreases, the other also changes. When both change in the same direction (e.g., both increase), this is a positive correlation. A negative correlation exists when one factor increases at the same time that the other decreases, as in the example of an increasing number of hours of television watched by children and the decreasing number of books read. Correlation is a statistical test.

cross-pressure: A term used in child development to mean that a child or an adolescent is subjected to influences that oppose each other. This concept applies particularly to parents and peers who may both influence or pressure a child toward opposite goals. Parents may teach the value of hard work while peers may put pressure on a youngster to "party" rather than study.

cross-sectional designs: Those in which a group of persons with certain known characteristics are compared with another group with a lower or a higher level of the same characteristics. For instance, children at age five can be compared to other children at age ten in terms of the types of demonstrations of affection they give their parents. Cross-sectional designs are snapshot studies and differ from longitudinal designs.

dizygotic twins: Fraternal twins. Twins that result from two ova fertilized by two spermatozoa.

dysfunctional: This adjective is used in this text to describe both behaviors and persons. Dysfunctional behaviors are those that impair a person's functioning and success. They are maladaptive either for society, a particular group or the person concerned–or all of these. Dysfunctional persons are those who have not adapted to their various roles, are impaired in their behaviors, and are inadequate in certain aspects of their lives. Dysfunctional behaviors are deemed to be so within a particular context.

genetic loading: When several relatives share the same trait or illness, a high genetic loading exists. When only one person in an extended family suffers from an illness, the genetic loading is low. However, a perhaps more realistic definition for the future should simply be that the greater the number of genes leading to a particular illness that a person has inherited, the greater that person's own genetic loading for that illness. A more appropriate term for the first type of loading may be "familial" loading.

goodness of fit: A concept that is used to describe how a child's personality characteristics fit environmental demands. Or, conversely, how environmental demands, such as family rules and school requirements, agree with a person's temperament. There is a lack of fit when the two do not conform to each other easily; maladjustment is likely to occur. (This term is used with an entirely different meaning in statistics.)

hegemony: Dominance.

ideology: Refers to a set of beliefs concerning a social situation and how it should be. These beliefs are generally shared by a group of people and guide their behavior or at least their thinking concerning that particular situation. Groups can hold ideologies pertaining to race relations, welfare, international politics, gender relations, etc.

indicators: Indicators are used to measure variables. They are sentences, numbers, or observations that serve to illustrate a variable. Indicators are often coded to derive statistics. An indicator of educational achievement is the number of years of schooling a person has received.

longitudinal studies: (Or designs) consist of studying the same people over time. For instance, children may be tested at age ten and restudied again at age 15 and then 20. This research design contrasts with cross-sectional or one-time studies and surveys. A synonym is a panel study.

monozygotic twins: Identical twins originating from one ovum fertilized by one sperm, which separates to produce identical embryos.

morbidity: Presence of illness or psychiatric disorder.

nonshared environment: This is in contrast to the environment shared by all siblings in a family. The nonshared environment refers to those experiences that siblings do not share, such as different peers and schools.

passive genotype-environment correlation: A concept used by behavior geneticists to explain the similarity that exists between biological parents and children on certain traits. This similarity leads to child-rearing practices that correlate with certain child outcomes because parents and children share both genes and a family environment in part created by these same genes.

polygenetic: Refers to a trait or characteristic caused by several genes. Most traits are polygenetic.

prospective studies: Are also longitudinal. The term prospective means that we can take a variable, such as mental illness at age 30, and go back to earlier stages of respondents' lives to seek other variables, such as behavior problems, that may have been present and might serve as antecedents to or predictors for mental illness. This contrasts with retrospective studies based on recollections of the past.

psychosomatic symptoms: Refer to physical ailments, such as headaches, upset stomach, diarrhea, or rapid heartbeat, that people may develop as a result of psychological stress or problems.

reactive genotype-environment correlation: A term used by behavior geneticists for situations in which people's (parents, teachers, peers) reactions to a child are influenced or determined by the child's characteristics and behaviors.

relative deprivation: Refers to the feelings that people have when they compare themselves to persons who are better off than they are and, as a consequence, see themselves as being less rich, less healthy, etc. They feel deprived relative to other people whom they use as a reference point. One can see that even the rich could feel relatively deprived!

retrospective studies: These use people's recollections of their past either to research their past or to link past experiences to current conditions.

rites of passage (rite de passage): Refers to ceremonies that accompany the passage of a person from one status to another status. These include wedding ceremonies, puberty initiations in many countries, and even court rulings concerning a new divorce. Rites of passage are more elaborate for those transitions considered important by a society in terms of its members' trajectory through the life course.

socioeconomic status or SES: The ranking of people on a scale of prestige for occupation, income, and education. Often used as a synonym for social class.

social construct: Refers to how a society defines an experience or a group of persons. For instance, adolescence is defined by Western societies as a difficult and stormy period. This is a cultural definition of adolescence that does not necessarily apply everywhere. We "construct" and "reconstruct" reality depending on who and what we are.

social mobility: The passage from one social stratum to another, or from one social class to another. *Downward* mobility occurs when individuals fall below their parents' stratum or below the one they themselves occupied earlier. *Upward mobility* is the opposite.

systemic: Refers to a problem that is built into a system, an institution, or a society. Solutions to such problems require a restructuring of the institution, a very difficult enterprise at best.

Bibliography

Abel, E. K. 1991. *Who cares for the elderly? Public policy and the experiences of adult daughters.* Philadelphia, PA: Temple University Press.

Abelman, R., and Pettey, G. R. 1989. Child attributes as determinants of parental television-viewing mediation. *Journal of Family Issues,* 10, 251-266.

Abramovitch, R., Pepler, D. J., and Corter, C. 1982. Patterns of sibling interactions among preschool-age children. In M. E. Lamb and B. Sutton-Smith (Eds.), *Sibling relationships: The nature and significance across the lifespan* (pp. 61-68). Hillsdale, NJ: Lawrence Erlbaum.

Agnew, R. 1991. A longitudinal test of social control and delinquency. *Journal of Research in Crime and Delinquency,* 28, 126-156.

Agnew, R., and White, H. R. 1992. An empirical test of general strain theory. *Criminology,* 30, 475-499.

Ainsworth, M. 1973. The development of mother-infant attachment. In B. Caldwell and H. N. Ricciue (Eds.), *Review of child development research,* vol. 3 (pp. 1-94). Chicago: University of Chicago Press.

Ainsworth, M. D. S. 1979. Attachment as related to mother-infant interaction. In J. S. Rosenblatt et al. (Eds.), *Advances in the study of behavior,* Vol. 9. New York: Academic Press.

Aldous, J. 1987. New views on the family life of the elderly and the near elderly. *Journal of Marriage and the Family,* 49, 227-234.

Aldous, J., Klaus, E., and Klein, D. M. 1985. The understanding heart: Aging parents and their favorite children. *Child Development,* 56, 303-316.

Alwin, D. F. 1986. From obedience to autonomy: Changes in traits desired in children, 1924-1978. *Public Opinion Quarterly,* 52, 33-52.

Alwin, D. F. 1990. Cohort replacement and changes in parental socialization values. *Journal of Marriage and the Family,* 52, 347-360.

Alwin, D. F. 1995. Taking time seriously: Social change, social structure, and human lives. In P. Moen, G. H. Elder, Jr., and K. Lüscher (Eds.), *Examining lives in context* (pp. 211-262). Washington, DC: American Psychological Association.

Amato, P. R. 1990. Dimensions of the family environment as perceived by children: A multidimensional scaling analysis. *Journal of Marriage and the Family,* 52, 613-620.

Amato, P. R. 1994. Father-child relations, mother-child relations, and off-spring psychological well-being in early adulthood. *Journal of Marriage and the Family*, 56, 1031-1042.

Amato, P. R. 1995. Single-parent households as settings for children's development, well-being, and attainment: A social network/resources perspective. *Sociological Studies of Children*, 7, 19-46.

Amato, P. R., and Keith, B. 1991. Parental divorce and adult well-being: A meta-analysis. *Journal of Marriage and the Family*, 53, 43-58.

Amato, P. R., and Rezac, S. J. 1994. Contact with nonresident parents, interparental conflict, and children's behavior. *Journal of Family Issues*, 15, 191-207.

Amato, P. R., Loomis, L. S., and Booth, A. 1995. Parental divorce, marital conflict, and offspring well-being during early adulthood. *Social Forces*, 73, 895-915.

Ambert, A.-M. 1982. Differences in children's behavior toward custodial mothers and custodial fathers. *Journal of Marriage and the Family*, 44, 73-86.

Ambert, A.-M. 1984. Longitudinal changes in children's behavior toward custodial parents. *Journal of Marriage and the Family*, 46, 463-468.

Ambert, A.-M. 1989. *Ex-spouses and new spouses: A study of relationships*. Greenwich, CT: JAI Press.

Ambert, A.-M. 1992. *The effect of children on parents*. Binghamton, NY: The Haworth Press.

Ambert, A.-M. 1994a. A qualitative study of peer abuse and its effects: Theoretical and empirical implications. *Journal of Marriage and the Family*, 56, 119-130.

Ambert, A.-M. 1994b. An international perspective on parenting: Social change and social constructs. *Journal of Marriage and the Family*, 56, 529-543.

Ambert, A.-M. 1995. A critical perspective on the research on parents and adolescents: Implications for research, intervention, and social policy. In D. H. Demo and A.-M. Ambert (Eds.), *Parents and adolescents in changing families* (pp. 291-306). Minneapolis, MN: National Council on Family Relations.

Ambert, A.-M. (in press). *The web of poverty: Psychosocial perspectives*. Binghamton, NY: The Haworth Press.

Ambert, A.-M., and Gagnon, L. D. 1995. Que sait-on de l'expérience existentielle des parents des jeunes contrevenants? *Criminologie*, 28, 131-142.

Ambert, A.-M., and Saucier, J.-F. 1984. Adolescents' academic success and aspirations by parental marital status. *Canadian Review of Sociology and Anthropology*, 21, 62-74.

Anastasi, A. 1958. Heredity, environment and the question "How?" *Psychological Review*, 65, 197-208.

Anastopoulos, A. D., et al. 1993. Parent training for attention deficit hyperactivity disorder: Its impact on child and parent functioning. *Journal of Abnormal Child Psychology*, 21, 581-596.

Anderson, E. 1989. Sex codes and family life among poor inner-city youth. *Annals*, 501, 59-78.

Anderson, E. A., and Lynch, M. M. 1984. A family impact analysis: The deinstitutionalization of the mentally ill. *Family Relations*, 33, 41-46.

Anderson, E. R., and Hetherington, M. E. 1989. Transformations in family relations at puberty: Effects of family context. *Journal of Early Adolescence*, 9, 310-334.

Anderson, K. E., Lytton, H., and Romney, D. M. 1986. Mothers' interactions with normal and conduct-disordered boys: Who affects whom? *Developmental Psychology*, 22, 604-609.

Anderson, S. A., and Sabatelli, R. M. 1990. Differentiating differentiation and individuation: Conceptual and operational challenges. *American Journal of Family Therapy*, 18, 32-50.

Angold, A. 1993. Why do we not know the cause of depression in children? In D. F. Hay and A. Angold (Eds.), *Precursors and causes in development and psychopathology* (pp. 265-292). Chichester, UK: John Wiley.

Anthony, E., and Cohler, B. (Eds.). 1987. *The invulnerable child*. New York: Guilford Press.

Apfel, R. J., and Handel, M. H. 1993. *Madness and loss of motherhood*. Washington, DC: American Psychiatric Press.

Aquilino, W. S. 1990. The likelihood of parent-adult child coresidence: Effects of family structure and parental characteristics. *Journal of Marriage and the Family*, 52, 405-419.

Aquilino, W. S. 1991. Family structure and home leaving: A further specification of the relationship. *Journal of Marriage and the Family*, 53, 999-1010.

Aquilino, W. S. 1994a. Later life parental divorce and widowhood: Impact on young adults' assessment of parent-child relations. *Journal of Marriage and the Family*, 56, 908-922.

Aquilino, W. S. 1994b. Impact of childhood family disruption on young adults' relationships with parents. *Journal of Marriage and the Family*, 56, 295-313.

Aquilino, W. S., and Supple, K. R. 1991. Parent-child relations and parents' satisfaction with living arrangements when adult children live at home. *Journal of Marriage and the Family*, 53, 13-28.

Arey, S., and Warheit, G. J. 1980. Psychosocial costs of living with psychologically disturbed family members. In L. Robins, P. J. Clayton, and J. K. Wing (Eds.), *The social consequences of psychiatric illness.* New York: Brunner/Mazel.

Ariès, P. 1962. *Centuries of childhood.* New York: Vintage.

Aro, H. M., and Palosaari, U. K. 1991. Parental divorce, adolescence, and transition to young adulthood: A follow-up study. *American Journal of Orthopsychiatry,* 62, 421-429.

Asarnow, J. R. 1994. Annotation: Childhood-onset schizophrenia. *Journal of Child Psychology and Psychiatry,* 35, 1345-1371.

Asher, S. R. 1990. Recent advances in the study of peer rejection. In S. R. Asher and J. D. Coie (Eds.), *Peer rejection in childhood* (pp. 3-14). Cambridge: Cambridge University Press.

Asher, S. R., and Coie, J. D. (Eds.). 1990. *Peer rejection in childhood.* Cambridge: Cambridge University Press.

Astone, N. M., and McLanahan, S. S. 1991. Family structure, parental practice and high school completion. *American Sociological Review,* 56, 309-320.

Atkin, C. 1978. Observation of parent-child interaction in supermarket decision making. *Journal of Marketing,* 42, 41-45.

Attar, B. K., Guerra, N. G., and Tolan, P. H. 1994. Neighborhood disadvantage, stressful life events, and adjustment in urban elementary-school children. *Journal of Clinical Child Psychology,* 23, 391-400.

Avery, R., Goldscheider, F., and Speare, A., Jr. 1992. Feathered nest/gilded cage: The effects of parental income on young adults leaving home. *Demography,* 29, 375-388.

Azmitia, M., and Hesser, J. 1993. Why siblings are important agents of cognitive development: A comparison of siblings and peers. *Child Development,* 64, 430-444.

Baethge, M. 1989. Individualization as hope and as disaster: A socioeconomic perspective. In K. Hurrelman and V. Engel (Eds.), *The social world of adolescents* (pp. 27-42). Berlin: Walter de Gruyter.

Bailey, J. M., and Pillard, R. C. 1991. A genetic study of male sexual orientation. *Archives of General Psychiatry,* 48, 1089-1096.

Bailey, J. M., Pillard, R. C., Neale, M. C., and Agyei, Y. 1993. Heritable factors influence sexual orientation in women. *Archives of General Psychiatry,* 50, 217-223.

Baines, C., Evans, P., and Neysmith, S. 1991. Caring: Its impact on the lives of women. In C. Baines, P. Evans, and S. Neysmith (Eds.), *Women caring: Feminist perspectives* (pp. 11-35). Toronto: McLelland and Stewart.

Baker, L. A., and Daniels, D. 1990. Nonshared environmental influences and personality differences in adult twins. *Journal of Personality and Social Psychology*, 58, 103-110.

Baker, D. P., and Stevenson, D. R. 1986. Mothers' strategies for children's school achievement: Managing the transition to high school. *Sociology of Education*, 59, 156-166.

Baker, L. A., Ho, H., and Reynolds, C. 1994. Sex differences in genetic and environmental influences for cognitive abilities. In J. C. DeFries, R. Plomin, and D. W. Fulker (Eds.), *Nature and nurture during middle childhood* (pp. 181-200). Cambridge, MA: Blackwell.

Baldwin, A. 1965. A is happy–B is not. *Child Development*, 36, 583-600.

Baltes, P. B., and Baltes, M. M. 1980. Plasticity and variability in psychological aging: Methodological and theoretical issues. In G. E. Gurski (Ed.), *Determining the effects of aging on the central nervous system*. Berlin: Schering A. G.

Bane, M. J. 1986. Household composition and poverty. In S. H. Danziger and D. H. Weinberg (Eds.), *Fighting poverty* (pp. 209-231). Cambridge, MA: Harvard University Press.

Bane, M. J., and Ellwood. D. T. 1986. Slipping into and out of poverty: The dynamics of spells. *Journal of Human Resources*, 21, 1-23.

Bank, L., Forgatch, M. S., Patterson, G. R., and Fetrow, R. A. 1993. Parenting practices of single mothers: Mediators of negative contextual factors. *Journal of Marriage and the Family*, 55, 371-384.

Bank, L., Marlowe, J. H., Reid, J. B., Patterson, G. R., and Weinrott, M. R. 1991. A comparative evaluation of parent training interventions for families of chronic delinquents. *Journal of Abnormal Child Psychology*, 19, 15-33.

Baranowski, M. D., Schilmoeller, G. L., and Higgins, B. S. 1990. Parenting attitudes of adolescent and older mothers. *Adolescence*, 25, 782-790.

Barber, B. K. 1992. Family, personality, and adolescent problem behaviors. *Journal of Marriage and the Family*, 54, 69-79.

Barber, B. K. 1994. Cultural, family, and personal contexts of parent-adolescent conflict. *Journal of Marriage and the Family*, 56, 375-386.

Barkley, R. A. 1981. The use of psychopharmacology to study reciprocal influences in parent-child interaction. *Journal of Abnormal Child Psychology*, 9, 303-310.

Barkley, R. A., Karlsson, J., Pollard, S., and Murphy, J. V. 1985. Developmental changes in the mother-child interactions of hyperactive boys: Effects of two dose levels of Ritalin. *Journal of Child Psychology and Psychiatry*, 26, 705-715.

Barkley, R. A., McMurray, M. B., Edelbrock, C. S., and Robbins, K. 1989.

The response of aggressive and nonaggressive ADHD children to two doses of methylphenidate. *Journal of the American Academy of Child and Adolescent Psychiatry*, 28, 873-881.

Barkley, R. A., Anastopoulos, A. D., Guevremont, D. C., and Fletcher, K. E. 1991. Adolescents with ADHD: Patterns of behavioral adjustment, academic functioning, and treatment utilization. *Journal of the American Academy of Child and Adolescent Psychiatry*, 30, 752-761.

Barkley, R. A., Guevremont, D. C., Anastopoulos, A. D., and Fletcher, K. E. 1992. A comparison of three family therapy programs for treating family conflicts in adolescents with Attention-Deficit Hyperactivity Disorder. *Journal of Consulting and Clinical Psychology*, 60, 450-462.

Barnett, R. C. 1994. Home-to-work spillover revisited: A study of full-time employed women in dual-earner couples. *Journal of Marriage and the Family*, 56, 647-656.

Barnett, R. C., and Baruch, G. K. 1987. Determinants of fathers' participation in family work. *Journal of Marriage and the Family*, 49, 29-40.

Barnett, R. C., Marshall, N. L., and Pleck, J. H. 1992. Adult son-parent relationships and their associations with son's psychological distress. *Journal of Family Issues*, 13, 505-525.

Baruch, G., and Barrett, R. 1983. Adult daughters' relationships with their mothers. *Journal of Marriage and the Family*, 45, 601-606.

Baskett, L. M. 1985. Sibling status effects: Adult expectations. *Developmental Psychology*, 21, 441-445.

Bassuk, E. L. 1995. In the mouths of babes. *American Journal of Orthopsychiatry*, 65, 4-5.

Bates, J. E. 1975. The effects of a child's imitation versus nonimitation on adults' verbal and nonverbal positivity. *Journal of Personality and Social Psychology*, 31, 840-851.

Bates, J. E. 1987. Temperament in infancy. In J. D. Osofsky (Ed.), *Handbook of infant development*, 2nd ed. (pp. 1101-1149). New York: Wiley.

Bates, J. E., Bayles, K., Bennett, D. S., Ridge, B., and Brown, M. M. 1991. Origins of externalizing behavior problems at eight years of age. In D. Pepler and K. H. Rubin (Eds.), *The development and treatment of childhood aggression* (pp. 93-120). Hillsdale, NJ: Lawrence Erlbaum.

Bates, J. E., Freeland, C. A. B., and Lounsbury, M. L. 1979. Measurement of infant difficultness. *Child Development*, 50, 794-802.

Bateson, G., et al. 1958. Toward a theory of schizophrenia. *Behavioral Sciences*, 1, 251-261.

Baum, C. G., and Forehand, R. 1991. Long-term follow-up assessment of parent training by use of multiple outcome measures. *Behavioral Therapy*, 12, 643-652.

Baumeister, R. F., Smart, L., and Boden, J. M. 1996. Relation of threatened egotism to violence and aggression: The dark side of high self-esteem. *Psyhological Review*, 103, 5-33.

Baumrind, D. 1967. Child care practices anteceding three patterns of preschool behavior. *Genetic Psychology Monographs*, 75, 43-88.

Baumrind, D. 1972. An exploratory study of socialization effects of black children: Some black-white comparisons. *Child Development*, 43, 261-267.

Baumrind, D. 1991a. Effective parenting during the early adolescent transition. In P.A. Cowan and E. M. Hetherington (Eds.), *Family transitions* (pp. 111-163). Hillsdale, NJ: Lawrence Erlbaum.

Baumrind, D. 1991b. The influence of parenting style on adolescent competence and substance abuse. *Journal of Early Adolescence*, 11, 56-94.

Baumrind, D. 1993. The average expectable environment is not good enough. A response to Scarr. *Child Development*, 64, 1299-1317.

Baumrind, D., and Black, A. E. 1967. Socialization practices associated with dimensions of competence in preschool boys and girls. *Child Development*, 38, 291-327.

Baydar, N., and Brooks-Gunn, J. 1991. Profiles of America's grandmothers: Those who provide care and those who do not. In *Grandmothers' lives, grandchildren's lives: An interdisciplinary approach to multigenerational parenting*. Symposium at the Biennial Meeting of the Society for Research in Child Development, Seattle.

Beane, J. A. 1990. *Affect in the curriculum: Toward democracy, dignity, and diversity*. New York: Teachers College Press.

Beardsall, L., and Dunn, J. 1992. Adversities in childhood: Siblings' experience, and their relations to self-esteem. *Journal of Child Psychology and Psychitary*, 33, 349-359.

Bebbington, P. E., Tennant, C., and Hurry, J. 1991. Adversity in groups with an increased risk of minor affective disorder. *British Journal of Psychiatry*, 158, 33-40.

Beels, C. C. 1974. Family and social management of schizophrenia. In P. Guerin (Ed.), *Family therapy: Theory and practice*. New York: Gardner Press.

Befera, M. S., and Barkley, R. A. 1985. Hyperactive and normal girls and boys: Mother-child interaction, parent psychiatric status and child psychopathology. *Journal of Child Psychology and Psychiatry*, 26, 439-452.

Bell, C. C., and Jenkins, E. J. 1993. Community violence and children on Chicago's southside. *Psychiatry*, 56, 46-54.

Bell, R. Q. 1968. A reinterpretation of the direction of effects in studies of socialization. *Psychological Review*, 75, 81-85.

Bell, R. Q., and Chapman, M. 1986. Child effects and studies using experimental or brief longitudinal approaches to socialization. *Developmental Psychology*, 22, 595-603.

Bell, R. Q., and Harper, L. V. 1977. *Child effects on adults*. Hillsdale, NJ: Lawrence Earlbaum.

Belle, D. (Ed.). 1989. *Children's social networks and social supports*. New York: John Wiley & Sons.

Belsky, J. 1981. Early human experience: A family perspective. *Developmental Psychology*, 17, 3-23.

Belsky, J. 1984. The determinants of parenting: A process model. *Child Development*, 55, 83-96.

Belsky, J. 1990. Parental and nonparental child care and children's socioemotional development: A decade in review. *Journal of Marriage and the Family*, 52, 885-903.

Belsky, J., and Eggebeen, D. 1991. Early and extensive maternal employment and young children's socioemotional development: Children of the National Longitudinal Survey of Youth. *Journal of Marriage and the Family*, 53, 1083-1110.

Belsky, J., and Isabella, R. 1988. Maternal, infant, and social contextual determinants of attachment security. In J. Belsky and T. Nezworski (Eds.), *Clinical implications of attachment* (pp. 41-94). Hillsdale, NJ: Lawrence Erlbaum.

Belsky, J., and Rovine, M. 1990. Patterns of marital change across the transition to parenthood: Pregnancy to three years postpartum. *Journal of Marriage and the Family*, 52, 5-19.

Belsky, J., and Vondra, J. 1989. Lessons from child abuse: The determinants of parenting. In D. Cicchetti and V. Carlson (Eds.), *Child maltreatment* (pp. 153-202). Cambridge: Cambridge University Press.

Belsky, J., Crnic, K., and Woodworth, S. 1995. Personality and parenting: Exploring the mediating role of transiant mood and daily hassles. *Journal of Personality*, 63, 904-929.

Belsky, J., Fish, M., and Isabella, R. 1991. Continuity and discontinuity in infant negative and positive emotionality: Family antecedents and attachment consequences. *Developmental Psychology*, 27, 421-431.

Belsky, J., Gilstrap, B., and Rovine, M. 1984. The Pennsylvania Infant and Family Development Project. I: Stability and change in mother-infant and father-infant interaction in a family setting at one, three, and nine months. *Child Development*, 55, 692-705.

Belsky, J., Lang, M. E., and Rovine, M. 1985. Stability and change in marriage across the transition to parenthood. A second study. *Journal of Marriage and the Family*, 47, 855-865.

Belsky, J., Lerner, R. M., and Spanier, G. B. 1984. *The child in the family.* Reading, MA: Addison-Wesley.

Belsky, J., Robins, E., and Gamble, W. 1984. The determinants of parental competence. In M. Lewis (Ed.), *Beyond the dyad* (pp. 251-279). New York: Plenum.

Belsky, J., Youngblade, L., Rovine, M., and Volling, B. 1991. Patterns of marital change and parent-child interaction. *Journal of Marriage and the Family,* 53, 487-498.

Bengtson, V. L. 1985. Diversity and symbolism in grandparental roles. In V. L. Bengtson and J. F. Robertson (Eds.), *Grandparenthood* (pp. 11-25). Beverly Hills, CA: Sage.

Bennett, N. G., Bloom D. E., and Craig, P. H. 1989. The divergence of Black and White marriage patterns. *American Journal of Sociology,* 95, 692-722.

Bentler, L., Arizmendi, T., Crago, M., Stanfield, S., and Hagaman, R. 1983. The effect of value similarity and clients' persuability on value convergence and psychotherapy improvement. *Journal of Social and Clinical Psychology,* 1, 231-245.

Berger, E. H. 1991. *Parents as partners in education.* New York: Merrill.

Berk, L. A. 1994. *Child Development,* 3rd ed. Boston: Allyn and Bacon.

Berndt, T. J., and Bulleit, T. N. 1985. Effects of sibling relationships on preschoolers' behavior at home and at school. *Developmental Psychology,* 21, 761-767.

Berndt, T. J., and Ladd, G. W. (Eds.). 1989. *Peer relationships in child development.* New York: Wiley.

Bertelsen, A., Harvald, B., and Hauge, M. A. 1977. A Danish twin study of manic-depressive disorders. *British Journal of Psychiatry,* 130, 330-351.

Besag, V. E. 1989. *Bullies and victims in schools. A guide to understanding and management.* Philadelphia: Open University Press.

Beutler, L. E., Machado, P. P. P., and Neufeldt, S. A. 1994. Therapist variables. In A. E. Bergin and S. L. Garfield (Eds.), *Handbook of psychotherapy and human change,* 3rd ed. (pp. 229-269). New York: Wiley.

Biglan, A., Hops, H., Sherman, L., Friedman, L., Arthur, D., and Osten, V. 1985. Problem-solving interactions of depressed women and their husbands. *Behavior Therapy,* 16, 431-451.

Billings, A., and Moos, R. 1983. Comparison of children of depressed and non-depressed parents. *Journal of Abnormal Child Psychology,* 11, 463-486.

Bird, G. W., Stith, S., and Schladale, J. 1991. Psychological resources, coping strategies, and negotiation styles as discriminators of violence in dating relationships. *Family Relations,* 40, 45-50.

Blake, J. 1989. *Family size and achievement*. Berkeley: University of California Press.

Blankenhorn, D., Bayme, S., and Elshtain, J. B. (Eds.). 1990. *Rebuilding the nest: A new commitment to the American family*. Milwaukee: Family Service of America.

Blanz, B., Schmidt, M. A., and Esser, G. 1991. Familial adversities and child psychiatric disorders. *Journal of Child Psychology and Psychiatry*, 32, 939-950.

Blatchford, P., et al. 1989. Teacher expectations in infant school: Associations with attainment and progress, curriculum coverage and classroom interaction. *British Journal of Educational Psychology*, 59, 19-30.

Block, J. 1971. *Lives through time*. Berkeley, CA: Bancroft Books.

Block, J., and Block, J. H. 1980. *The California Child Q-set*. Palo Alto, CA: Consulting Psychological Press.

Block, J. H, Block. J., and Gjerde, P. F. 1986. The personality of children prior to divorce: A prospective study. *Child Development*, 57, 827-840.

Block, J. H., Block. J., and Gjerde, P. F. 1988. Parental functioning and the home environment of families of divorce: Prospective and current analyses. *Journal of the American Academy of Child and Adolescent Psychiatry*, 27, 207-213.

Block, J., Block, J. H., and Keyes, S. 1988. Longitudinally foretelling drug useage in adolescence: Early childhood personality and environmental precursors. *Child Development*, 59, 336-355.

Block, J. H., Gjerde, P. F., and Block, J. 1991. Personality antecedents of depressive tendencies in 18-year-olds: A prospective study. *Journal of Personality and Social Psychology*, 60, 726-738.

Blos, P. 1979. *The adolescent passage*. New York: International Universities Press.

Boer, F. 1990. *Sibling relationships in middle childhood*. Leiden: DSWO University of Leiden Press.

Boer, F., Goedhart, A. W., and Treffers, P. D. A. 1992. Siblings and their parents. In F. Boer and J. Dunn (Eds.), *Children's sibling relationships* (pp. 41-54). Hillsdale, NJ: Lawrence Erlbaum.

Bohman, M., and Sigvardsson, S. 1978. An 18-year, prospective, longitudinal study of adopted boys. In E. J. Anthony and C. C. Koupernik (Eds.), *The child in his family* (pp. 473-486). Huntington, NY: Krieger.

Bohman, M., and Sigvardsson, S. 1980. A prospective longitudinal study of children registered for adoption. A 15-year follow-up. *Acta Psychiatrica Scandinavica*, 61, 339-353.

Bolgar, R., Zweig-Frank, H., and Paris, J. 1995. Childhood antecedents of interpersonal problems in young adult children of divorce. *Journal of the American Academy of Child and Adolescent Psychiatry*, 34, 143-150.

Bolger, K. E., Patterson, C. J., and Thompson, W. M. 1995. Psychosocial adjustment among children experiencing persistent and intermittent family economic hardship. *Child Development*, 66, 1107-1129.

Boney-McCoy, S., and Finkelhor, D. 1995. Psychosocial sequelae of violent victimization in a national youth sample. *Journal of Consulting and Clinical Psychology*, 63, 726-736.

Booth, A., and Amato, P. R. 1994. Parental marital quality, parental divorce, and relations with parents. *Journal of Marriage and the Family*, 56, 21-33.

Booth, A., and Dunn, J. (Eds.). 1994. *Stepfamilies: Who benefits? Who does not?* Hillsdale, NJ: Lawrence Erlbaum.

Borduin, C. M., et al. 1995. Multisystemic treatment of serious juvenile offenders: Long-term prevention of criminality and violence. *Journal of Consulting and Clinical Psychology*, 63, 569-578.

Bornstein, R. F. 1995. Active dependency. *The Journal of Nervous and Mental Disease*, 183, 64-77.

Bouchard, T. J., Jr., Lykken, D. T., McGue, M., Segal, N. L., and Tellegen, A. 1990. Sources of human psychological difference: The Minnesota study of twins reared apart. *Science*, 250, 223-228.

Bowlby, J. 1969. *Attachment and loss, Vol. 1. Attachment*. New York: Basic Books.

Bowlby, J. 1973. *Attachment and loss, Vol. 2: Separation: Anxiety and anger*. New York: Basic Books.

Bowlby, J. 1980. *Attachment and loss, Vol. 3: Loss, sadness and depression*. New York: Basic Books.

Bowles, S., and Gintis, H. 1976. *Schooling in capitalist America: Educational reform and the contradictions of economic life*. New York: Basic Books.

Bowman, P. J. 1990. The adolescent-to-adult transition: Discouragement among jobless Black youth. In V. C. McLoyd and C. A. Flanagan (Eds.), *Economic stress: Effects on family life and child development* (pp. 87-105). San Francisco: Jossey-Bass.

Boyd, M., and Norris, D. 1995. Leaving the nest? The impact of family structure. *Canadian Social Trends*, 38, Autumn, 14-19.

Boykin, A. W. 1986. The triple quandary and the schooling of Afro-American children. In U. Neisser (Ed.), *The school achievement of minority children* (pp. 57-92). Hillsdale, NJ: Lawrence Erlbaum.

Boyle, M. M., and Offord, D. R. 1988. Prevalence of childhood disorder, perceived need for help, family dysfunction, and resource allocation for child welfare and children's mental health services in Ontario. *Canadian Journal of Behavioural Sciences*, 20, 374-388.

Bozett, F., and Hanson, S. (Eds.). 1991. *Fatherhood and families in cultural context*. New York: Springer.

Bozon, M. 1990. Les loisirs forment la jeunesse (Leisure activities shape youth). *Données sociales 1990*. Paris: Insee.

Bradley, R. H., and Caldwell, B. M. 1991. Like images refracted: A view from the interactionist perspective. *Behavioral and Brain Sciences*, 14, 389-390.

Bradley, R., Caldwell, B., Rock, S., Casey, P., and Nelson, J. 1987. The early development of low birth weight infants. *International Journal of Behavioral Development*, 10, 301-318.

Brand, E., Clingempeel, W. G., and Bowen-Woodword, K. 1988. Family relationships and children's psychological adjustment in stepmother and stepfather families: Findings and conclusions from the Philadelphia Stepfamily Research Project. In E. M. Hetherington and J. D. Arasteh (Eds.), *Impact of divorce, single parenting and stepparenting on children* (pp. 299-324). Hillsdale, NJ: Lawrence Erlbaum.

Brantlinger, E. A. 1993. *The politics of social class in secondary school*. New York: Teachers College Press.

Braungart-Rieker, J., et al. 1995. Genetic mediation of longitudinal associations between family environment and childhood behavior problems. *Development and Psychopathology*, 7, 233-245.

Bray, J. H. 1988. Children's development during early remarriage. In E. M. Hetherington and J. D. Arasteh (Eds.), *Impact of divorce, single parenting and stepparenting on children* (pp. 279-298). Hillsdale, NJ: Lawrence Erlbaum.

Breitmayer, B. J., and Ricciuti, H. N. 1988. The effect of neonatal temperament on caregiver behavior in the newborn nursery. *Infant Mental Health Journal*, 9, 158-172.

Breslau, N., Weitzman, M., and Messenger, K. 1981. Psychological functioning of siblings of disabled children. *Paediatrics*, 67, 344-353.

Bretherton, I., and Waters, E. (Eds.). 1985. Growing points of attachment theory and research. *Monographs for the Society for Research in Child Development*, 50, no. 209.

Bridges, E. 1992. *The incompetent teacher: Managerial responses*. New York: Falmer Press.

Briere, J. 1992. *Child abuse trauma*. Newbury Park, CA: Sage.

Bristowe, E., and Collins, J. B. 1989. Family mediated abuse of non-institutionalized frail elderly men and women living in British Columbia. *Journal of Elder Abuse and Neglect*, 1, 45-64.

Britton, B. K., Woodward, A., and Binkley, M. (Eds.). 1993. *Learning from textbooks: Theory and practice.* Hillsdale, NJ: Lawrence Erlbaum.

Brody, N. 1993. Intelligence and the behavioral genetics of personality. In R. Plomin and G. E. McClearn (Eds.), *Nature, nurture & psychology* (pp. 161-178). Washington, DC: American Psychological Association.

Brody, G. H., Pillegrini, A. D., and Sigel, I. E. 1986. Marital quality and mother-child and father-child interactions with school-aged children. *Developmental Psychology, 22,* 291-296.

Brody, G. H., Stoneman, Z., and Burke, M. 1987. Child temperament, maternal differential behavior, and sibling relationships. *Developmental Psychology, 23,* 354-362.

Brody, G. H., Stoneman, Z., and McCoy, J. K. 1992. Parental differential treatment of siblings and sibling differences in negative emotionality. *Journal of Marriage and the Family, 54,* 643-651.

Brody, G. H., Stoneman, Z., McCoy, J. K., and Forehand, R. 1992. Contemporaneous and longitudinal associations of sibling conflict with family relationship assessments and family discussions about sibling problems. *Child Development, 63,* 391-400.

Bronfenbrenner, U. 1979. *The ecology of human development.* Cambridge, MA: Harvard University Press.

Bronfenbrenner, U. 1985. Freedom and discipline across the decades. In G. Becker, H. Becker, and L. Huber (Eds.), *Ordnung und Unordnung (Order and Disorder)* (pp. 326-339). Berlin: Beltz.

Bronfenbrenner, U. 1986. Ecology of the family as a context for human development: Research perspectives. *Developmental Psychology, 22,* 723-742.

Bronfenbrenner, U. 1988. Interacting systems in human development: Research paradigm: Present and future. In N. Bolger, A. Caspi, G. Downey, and M. Moorehouse (Eds.), *Persons in context: Developmental processes* (pp. 25-49). New York: Cambridge University Press.

Bronfenbrenner, U. 1989. Ecological systems theory. In R. Vasta (Ed.), *Six theories of child development* (pp. 185-246). Greenwich, CT: JAI Press.

Bronfenbrenner, U. 1990. Discovering what families do. In D. Blankenhorn et al. (Eds.), *Rebuilding the nest: A new commitment to the American family* (pp. 27-38). Milwaukee: Family Service America.

Bronfenbrenner, U. 1994. Ecological models of human development. In T. Husen and T. N. Postlethwaite (Eds.), *International Encyclopedia of Education,* 2nd ed. (pp. 1643-1647). Oxford, UK: Pergamon/Elsevier.

Bronfenbrenner, U., and Ceci, S. J. 1993. Heredity, environment, and the question "how?"—A first approximation. In R. Plomin and G. E. McClearn (Eds.), *Nature, nurture & psychology* (pp. 313-324). Washington, DC: American Psychological Association.

Bronfenbrenner, U., and Ceci, S. J. 1994. Nature-nurture reconceptualized in developmental perspective: A bioecological model. *Psychological Review*, 101, 568-586.

Bronfenbrenner, U, and Crouter, A. 1983. The evolution of environmental models in developmental research. In W. Kessen (Ed.), *Handbook of child psychology*, 1, (pp. 357-476). New York: John Wiley.

Bronfenbrenner, U., Kessel, F., Kessen, W., and White, S. 1986. Toward a critical social history of developmental psychology: A propaedeutic discussion. *American Psychologist*, 41, 1218-1230.

Bronfenbrenner, U., Moen, P., and Garbarino, J. 1984. Child, family, and community. In R. Parke (Ed.), *Review in child development research: Vol. 7. The family* (pp. 283-328). Chicago: University of Chicago Press.

Brook, J. S., Whiteman, M., and Finch, S. 1993. Role of mutual attachment in drug use: A longitudinal study. *Journal of the American Academy of Child and Adolescent Psychiatry*, 32, 982-989.

Brooks-Gunn, J. 1995. Children in families in communities: Risk and intervention in the Bronfenbrenner tradition. In P. Moen, G. H. Elder, Jr., and K. Luscher (Eds.), *Examining lives in context* (pp. 467-519). Washington, DC: American Psychological Association.

Brooks-Gunn, J., and Furstenberg, F. F., Jr. 1986. The children of adolescent mothers: Physical, academic, and psychological outcomes. *Developmental Review*, 6, 224-251.

Brooks-Gunn, J., and Petersen, A. C. 1991. Studying the emergence of depression and depressive symptoms during adolescence. *Journal of Youth and Adolescence*, 20, 115-119.

Brooks-Gunn, J., Duncan, G. J., Klebanov, P. K., and Sealand, N. 1993. Do neighborhoods influence child and adolescent development? *American Journal of Sociology*, 99, 353-395.

Brophy, J. 1988. Teacher influences on student achievement. *American Psychologist*, 41, 1069-1077.

Brown, B. B. 1990. Peer groups and peer cultures. In S. S. Feldman and G. R. Elliott (Eds.), *At the threshold: The developing adolescent* (pp. 171-196). Cambridge, MA: Harvard University Press.

Brown, B. B., Mounts, N., Lamborn, S. D., and Steinberg, L. 1993. Parenting practices and peer group affiliation in adolescence. *Child Development*, 64, 467-482.

Brown, G. R. J., Birley, L. T., and Winey, J. K. 1972. Influence of family life on the course of schizophrenic disorders: A replication. *British Journal of Psychiatry*, 121, 241-258.

Brown, R. T., Borden, K. A., Clingerman, S. R., and Jenkins, P. 1988.

Depression in attention deficit-disordered and normal children and their parents. *Child Psychiatry and Human Development*, 18, 119-132.

Bruce, M. L., Takeuchi, D. T., and Leaf, P. J. 1991. Poverty and psychiatric status. *Archives of General Psychiatry*, 48, 470-474.

Brunk, M. A., and Henggeler, S. W. 1984. Child influences on adult controls: An experimental investigation. *Developmental Psychology*, 20, 1074-1081.

Bryant, B. K. 1989. The child's perspective of sibling caretaking and its relevance to understanding socio-emotional functioning and development. In P. G. Zukow (Ed.), *Sibling interaction across cultures* (pp. 143-164). New York: Springer-Verlag.

Bryant, B. K., and DeMorris, K. A. 1992. Beyond parent-child relationships: Potential links between family environments and peer relations. In R. D. Parke and G. W. Ladd (Eds.), *Family-peer relationships: Models of linkage* (pp. 191-212). Hillsdale, NJ: Lawrence Erlbaum.

Buchanan, C. M., Maccoby, E. E., and Dornbusch, S. M. 1991. Caught between parents: Adolescents' experience in divorced homes. *Child Development*, 62, 1008-1029.

Buck, N., and Scott, J. 1993. She's leaving home: But why? An analysis of young people leaving the parental home. *Journal of Marriage and the Family*, 55, 863-874.

Buckhault, J. A., Rutherford, R. B., and Goldberg, K. E. 1978. Verbal and nonverbal interaction of mothers with their Down's syndrome and non-retarded infants. *American Journal of Mental Deficiency*, 82, 337-343.

Budoff, M. 1975. Engendering changes in special education practices. *Harvard Educational Review*, 45, 507-526.

Bugental, D. B., and Shennum, W. A. 1984. "Difficult" children as elicitors and targets of adult communication patterns: An attributional-transactional analysis. *Monographs of the Society for Research and Development*, 49, no. 205.

Bugental, D., Blue, J., and Cruzcosa, M. 1989. Perceived control over caregiving outcomes: Implications for child abuse. *Developmental Psychology*, 25, 532-539.

Buhrmester, D., and Furman, W. 1987. The development of companionship and intimacy. *Child Development*, 58, 1101-1113.

Buhrmester, D., and Furman, W. 1990. Perceptions of sibling relationships during middle childhood and adolescence. *Child Development*, 61, 1387-1398.

Buhrmester, D., et al. 1992. Mothers and fathers interacting in dyads and triads with normal and hyperactive sons. *Developmental Psychology*, 28, 500-509.

Bulcroft, K., and Bulcroft, R. 1991. The timing of divorce: Effects on parent-child relationships in later life. *Research on Aging*, 13, 226-243.

Bumpass, L. L. 1984. Children and marital disruption: A replication and update. *Demography*, 21, 71-82.

Bumpass, L. L., Martin, T. C., and Sweet, J. A. 1991. The impact of family background and early marital factors on marital disruption. *Journal of Family Issues*, 12, 22-42.

Burcky, W., Reuterman, N., and Kopsky, S. 1988. Dating violence among high school students. *The School Counselor*, 35, 353-358.

Burgoyne, J., Ormrod, R., Richards, M. P. M. 1987. *Divorce matters.* London: Penguin Books.

Burke, K. C., Burke, J. D., Regier, D. A., and Rae, D. S. 1990. Age at onset of selected mental disorders in five community populations. *Archives of General Psychiatry*, 47, 511-518.

Burkett, L. P. 1991. Parenting behaviors of women who were sexually abused as children in their families of origin. *Family Process*, 30, 421-434.

Burman, B., John, R. S., and Margolin, G. 1987. Effects of marital and parent-child relations on children's adjustment. *Journal of Family Psychology*, 1, 91-108.

Bursik, R. J., Jr. 1988. Social disorganization and theories of crime and delinquency: Problems and prospects. *Criminology*, 26, 519-552.

Burton, L. M. 1990. Teenage childbearing as an alternative life-course strategy in multigeneration black families. *Human Nature*, 1, 123-143.

Burton, L. M., and Bengtson, V. L. 1985. Black grandmothers: Issues of timing and continuity of roles. In V. L. Bengston and J. F. Robertson (Eds.), *Grandparenthood* (pp. 61-80). Beverly Hills, CA: Sage.

Buss, D. M. 1981. Predicting parent-child interactions from children's activity level. *Developmental Psychology*, 17, 59-65.

Butler, S. M., MacKay, S. A., and Dickens, S. E. 1995. Maternal and adolescent ratings of psychopathology in young offender and non-clinical males. *Canadian Journal of Behavioural Science*, 27, 333-342.

Cadoret, R. J. 1985. Genes, environment, and their interaction in the development of psychopathology. In T. Sakai and T. Tsuboi (Eds.), *Genetic aspects of human behavior* (pp. 165-175). Tokyo: Ogaku-Shoin.

Cadoret, R. J., Cain, C. A., and Crowe, R. R. 1983. Evidence for gene-environment interaction in the development of adolescent antisocial behavior. *Behavior Genetics*, 13, 301-310.

Cadoret, R. J., Yates, W. R., Troughton, E., Woodworth, G., and Stewart,

M. A. 1995a. Adoption study demonstratring two genetic pathways to drug abuse. *Archives of General Psychiatry*, 52, 42-52.

Cadoret, R. J., Yates, W. R., Troughton, E., Woodworth, G., and Stewart, M. A. 1995b. Genetic-environmental interaction in genesis of aggressivity and conduct disorders. *Archives of General Psychiatry*, 52, 916-924.

Cairns, R. B., McGuire, A. M., and Gariépy, J. L. 1993. Developmental behavior genetics: Fusion, correlated constraints, and timing. In D. F. Hay and A. Angold (Eds.), *Precursors and causes in development and psychopathology* (pp. 87-122). Chichester, England: John Wiley and Sons.

Call, K., Mortimer, J. T., and Shanahan, M. J. 1995. Helpfulness and the development of competence in adolescence. *Child Development*, 66, 129-138.

Camara, K. A., and Resnick, G. 1988. Interparental conflict and cooperation: Factors moderating children's post-divorce adjustment. In E. M. Hetherington and J. D. Arasteh (Eds.), *Impact of divorce, single parenting, and stepparenting on children* (pp. 169-195). Hillsdale, NJ: Lawrence Erlbaum.

Campbell, S. 1979. Mother-infant interaction as a function of maternal ratings of temperament. *Child Psychiatry and Human Development*, 10, 67-76.

Cantor, N. L., and Gelfand, D. M. 1977. Effects of responsiveness and sex of children on adults' behavior. *Child Development*, 48, 232-238.

Capaldi, D. M., and Patterson, G. R. 1991. Relation of parental transitions to boys' adjustment problems: I. A linear hypothesis: II. Mothers at risk for transitions and unskilled parenting. *Developmental Psychology*, 27, 489-251.

Caplan, H. L., et al. 1989. Maternal depression and the emotional development of the child. *British Journal of Psychiatry*, 154, 818-822.

Caplan, P. J., and Hall-McCorquodale, I. 1985. Mother-blaming in major clinical journals. *American Journal of Orthopsychiatry*, 55, 345-353.

Cardon, L. R., and Fulker, D. W. 1993. Genetics of specific cognitive abilities. In R. Plomin and G. E. McClearn (Eds.), *Nature, nurture & psychology* (pp. 99-120). Washington, DC: American Psychological Association.

Carlson, B. E. 1990. Adolescent observers of marital violence. *Journal of Family Violence*, 5, 285-299.

Caspi, A. 1987. Personality in the life course. *Journal of Personality and Social Psychology*, 53, 1203-1213.

Caspi, A., and Bem, D. 1990. Personality continuity and change across the life course. In L. A. Pervin (Ed.), *Handbook of personality: Theory and research* (pp. 549-575). New York: Guilford Press.

Caspi, A., and Herbener, E. S. 1990. Continuity and change: Assortative marriage and the consistency of personality in adulthood. *Journal of Personality and Social Psychology*, 58, 250-258.

Caspi, A., and Moffitt, T. 1991. The continuity of maladaptive behavior: From description to understanding in the study of antisocial behavior. In D. Cicchetti and D. Cohen (Eds.), *Manual of developmental psychopathology*. New York: Wiley.

Caspi, A., and Silva, P. A. 1995. Temperamental qualities at age three predict personality traits in young adulthood: Longitudinal evidence from a birth cohort. *Child Development*, 66, 486-498.

Caspi, A., Bem, D. J., and Elder, G. H., Jr. 1989. Continuities and consequences of interactional styles across the life course. *Journal of Personality*, 57, 375-406.

Caspi, A., Elder, G. H., Jr., and Bem, D. J. 1987. Moving against the world: Life-course patterns of explosive children. *Developmental Psychology*, 23, 308-317.

Caspi, A., Elder, G. H., Jr., and Herbener, E. S. 1990. Childhood personality and the prediction of life-course patterns. In M. Rutter and L. Robins (Eds.), *Straight and devious pathways from childhood to adulthood* (pp. 13-35). Cambridge: Cambridge University Press.

Caspi, A., Herbener, E. S., and Ozer, D. J. 1992. Shared experiences and the similarity of personalities: A longitudinal study of married couples. *Journal of Personality and Social Psychology*, 62, 281-291.

Caspi, A., Moffitt, T. E., Silva, P. A., Stouthamer-Loeber, M., Krueger, R. F., and Schmutte, P. S. 1994. Are some people crime-prone? Replications of the personality-crime relationship across countries, genders, races, and methods. *Criminology*, 32, 163-195.

Caspi, A., Henry, B., McGee, R., Moffitt, T. E., and Silva, P. A. 1995. Temperamental origins of child and adolescent behavior problems: From age three to fifteen. *Child Development*, 66, 55-68.

Castle, D. F. 1986. Early emancipation statutes: Should they protect parents as well as children? *Family Law Quarterly*, 20, 343-372.

Causey, D., and Dubow, E. 1992. Development of a self-report coping measure for elementary school children. *Journal of Clinical Child Psychology*, 21, 47-59.

Cavalli-Sforza, L. L., and Feldman, M. W. 1973. Cultural versus biological inheritance: Phenotypic transmission from parents to children (a theory of the effect of parental phenotypes on children's phenotypes). *American Journal of Human Genetics*, 25, 618-637.

Cawthron, P., James, A., Dell, J., and Seagroatt, V. 1994. Adolescent onset psychosis. A clinical and outcome study. *Journal of Child Psychology and Psychiatry*, 35, 1321-1332.

Chappell, N. L. 1985. Social support and the receipt of home care services. *The Gerontologist*, 25, 47-54.

Chappell, N. L., Strain, L. A., and Blandford, A. A. 1986. *Aging and health care. A social perspective.* Toronto: Holt, Rinehart and Winston of Canada.

Chase-Lansdale, P. L., Brooks-Gunn, J., and Paikoff, R. L. 1991. Research and programs for adolescent mothers: Missing links and future promises. *Family Relations*, 40, 396-403.

Chase-Lansdale, P. L., Brooks-Gunn, J., and Zamsky, E. J. 1991. Grandmothers, young mothers, and 3-year-olds: Interrelations among grandmothers' presence, quality of parenting, and child development. In *Grandmothers' lives, grandchildren's lives: An interdisciplinary approach to multigenerational parenting.* Symposium at the Biannual Meeting of the Society for Research in Child Development, Seattle.

Chassin, L., Curran, P. J., Hussong, A. M., and Colder, C. R. 1996. The relation of parent alcoholism to adolescent substance use: A longitudinal follow-up study. *Journal of Abnormal Psychology*, 105, 70-80.

Chatters, L. M., Taylor, R. J., and Neighbors, H. W. 1989. Size of informal helper network mobilized during a serious personal problem among black Americans. *Journal of Marriage and the Family*, 51, 667-676.

Cherlin, A., and Furstenberg, F. F., Jr. 1994. Stepfamilies in the United States: A reconsideration. *Annual Review of Sociology*, 20, 359-381.

Chess, S., and Thomas, A. 1984. *Origins and evolution of behavior disorders.* New York: Brunner/Mazel.

Chisholm, L., Brown, P., Büchner, P., and Krüger, H.-H. Childhood and youth studies in the United Kingdom and West Germany: An introduction. In L. Chisholm, P. Büchner, H.-H. Krüger, and P. Brown (Eds.), *Childhood, youth and social change: A comparative perspective.* London: Falmer Press.

Christensen, A., and Margolin, G. 1988. Conflict and alliance in distressed and non distressed families. In R. A. Hinde and J. S. Hinde (Eds.), *Relationships within families: Mutual influences* (pp. 263-282). New York: Oxford University Press.

Christensen, S. L., Rounds, T., and Gorney, D. 1992. Family factors and student achievement: An avenue to increase students' success. *School Psychology Quarterly*, 7, 178-206.

Cicchetti, D., and Lynch, M. 1993. Toward an ecological/transactional model of community violence and child maltreatment: Consequences for children's development. *Psychiatry*, 56, 96-118.

Cicirelli, V. G. 1980. Sibling relationships in adulthood: A life span perspective. In L. W. Poon (Ed.), *Aging in the 1980s: Psychological issues* (pp. 445-462). Washington, DC: American Psychological Association.

Cicirelli, V. G. 1983. Adult children and their elderly parents. In T. Brubaker (Ed.), *Family relationships in later life*. Beverly Hills, CA: Sage.

Cicirelli, V. G. 1989. Feelings of attachment to siblings and well-being in later life. *Psychology and Aging*, 4, 211-216.

Cicirelli, V. G. 1991. Attachment theory in old age: Protection of the attached figure. In K. Pillemer and K. McCartney (Eds.), *Parent-child relations throughout life* (pp. 25-42). Hillsdale, NJ: Lawrence Erlbaum.

Cicirelli, V. G. 1994. Sibling relationships in cross-cultural perspective. *Journal of Marriage and the Family*, 56, 7-20.

Cicirelli, V. G. 1995. *Sibling relationships across the life span*. New York: Plenum.

Cicirelli, V. G., Coward, R. T., and Dwyer, J. W. 1992. Siblings as caregivers for impaired elders. *Research on Aging*, 14, 331-350.

Claes, M. 1990. Les relations entre parents et enfants dans une famille en changement. In D. Lemieux (Ed.), *Familles d'aujourd'hui*. Québec: Institut québecois de recherche sur la culture.

Clark, J., and Barber, B. L. 1994. Adolescents in postdivorce and always-married families: Self-esteem and perceptions of fathers' interest. *Journal of Marriage and the Family*, 56, 608-614.

Clarke, A. M., and Clarke, A. D. B. 1992. How modifiable is the human life path? In N. W. Bray (Ed.), *International review of research in mental retardation*, 18, 137-157. New York: Academic Press.

Clarke-Stewart, K. A. 1987a. In search of consistencies in child care research. In D. Phillips (Ed.), *Quality day care* (pp. 105-120). Washington, DC: NAEYC.

Clarke-Stewart, K. A. 1987b. Predicting child development from child care forms and features: The Chicago study. In D. Phillips (Ed.), *Quality day care* (pp. 21-42). Washington, DC: NAEYC.

Clausen, J. A. 1986. *The life course: A sociological perspective*. Englewood Cliffs, NJ: Prentice-Hall.

Clausen, J. 1991. Adolescent competence and the shaping of the life course. *American Journal of Sociology*, 96, 805-842.

Claussen, A. I. E., and Crittenden, P. M. 1991. Physical and psychological maltreatment: Relations among types of maltreatment. *Child Abuse and Neglect*, 15, 5-18.

Clemens, A., and Axelson, L. 1985. The not so empty nest: The return of the fledgling adult. *Family Relations*, 34, 259-264.

Clingempeel, W. G., Brand, E., and Segal, S. 1987. A multi-level-multivariable-developmental perspective for future research on stepfamilies. In K. Pasley and M. Ihinger-Tallman (Eds.), *Remarriage and stepparenting: Current research and theory* (pp. 65-93). New York: Guilford.

Cloninger, C. R., Sigvardsson, S., Bohman, M., and von Knorring, A.-L. 1982. Predisposition to petty criminality in Swedish adoptees: II. Cross-parenting analysis of gene-environment interaction. *Archives of General Psychiatry*, 39, 1242-1247.

Cochran, M., and Riley, D. 1988. Mother reports of children's personal networks: Antecedents, concomitants, and consequences. In S. Salzinger, J. Antrobus, and M. Hammer (Eds.), *Social networks of children, adolescents, and college students* (pp. 113-148). Hillsdale, NJ: Lawrence Erlbaum.

Coleman, J. S. 1988. Social capital in the creation of human capital. *American Journal of Sociology*, 94, S95-S120.

Coleman, J. S., and Hoffer, T. 1987. *Public and private schools: The impact of communities*. New York: Basic Books.

Coleman, M., and Ganong, L. H. 1990. Remarriage and stepfamily research in the 1980s: Increased interest in an old family form. *Journal of Marriage and the Family*, 52, 925-940.

Collins, W. A. 1990. Parent-child relationships in the transition to adolescence: Continuity and change in interaction, affect, and cognition. In R. Montemayor, G. R. Adams, and T. P. Gullotta (Eds.), *From childhood to adolescence* (pp. 85-106). Newbury Park, CA: Sage.

Collins, W. A., and Gunnar, M. R. 1990. Social and personality development. *Annual Review of Psychology*, 41, 387-416.

Collins, W. A., and Repinski, D. J. 1994. Relationships during adolescence: Continuity and change in interpersonal perspective. In R. Montemayor, G. R. Adams, and T. P. Gullotta (Eds.), *Personal relationships during adolescence* (pp. 7-36). Thousand Oaks, CA: Sage.

Collins, W. A., and Russell, G. 1991. Mother-child and father-child relationships in middle childhood and adolescence: A developmental analysis. *Developmental Review*, 11, 99-136.

Compas, B. E. 1987. Coping with stress during childhood and adolescence *Psychological Bulletin*, 101, 393-403.

Compas, B. E., Howell, D. C., Phares, V., Williams, R. A., and Ledoux, N. 1989. Parent and child stress symptoms: An integrative analysis. *Developmental Psychology*, 25, 550-559.

Conger, R. D., and Elder, G. H. Jr., 1994. *Families in troubled times. Adapting to rural change in America.* New York: Aldine de Gruyter.

Conger, R. D., Patterson, G. R., and Ge, X. 1995. It takes two to replicate: A mediational model for the impact of parents' stress on adolescent adjustment. *Child Development*, 66, 80-97.

Conger, R. D., Conger, K. J., Elder, G. H., Jr., Lorenz, F. O., Simons, R. L., and Whitbeck, L. B. 1992. A family process model of economic hardship and adjustment of early adolescent boys. *Child Development*, 63, 526-554.

Conger, R. D., Conger, K. J., Elder, G. H., Jr., Lorenz, F. O., Simons, R. L., and Whitbeck, L. B. 1993. Family economic stress and adjustment of early adolescent girls. *Developmental Psychology*, 29, 206-219.

Conger, R. D., et al. 1992. A family process model of economic hardship and adjustment of early adolescent boys. *Child Development*, 63, 526-541.

Congressional Budget Office, 1990. *Sources of support for adolescent mothers.* Washington, DC: U.S. Government Printing Office.

Connidis, I. A. 1989. Siblings as friends in later life. *American Behavioral Scientist*, 33, 81-93.

Cook, J. 1988. Who "mothers" the chronically mentally ill? *Family Relations*, 37, 42-49.

Cook, J., and Cohler, B. J. 1986. Reciprocal socialization and the care of offspring with cancer and with schizophrenia. In N. Datan, A. Greene, and H. Reese (Eds.), *Life-span developmental psychology: Intergenerational relations* (pp. 223-243). Hillsdale, NJ: Lawrence Erlbaum.

Cook, W. L., et al. 1990. Mother-child dynamics in early-onset depression and childhood schizophrenia spectrum disorders. *Development and Psychopathology*, 2, 71-84.

Coon, H., and Carey, G. 1989. Genetic and environmental determinants of mutual ability in twins. *Behavioral Genetics*, 19, 183-193.

Cooney, T. M. 1994. Young adults' relations with parents: The influence of recent parental divorce. *Journal of Marriage and the Family*, 56, 46-56.

Cooney, T. M., and Uhlenberg, P. 1990. The role of divorce in men's relations with their adult children after mid-life. *Journal of Marriage and the Family*, 52, 677-688.

Cooney, T. M., and Uhlenberg, P. 1992. Support from parents over the life course: The adult child's perspective. *Social Forces*, 71, 63-84.

Cooney, T. M., Pedersen, F. A., Indelicato, S., and Palkovitz, R. 1993. Timing of fatherhood: Is "on-time" optional? *Journal of Marriage and the Family*, 55, 205-215.

Cooper, C. R., and St. John, L. 1990. Children helping children in the family: Developmental perspectives on sibling relationships. In H. C. Foot, M. J. Morgan, and R. H. Shute (Eds.), *Children helping children* (pp. 259-273). New York: Wiley.

Copron, C., and Dwyne, M. 1989. Assessment of effects of socioeconomic status on IQ in a cross-fostering study. *Nature*, 340, 552-554.

Corsaro, W. A., and Eder, D. 1990. Children's peer cultures. *Annual Review of Sociology*, 16, 197-220.

Corsaro, W. A., and Rizzo, T. A. 1990. Disputes in the peer culture of American and Italian nursery school children. In A. D. Grinshaw (Ed.), *Conflict talk* (pp. 21-66). Cambridge: Cambridge University Press.

Corteen, R. S., and Williams, T. 1986. Television and reading skills. In T. Williams (Ed.), *The impact of television: A natural experiment in three communities* (pp. 39-84). Orlando, FL: Academic Press.

Corter, C., Pepler, D., Stanhope, L., and Abramovitch, R. 1992. Home observations of mothers and sibling dyads comprised of Down's Syndrome and nonhandicapped children. *Canadian Journal of Behavioural Science*, 24, 1-13.

Costa, P. T., Jr., and McCrae, R. R. 1992. *NEO-PI-R: Revised personality inventory*. Odessa, FL: Psychological Assessment Resources.

Coulton, C. J., Korbin, J. E., Su, M., and Chow, J. 1995. *Community level factors and child maltreatment rates, Child Development*, 66, 1262-1276.

Cowan, C. P., Cowan, P. A., Heming, G., and Miller, N. B. 1991. Becoming a family: Marriage, parenting, and child development. In P. A. Cowan and E. M. Hetherington (Eds.), *Family transitions* (pp. 79-110). Hillsdale, NJ: Lawrence Erlbaum.

Cowan, P. A., Cowan, C. P., and Kerig, P. K. 1992. Mothers, fathers, sons, and daughters: Gender differences in family formation and parenting style. In P. A. Cowan et al. (Eds.), *Family, self, and society: Towards a new agenda for family research* (pp. 165-195). Hillsdale, NJ: Lawrence Erlbaum.

Cox, A. D., Puckering, C., Pound, A., and Mills, M. 1987. The impact of maternal depression on young people. *Journal of Child Psychology and Psychiatry*, 28, 917-928.

Coyne, J. C., and Whiffen, V. E. 1995. Issues in personality as diathesis for depression: The case of sociotropy-dependency and autonomy-self criticism. *Psychological Bulletin*, 118, 358-378.

Coyne, J. C., Downey, G., and Boergers, J. 1992. Depression in families. A systems perspective. In D. Cicchetti and S. Toth (Eds.), *Rochester symposium on developmental psychopathology: Vol. 4. A developmen-*

tal approach to affective disorders (pp. 211-249). Rochester, NY: University of Rochester Press.

Crane, J. 1991. The epidemic theory of ghettos and neighborhood effects on dropping out and teenage childbearing. *American Journal of Sociology*, 96, 1226-1259.

Creasey, G., Mitts, N., and Catanzaro, S. 1995. Associations among daily hassles, coping, and behavior problems in nonreferred kindergartners. *Journal of Clinical Child Psychology*, 24, 311-319.

Crimmins, E., Easterlin, R., and Saito, Y. 1991. Preference changes among American youth: Family, work, and goods aspirations, 1976-87. *Population and Development Review*, 17, 115-133.

Crockenberg, S. B. 1986. Are temperamental differences in babies associated with predictable differences in care-giving? In J. V. Lerner and R. M. Lerner (Eds.), *Temperament and social interaction in infants and children* (pp. 75-88). San Francisco: Jossey-Bass.

Crook, T., Raskin, A., and Eliot, J. 1981. Parent-child relationship and adult depression. *Child Development*, 52, 950-957.

Crouter, A. C. 1994. Processes linking families and work: Implications for behavior and development in both settings. In R. D. Parke and S. G. Kellam (Eds.), *Exploring family relationships with other social contexts* (pp. 9-28). Hillsdale, NJ: Lawrence Erlbaum.

Crouter, A. C., MacDermid, S. M., McHale, S. M., and Perry-Jenkins, M. 1990. Parental monitoring and perception of children's school performance and conduct in dual- and single-earner families. *Developmental Psychology*, 26, 649-657.

Crowe, R. R. 1974. An adoption study of antisocial personality. *Archives of General Psychiatry*, 31, 785-791.

Cuber, J. F., and Harroff, P. B. 1965. *The significant American*. New York: Hawthorn Books.

Culp, R. E., Culp, A. M., Osofsky, J. D., and Osofsky, H. J. 1991. Adolescent and older mothers' interaction patterns with their six-month-old infants. *Journal of Adolescence*, 14, 195-200.

Cummings, E. M., and Cicchetti, D. 1990. Towards a transactional model of relations between attachment and depression. In M. Greenberg et al. (Eds.), *Attachment in the preschool years* (pp. 339-372). Chicago: The University of Chicago Press.

Cummings, E. M., and Davies, P. T. 1994a. *Children and marital conflict: The impact of family dispute and resolution*. New York: Guilford.

Cummings, E. M., and Davies, P. T. 1994b. Maternal depression and child development. *Journal of Child Psychology and Psychiatry*, 35, 73-112.

Cummings, E. M., Hennessy, K., Rabideau, G., and Cicchetti, D. 1994.

Responses of physically abused boys to interadult anger involving their mothers. *Developmental Psychopathology*, 6, 31-41.

Cummings, N. 1986. The dismantling of our health system: Strategies for the survival of psychological practice. *American Psychologist*, 41, 426-431.

Cunningham, C. E., Bremmer, R., and Boyle, M. 1995. Large group community-based parenting programs for families of preschoolers at risk for disruptive behavior disorders: Utilization, cost effectiveness, and outcome. *Journal of Child Psychology and Psychiatry*, 36, 1141-1159.

Cunningham, C. E., Benness, B., and Siegel, L. S. 1988. Family functioning, time allocation, and parental depression in the families of normal and ADDH children. *Journal of Clinical Child Psychology*, 17, 169-177.

Curtner-Smith, M. E., and MacKinnon-Lewis, C. E. 1994. Family process effects on adolescent males' susceptibility to antisocial peer pressure. *Family Relations*, 43, 462-468.

Cutrona, C., and Troutman, B. 1986. Social support, infant temperament and parenting self-efficacy: A mediational model of post-partum depression. *Child Development*, 57, 1507-1518.

Daly, M., and Wilson, M. 1994. Some differential attributes of lethal assaults on small children by stepfathers versus genetic fathers. *Ethology and Sociobiology*, 15, 381-389.

Dandurand, R. B. 1994. Divorce et nouvelle monoparentalité. In F. Dumont et al. (Eds.), *Traité des problèmes sociaux*. Québec: Institut québecois de recherche sur la culture.

Daniels, D. 1987. Differential experiences of children in the same family as predictors of adolescent sibling personality differences. *Journal of Personality and Social Psychology*, 51, 339-346.

Daniels, D., and Plomin, R. 1985. Differential experience of siblings in the same family. *Developmental Psychology*, 21, 747-760.

Danziger, S. K., and Radin, N. 1990. Absent does not equal uninvolved: Predictors of fathering in teen mother families. *Journal of Marriage and the Family*, 52, 636-642.

Darling, N., and Steinberg, L. 1993. Parenting style as context: An integrative model. *Psychological Bulletin*, 113, 487-496.

Darling, R. B. 1987. The economic and psychosocial consequences of disability: Family-society relationships. *Marriage and Family Review*, 11, 45-61.

Da Vanzo, J., and Goldscheider, F. K. 1990. Coming home again: Returns to the parental home of young adults. *Population Studies*, 44, 241-255.

Davidson, R. J. 1992. Emotion and affective style: Hemispheric substrates. *Psychological Science*, 3, 39-43.

Davies, K., and Read, A. P. 1991. *Molecular basis of inherited disease*, 2nd ed. Oxford: Oxford University Press.

Dawson, D. A. 1991. Family structure and children's health and well-being: Data from the 1988 National Health Interview Survey on Child Health. *Journal of Marriage and the Family*, 53, 573-584.

Day, R. 1992. The transition to first intercourse among racially and culturally diverse youth. *Journal of Marriage and the Family*, 54, 749-762.

DeBaryshe, B. D., Patterson, G. R., and Capaldi, D. M. 1993. A performance model for academic achievement in early adolescent boys. *Developmental Psychology*, 29, 795-804.

DeFries, J. C., Plomin, R., and Fulker, D. W. 1994. *Nature and nurture during middle childhood*. Cambridge, MA: Blackwell.

Demo, D. H. 1992. Parent-child relations: Assessing recent changes. *Journal of Marriage and the Family*, 54, 104-117.

Demo, D. H. 1993. The relentless search for effects of divorce: Forging new trails or tumbling down the beaten path? *Journal of Marriage and the Family*, 55, 42-45.

Demos, J. 1971. Developmental perspectives on the history of childhood. *The Journal of Interdisciplinary History*, 2, 315-327.

Depue, R. A., and Monroe, S. M. 1986. Conceptualization and measurement of human disorder in life stress research: The problem of chronic disturbance. *Psychological Bulletin*, 99, 36-51.

de Vries, M. W. 1987. Cry babies, culture, and catastrophe: Infant temperament among the Masai. In N. Scheper-Hughes (Ed.), *Child survival* (pp. 165-186). Dordrecht: D. Reidel Publishing.

Diaz, R. M., and Berndt, T. J. 1982. Children's knowledge of a best friend: Fact or fancy? *Developmental Psychology*, 18, 787-794.

DiLalla, L. J., and Gottesman, I. I. 1989. Heterogeneity of causes for delinquency and criminality: Lifespan perspectives. *Development and Psychopathology*, 1, 339-349.

DiLalla, L. J., and Gottesman, I. I. 1991. Biological and genetic contributors to violence–Widom's untold tale. *Psychological Bulletin*, 109, 125-129.

Dilworth-Anderson, P., Burton, L., and Johnson, L. 1993. Reframing theories for understanding race, ethnicity and families. In P. G. Boss et al. (Eds.), *Sourcebook of family theories and methods: A contextual approach* (pp. 627-665). New York: Plenum.

Dilworth-Anderson, P., Burton, L. M., and Turner, W. L. 1993. The importance of values in the study of culturally diverse families. *Family Relations*, 42, 238-242.

Dishion, T. J., and Andrews, D. W. 1995. Preventing escalation in problem behaviors with high-risk young adolescents: Immediate and 1-year outcomes. *Journal of Consulting and Clinical Psychology*, 63, 538-548.

Dishion, T. J., Andrews, D. W., and Crosby, L. 1995. Adolescent boys and their friends in early adolescence: I. Relationship characteristics, quality, and interactional process. *Child Development*, 66, 139-151.

Dix, T. 1991. The affective organization of parenting: Adaptive and maladaptive processes. *Psychological Bulletin*, 110, 3-25.

Dix, T., and Lochman, J. 1990. Social cognition and negative reactions to children: A comparison of mothers of aggressive and nonagressive boys. *Journal of Social and Clinical Psychology*, 9, 418-438.

Dodge, K. A. 1990a. Developmental psychopathology in children of depressed mothers. *Developmental Psychology*, 26, 3-6.

Dodge, K. A. 1990b. Nature versus nurture in childhood conduct disorder: It is time to ask a different question. *Developmental Psychology*, 26, 698-901.

Dodge, K. A., and Frame, C. L. 1982. Social cognitive biases and deficits in aggressive boys. *Child Development*, 53, 620-635.

Dodge, K. A., Bates, J. E., and Pettit, G. S. 1990. Mechanisms in the cycle of violence. *Science*, 250, 1678-1683.

Doherty, W. J., and Needle, R. H. 1991. Psychological adjustment and substance use among adolescents before and after a parental divorce. *Child Development*, 62, 328-337.

Donnelly, D., and Finkelhor, D. 1992. Does equality in custody arrangements improve the parent-child relationship? *Journal of Marriage and the Family*, 54, 837-845.

Donzelot, J. 1979. *The policing of families*. New York: Random House.

Doris, J. L. (Ed.). 1991. *The suggestibility of children's recollections*. Washington, DC: American Psychological Association.

Dornbusch, S. M., Ritter, L. P., and Steinberg, L. 1991. Community influences on the relation of family statuses to adolescent school performance: Differences between African Americans and non-Hispanic whites. *American Journal of Education*, 38, 543-567.

Dornbusch, S. M., Carlsmith, J., Bushwall, S., Ritter, P., Leiderman, P., Hastorf, A., and Gross, R. 1985. Single parents, extended household and the control of adolescents. *Child Development*, 56, 326-341.

Dornbusch, S. M., Ritter, P. L., Leiderman, P. H., Roberts, D. F., and Fraleigh, M. J. 1987. The relation of parenting style to adolescent school performance. *Child Development*, 58, 1244-1257.

Downey, D. B., and Powell, B. 1993. Do children in single-parent households fare better living with same-sex parents? *Journal of Marriage and the Family*, 55, 55-71.

Downey, G., and Coyne, J. C. 1990. Children of depressed parents: An integrative review. *Psychological Bulletin*, 108, 50-76.

Downs, W. R., Miller, B. A., Testa, M., and Panek, D. 1992. Long-term effects of parent-to-child violence for women. *Journal of Interpersonal Violence*, 7, 365-382.

Dubois, D., et al. 1992. A prospective study of life stress, social support, and adaptation in early adolescence. *Child Development*, 63, 542-557.

Dubow, E. F., and Luster, T. 1990. Adjustment of children born to teenage mothers: The contribution of risk and protective factors. *Journal of Marriage and the Family*, 52, 393-403.

Dubow, E. F., and Tisak, J. 1989. The relation between stressful life events and adjustment in elementary school children: The role of social support and social problem-solving skills. *Child Development*, 60, 1412-1423.

Dubow, E., Tisak, J., Causey, D., Hryshko, A., and Reid, G. 1991. A two-year longitudinal study of stressful life events, social support, and social problem solving skills: Contributions to children's behavioral and academic adjustment. *Child Development*, 62, 583-599.

Dumas, J. E. 1989. Treating antisocial behavior in children: Child and family approaches. *Clinical Psychology Review*, 9, 197-222.

Duncan, G. J. 1988. The volatility of family income over the life course. In P. B. Baltes, D. L. Featherman, and R. M. Lerner (Eds.), *Life-span development and behavior*, Vol. 9 (pp. 317-358). Hillsdale, NJ: Lawrence Erlbaum.

Duncan, G. J. 1991. The economic environment of childhood. In A. C. Huston (Ed.), *Children in poverty, child development and public policy* (pp. 23-50). Cambridge, UK: Cambridge University Press.

Duncan, G. J. 1994. Families and neighbors as sources of disadvantage in the schooling decisions of white and black adolescents. *American Journal of Education*, 103, 20-53.

Duncan, G. J., and Hoffman, S. D. 1985. Economic consequences of marital instability. In M. David and T. Smeeding (Eds.), *Horizontal equity, uncertainty and well-being* (pp. 427-470). Chicago: University of Chicago Press.

Duncan, G. J., and Yeung, W.-J. J. 1995. Extent and consequences of welfare dependence among America's children. *Children and Youth Services Review*, 17, 159-186.

Duncan, G. J., Brooks-Gunn, J., and Klebanov, P. K. 1994. Economic deprivation and early childhood development. *Child Development*, 65, 296-318.

Duncan, G. J., Hill, M. S., and Hoffman, S. D. 1988. Welfare dependence within and across generations. *Science*, 239, January 29, 467-471.

Duncan, G. J., Smeeding, T., and Rodgers, W. 1991. *Whither the middle class: A dynamic view.* Ann Arbor, MI: Survey Research Center, University of Michigan.

Dunlap, E. 1992. The impact of drugs on family life and kin networks in the inner-city African-American single-parent household. In A. V. Harrell and G. E. Peterson (Eds.), *Drugs, crime, and social isolation* (pp. 181-208). Washington, DC: The Urban Institute Press.

Dunn, J. 1994. Temperament, siblings, and the development of relationships. In W. B. Carey and S. C. McDevitt (Eds.), *Prevention and early intervention* (pp. 50-58). New York: Bruner/Mazel.

Dunn, J., and Kendrick, C. 1982. *Siblings: Love, envy and understanding.* Cambridge, MA: Harvard University Press.

Dunn, J., and McGuire, S. 1994. Young children's nonshared experiences: A summary of studies in Cambridge and Colorado. In E. M. Hetherington, D. Reiss, and R. Plomin (Eds.), *Separate social worlds of siblings* (pp. 111-128). Hillsdale, NJ: Lawrence Erlbaum.

Dunn, J., and Plomin, R. 1990. *Separate lives: Why siblings are so different.* New York: Basic Books.

Dunn, J., and Stocker, C. 1989. The significance of differences in siblings' experiences within the family. In K. Kreppner and R. Lerner (Eds.), *Family systems and life-span development* (pp. 289-301). Hillsdale, NJ: Lawrence Erlbaum.

Dunn, J., Kendrick, C., and McNamee, R. 1981. The reaction of first born children to the birth of a sibling. *Journal of Child Psychology and Psychiatry,* 22, 1-18.

Dunn, J., Plomin, R., and Daniels, D. 1986. Consistency and change in mothers' behavior to two-year-old siblings. *Child Development,* 57, 348-356.

Dunn, J., Stocker, C., and Plomin, R. 1990. Nonshared experiences within the family: Correlates of behavioral problems in middle childhood. *Development and Psychopathology,* 2, 113-126.

Dunn, J., Slomkowski, C., Beardsall, L., and Rende, R. 1994. Adjustment in middle childhood and early adolescence: Links with earlier and contemporary sibling relationships. *Journal of Child Psychology and Psychiatry,* 35, 491-504.

Dupont, A. 1980. A study concerning the time-related and other burdens when severely handicapped children are reared at home. *Acta Psychiatrica Scandinavica,* 62, Supplement, 205, 249-257.

Duran-Aydintug, C., and Ihinger-Tallman, M. 1995. Law and stepfamilies. *Marriage and Family Review,* 21, 169-192.

Dwyer, J. W., Lee, G. R., and Jankowski, T. B. 1994. Reciprocity, elder satisfaction, and caregiver stress and burden: The exchange of aid in the family caregiving relationship. *Journal of Marriage and the Family*, 56, 35-43.

Eagles, J. M., Craig, A., Rawlinson, F., Restall, D. B., Beattie, J. A. G., and Besson, J. A. O. 1987. The psychological well-being of supporters of the demented elderly. *British Journal of Psychiatry*, 150, 293-298.

Earls, F. 1994. Oppositional-defiant and conduct disorders. In M. Rutter, E. Taylor, and L. Hersov (Eds.), *Child and adolescent psychiatry*, 3rd ed. (pp. 308-329). Oxford: Blackwell.

Earls, F., Reich, W., Jung, K., and Cloninger, R. 1988. Psychopathology in children of alcoholic and anti-social parents. *Alcoholism and Experimental Research*, 12, 481-487.

East, P. L., and Rook, K. S. 1992. Compensatory patterns of support among children's peer relationships: A test using school friends, non-school friends, and siblings. *Developmental Psychology*, 28, 163-172.

East, P. L., Felice, M. E., and Morgan, M. C. 1993. Sisters' and girlfriends' sexual and childbearing behavior: Effects on early adolescent girls' sexual outcomes. *Journal of Marriage and the Family*, 55, 953-963.

Easterbrook, M. A., and Emde, R. N. 1988. Marital and parent-child relationships: The role of affect in the family system. In R. A. Hinde and J. S. Hinde (Eds.), *Relationships within families: Mutual influences* (pp. 83-103). New York: Oxford University Press.

Eaves, L. J., Eysenck, H. J., and Martin, N. G. 1989. *Genes, culture, and personality: An empirical approach*. San Diego, CA: Academic Press.

Eaves, L. J., Long, J., and Heath, A. C. 1986. A theory of developmental change in quantitative phenotypes applied to cognitive development. *Behavior Genetics*, 16, 143-162.

Eccles, J. S., and Hoffman, L. W. 1984. Sex roles, socialization, and occupational behavior. In H. W. Stevenson and A. E. Siegel (Eds.), *Child development research and social policy* (pp. 367-420). Chicago: University of Chicago Press.

Eccles, J. S., and Midgley, C. 1990. Changes in academic motivation and self-perception during early adolescence. In R. Montemayor, G. R. Adams, and T. P. Gullotta (Eds.), *From childhood to adolescence* (pp. 134-155). Newbury Park, CA: Sage.

Eckenrode, J., Laird, M., and Doris, J. 1993. School performance and disciplinary problems among abused and neglected children. *Developmental Psychology*, 29, 53-62.

Edelbrock, C. et al. 1995. A twin study of competence and problem behavior in childhood and early adolescence. *Journal of Child Psychology and Psychiatry*, 36, 775-785.

Eder, D. 1985. The cycle of popularity: Interpersonal relations among female adolescents. *Sociology of Education*, 58, 154-165.

Eder, D. 1991. The role of teasing in adolescent peer group culture. *Sociological Studies of Child Development*, 4, 181-197.

Edwin, J. C. G., et al. 1995. A twin-singleton comparison of problem behavior in 2-3-year-olds. *Journal of Child Psychology and Psychiatry*, 36, 449-458.

Egeland, B., and Hiester, M. 1995. The long-term consequences of infant day-care and mother-infant attachment. *Child Development*, 66, 474-485.

Egeland, B., Jacobvitz, D., and Papatola, K. 1987. Intergenerational continuity of abuse. In R. J. Gelles and J. B. Lancaster (Eds.), *Child abuse and neglect: Biosocial dimensions* (pp. 255-276). New York: Aldine de Gruyter.

Egeland, B., Jacobvitz, D., and Sroufe, L. A. 1988. Breaking the cycle of abuse. *Child Development*, 59, 1080-1088.

Eggebeen, D. J., and Hogan, D. P. 1990. Giving between generations in American families. *Human Nature*, 1, 211-232.

Eggebeen, D. J., Crockett, L. J., and Hawkins, A. J. 1990. Patterns of adult male coresidence among young children of adolescent mothers. *Family Planning Perspectives*, 22, 219-223.

Elder, G. H., Jr. 1974. *Children of the Great Depression: Social change in life experience*. Chicago: University of Chicago Press.

Elder, G. H., Jr. 1979. Historical change in life patterns and personality. In P. B. Baltes and O. G. Brim (Eds.), *Lifespan development and behavior*, vol. 2 (pp. 117-159). New York: Academic Press.

Elder, G. H., Jr. 1985. Perspectives on the life course. In G. H. Elder, Jr. (Ed.), *Life course dynamics* (pp. 23-49). Ithaca: Cornell University.

Elder, G. H., Jr. 1993. The life course paradigm and social change: Historical and developmental perspectives. In P. Moen, G. H. Elder, Jr., and K. Luscher (Eds.), *Perspectives on the ecology of human development* (pp. 101-140). Washington, DC: American Psychological Association.

Elder, G. H., Jr. 1995. The life course paradigm and social change: Historical and developmental perspectives. In P. Moen, G. H. Elder, Jr., and K. Luscher (Eds.), *Perspectives on the ecology of human development* (pp. 101-140). Washington, DC: American Psychological Association.

Elder, G. H., Jr., and Caspi, A. 1988. Economic stress in lives: Developmental perspectives. *Journal of Social Issues*, 44, 25-45.

Elder, G. H., Jr., Caspi, A., and Burton, L. M. 1988. Adolescent transition in developmental perspective: Sociological and historical insights. In M. R. Gunnar and W. A. Collins (Eds.), *Development during the transition to adolescence* (pp. 151-180). Hillsdale, NJ: Lawrence Erlbaum.

Elder, G. H., Jr., Caspi, A., and Nguyen, T. V. 1994. Resourceful and vulnerable children: Family influences in stressful times. In R. K. Silbereisen and K. Eyferth (Eds.), *Development in context: Integrative perspectives on youth development.* New York: Springer-Verlag.

Elder, G. H., Jr., Foster, E. M., and Ardelt, M. 1994. Children in the household economy. In R. D. Conger and G. H. Elder, Jr. (Eds.), *Families in troubled times* (pp. 127-146). New York: Aldine de Gruyter.

Elder, G. H., Jr., Modell, J., and Parke, R. D. 1993a. Studying children in a changing world. In G. H. Elder, Jr., J. Modell, and R. D. Parke (Eds.), *Children in time and place: Developmental and historical insights* (pp. 3-22). Cambridge: Cambridge University Press.

Elder, G. H., Jr., Modell, J., and Parke, R. D. 1993b. Epilogue: An emerging framework for dialogue between history and developmental psychology. In G. H. Elder, Jr., J. Modell, and R. D. Parke (Eds.), *Children in time and place: Developmental and historical insights* (pp. 241-249). Cambridge: Cambridge University Press.

Elder, G. H., Jr., Eccles, J. S., Ardelt, M., and Lord, S. 1995. Inner-city parents under economic pressure: Perspectives on the strategies of parenting. *Journal of Marriage and the Family,* 57, 771-784.

Elder, G. H., Jr., et al. 1992. Families under economic pressure. *Journal of Family Issues,* 13, 5-37.

Elias, M. J. 1989. Schools as a source of stress to children: An analysis of causal and ameliorative influences. *Journal of School Psychology,* 27, 393-407.

Elliott, B. J., and Richards, M. P. M. 1991. Children and divorce: Educational performance and behavior before and after parental separation. *International Journal of Law and the Family,* 5, 258-276.

Elliott, D. S., Huizinga, D., and Ageton, S. S. 1985. *Explaining delinquency and drug use.* Beverly Hills, CA: Sage.

Elshtain, J. B. 1990. The family and civic life. In D. Blankenhorn et al. (Eds.), *Rebuilding the nest: A new commitment to the American family* (pp. 119-132). Milwaukee: Family Service America.

Ellwood, D. T. 1988. *Poor support: Poverty in the American family.* New York: Basic Books.

Ellwood, D. T. 1989. The origins of "dependency": Choices, confidence or culture? *Focus,* 12, 6-13.

Elster, E. B., and Lamb, M. E. (Eds.). 1986. *Adolescent fatherhood.* Hillsdale, NJ: Lawrence Erlbaum.

Engelbert, A. 1994. Worlds of childhood: Differentiated but different. In J. Qvortrup et al. (Eds.), *Childhood matters* (pp. 285-298). Aldershot, UK: Avebury.

Enos, D. M., and Handal, P. J. 1986. The relation of parental marital status and perceived family conflict to adjustment in white adolescents. *Journal of Counseling and Clinical Psychology*, 54, 820-824.

Ensminger, M. E., and Slusarcick, A. L. 1992. Paths to high school graduation or dropout: A longitudinal study of a first grade cohort. *Sociology of Education*, 65, 95-113.

Ensminger, M. E., Kellam, S. G., and Rubin, B. R. 1983. School and family origins of delinquency: Comparisons by sex. In K. T. Van Dusen and S. A. Mednick (Eds.), *Prospective studies of crime and delinqency* (pp. 73-97). Boston: Kluwer-Nijhoff.

Entwisle, D. R., and Alexander, K. L. 1992. Summer setback: Race, poverty, school composition, and mathematical achievement in the first two years of school. *American Sociological Review*, 57, 72-84.

Entwisle, D. R., and Alexander, K. L. 1995. A parent's economic shadow: Family structure versus family resources as influences on early school achievement. *Journal of Marriage and the Family*, 57, 399-409.

Epstein, J. L. 1987. Toward a theory of family-school connections: Teacher practices and parent involvement across the school years. In K. Hurrelmann, F. Kaufmann, and F. Losel (Eds.), *Potential and contraints*. New York: de Gruyter.

Erel, O., and Burman, B. 1995. Interrelatedness of marital relations and parent-child relations: A meta-analytic review. *Psychological Bulletin*, 118, 108-132.

Eron, L. D., and Huesmann, L. R. 1990. The stability of aggressive behavior—Even unto the third generation. In M. Lewis and S. M. Miller (Eds.), *Handbook of developmental psychopathology* (pp. 147-156). New York: Plenum Press.

Eron, L. D., Gentry, J. H., and Schlegel, P. (Eds.) 1994. *Reason to hope: A psychosocial perspective on violence and youth*. Washington, DC: American Psychological Association.

Escalona, S. 1982. Babies at double hazard: Early development of infants at biological and social risk. *Pediatrics*, 70, 670-676.

Esser, G., Schmidt, M., and Woerner, W. 1990. Epidemiology and course of psychiatric disorder in school-age children—results of a longitudinal study. *Journal of Child Psychology and Psychiatry*, 31, 243-263.

Etzioni, A. (Ed). 1994. *Rights and the common good: The communitarian perspective*. New York: St. Martin's.

Evans, G. W., Hygge, S., and Bullinger, M. 1995. Chronic noise and psychological stress. *Psychological Science*, 6, 333-338.

Fabrega, H., Jr., Ulrich, R., and Loeber, R. 1996. Adolescent psychopathology as a function of informant and risk status. *Journal of Nervous and Mental Disease*, 184, 27-34.

Falconer, D. S. 1989. *Introduction to quantitative genetics*, 3rd ed. New York: Wiley.

Faller, K. C. 1990. *Understanding child sexual maltreatment*. Newbury Park, CA: Sage.

Falloon, I. R. H., and Pederson, J. 1985. Family management in the prevention of morbidity of schizophrenia: The adjustment of the family unit. *British Journal of Psychiatry*, 147, 156-163.

Farrington, D. P. 1978. Family background of aggressive youths. In L. Hersov, M. Berger, and D. Shaffer (Eds.), *Aggressive and anti-social behavior in childhood and adolescence*. New York: Pergamon Press.

Farrington, D. P. 1987. Early precursors of frequent offending. In J. Q. Wilson and G. C. Loury (Eds.), *From children to citizens: Families, schools, and delinquency prevention* (pp. 21-50). New York: Springer-Verlag.

Farrington, D. P. 1991. Childhood aggression and adult violence: Early precursors and later life outcomes. In D. Pepler and H. Rubin (Eds.), *The development and treatment of childhood aggression* (pp. 5-29). Hillsdale, NY: Lawrence Erlbaum.

Farrington, D. P. 1993. Understanding and preventing bullying. In M. Tonry (Ed.), *Crime and justice: A review of research*. Vol. 17, Chicago: University of Chicago Press.

Farrington, D. P., Gallagher, B., Morley, L. St. Ledger, R. J., and West, D. J. 1988. Are there any successful men from criminogenic backgrounds? *Psychiatry*, 51, 116-130.

Fasick, F. A. 1984. Parents, peers, youth culture and autonomy in adolescence. *Adolescence*, 19, 143-157.

Fauber, R., Forehand, R., Thomas, A., and Wierson, M. 1990. A mediational model of the impact of marital conflict on adolescent adjustment in intact and divorced families: The role of disrupted parenting. *Child Development*, 61, 1112-1123.

Featherman, D. L., Spenner, K. I., and Tsunematsu, N. 1988. Class and socialization of children: Constancy, change, or irrelevance? In E. M. Hetherington, R. M. Lerner, and M. Perlmutter (Eds.), *Child development in life-span perspective* (pp. 67-90). Hillsdale, NJ: Lawrence Erlbaum.

Federal Bureau of Investigation. 1993. *Uniform crime reports for the United States: Crime in the United States*. Washington, DC: U.S. Government Printing Office.

Fehrman, P. G., Keith, T. Z., and Reimer, T. M. 1987. Home influence on school learning: Direct and indirect effects of parental involvement on high school grades. *Journal of Educational Research*, 80, 330-337.

Feldman, S. S., and Elliott, G. R. (Eds.). 1990. *At the threshold: The developing adolescent*. Cambridge: Harvard University Press.

Feldman, S. S., and Rosenthal, D. A. 1994. Culture makes a difference . . . or does it? A comparison of adolescents in Hong Kong, Australia, and the United States. In R. K. Silbereisen and E. Todt (Eds.), *Adolescence in context* (pp. 99-113). New York: Springer-Verlag.

Fergusson, D. M., Horwood, L. J., and Lynskey, M. 1994. The childhoods of multiple problem adolescents: A 15-year longitudinal study. *Journal of Child Psychology and Psychiatry*, 35, 1123-1140.

Fergusson, D. M., Horwood, L. J., and Lynskey, M. T. 1995. Maternal depressive symptoms and depressive symptoms in adolescents. *Journal of Child Psychology and Psychiatry*, 36, 1161-1178.

Fergusson, D. M., Lynskey, M., and Horwood, L. J. 1995. The adolescent outcomes of adoption: A 16-year longitudinal study. *Journal of Child Psychology and Psychiatry*, 36, 597-615.

Fincham, F. D. 1994. Understanding the association between marital conflict and child adjustment: Overview. *Journal of Family Psychology*, 8, 123-127.

Fincham, F. D., Beach, S. R. H., Moore, T., and Diener, C. 1994. The professional response to child sexual abuse. Whose interests are served? *Family Relations*, 43, 244-254.

Fine, G. A., Mortimer, J. T., and Roberts, D. F. 1990. Leisure, work, and the mass media. In S. S. Feldman and G. R. Elliott (Eds.), *At the threshold: The developing adolescent* (pp. 225-252). Cambridge, MA: Harvard University Press.

Fine, M. 1991. *Framing dropouts: Notes on the politics of an urban public high school*. Albany: State University of New York Press.

Fine, M. A., and Fine, D. R. 1992. Recent changes in law affecting stepfamilies: Suggestions for legal reform. *Family Relations*, 41, 334-340.

Fine, M. A., McKenry, P. C., Donnelly, B. W., and Voydanoff, P. 1992. Perceived adjustment of parents and children: Variations by family structure, race, and gender. *Journal of Marriage and the Family*, 54, 118-127.

Fingerhut, L. A., Ingram, D. D., and Feldman, J. J. 1992. Firearm and nonfirearm homicide among persons 15 through 19 years of age: Differences by level of urbanization, United States, 1979 through 1989. *Journal of the American Medical Association*, 267, 3048-3053.

Finkelhor, D., and Dziuba-Leatherman, J. 1994. Victimization of children. *American Psychologist*, 49, 173-183.

Finnie, R. 1993. Women, men, and the economic consequences of divorce: Evidence from Canadian longitudinal data. *Canadian Review of Sociology and Anthropology*, 30, 205-241.

Fischer, J. L., and Wampler, R. S. 1994. Abusive drinking in young adults: Personality type and family role as moderators of family-of-origin influences. *Journal of Marriage and the Family*, 56, 469-479.

Fishbein, D. H. 1990. Biological perspectives in criminology. *Criminology*, 28, 27-57.

Fitzgerald, H. E., et al. 1993. Predictors of behavior problems in three-year-old sons of alcoholics: Early evidence for the onset of risk. *Child Development*, 64, 110-123.

Fleming, A. S., Ruble, D. N., Flett, G. L., and Shaul, D. L. 1988. Postpartum adjustment in first-time mothers: Relations between mood, maternal attitudes, and mother-infant interaction. *Developmental Psychology*, 24, 71-81.

Fletcher, A. C., Darling, N. E., Dornbusch, S. M., and Steinberg, L. 1995. The company they keep: Relation of adolescents' adjustment and behavior to their friends' perceptions of authoritative parenting in the social network. *Developmental Psychology*, 31, 300-310.

Fluitt, M. S., and Paradise, L. V. 1991. The relationship of current family structure to young adults' perceptions of stepparents. *Journal of Divorce and Remarriage*, 15, 159-174.

Folk, K. F., and Yi, Y. 1994. Piecing together child care with multiple arrangements: Crazy quilt or preferred pattern of employed parents of preschool children? *Journal of Marriage and the Family*, 56, 669-680.

Forcier, K. I. 1990. Management and care of pregnant psychiatric patients. *Journal of Psychosocial Nursing*, 28, 11-16.

Forehand, R., McCombs, A., and Brody, G. H. 1987. The relationship between parental depressive mood states and child functioning. *Advances in Behaviour Research and Therapy*, 9, 1-20.

Forehand, R., Neighbors, B., Devine, D., and Armistead, L. 1994. Interparental conflict and parental divorce. The individual, relative, and interactive effects on adolescents across four years. *Family Relations*, 43, 387-393.

Forehand, R., McCombs, A., Long, N., Brody, G., and Fauber, R. 1988. Early adolescent adjustment to recent parental divorce: The role of interparental conflict and adolescent sex as mediating variables. *Journal of Consulting and Clinical Psychology*, 56, 624-627.

Forgatch, M. S. 1989. Patterns and outcomes in family problem solving: The disrupting effect of negative emotion. *Journal of Marriage and the Family*, 51, 115-124.

Frank, S., Laman, M., and Avery, C. 1988. Young adults' perceptions of their relationship with their parents: Individual differences in connectedness, competence, and emotional autonomy. *Developmental Psychology*, 24, 729-737.

Franklin, D. L., Smith, S. E., McMiller, W. E. P. 1995. Correlates of marital status among African American mothers in Chicago neighborhoods of concentrated poverty. *Journal of Marriage and the Family*, 57, 141-152.

Freeman, J. 1995. Annotation: Recent studies of giftedness in children. *Journal of Child Psychology and Psychiatry*, 36, 531-547.

Freedman, V. A. 1991. Intergenerational transfers: A question of perspectives. *The Gerontologist*, 31, 640-647.

Freud, A. 1969. Adolescence as a developmental disturbance. In G. Caplan and S. Lebovici (Eds.), *Adolescence: Psychological perspectives*. New York: Basic Books.

Frick, P. J., Lahey, B. B., Loeber, R., Stouthamer-Lober, M., Christ, A. G., and Hanson, K. 1992. Familial risk factors to oppositional defiant disorder and conduct disorder: Parental psychopathology and maternal parenting. *Journal of Consulting and Clinical Psychology*, 60, 49-55.

Friedman, H. S., Tucker, J. S., Schwartz, J. E., Tomlinson-Keasey, C., Martin, L. R., Wingard, D. L., and Criqui, M. H. 1995. Psychological and behavioral predictors of longevity. The aging and death of the "Termites." *American Psychologist*, 50, 69-78.

Friedrich-Cofer, L., and Huston, A. C. 1986. Television violence and aggression: The debate continues. *Psychological Bulletin*, 15, 1-20.

Fromm-Reichmann, F. 1948. Notes on the development of treatment of schizophrenics by psychoanalytic psychotherapy. *Psychiatry*, 11, 263-273.

Fuchs, V. R. 1990. Are Americans underinvesting in children? In D. Blankenhorn et al. (Eds.), *Rebuilding the nest: A new commitment to the American family* (pp. 53-72). Milwaukee: Family Service America.

Fuchs, V., and Reklis, D. 1992. America's children: Economic perspectives and policy options. *Science*, 255, 41-46.

Fuhrman, T., and Holmbeck, G. N. 1995. A contextual-moderator analysis of emotional autonomy and adjustment in adolescence. *Child Development*, 66, 793-811.

Funder, D. C., Block, J. H., and Block, J. 1983. Delay of gratification: Some longitudinal personality correlates. *Journal of Personality and Social Psychology*, 44, 1198-1213.

Furman, W., and Buhrmester, D. 1992. Age and sex differences in perceptions of networks of personal relationships. *Child Development*, 63, 103-115.

Furman, W., and Robbins, P. 1985. What's the point? Issues in the selection of treatment objectives. In B. Schneider, K. H. Rubin, and J. T. Ledingham (Eds.), *Children's peer relations: Issues in assessment and intervention* (pp. 41-50). New York: Springer.

Furstenberg, F. F., Jr. 1991. As the pendulum swings: Teenage childbearing and social concern. *Family Relations*, 40, 127-138.

Furstenberg, F. F., Jr. 1993. How families manage risk and opportunity in dangerous neighborhoods. In W. J. Wilson (Ed.), *Sociology and the public agenda* (pp. 231-258). Newbury Park, CA: Sage.

Furstenberg, F. F., Jr., and Cherlin, A. 1991. *Divided families. What happens to children when parents part?* Cambridge, MA: Harvard University Press.

Furstenberg, F. F., Jr., and Hughes, M. E. 1995. Social capital and successful development among at-risk youth. *Journal of Marriage and the Family*, 57, 580-592.

Furstenberg, F. F., Jr., Brooks-Gunn, J., and Chase-Lansdale, P. L. 1987. Teenaged pregnancy and childbearing. *American Psychologist*, 44, 313-320.

Furstenberg, F. F., Jr., Brooks-Gunn, J., and Morgan, S. P. 1987. *Adolescent mothers in later life.* New York: Cambridge University Press.

Gable, S., Belsky, J., and Crnic, K. 1992. Marriage, parenting, and child development: Progress and prospects. *Journal of Family Psychology*, 5, 276-294.

Gable, S., Crnic, K., and Belsky, J. 1994. Coparenting within the family system. Influences on children's development. *Family Relations*, 43, 380-386.

Galambos, N. L., Sears, H. A., Almeida, D. M., and Kolaric, G. C. 1995. Parents' work overload and problem behavior in young adolescents. *Journal of Research on Adolescence*, 5, 201-223.

Galinsky, E., Howes, C., Kontos, S., and Shinn, M. 1994. *The study of children in family child care and relative care.* New York: Family and Work Institute.

Gallagher, J. 1991. Educational reform, values, and gifted students. *Gifted Child Quarterly*, 35, 12-19.

Galland, O. 1991. Sociologie de la jeunesse. Paris: Armand Collin.

Ganong, L. H., and Coleman, M. 1983. Stepparent: A pejorative term? *Psychology Reports*, 52, 919-922.

Ganong, L. H., and Coleman, M. 1994. *Remarried family relationships.* Thousand Oaks, CA: Sage.

Ganong, L. H., Coleman, M., and Demo, D. H. 1995. Issues in training family scientists. *Family Relations*, 44, 501-508.

Garbarino, J. 1989. Troubled youth, troubled families: The dynamics of adolescent maltreatment. In D. Cicchetti and V. Carlson (Eds.), *Child maltreatment* (pp. 685-706). Cambridge: Cambridge University Press.

Garbarino, J., and Kostelny, K. 1992. Child maltreatment as a community problem. *Child Abuse & Neglect*, 16, 455-464.

Garbarino, J., and Plantz, M. C. 1986. Child abuse and juvenile delinquency. In J. Garbarino, C. J. Schellenback, and J. M. Sebes (Eds.), *Troubled youth, troubled families* (pp. 27-40). New York: Aldine.

Garbarino, J., Kostelny, K., and Dubrow, N. 1991. *No place to be a child: Growing up in a war zone.* Lexington, MA: Lexington Books.

Garbarino, J., Dubrow, N., Kostelny, K., and Pardo, C. 1992. *Children in danger: Coping with the consequence of community violence.* San Francisco: Jossey-Bass.

Garmezy, N. 1983. Stressors of childhood. In N. Garmezy and M. Rutter (Eds.), *Stress, coping, and development in children* (pp. 43-84). New York: Plenum.

Garmezy, N., and Masten, A. 1991. The protective role of competence indicators in children at risk. In E. M. Cummings, A. L. Greene, and K. K. Kanaker (Eds.), *Life-span developmental psychology: Perspectives on stress and coping* (pp. 151-176). Hillsdale, NJ: Lawrence Erlbaum.

Garmezy, N., and Masten, A. S. 1994. Chronic adversities. In M. Rutter, E. Taylor, and L. Hersov (Eds.), *Child and adolescent psychiatry*, 3rd ed. (pp. 191-208). Oxford: Blackwell.

Gartner, A., and Lipsky, D. K. 1987. Beyond special education: Toward a quality system for all students. *Harvard Educational Review*, 57, 367-395.

Gartner, R., and Piliavin, I. 1988. The aging offender and the aged offender. In P. B. Baltes, D. L. Featherman, and R. M. Lerner (Eds.), *Life-span development and behavior*, vol. 9 (pp. 289-316), Hillsdale, NJ: Lawrence Erlbaum.

Gately, D. W., and Schwebel, A. I. 1991. The challenge model of children's adjustment to parental divorce. *Journal of Family Psychology*, 5, 60-81.

Gath, A., and Gumley, D. 1986. Family background of children with Down's syndrome and of children with a similar degree of mental retardation. *British Journal of Psychiatry*, 149, 161-171.

Ge, X., Conger, R., Lorenz, F., and Simons, R. 1994. Parents' stress and adolescent depressive symptoms: Mediating processes. *Journal of Health and Social Behavior*, 35, 28-44.

Gecas, V., and Seff, M. A. 1990. Families and adolescents: A review of the 1980s. *Journal of Marriage and the Family*, 52, 941-958.

Gee, E. M., and Kimball, M. M. 1987. *Women and aging*. Toronto: Butterworths.

Gehring, T. M., Wentzel, K. R., Feldman, S. S., and Munson, J. 1990. Conflict in families of adolescents: The impact on cohesion and power structures. *Journal of Family Psychology*, 3, 290-309.

Geldman, S. S., and Rosenthal, D. A. 1994. Culture makes a difference . . . or does it? A comparison of adolescents in Hong Kong, Australia, and the United States. In R. K. Silbereisen and E. Todt (Eds.), *Adolescence in context* (pp. 99-113). New York: Springer-Verlag.

Geller, J., and Johnson, C. 1995. Predictors of mothers' responses to child noncompliance: Attributions and attitudes. *Journal of Clinical Child Psychology*, 24, 272-278.

General Household Survey. 1992. London, UK. OPCS, HMSO.

Gergen, K. J. 1973. Social psychology as history. *Journal of Presonality and Social Psychology*, 26, 309-320.

Gergen, K. J. 1985. The social constructionist movement in modern psychology. *American Psychologist*, 40, 266-275.

Gergen, K. J. 1992. Toward a postmodern psychology. In S. Kvale (Ed.), *Psychology and postmodernism* (pp. 1-16). Newbury Park, CA: Sage.

Gershon, E. S., Targum, S. D., Kessler, L. R., Mazure, C. M., and Bunney, W. E., Jr. 1977. Genetics studies and biologic strategies in affective disorders. *Progress in Medical Genetics*, 2, 103-164.

Gerstel, N., and Gallagher, S. K. 1993. Kinkeeping and distress: Gender, recipients of care, and work-family conflict. *Journal of Marriage and the Family*, 55, 598-607.

Ghodsian-Carpey, J., and Baker. L. A. 1987. Genetic and environmental influences on aggression in 4- and 7-year-old twins. *Aggressive Behavior*, 13, 173-186.

Gibbs, J. T., et al. (Eds.). 1988. *Young, black, and male in America: An endangered species*. Dover, MA: Auburn House.

Gibson, M. A., and Ogbu, J. V. (Eds.) 1991. *Minority status and schooling*. New York: Garland.

Giles-Sims, J., and Crosbie-Burnett, M. 1989. Adolescent power in stepfather families: A test of normative-resource theory. *Journal of Marriage and the Family*, 57, 1065-1078.

Gilgun, J. F. 1995. We shared something special: The moral discourse of incest perpetrators. *Journal of Marriage and the Family*, 57, 265-282.

Gilleard, C. J., Gilleard, E., and Whittig, J. E. 1992. Impact of psychogeriatric day hospital care on the patient's family. *British Journal of Psychiatry*, 161, 487-492.

Gilleard, C. J., Belford, H., Gilleard, E., Whittiek, J. E., and Gledhill, K.

1984. Emotional distress amongst the supporters of the elderly mentally infirm. *British Journal of Psychiatry*, 145, 172-177.

Giordano, P. C., Cernkovich, S. A., and DeMaris, A. 1993. The family and peer relations of black adolescents. *Journal of Marriage and the Family*, 55, 277-287.

Gjerde, P. F. 1986. The interpersonal structure of family interaction settings: Parent-adolescent relations in dyads and triads. *Developmental Psychology*, 22, 297-304.

Gold, D. T. 1989. Generational solidarity. *American Behavioral Scientist*, 33, 19-32.

Goldberg, L. R. 1993. The structure of phenotypic personality traits. *American Psychologist*, 48, 26-34.

Goldberg, W. A., and Easterbrook, M. A. 1984. Role of marital quality in toddler development. *Developmental Psychology*, 20, 504-514.

Goldscheider, F., and Goldscheider, C. 1987. Moving out and marriage: What do young adults expect? *American Sociological Review*, 52, 278-285.

Goldscheider, F., and Goldscheider, C. 1993a. *Leaving home before marriage*. Madison: University of Wisconsin.

Goldscheider, F., and Goldscheider, C. 1993b. Whose nest? A two-generational view of leaving home during the 1980s. *Journal of Marriage and the Family*, 55, 851-862.

Goldscheider, F. K., and Waite, L. 1991. *New families, no families? The transformation of the American home*. Berkeley: University of California Press.

Goldscheider, F. K., Thornton, A., and Young-DeMarco, L. 1993. A portrait of the nest-leaving process in early adulthood. *Demography*, 30, 683-699.

Goldsmith, H. H. 1989. Behavior-genetic approaches to temperament. In G. A. Kohnstamm, J. E. Bates, and M. K. Rothbart (Eds.), *Temperament in childhood* (pp. 111-132). New York: John Wiley.

Goldsmith, H. H. 1993. Nature-nurture issues in the behavioral genetics context: Overcoming barriers to communication. In R. Plomin and G. E. McClearn (Eds.), *Nature, nurture & psychology* (pp. 325-340). Washington, DC: American Psychological Association.

Goldsmith, H. H., Buss, A. H., Plomin, R., Rothbart, M. K., Thomas, A., Chess, S., Hinde, R. A., and McCall, R. B. 1987. Roundtable: What is temperament? Four approaches. *Child Development*, 58, 505-529.

Goldstein, H. S. 1984. Parental composition, supervision, and conduct problems in youth 12 to 17 years old. *Journal of the American Academy of Child Psychiatry*, 23, 679-684.

Goldstein, M. J., and Tuma, A. H. 1987. High-risk research. *Schizophrenia Bulletin*, 13, 369-531.

Goldstein, M. J., Talovic, S. A., Nvechterlein, K. H., Fogelson, D. L., Subotnik, K. L., and Asarnow, R. F. 1992. Family interaction versus individual psychopathology: Do they indicate the same processes in the families of schizophrenics? *British Journal of Psychiatry*, 161, 97-102.

Golombok, S., and Tasker, F. 1996. Do parents influence the sexual orientation of their children? Findings from a longitudinal study of lesbian mothers. *Developmental Psychology*, 32, 3-11.

Gomez-Schwartz, B., Horowitz, J. M., and Cardarelli, A. P. 1990. *Child sexual abuse: Initial effects*. Newbury Park, CA: Sage.

Good, T. L., Slavings, R. L., Harel, K. H., and Emerson, H. 1987. Student passivity: A study of question asking in K-12 classrooms. *Sociology of Education*, 60, 181-199.

Goodman, R. 1991. Growing together and growing apart: The nongenetic influences on children in the same family. In A. McGriffin and R. M. Murray (Eds.), *The new genetics of mental illness* (pp. 212-224). Oxford: Butterworth-Heinemann.

Goodman, R., and Stevenson, J. 1989. A twin study of hyperactivity II. The aetiological role of genes, family relationship and perinatal adversity. *Journal of Child Psychology and Psychiatry*, 30, 691-709.

Goodman, R., and Stevenson, J. 1991. Parental criticism and warmth toward unrecognized monozygotic twins. *Behavioral and Brain Sciences*, 14, 394-395.

Goodman, S. H., et al. 1993. Social and emotional competence in children of depressed mothers. *Child Development*, 64, 516-531.

Goodwin, M. H., and Goodwin, C. 1988. Children's arguing. In S. Phillips, S. Steele, and C. Tantz (Eds.), *Language, gender and sex in a comparative perspective* (pp. 200-248). New York: Cambridge University Press.

Goodyear, I. M., Kolvin, I., and Gatzanis, S. 1987. The impact of recent undesirable life events on psychiatric disorders in childhood and adolescence. *British Journal of Psychiatry*, 151, 179-184.

Goodyear, I. M., Cooper, P. J., Vize, C., and Ashby, L. 1993. Depression in 11 to 16 year old girls: The role of past parental psychopathology and exposure to recent life events. *Journal of Child Psychology and Psychiatry*, 34, 1103-1115.

Gordon, L. 1988. *Heroes of their own lives*. New York: Viking Penguin.

Gore, S., and Aseltine, R. H. Jr. 1995. Protective processes in adolescence: Matching stressors with social resources. *American Journal of Community Psychology*, 23, 301-327.

Gottesman, I. I. 1991. *Schizophrenia genesis. The origins of madness.* New York: W. H. Freeman.

Gottesman, I. I., and Bertelsen, A. 1989. Confirming unexpressed genotypes for schizophrenia: Risks in the offspring of Fischer's Danish identical and fraternal discordant twins. *Archives of General Psychiatry,* 46, 867-872.

Gottfredson, D. C., Gottfredson, G. D., and Hybl, L. G. 1993. Managing adolescent behavior: A multiyear, multischool study. *American Educational Research Journal,* 30, 179-215.

Gottfredson, M. R., and Hirschi, T. 1990. *A general theory of crime.* Stanford, CA: Stanford University Press.

Gottlieb, B. H. 1989. A contextual perspective on stress in family care of the elderly. *Canadian Psychology,* 30, 596-607.

Gottlieb, G. 1995. Some conceptual deficiencies in "developmental" behavior genetics. *Human Development,* 38, 131-141.

Gottlieb, L. N., and Mendelson, M. J. 1990. Parental support and firstborn girls' adaptation to the birth of a sibling. *Journal of Applied Developmental Psychology,* 11, 29-48.

Gottman, J. M., and Levenson, R. W. 1988. The social psychophysiology of marriage. In P. Noller and M. A. Fitzpatrick (Eds.), *Perspectives on marital interaction* (pp. 182-200). Philadelphia: Multilingual Matters.

Graber, J. A., Brooks-Gunn, J., and Warren, M. P. 1995. The antecedents of menarchal age: Heredity, family environment, and stressful life events. *Child Development,* 66, 346-359.

Graham, P., Rutter, M., and George, S. 1973. Temperamental characteristics as predictors of behavior disorders in children. *American Journal of Orthopsychiatry,* 43, 328-339.

Gramlich, E., Laren, D., and Sealand, N. 1992. Moving into and out of poor urban areas. *Journal of Policy Analysis and Management,* 11, 273-287.

Grasmick, H. S., Tittle, C. R., Bursik, R. J., Jr., and Arneklev, B. J. 1993. Testing the core empirical implications of Gottfredson and Hirschi's general theory of crime. *Journal of Research in Crime and Delinquency,* 30, 5-29.

Greenberg, J. S., and Becker, M. 1988. Aging parents as family resources. *The Gerontologist,* 28, 786-791.

Greenberg, J. S., et al. 1993. Mothers caring for an adult child with schizophrenia. *Family Relations,* 42, 205-211.

Greenberger, E., and O'Neil, R. 1990. Parents' concerns about their child's development: Implications for fathers' and mothers' well-being and attitudes toward work. *Journal of Marriage and the Family*, 52, 621-635.

Greenberger, E., and Steinberg, L. D. 1986. *When teenagers work: The psychological and social costs of adolescent employment.* New York: Basic Books.

Greenburg, J. S., Siltzer, M. M., and Greenlay, J. R. 1993. Aging parents of adults with disabilities: The gratifications and frustrations of later-life caregiving. *The Gerontologist*, 33, 542-549.

Greenstein, T. N. 1995. Are the "most advantaged" children truly disadvantaged by early maternal employment? Effects on child cognitive outcomes. *Journal of Family Issues*, 16, 149-169.

Griffin, L. W. 1994. Elder maltreatment among rural African-Americans. *Journal of Elder Abuse & Neglect*, 6, 1-27.

Grigsby, J. 1989. Adult children in the parental household: Who benefits? *Lifestyles*, 10, 293-309.

Gringlas, M., and Weinraub, M. 1995. The more things change. . . . Single parenting revisitsed. *Journal of Family Issues*, 16, 29-52.

Grotevant, H. D. 1979. Environmental influences on vocational interest development in adolescents from adoptive and biological families. *Child Development*, 50, 854-860.

Gruber-Baldini, A. L., Schaie, K. W., and Willis, S. L. 1995. Similarity in married couples: A longitudinal study of mental abilities and rigidity-flexibility. *Journal of Personality and Social Psychology*, 69, 191-203.

Grych, J. H., and Fincham, F. D. 1990. Marital conflict and children's adjustment: A cognitive-contextual framework. *Psychological Bulletin*, 108, 267-290.

Gubman, G. D., and Tessler, R. C. 1987. The impact of mental illness on families. *Journal of Family Issues*, 8, 226-245.

Guerra, N. G., Huesmann, L. R., Tolan, P. H., Van Acker, R., and Eron, L. D. 1995. Stressful events and individual beliefs as correlates of economic disadvantage and aggression among urban children. *Journal of Consulting and Clinical Psychology*, 63, 518-528.

Guerra, N. G., Tolan, P. H., and Hammond, W. R. 1994. Prevention and treatment of adolescent violence. In L. D. Eron, J. H. Gentry, and P. Schlegel (Eds.), *Reason to hope: A psychosocial perspective on violence and youth* (pp. 383-403). Washington, DC: American Psychological Association.

Hagestad, G. O. 1984. The continuous bond: A dynamic multigenerational perspective on parent-child relations between adults. In M. Perlmutter (Ed.), *Parent-child relations in child development* (pp. 129-158), 17, The Minnesota Symposium on Child Psychology.

Hagestad, G. O. 1986. Dimensions of time and the family. *American Behavior Scientist*, 29, 679-694.

Hagestad, G. O., Smyer, M. A., and Stierman, K. L. 1984. Parent-child relations in adulthood: The impact of divorce in middle age. In R. Cohen et al. (Eds.), *Parenthood: A psychodynamic perspective* (pp. 247-262). New York: Guilford.

Hahn, M. E., Hewitt, J. E., Henderson, N. D., and Benno, R. H. 1990. *Developmental behavior genetics: Neural, biochemical, and evolutionary approaches*. New York: Oxford University Press.

Halcombe, A., Wolery, M., and Katzenmeyer, J. 1995. Teaching preschoolers to avoid abduction by strangers: Evaluation of maintenance strategies. *Journal of Child and Family Studies*, 4, 177-191.

Hallinan, M. T., and Williams, R. A. 1989. Interracial friendship choices in secondary school. *American Sociological Review*, 54, 67-78.

Halverson, C. F., Jr. 1988. Remembering your parents: Reflections on the retrospective method. *Journal of Personality*, 56, 435-443.

Hammen, C. 1988. Self-cognition, stressful events, and the prediction of depression in children of depressed mothers. *Journal of Abnormal Child Psychology*, 16, 347-367.

Hammen, C. 1992a. The family-environmental context of depression: A perspective on children's risk. In D. Cicchetti and S. Toth (Eds.), *Rochester symposium on developmental psychopathology: Vol. 4. A developmental approach to affective disorders* (pp. 251-281). Rochester, NY: University of Rochester Press.

Hammen, C. 1992b. Cognitive, life stress, and interpersonal approaches to a developmental psychopathology model of depression. *Development and Psychopathology*, 4, 189-206.

Hansen, D. A. 1986. Family-school articulations: The effects of interaction rule mismatch. *American Educational Research Journal*, 23, 643-659.

Hanson, T. L. 1993. *Family structure, parental conflict, and child well-being*. Doctoral dissertation, Department of Sociology, Madison: University of Wisconsin.

Hardy, J. B., Duggan, A. K., Masnyk, K., and Pearson, C. 1989. Fathers of children born to young urban mothers. *Family Planning Perspective*, 21, 159-163.

Hareven, T. K. 1989. Historical changes in children's networks in the family and community. In D. Belle (Ed.), *Children's social networks and social supports* (pp. 15-36). New York: John Wiley.

Hareven, T. K. 1994. Aging and generational relations: A historical and life course perspective. *Annual Review of Sociology*, 20, 437-461.

Harrington, R. C., Fudge, H., Rutter, M. L., Bredenkamp, D., Groothues, C., and Pridham, J. 1993. Child and adult depression: A test of continuities with data from a family study. *British Journal of Psychiatry*, 162, 627-633.

Harris, J. R. 1995. Where is the child's environment? A group socialization theory of development. *Psychological Review*, 102, 458-489.

Harris, K. M., and Morgan, S. P. 1991. Fathers, sons, and daughters: Differential paternal involvement in parenting. *Journal of Marriage and the Family*, 51, 531-544.

Hart, C. H., Ladd, G. W., and Burleson, B. R. 1990. Children's expectations of the outcomes of social strategies: Relations with sociometric status and maternal disciplinary styles. *Child Development*, 61, 127-137.

Hartup, W. W. 1996. The company they keep: Friendships and their developmental significance. *Child Development*, 67, 1-13.

Haskett, M. E., Johnson, C. A., and Miller, J. W. 1994. Individual differences in risk of child abuse by adolescent mothers: Assessment in the perinatal period. *Journal of Child Psychology and Psychiatry*, 35, 461-476.

Haskins, R. 1985. Public aggression among children with varying day care experience. *Child Development*, 57, 689-703.

Hatfield, A. B. 1987. Families as caregivers: A historical perspective. In A. B. Hatfield and H. B. Lefley (Eds.), *Families of the mentally ill* (pp. 3-29). New York: Guilford.

Hatfield, A. B., and Lefley, H. P. (Eds.). 1987. *Families of the mentally ill. Coping and adaptation*. New York: Guilford.

Hawkins, J. D., Catalano, R. F., and Miller, J. Y. 1992. Risk and protective factors for alcohol and other drug problems in adolescence and early adulthood: Implications for substance abuse prevention. *Psychological Bulletin*, 112, 64-105.

Hawley, T. L., Halle, T. G., and Drasin, R. E. 1995. Children of addicted mothers: Effects of the "crack epidemic" on the caregiving environment and the development of preschoolers. *American Journal of Orthopsychiatry*, 65, 364-379.

Hayes, B. C., and Pittelkow, Y. 1993. Religious belief, transmission, and the family: An Australian study. *Journal of Marriage and the Family*, 55, 755-766.

Hayes, C. D. 1987. Adolescent pregnancy and childbearing : An emerging research focus. In S. L. Hofferth and C. D. Hayes (Eds.), *Risking the future: Adolescent sexuality, pregnancy, and childrearing*, vol. 2 (pp. 126). Washington, DC: National Academy Press.

Heath, S. B. 1981. Questioning at home and at school: A comparative study. In G. Spindler (Ed.), *Doing ethnography: Educational anthropology in action*. New York: Holt, Rinehart & Winston.

Heaton, T. B., and Albrecht, S. L. 1991. Stable unhappy marriages. *Journal of Marriage and the Family*, 53, 747-758.

Helm, J., et al. 1990. Adolescent and adult mothers of handicapped children: Maternal involvement in play. *Family Relations*, 39, 432-437.

Heming, G. 1985. *Predicting adaptation in the transition to parenthood*. Doctoral dissertation, Berkeley: University of California.

Henggeler, S. W. 1989. *Delinquency in adolescence*. Newbury Park, CA: Sage.

Henggeler, S. W., and Borduin, C. M. 1990. *Family therapy and beyond: A multisystemic approach to treating the behavior problems of children and adolescents*. Pacific Grove, CA: Brooks/Cole.

Henggeler, S. W., Melton, G. B., and Smith, L. A. 1992. Family preservation using multisystemic therapy: An effective alternative to incarcerating serious juvenile offenders. *Journal of Consulting and Clinical Psychology*, 60, 953-961.

Henggeler, S. W., Schoenwald, S. K., and Pickrel, S. G. 1995. Multisystemic therapy: Bridging the gap between university- and community-based treatment. *Journal of Consulting and Clinical Psychology*, 63, 709-717.

Henry, C. S. 1994. Family system characteristics, parental behaviors, and adolescent family life satisfaction. *Family Relations*, 43, 447-455.

Henry, C. S., and Peterson, G. W. 1995. Adolescent social competence, parental qualities, and parental satisfaction. *American Journal of Orthopsychiatry*, 65, 249-262.

Henry, S. L., and Pepper, F. C. 1990. Cognitive, social, and cultural effects on Indian learning style: Classroom implications. *The Journal of Educational Issues of Language Minority Students*, 7, 85-92.

Herbert, M. 1987. *Conduct disorders of childhood and adolescence*, 2nd ed. Chichester, UK: John Wiley and Sons.

Hernandez, D. J. 1993. *America's children*. New York: Russell Sage.

Heston, L. L. 1966. *Family interaction and psychopathology: Theories, methods and findings*. New York: Plenum.

Hetherington, E. M. 1988. Parents, children, and siblings: Six years after divorce. In R. A. Hinde and J. Stevenson-Hinde (Eds.), *Relationships within families: Mutual influences* (pp. 311-331). Oxford: Oxford University Press.

Hetherington, E. M. 1989. Coping with family transitions: Winners, losers and survivors. *Child Development*, 60, 1-14.

Hetherington, E. M. 1991. The role of individual differences and family relationships in children's coping with divorce and remarriage. In P. A. Cowan and E. M. Hetherington (Eds.), *Family Transitions* (pp. 165-194). Hillsdale, NJ: Lawrence Erlbaum.

Hetherington, E. M. 1993. An overview of the Virginia longitudinal study of divorce and remarriage with a focus on early adolescence. *Journal of Family Psychology*, 7, 39-56.

Hetherington, E. M., and Camara, K. A. 1984. Families in transition. In R. D. Parke (Ed.), *Review of Child Development Research*, vol. 7 (pp. 398-439). Chicago: University of Chicago Press.

Hetherington, E. M., Cox, M., and Cox, R. 1982. Effects of divorce on parents and children. In M. E. Lamb (Ed.), *Nontraditional families* (pp. 233-288). Hillsdale, NJ: Lawrence Erlbaum.

Hetherington, E. M., Cox, M., and Cox, R. 1985. Long-term effects of divorce and remarriage on the adjustment of children. *Journal of the American Academy of Child and Adolescent Psychiatry*, 24, 518-530.

Hetherington, E. M., Clingempeel, W. G., et al. 1992. Coping with marital transitions. *Monographs of the Society for Research in Child Development*, 57, nos 2-3.

Heyns, B. 1988. Schooling and cognitive development: Is there a season for learning? *Child Development*, 58, 1151-1160.

Hill, J. P. 1993. Recent advances in selected aspects of adolescent development. *Journal of Child Psychology and Psychiatry*, 34, 69-99.

Hill, J., Holmbeck, G., Marlow, L., Green, T., and Lynch, M. 1985a. Menarcheal status and parent-child relations in families of seventh-grade girls. *Journal of Youth and Adolescence*, 14, 314-330.

Hill, J., Holmbeck, G., Marlow, L., Green, T., and Lynch, M. 1985b. Pubertal status and parent-child relations in families of seventh-grade boys. *Journal of Early Adolescence*, 5, 31-44.

Hills, H. I., and Stozier, A. L. 1992. Multicultural training in APA-approved counseling psychology programs: A survey. *Professional Psychology: Research and Practice*, 23, 43-51.

Hirsch, J., McGuire, T. R., and Vetta, A. 1980. Concepts of behavior genetics and misapplications to humans. In J. Lockard (Ed.), *The evolution of human social behavior* (pp. 215-238). New York: Elsevier.

Hirsch, S. R., and Leff, J. P. 1975. *Abnormalities in parents of schizophrenics*. London: Oxford University Press.

Hjelle, L. A., and Ziegler, D. J. 1992. *Personality theories. Basic assumptions, research, and applications*, 3rd ed. New York: McGraw-Hill.

Hobart, C. W. 1988. Perception of parent-child relationships in first married and remarried families. *Family Relations*, 37, 175-182.

Hochschild, A. 1989. *The second shift: Working parents and the revolution at home.* New York: Viking Press.

Hoffman, J. 1984. Psychological separation of late adolescents from their parents. *Journal of Counseling Psychology*, 3, 170-178.

Hoffman, L. W. 1985. The changing genetics/socialization balance. *Journal of Social Issues*, 41, 127-148.

Hoffman, L. W. 1986. Moral development. In M. H. Bornstein and M. E. Lamb (Eds.), *Developmental psychology*, 2nd ed. (pp. 309-366). Hillsdale, NJ: Lawrence Erlbaum.

Hoffman, L. W. 1991. The influence of the family environment on personality: Accounting for sibling differences. *Psychological Bulletin*, 110, 187-203.

Hoffman, L. W. 1994. A proof and a disproof questioned. *Social Development*, 3, 60-63.

Hogan, D. 1980. The transition to adulthood as a career contingency. *American Sociological Review*, 45, 261-276.

Hogan, D. P., and Kitagawa, E. M. 1985. The impact of social status, family structure and neighborhood on the fertility of black adolescents. *American Journal of Sociology*, 90, 825-855.

Hogan, D., Eggebeen, D., and Clogg, C. 1993. The structure of intergenerational exchange in American families. *American Journal of Sociology*, 98, 1428-1458.

Hollinan, M. T., and Williams, R. A. 1989. Interracial friendship choices in secondary school. *American Sociological Review*, 54, 67-78.

Hollingshead, A. B., and Redlich, F. C. 1958. *Social class and mental illness: A community study.* New York: John Wiley.

Hollnsteiner, M. R., and Taçon, P. 1983. Urban migration in developing countries: Consequences for families and their children. In D. A. Wagner (Ed.), *Child development and international development: Research-policy interfaces* (pp. 5-26). San Francisco: Jossey-Bass.

Holmbeck, G. N., and Hill, J. P. 1988. Storm and stress beliefs about adolescence: Prevalence, self-reported antecedents, and effects of an undergraduate course. *Journal of Youth and Adolescence*, 17, 285-306.

Holt, G. S. 1972. Stylin' outta the black pulpit. In T. Kochman (Ed.), *Rappin' and stylin' out: Communicating in urban black America.* Chicago: University of Chicago Press.

Hoover-Dempsey, V., Bassler, O. C., and Brissie, J. S. 1987. Parent-involvement: Contributions of teacher efficacy, school socio-economic status, and other school characteristics. *American Educational Research Journal*, 24, 417-435.

Hops, H., Biglan, A., Sherman, L., Arthur, J., Friedman, L., and Osteen, V.

1987. Home observations of family interactions of depressed women. *Journal of Consulting and Clinical Psychology*, 55, 341-346.

Hops, H., Sherman, L., and Biglan, A. 1990. Maternal depression, marital discord, and children's behavior: A developmental perspective. In G. R. Patterson (Ed.), *Depression and aggression in family interaction* (pp. 185-208). Hillsdale, NJ: Lawrence Erlbaum.

Horowitz, B., and Wolock, I. 1985. Material deprivation, child maltreatment, and agency in interventions among poor families. In L. Pelton (Ed.), *The social context of child abuse and neglect* (pp. 137-184). New York: Human Sciences Press.

Horwitz, A. V. 1993. Adult siblings as sources of social support for the seriously mentally ill: A test of the serial model. *Journal of Marriage and the Family*, 55, 623-632.

Horwitz, A. V. 1994. Predictors of adult sibling social support for the seriously mentally ill. An exploratory study. *Journal of Family Issues*, 15, 272-289.

Hotalling, G. T., Strauss, M. A., and Lincoln, A. J. 1990. Intrafamily violence and crime and violence outside the family. In M.A. Strauss and R. J. Gelles (Eds.), *Physical violence in American families*. New Brunswick, NJ: Transaction Books.

Howes, C. 1988. Abused and neglected children with their peers. In G. T. Hotalling et al. (Eds.), *Family abuse and its consequences* (pp. 99-108). Beverly Hills, CA: Sage.

Howes, C. 1990. Can the age of entry into child care and the quality of child care predict adjustment in kindergarten? *Developmental Psychology*, 26, 292-303.

Howes, C., and Stewart, P. 1987. Child's play with adults, toys, and peers: An examination of family and child-care influences. *Developmental Psychology*, 23, 423-430.

Howes, P., and Markham, H. J. 1989. Marital quality and child functioning: A longitudinal investigation. *Child Development*, 60, 1044-1051.

Hubert, N., and Wachs, T. D. 1985. Parental perceptions of the behavioral components of infant easiness-difficultness. *Child Development*, 56, 1525-1537.

Hudley, C. A. 1995. Assessing the impact of separate schooling for African American male adolescents. *Journal of Early Adolescence*, 15, 38-57.

Huesmann, L. R. 1986. Psychological processes promoting the relation between exposure to media violence and aggressive behavior by the viewer. *Journal of Social Issues*, 42, 125-139.

Huesmann, L. R., Eron, L. D., Lefkowitz, M. M., and Walder, L. O. 1984.

Stability of aggression over time and generations. *Developmental Psychology*, 20, 1120-1134.

Hur, Y.-M., and Bouchard, T. J., Jr. 1995. Genetic influences on perceptions of childhood family environment: A reared apart twin study. *Child Development*, 66, 330-345.

Huston, A. C. 1985. The development of sex-typing. *Developmental Review*, 5, 1-17.

Huston, A. C. 1991. Children in poverty: Developmental and policy issues. In A. C. Huston, (Ed.), *Children in poverty: Child development and public policy* (pp. 1-22). Cambridge: Cambridge University Press.

Huston, A., and Wright, J. 1994. Educating children with television: The forms of the medium. In D. Zillman, J. Bryant, and A. Huston (Eds.), *Media, children, and the family: Social scientific, psychodynamic, and clinical perspectives*. Hillsdale, NJ: Lawrence Erlbaum.

Hutchings, B., and Mednick, S. A. 1975. Registered criminality in the adoptive and biological parents of registered male criminal adoptees. In R. R. Fieve, D. Rosenthal, and H. Brill (Eds.), *Genetic research in psychiatry* (pp. 105-116). Baltimore: John Hopkins University Press.

Hymel, S., Rubin, K. H., Rowden, L., and Le Mare, L. 1990. Children's peer relationships: Longitudinal prediction of internalizing and externalizing problems from middle to late childhood. *Child Development*, 61, 2004-2021.

Jacob, T., Krahn, F. L., and Leonard, K. 1991. Parent-child interactions in families with alcoholic fathers. *Journal of Consulting and Clinical Psychology*, 59, 176-187.

Jackson, J. F. 1993. Human behavior genetics, Scarr's theory, and her views on interventions: A critical review and commentary on their implications for African American children. *Child Development*, 64, 1318-1330.

Jankowski, M. S. 1991. *Islands in the street: Gangs and American urban society*. Berkeley, CA: University of California Press.

Jencks, C. 1992. *Rethinking social policy*. Cambridge, MA: Harvard University Press.

Jencks, C., and Mayer, S. E. 1990. The social consequences of growing up in a poor neighborhood. In L. E. Lynn, Jr. and G. H. McGeary (Eds.), *Inner city poverty in the United States* (pp. 111-186). Washington, DC: National Academy Press.

Jencks, C., and Peterson, P. E. 1991. *The urban underclass*. Washington, DC: Brookings Institution.

Jenkins, J. 1992. Sibling relationships in disharmonious homes: Potential difficulties and protective effects. In F. Boer and J. Dunn (Eds.), *Children's sibling relationships*. Hillsdale, NJ: Lawrence Erlbaum.

Jenkins, J. M., and Smith, M. A. 1990. Factors protecting children living in disharmonious homes: Maternal reports. *Journal of American Academy of Child and Adolescent Psychiatry*, 29, 60-69.

Jenkins, J. M., and Smith, M. A. 1993. A prospective study of behavioral disturbance in children of parental divorce: A research note. *Journal of Divorce and Remarriage*, 19, 143-159.

Jenkins, J. M., Smith, M. A., and Graham, P. J. 1989. Coping with parental quarrels. *Journal of American Academy of Child and Adolescent Psychiatry*, 28, 182-189.

Jennings, J. 1987. Elderly parents as caregivers for their adult dependent children. *Social Work*, 32, 430-433.

Jensen-Campbell, L. A., Graziano, W. G., and Hair, R. C. 1996. Personality and relationships as moderators of interpersonal conflict in adolescence. *Merrill-Palmer Quarterly*, 42, 148-164.

Jessor, R., Donovan, J., and Costa, F. 1991. *Beyond adolescence: Problem behavior and young adult development*. Cambridge: Cambridge University Press.

Johnson, C. L. 1985. *Growing up and growing old in Italian-American families*. New Brunswick, NJ: Rutgers University Press.

Johnson, D., and Johnson, R. 1989. *Cooperation and competition: Theory and research*. Edina, MN: Interaction Book Co.

Johnson, W. R., and Warren, D. M. 1994. *Inside the mixed marriage*. Lanham, MD: University Press of America.

Johnston, C., and Pelham, W. E. 1990. Maternal characteristics, ratings of child behavior, and mother-child interactions in families of children with externalizing disorders. *Journal of Abnormal Child Psychology*, 18, 407-417.

Jones, M. B., and Szatmari, P. 1988. Stoppage rules and the genetics of autism. *Journal of Autism and Developmental Disorders*, 18, 31-41.

Jouriles, E. N., Bourg, W. J., and Farris, A. M. 1991. Marital adjustment and child conduct problems: A comparison of the correlation across subsamples. *Journal of Consulting and Clinical Psychology*, 59, 354-357.

Jouriles, E. N., Farris, A. M., and McDonald, R. 1991. Marital functioning and child behavior: Measuring specific aspects of the marital relationship. In J. P. Vincent (Ed.), *Advances in family intervention, assessment, and theory*, Vol. 5 (pp. 25-46). London: Jessica Kingsley.

Joy, L. A., Kimball, M. M., and Zabrack, M. L. 1986. Television and children's aggressive behavior. In T. M. Williams (Ed.), *The impact of television: A natural experiment in three communities* (pp. 303-360). Orlando, FL: Academic Press.

Kagan, J. 1992. Yesterday's premises, tomorrow's promises. *Developmental Psychology*, 28, 990-997.

Kagan, J. 1994. *Galen's prophecy: Temperament in human nature*. New York: Basic Books.

Kagan, J., and Snidman, N. 1991. Temperamental factors in human development. *American Psychologist*, 46, 856-862.

Kagan, J., Reznick, J. S., and Snidman, N. 1988. Biological bases of childhood shyness. *Science*, 240, 167-171.

Kagan, J., Reznick, J. S., and Snidman, N. 1989. Issues in the study of temperament. In G. A. Kohnstamm, J. E. Bates, and M. K. Rothbart (Eds.), *Temperament in childhood* (pp. 133-152). New York: John Wiley.

Kagan, S., et al. 1985. Classroom structural bias: Impact of cooperative and competitive classroom structures on cooperative and competitive individuals and groups. In R. E. Slavin et al. (Eds.), *Learning to cooperate, cooperating to learn*. New York: Plenum.

Kallman, F. J., and Roth, B. 1956. Genetic aspects of preadolescent schizophrenia. *American Journal of Psychiatry*, 112, 599-606.

Kalmijn, M. 1993. Trends in black/white intermarriage. *Social Forces*, 72, 119-146.

Kandel, D. B. 1990. Parenting styles, drug use, and children's adjustment in families of young adults. *Journal of Marriage and the Family*, 52, 183-196.

Kandel, D. B., and Davies, M. 1996. High school students who use crack and other drugs. *Archives of General Psychiatry*, 53, 71-80.

Kanter, J., Lamb, H. R., and Loeper, C. 1987. Expressed emotion in families: A critical review. *Hospital and Community Psychiatry*, 38, 374-380.

Kao, G. 1995. Asian Americans as model minorities? A look at their academic performance. *American Journal of Education*, 103, 121-159.

Kasarda, J. D. 1990. City jobs and residents on a collision course: The urban underclass dilemma. *Economic Development Quarterly*, 4, 313-319.

Kasarda, J. D. 1993. The severely distressed in economically transforming cities. In A. V. Harrell and G. E. Peterson (Eds.), *Drugs, crime, and social isolation* (pp. 45-98). Washington, DC: The Urban Institute.

Kashani, J. H., et al. 1987. Psychiatric disorders in a community sample of adolescents. *American Journal of Psychiatry*, 144, 584-589.

Katz, L. F., and Gottman, J. M. 1994. Patterns of marital interaction and children's emotional development. In R. D. Parke and S. G. Kellam (Eds.),

Exploring family relationships with other social contexts (pp. 49-74). Hillsdale, NJ: Lawrence Erlbaum.

Katz, L. F., and Gottman, J. M. 1995. Vagal tone protects children from marital conflict. *Development and Psychopathology*, 7, 83-92.

Kaufman, J., and Zigler, E. 1987. Do abused children become abusive parents? *American Journal of Orthopsychiatry*, 57, 186-192.

Kazak, A. E., and Marvin, R. S. 1984. Differences, difficulties and adaptation: Stress and social networks in families with a handicapped child. *Family Relations*, 33, 66-77.

Kazdin, A. E. 1987. Treatment of antisocial behavior in children: Current status and future directions. *Psychological Bulletin*, 102, 187-203.

Kazdin, A. E. 1991. Effectiveness of psychotherapy with children and adolescents. *Journal of Consulting and Clinical Psychology*, 59, 785-798.

Kazdin, A. E., Bass, D., Ayers, W. A., and Rodgers, A. 1990. Empirical and clinical focus of child and adolescent psychotherapy research. *Journal of Consulting and Clinical Psychology*, 58, 729-740.

Kazdin, A. E., Esveldt-Dawson, K., Sherick, R. B., and Colbus, D. 1985. Assessment of overt behavior and childhood depression among psychiatrically disturbed children. *Journal of Consulting and Clinical Psychology*, 53, 201-210.

Kazdin, A. E., Esveldt-Dawson, K., French, N. H., and Unis, A. S. 1987. Effects of parent management training and problem-solving skills training combined in the treatment of antisocial child behavior. *Journal of the American Academy of Child and Adolescent Psychiatry*, 26, 416-424.

Kellam, S. G. 1994. The social adaptation of children in classrooms: A measure of family childrearing effectiveness. In R. D. Parke and S. G. Kellam (Eds.), *Exploring family relationships with other social contexts* (pp. 147-168). Hillsdale, NJ: Lawrence Erlbaum.

Keller, B. B., and Bell, R. Q. 1979. Child effects on adults' methods of eliciting altruistic behavior. *Child Development*, 50, 1004-1009.

Keller, M. B., Beardslee, W. R., Dorer, D. J., Lavori, P. W., Samuelson, H., and Klerman, G. R. 1986. Impact of severity and chronicity of parental affective illness on adaptive functioning and psychopathology in children. *Archives of General Psychiatry*, 43, 930-937.

Kelley, P. 1976. The relation of infant's temperament and mother's psychopathology to interactions in early infancy. In K. R. Riegel and J. A. Meacham (Eds.), *The developing individual in a changing world*, Vol. 2. Chicago: Aldine.

Kelly, L., Regan, L., and Burton, S. 1991. *An exploratory study of the prevalence of sexual abuse in a sample of 16-21 year olds.* London: Polytechnic of North London.

Kendall, P. C., and Stoutham-Gerow, M. A. 1995. Issues in the transportability of treatment: The case of anxiety disorders in youths. *Journal of Consulting and Clinical Psychology*, 63, 702-708.

Kendall, P. C., Lerner, R. M., and Craighead, W. E. 1984. Human development and intervention in childhood psychopathology. *Child Development*, 55, 71-82.

Kendall-Tackett, K. A., Williams, L. M., and Finkelhor, D. 1993. Impact of sexual abuse on children: A review and synthesis of recent empirical studies. *Psychological Bulletin*, 113, 164-180.

Kendler, K. S. 1988. The genetics of schizophrenia: An overview. In M. T. Tsuang and J. C. Simpson (Eds.), *Handbook of schizophrenia, vol. 3. Nosology, epidemiology and genetics of schizophrenia* (pp. 437-462), Amsterdam: Elsevier.

Kendler, K. S. 1991. A psychiatric perspective on the "nature of nurture." *Behavioral and Brain Sciences*, 14, 398-399.

Kendler, K. S. 1996. Parenting: A genetic-epidemiologic perspective. *American Journal of Psychiatry*, 153, 11-20.

Kendler, K. S., et al. 1992. Life events and depressive symptoms: A twin study perspective. In P. McGriffin and R. Murray (Eds.), *The new genetics of mental illness* (pp. 146-164). Oxford: Butterworth-Heinemann.

Kendler, K. S. 1995a. Genetic epidemiology in psychiatry. Taking both genes and environment seriously. *Archives of General Psychiatry*, 52, 895-899.

Kendler, K. S. 1995b. Stressful life events, genetic liability and onset of an episode of major depression in women. *American Journal of Psychiatry*, 152, 833-842.

Kerbow, D., and Bernhardt, A. 1993. Parental intervention in the school: The context of minority involvement. In B. Schneider and J. S. Coleman (Eds.), *Parents, their children, and schools* (pp. 115-146). San Francisco: Westview Press.

Kessen, W. 1979. The American child and other cultural inventions. *American Psychologist*, 34, 815-820.

Kessler, R. C., McGonagle, K. A., Zhao, S., Nelson, C. B., Hughes, M., Eshleman, S., Wittchen, H. O., and Kendler, K. S. 1994. Lifetime and 12-month prevalence of DSM-III-R psychiatric disorders in the United States: Results from the National Comorbidity Survey. *Archives of General Psychiatry*, 51, 8-19.

Kett, J. F. 1977. *Rites of passage: Adolescence in America 1790 to present.* New York: Basic Books.

Ketterlinus, R. D., Henderson, S., and Lamb, M. E. 1991. The effects of maternal age-at-birth on children's cognitive development. *Journal of Research on Adolescence*, 1, 173-188.

Kety, S. S., Rosenthal, D., Wender, P. H., and Schulsinger, F. 1968. The types and prevalence of mental illness in the biological and adoptive families of adopted schizophrenics. *Journal of Psychiatric Research*, 6, 345-362.

Kiernan, K. 1992. The impact of family disruption in childhood on transitions made in young adult life. *Population Studies*, 46, 218-234.

Killbride, P. L., and Killbride, J. C. 1990. *Changing family life in East Africa: Women and Children at risk.* University Park: The Pennsylvania State University Press.

Kimball, M. M. 1986. Television and sex-role attitudes. In T. M. Williams (Ed.), *The impact of television* (pp. 265-301). New York: Academic Press.

Kingston, E. R., Hirshorn, B. A., and Cornman, J. M. 1986. *Ties that bind: The interdependence of generations.* Washington, DC: Seven Locks Press.

Kinney, D. A. 1993. From nerds to normals: The recovery of identity among adolescents from middle school to high school. *Sociology of Education*, 66, 21-40.

Kitchen, B. 1995. Children and the case for distributive justice between generations in Canada. *Child Welfare*, 74, 430-458.

Kitson, G. C. 1992. *Portrait of divorce.* New York: Guilford Press.

Kitson, G. C., and Morgan, L. A. 1990. The multiple consequences of divorce. *Journal of Marriage and the Family*, 52, 913-924.

Klebanov, P. K., Brooks-Gunn, J., and Duncan, G. J. 1994. Does neighborhood and family poverty affect mothers' parenting, mental health, and social support? *Journal of Marriage and the Family*, 56, 441-455.

Klein, R. G. 1994. Anxiety disorders. In M. Rutter, E. Taylor, and L. Hersov (Eds.), *Child and adolescent psychiatry: Modern approaches*, 3rd ed. (pp. 351-374). Oxford: Balckwell.

Klerman, L. V. 1991. The association between adolescent parenting and childhood poverty. In A. C. Huston (Ed.), *Children in poverty. Child development and public policy* (pp. 79-104). Cambridge: Cambridge University Press.

Kline, M., Johnston, J., and Tschann, J. 1991. The long shadow of marital conflict: A model of children's postdivorce adjustment. *Journal of Marriage and the Family*, 53, 297-309.

Knitzer, J., and Aber, J. L. 1995. Young children in poverty: Facing the facts. *American Journal of Orthopsychiatry*, 65, 174-176.

Kochanska, G. 1990. Maternal belief as long-term predictors of mother-child interactions and report. *Child Development*, 61, 1934-1943.

Kochanska, G. 1993. Toward a synthesis of parental socialization and child temperament in early development of conscience. *Child Development*, 64, 325-347.

Kochanska, G. 1995. Children's temperament, mother's discipline, and security of attachment: Multiple pathways to emerging internalization. *Child Development*, 66, 597-615.

Kochanska, G., and Aksan, N. 1995. Mother-child mutually positive affect, the quality of child compliance to requests and prohibitions, and maternal control as correlates of early internalization. *Child Development*, 66, 236-254.

Kochanska, G., Kuczynski, L., and Radke-Yarrow, M. 1989. Correspondence between mothers' self-reported and observed child-rearing practices. *Child Development*, 60, 56-63.

Kohn, M. L. 1969. *Class and conformity: A study in values.* Homewood, IL: Dorsey Press.

Kohn, M. L., and Schooler, C. 1983. *Work and personality: An inquiry into the impact of social stratification.* Norwood, NJ: Ablex.

Kohn, M. L., Slomczynski, K. M., and Schoenbach, C. 1986. Social stratification and the transmission of values in the family: A cross-national assessment. *Sociological Forum*, 1, 73-101.

Kolvin, I., et al. 1988a. Risk/protective factors for offending with particular reference to deprivation. In M. Rutter (Ed.), *Studies of psychosocial risk: The power of longitudinal data* (pp. 77-95). Cambridge: Cambridge University Press.

Kolvin, I., Miller, F. J. W., Fleeting, M., and Kolvin, P. A. 1988b. Social and parenting factors affecting criminal offence rates. Findings from the Newcastle Thousand Family Study (1947-1980). *British Journal of Psychiatry*, 152, 80-90.

Koocher, G. P., Goodman, G. S., White, C. S., Friedrich, W. N., Sivan, A. B., and Reynolds, C. R. 1995. Psychological science and the use of anatomically detailed dolls in child sexual-abuse assessments. *Psychological Bulletin*, 118, 199-222.

Korbin, J. E. 1986. Childhood histories of women imprisoned for fatal child maltreatment. *Child Abuse and Neglect: The International Journal*, 10, 331-338.

Korbin, J. E., Anetzberger, G., and Austin, C. 1995. The intergenerational cycle of violence in child and elder abuse. *Journal of Elder Abuse & Neglect*, 7, 1-15.

Kottler, J. 1991. *The compleat therapist.* San Francisco: Jossey-Bass.

Kouri, K. M., and Lasswell, M. 1993. Black-white marriages: Social change and intergenerational mobility. *Marriage and Family Review*, 19, 241-255.

Kramer, L., and Gottman, J. 1992. Becoming a sibling: "with a little help from my friends." *Developmental Psychology*, 28, 685-699.

Krauss, J. B., and Slavinsky, A. T. 1982. *The chronically ill psychiatric patient in the community.* Boston: Blackwell.

Kringlen, E., and Cramer, G. 1989. Offspring of monozygotic twins discordant for schizophrenia. *Archives of General Psychiatry*, 46, 873-877.

Krishnan, V. 1987. Preference for sex of children: A multivariate analysis. *Journal of Biosocial Science*, 19, 367-376.

Krueger, R. F., Schmutte, P. S., Caspi, A., and Moffitt, T. 1994. Personality traits are linked to crime among men and women: Evidence from a birth cohort. *Journal of Abnormal Psychology*, 103, 328-338.

Kuczynski, L., and Kochanska, G. 1995. Function and content of maternal demands: Developmental significance of early demands for competent action. *Child Development*, 66, 616-628.

Kupersmidt, J. B., and Coie, J. D. 1990. Preadolescent peer status, aggression, and school adjustment as predictors of externalizing problems in adolescence. *Child Development*, 61, 1350-1362.

Kupersmidt, J. B., Griesler, P. C., DeRosier, M. E., Patterson, C. J., and Davis, P. W. 1995. Childhood aggression and peer relations in the context of family and neighborhood factors. *Child Development*, 66, 360-375.

Ladd, G. W. 1992. Themes and theories: Perspectives on processes in family-peer relationships. In R. D. Parke and G. W. Ladd (Eds.), *Family-peer relationships: Modes of linkage* (pp. 1-34). Hillsdale, NJ: Lawrence Erlbaum.

Ladd, G. W., and Coleman, C. 1993. Young children's peer relationships: Forms, features, and functions. In B. Spodek (Ed.), *Handbook of research on the education of young children*, 2nd ed. New York: Macmillan.

Ladd, G. W., Le Sieur, K., and Profilet, S. M. 1993. Direct parental influences on young children's peers relations. In S. Duck (Ed.), *Learning about relationships*, vol. 2. Newbury Park, CA: Sage.

Lahey, B. B., Russo, M. F., Walker, J. L., and Piacentini, J. C. 1989. Personality characteristics of the mothers of children with disruptive behavior disorders. *Journal of Consulting and Clinical Psychology*, 57, 512-515.

Lahey, B. B., Piacentini, J. C., McBurnett, K., Stone, P., Hartdagen, S., and Hynd, G. W. 1988. Psychopathology in the parents of children with conduct disorder and hyperactivity. *Journal of the American Academy of Child and Adolescent Psychiatry*, 27, 163-170.

Lahey, B. B., Hartdagen, S. E., Frick, P. J., McBurnett, K., Connor, R., and Hynd, G. W. 1988a. Conduct disorder: Parsing the confounded relation to parental divorce and antisocial personality. *Journal of Abnormal Psychology*, 97, 334-337.

Lahey, B. B., Piacentini, J. C., McBurnett, K., Stone, P., Hartdagen, S., and Hynd, G. 1988b. Psychopathology in the parents of children with conduct disorder and hyperactivity. *Journal of the American Academy of Child and Adolescent Psychiatry*, 27, 163-170.

Laird, R. D., Pettit, G. S., Mize, J., Brown, E. G., and Lindsey, E. 1994. Mother-child conversations about peers. Contributions to competence. *Family Relations*, 43, 425-432.

Lamb, M. E. 1983. Fathers of exceptional children. In M. Seligman (Ed.), *The family with a handicapped child: Understanding and treatment.* New York: Grune and Stratton.

Lamb, M. E. 1987. Niche picking by siblings and scientists. *Behavioral and Brain Sciences*, 10, 30-31.

Lamb, M. E., and Ketterlinus, R. D. 1991. Parental behavior, adolescence. In R. M. Lerner, A. C. Peterson, and J. Brooks-Gunn (Eds.), *Encyclopedia of adolescence*, Vol. 2 (pp. 735-738). New York: Garland.

Lamb, M. E., and Teti, D. M. 1991. Parenthood and marriage in adolescence: Associations with educational and occupational attainment. In R. M. Lerner, A. C. Peterson, and J. Brooks-Gunn (Eds.), *Encyclopedia of adolescence*, Vol. 2 (pp. 742-745). New York: Garland.

Lamb, M. E., Hwang, C. P., and Brody, A. 1989. Associations between parental agreement regarding child-rearing and the characteristics of families and children in Sweden. *International Journal of Behavioral Development*, 12, 115-130.

Lamb, M. E., Pleck, J. H., and Levine, J. A. 1986. The role of the father in child development: The effects of increased paternal involvement. In M. Lamb (Ed.), *The father's role: Applied perspectives* (pp. 229-267). New York: Wiley.

Lamb, M. E., Pleck, J. H., and Levine, J. A. 1987. Effects of increased paternal involvement on fathers and mothers. In C. Lewis and M. O'Brien (Eds.), *Reassessing fatherhood: New observations on fathers and the modern family* (pp. 109-125). Beverly Hills, CA: Sage.

Lamborn, S. D., and Steinberg, L. 1993. Emotional autonomy redux: Revisiting Ryan and Lynch. *Child Development*, 64, 483-499.

Lamborn, S. D., Mounts, N. S., Steinberg, L. and Dornbusch, S. M. 1991. Patterns of competence and adjustment among adolescents from authoritative, authoritarian, indulgent, and neglected families. *Child Development*, 62, 1049-1065.

Lancaster, J. B., Altmann, J., Rossi, A. S., and Sherrod, L. R. (Eds.). 1987. *Parenting across the life span: Biosocial dimensions*. New York: Aldine de Gruyter.

Langmeier, J., and Matejcek, Z. 1975. *Psychological deprivation in childhood*. New York: John Wiley.

Lareau, A. 1989. *Home advantage: Social class and parental intervention in elementary education*. New York: Falmer Press.

Larson, R. W., and Richards, M. H. 1991. Boredom in the middle school years: Blaming schools versus blaming students. *American Journal of Education*, 91, 418-443.

Larson, R. W., and Richards, M. H. 1994. *Divergent realities: The emotional lives of mothers, fathers, and adolescents*. New York: Basic Books.

Lasko, J. K. 1954. Parent behavior toward first and second children. *Genetic Psychology Monographs*, 49, 97-137.

Laub, J. H., and Sampson, R. J. 1993. Turning points in the life course: Why change matters to the study of crime. *Criminology*, 31, 301-325.

Lavigueur, S., Tremblay, R. E., and Saucier, J.-F. 1995. Interactional processes in families with disruptive boys: Patterns of direct and indirect influence. *Journal of Abnormal Child Psychology*, 23, 359-378.

Lawton, L., Silverstein, M., and Bengtson, V. 1994. Affection, social contact, and geographic distance between adult children and their parents. *Journal of Marriage and the Family*, 56, 57-68.

Laursen, B., and Collins, W. A. 1994. Interpersonal conflict during adolescence. *Psychological Bulletin*, 115, 197-209.

Lazure, J. 1990. Mouvance des générations. Condition féminine et masculine. In F. Dumont (Ed.). *La société québécoise après 30 ans de changements*. Québec: Institut Québécois de Recherche sur la Culture.

Le Blanc, M., McDuff, P., and Tremblay, R. E. 1991. Types de familles, conditions de vie, fonctionnement du système familial et inadaptation sociale au cours de la latence et de l'adolescence dans les millieux défavorisés. *Santé Mentale au Québec*, 16, 45-75.

Le Blanc, M., and Fréchette, M. 1989. *Male criminal activity from childhood through youth: Multilevel and developmental perspectives*. New York: Springer/Verlag.

LeClere, F. B., and Kowalewski, B. M. 1994. Disability in the family: The effects on children's well-being. *Journal of Marriage and the Family*, 56, 457-468.

Lee, C. L., and Bates, J. E. 1985. Mother-child interaction at age two years and perceived difficult temperament. *Child Development*, 56, 1314-1325.

Lee, G. R. 1985. Kinship and social support of the elderly: The case of the United States. *Ageing and Society*, 5, 19-38.

Lee, G. R., Netzer, J. K., and Coward, R. T. 1995. Depression among older parents: The role of intergenerational exchange. *Journal of Marriage and the Family*, 57, 823-833.

Lee, S. A. 1993. Family structure effects on student outcomes. In B. Schneider and J. S. Coleman (Eds.), *Parents, their children, and schools* (pp. 43-75). San Francisco: Westview Press.

Lee, T. R., Mancini, J. A., and Maxwell, J. W. 1990. Sibling relationships in adulthood: Contact patterns and motivation. *Journal of Marriage and the Family*, 52, 431-440.

Lee, V., Brooks-Gunn, J., and Schnur, E. 1988. Does Head-Start work? A 1-year longitudinal follow-up comparison of disadvantaged children attending Head-Start, no pre-school, and other pre-school programs. *Developmental Psychology*, 24, 210-222.

Leff, J., Kuipers, L., Berkowitz, R., Eberlein-Vries, R., and Sturgeon, D. 1982. A controlled trial of social intervention in the families of schizophrenic patients. *British Journal of Psychiatry*, 141, 121-124.

LeMasters, E. E., and DeFrain, J. 1989. *Parents in contemporary America: A sympathetic view*, 5th ed. Belmont, CA: Wadsworth.

Lefley, H. P. 1987. Behavioral manifestations of mental illness. In A. B. Hatfield and H. B. Lefley (Eds.), *Families of the mentally ill: Coping and adaptation*. (pp. 107-127). New York: Guilford.

Lefley, H. P. 1989. Family burden and family stigma in major mental illness. *American Psychologist*, 44, 556-560.

Lefkowitz, M. M., Eron, L. D., Walder, L. O., and Huesmann, L. R. 1977. *Growing up to be violent: A longitudinal study of the development of aggression*. New York: Pergamon.

Lempers, J. D., Clark-Lempers, D., and Simons, R. L. 1989. Economic hardship, parenting, and distress in adolescence. *Child Development*, 60, 25-39.

Lenton, R. L. 1990. Techniques of child discipline and abuse by parents. *Canadian Review of Sociology and Anthropology*, 27, 157-185.

Lerner, J. V., and Lerner, R. M. 1994. Explorations of the goodness-of-fit model in early adolescence. In W. B. Carey and S. C. McDevitt (Ed.), *Prevention and early intervention. Individual differences as risk factors for the mental health of children* (pp. 161-169). New York: Brunner/ Mazel.

Lerner, R. M. 1978. Nature, nurture and dynamic interactionism. *Human Development*, 21, 1-20.

Lerner, R. M. 1982. Children and adolescents as producers of their own development. *Developmental Review*, 2, 342-370.

Lerner, R. M. 1987. The concept of plasticity in development. In J. J. Gallagher and C. T. Ramsey (Eds.), *The malleability of children* (pp. 3-14). Baltimore: Brookes Publishing.

Lerner, R. M. 1991. Changing organism-context relations as the basic process of development: A developmental contextual perspective. *Developmental Psychology*, 27, 27-32.

Lerner, R. M., and Busch-Rossnagel, N. A. (Eds.), 1981. *Individuals as producers of their own development: A life-span perspective*. New York: Academic Press.

Lerner, R. M., and Busch-Rossnagel, N. A 1981. Individuals as producers of their development: Conceptual and empirical bases. In R. M. Lerner and N. A. Busch-Rossnagel (Eds.), *Individuals as producers of their own development: A life-span perspective* (pp. 1-36). San Diego, CA: Academic Press.

Lerner, R. M., and Kauffman, M. B. 1985. The concept of development in contextualism. *Developmental Review*, 5, 309-333.

Lerner, R. M., and von Eye, A. 1992. Sociobiology and human development: Arguments and evidence. *Human Development*, 35, 12-33.

Lesthaeghe, R., and Surkyn, J. 1988. Cultural dynamics and economic theories of fertility change. *Population and Development Review*, 11, 1-45.

LeVine, R. A., and White, M. 1987. The social transformation of childhood. In J. B. Lancaster et al. (Eds.), *Parenting across the life span: Biosocial dimensions*. New York: Aldine de Gruyter.

Lewis, C. C. 1981. The effects of parental firm control: A reinterpretation of findings. *Psychological Bulletin*, 90, 547-563.

Lewis, C. E., Robins, L. N., and Rice, J. 1985. Associations of alcoholism with antisocial personality in urban men. *Journal of Nervous and Mental Disease*, 173, 166-174.

Lewis, D. O., Mallouh, C., and Webb, V. 1989. Child abuse, delinquency and violent criminality. In D. Cicchetti and V. Carlson (Eds.), *Child maltreatment: Research on the causes and consequences of child abuse and neglect* (pp. 707-721). New York: Cambridge University Press.

Lewis, D. O., et al. 1991. A follow-up of female delinquents: Maternal contributions to the perpetuation of deviance. *Journal of the American Academy of Child and Adolescent Psychiatry*, 30, 197-201.

Lewis, J. M., Owen, M. T., and Cox, M. J. 1988. The transition to parenthood: III. Incorporation of the child into the family. *Family Process*, 27, 411-421.

Lewis, M. 1992. Commentary. *Human Development*, 35, 44-51.

Lewontin, R. C., Rose, S., and Kamin, K. J. 1984. *Not in our genes*. New York: Pantheon Books.

Lichter, D. T., and Eggebeen, D. J. 1994. The effect of parental employment on child poverty. *Journal of Marriage and the Family*, 56, 633-645.

Lichter, D. T., and Lansdale, N. S. 1995. Parental work, family structure, and poverty among Latino children. *Journal of Marriage and the Family*, 57, 346-354.

Liebert, R. M., and Sprafkin, J. 1988. *The early window. Effects of television on children and youth*, 3rd ed. New York: Pergamon.

Liem, J. H. 1974. Effects of verbal communications of parents and children: A comparison of normal and schizophrenic families. *Journal of Consulting and Clinical Psychology*, 42, 438-450.

Liem, R., and Liem, J. H. 1989. The psychological effects of unemployment on workers and their families. *Journal of Social Issues*, 44, 87-105.

Lindsay, C. 1994. *Lone-parent families in Canada*. Ottawa: Statistics Canada, Housing, Family and Social Statistics Division, cat. no. 89-522E.

Link, B. G., et al. 1994. Life-time and five-year prevalence of homelessness in the United States. *American Journal of Public Health*, 84, 1907-1912.

Little, J., and Thompson, B. 1988. Descriptive epidemiology. In I. M. MacGillivray et al. (Eds.), *Twinning and twins* (pp. 37-66). Chichester: Wiley.

Lloyd, B., and Duveen, G. (Eds.). 1990. *Social representation and the development of knowledge*. Cambridge: Cambridge University Press.

Lochman, J. E., and Dodge, K. A. 1994. Social-cognitive processes of severely violent, moderately aggressive, and nonaggressive boys. *Journal of Consulting and Clinical Psychology*, 62, 366-374.

Lochman, J. E., Burch, P. R., Curry, J. F., and Lampron, L. B. 1984. Treatment and generalization effects of cognitive-behavioral and goal-setting interventions with aggressive boys. *Journal of Consulting and Clinical Psychology*, 52, 915-916.

Lo, O., and Gauthier, P. 1995. Housing affordability problems among mothers. *Canadian Social Trends*, 36, 14-17.

Loeber, R. 1982. The stability of antisocial and delinquent child behavior: A review. *Child Development*, 53, 1431-1446.

Loeber, R. 1988. The natural history of juvenile conduct problems, delinquency, and associated substance use: Evidence for developmental progressions. In B. B. Lahey and A. E. Kazdin (Eds.), *Advances in clinical child psychology*, 11, 73-124. New York: Plenum.

Loeber, R. 1991. Antisocial behavior: More enduring than changeable? *Journal of the American Academy of Child and Adolescent Psychiatry*, 30, 393-397.

Loeber, R., and Hay, D. F. 1994. Developmental approaches to aggression and conduct problems. In M. Rutter and D. F. Hay (Eds.), *Development through life: A handbook for clinicians* (pp. 488-516). Boston: Blackwell.

Loeber, R., and Le Blanc, M. 1990. Toward a developmental criminology. In M. Tonry and N. Morris (Eds.), *Crime and justice* (pp. 375-437). Chicago: University of Chicago Press.

Loeber, R., and Stouthamer-Loeber, M. 1986. Family factors as correlates and predictors of juvenile conduct problems and delinquency. In M. Tonry and N. Morris (Eds.), *Crime and justice*, Vol. 7. Chicago: University of Chicago Press.

Loeber, R., et al. 1993. Developmental pathways in disruptive child behavior. *Development and Psychopathology*, 5, 103-133.

Loehlin, J. C. 1992. *Genes and environment in personality development.* Newbury Park, CA: Sage.

Loehlin, J. C., and Rowe, D. C. 1992. Genes, environment and personality. In G. V. Caprara and G. L. Van Heck (Eds.), *Modern personality psychology. Critical reviews and new directions* (pp. 352-370). London: Harvester/Wheatsheaf.

Loehlin, J. C., Willerman, L., and Horn, J. M. 1987a. Personality resemblance in adoptive families: A 10-year follow-up. *Journal of Personality and Social Psychology*, 53, 961-969.

Loehlin, J. C., Willerman, L., and Horn, J. M. 1987b. Human behavior genetics. *Annual Review of Psychology*, 39, 101-133.

Long, N., Forehand, R., Fauber, R., and Brody, G. H. 1989. Self-perceived and independent observed competence of young adolescents as a function of parental marital conflict and recent divorce. *Journal of Abnormal Child Psychology*, 15, 15-27.

Longstad, L. F. 1989. Social class, marriage, and fertility in schizophrenia. *Schizophrenia Bulletin*, 15, 9-43.

Loomis, L. S., and Booth, A. 1995. Multigenerational caregiving and well-being: The myth of the beleaguered sandwich generation. *Journal of Family Issues*, 16, 131-148.

Lorion, R., and Saltzman, W. 1993. Children's exposure to community violence: Following a path from concern to research to action. In D.

Reiss et al. (Eds.), *Children and violence* (pp. 55-65). New York: Guilford Press.

Losel, F., and Bliesener, T. 1990. Resilience in adolescence: A study on the generalizability of protective factors. In K. Hurrelman and F. Losel (Eds.), *Health hazards in adolescence*. New York: Walter de Gruyter.

Lounsbury, M. L., and Bates, J. E. 1982. The cries of infants of differing levels of perceived temperamental difficultness: Acoustic properties and effects on listeners. *Child Development*, 53, 677-686.

Luckenbill, D. F., and Doyle, D. P. 1989. Structural position and violence: Developing a cultural explanation. *Criminology*, 27, 419-435.

Luster, T., and McAdoo, H. 1996. Family and child influences on educational attainment: A secondary analysis of the high/scope Perry Preschool data. *Developmental Psychology*, 32, 26-39.

Luthar, S. S. 1991. Vulnerability and resilience: A study of high-risk adolescents. *Child Development*, 62, 600-616.

Luthar, S. S. 1993. Methodological and conceptual issues in research on childhood resilience. *Journal of Child Psychology and Psychiatry*, 34, 441-453.

Luthar, S. S., and Zigler, E. 1991. Vulnerability and competence: A review of research on resilience in childhood. *American Journal of Orthopsychiatry*, 61, 6-22.

Lykken, D. 1987. An alternative explanation for low or zero sib correlations. *Behavioral and Brain Sciences*, 10, 31-32.

Lykken, D. T., McGue, M., Bouchard, T. J., Jr., and Tellegen, A. 1990. Does contact lead to similarity or similarity to contact? *Behavior Genetics*, 20, 547-561.

Lyons, M. J., True, W. R., Eisen, S. A., Goldberg, J., Meyer, J. M., Faraone, S. V., Eaves, L. J., and Tsuang, M. T. 1995. Differential heritability of adult and juvenile antisocial traits. *Archives of General Psychiatry*, 52, 906-915.

Lytton, H. 1977. Do parents create, or respond to differences in twins? *Developmental Psychology*, 13, 456-459.

Lytton, H. 1980. *Parent-child interaction: The socialization process observed in twin and singleton families*. New York: Plenum.

Lytton, H. 1990. Child and parents' effects in boys' conduct disorder: A reinterpretation. *Developmental Psychology*, 26, 683-697.

Maccoby, E. E. 1984. Socialization and developmental change. *Child Development*, 55, 317-328.

Maccoby, E. E. 1992a. Commentary. Family structure and children's adjustment: Is quality of parenting the major mediator? In E. M.

Hetherington et al., Coping with marital transitions. *Monographs of the Society for Research in Child Development*, 57, nos. 2-3, 230-238.

Maccoby, E. E. 1992b. The role of parents in the socialization of children: A historical overview. *Developmental Psychology*, 28, 1006-1017.

Maccoby, E. E. 1996. Peer conflict and intrafamily conflict: Are there conceptual bridges? *Merrill-Palmer Quarterly*, 42, 165-176.

Maccoby, E. E., and Jacklin, C. N. 1983. The "person" characteristics of children and the family as environment. In D. Magnusson and V. L. Allen (Eds.), *Human development. An interactional perspective* (pp. 76-92). New York: Academic Press.

Maccoby, E. E., and Martin, J. 1983. Socialization in the context of the family: Parent-child interaction. In E. M. Hetherington (Ed.), *Handbook of child psychology: Vol. 4. Socialization, personality, and social development* (pp. 1-101). New York: Wiley.

Maccoby, E. E., and Mnookin, R. H. 1992. *Dividing the child. Social & legal dilemmas of custody.* Cambridge: Harvard University Press.

Maccoby, E. E., Depner, C. E., and Mnookin, R. H. 1990. Coparenting in the second year after divorce. *Journal of Marriage and the Family*, 52, 141-155.

MacKinnon, C. E. 1989. An observational investigation of sibling interactions in married and divorced families. *Developmental Psychology*, 25, 36-44.

MacKinnon-Lewis, C. E., and Lamb, M. E. 1992. The relationship between biased maternal and filial attributions and the aggressiveness of their interactions. *Development and Psychopathology*, 4, 403-415.

MacLeod, C. Mathews, A., and Tata, P. 1986. Attentional bias in emotional disorders. *Journal of Abnormal Psychology*, 95, 15-20.

Madden, D. J., and Harbin, H. T. 1983. Family structure of assaultative adolescents. *Journal of Marital and Family Therapy*, 9, 311-316.

Madden, N. A., et al. 1993. Success for all: Longitudinal effects of a restructuring program of inner-city elementary schools. *American Educational Research Journal*, 30, 123-148.

Maddock, J. W. 1993. Ecology, ethics, and responsibility in family therapy. *Family Relations*, 42, 116-123.

Magnusson, D. 1990. Personality development from an interactional perspective. In L. A. Pervin (Ed.), *Handbook of personality theory and research* (pp. 193-222). New York: Guilford Press.

Magnusson, D. 1995. Individual development: A holistic, integrated model. In P. Moen, G. H. Elder, Jr., and K. Luscher (Eds.), *Examining lives in context* (pp. 19-60). Washington, DC: American Psychological Association.

Magnusson, D., and Bergman, L. R. 1990. A pattern approach to the study of pathways from childhod to adulthood. In L. N. Robins and M. Rutter (Eds.), *Straight and devious pathways from childhood to adulthood* (pp. 101-115). Cambridge, UK: Cambridge University Press.

Mancini, C., Van Ameringen, M., and Macmillan, H. 1995. Relationship of childhood sexual and physical abuse to anxiety disorders. *The Journal of Nervous and Mental Disease*, 183, 309-314.

Mancini, J. A. 1989. Family gerontology and the study of parent-child relationships. In J. A. Mancini (Eds.), *Aging parents and adult children* (pp. 3-12). Lexington, MA: Lexington Books.

Mancini, J. A., and Blieszner, R. 1989. Aging parents and adult children: Research themes in intergenerational relations. *Journal of Marriage and the Family*, 51, 275-290.

Mandell, N. 1986. Peer interaction in day care settings: Implications for social cognition. In P. A. Adler and P. Adler (Eds.), *Sociological Studies of Child Development*, (pp. 55-79). Greenwich, CT: JAI.

Mangelsdorf, S., Gunnar, M., Kestenbaum, R., Lang, S., and Andreas, D. 1990. Infant proneness-to-distress temperament, maternal personality, and mother-infant attachment: Associations and goodness of fit. *Child Development*, 61, 820-831.

Marans, S., and Cohen, D. 1993. Children and inner-city violence: Strategies for intervention. In L. Leavitt and N. Fox (Eds.), *Psychological effects of war and violence on children* (pp. 281-302). Hillsdale, NJ: Lawrence Erlbaum.

Margolin, G. 1988. Marital conflict is not marital conflict is not marital conflict. In R. DeV. Peters and R. J. MacMahon (Eds.), *Social learning and systems approaches to marriage and the family* (pp. 193-216). New York: Brunner/Mazel.

Marks, N. F. 1995. Midlife marital status differences in social support relationships with adult children and psychological well-being. *Journal of Family Issues*, 16, 5-28.

Marks, N. F. 1996. Caregiving across the lifespan. National prevalence and predictors. *Family Relations*, 45, 27-36.

Marotto, R. A. 1986. "Posin' to be chosen": An ethnographic study of inschool truancy. In D. M. Fetterman and M. A. Pitman (Eds.), *Educational evaluation: Ethnography in theory, practice, and politics* (pp. 193-211). Beverly Hills, CA: Sage.

Marsiglio, W. 1991. Paternal engagement activities with minor children. *Journal of Marriage and the Family*, 53, 973-986.

Martin, N., and Jardine, R. 1986. Eysenck's contributions to behaviour genetics. In S. Modgil and C. Modgil (Eds.), *Hans Eysenck: Consensus and controversy* (pp. 13-47). Philadelphia: Falmer Press.

Mash, E. J., and Johnson, C. 1983a. Sibling interactions of hyperactive and normal children and their relationship to reports of maternal stress and self-esteem. *Journal of Clinical Child Psychology*, 12, 91-99.

Mash, E. J., and Johnson, C. 1983b. Parental perception of child behavior problems, parenting self-esteem and mothers' reported stress in younger and older hyperactive and normal children. *Journal of Consulting and Clinical Psychology*, 51, 86-99.

Mash, E. J., and Johnson, C. 1990. Determinants of parenting stress: Illustrations from families of hyperactive children and families of physically abused children. *Journal of Clinical Child Psychology*, 19, 313-328.

Massat, C. R. 1995. Is older better? Adolescent parenthood and maltreatment. *Child Welfare*, 74, 325-336.

Masten, A. 1989. Resilience in development: Implications of the study of successful adaptation for developmental psychopathology. In D. Cichetti (Ed.), *Rochester symposium on developmental psychopathology*. Hillsdale, NJ: Lawrence Erlbaum.

Matsueda, R. L., and Heimer, K. 1987. Race, family structure and delinquency: A test of differential association and social control theories. *American Sociological Review*, 52, 826-840.

Matthews, S. H., and Sprey, J. 1989. Older family systems: Intra- and intergenerational relations. In J. Mancini (Eds.), *Aging parents and adult children* (pp. 63-77). Lexington, MA: Lexington Books.

Maziade, M. 1994. Temperament research and practical implications for clinicians. In W. B. Carey and S. C. McDevitt (Eds.), *Prevention and early intervention: Individual differences as risk factors for the mental health of children* (pp. 69-91). New York: Brunner/Mazel.

McAdoo, H. P. (Ed.). 1988. *Black family*. Newbury Park, CA: Sage.

McAdoo, J. L. 1988. The role of Black fathers in the socialization of Black children. In H. P. McAdoo (Ed.), *Black family* (pp. 257-269). Newbury Park, CA: Sage.

McCall, R. B. 1987. Developmental function, individual differences, and the plasticity of intelligence. In J. J. Gallagher and C. T. Ramsey (Eds.), *The malleability of children* (pp. 25-35). Baltimore: Brookes Publishing.

McCartney, K., Harris, M. J., and Bernieri, F. 1990. Growing up and growing apart: A developmental meta-analysis of twin studies. *Psychological Bulletin*, 107, 226-237.

McCartney, K., et al. 1991. Mothers' language with first- and second-born children: A within-family study. In K. Pillemer and K. McCartney (Eds.), *Parent-child relations throughout life* (pp. 125-142). Hillsdale, NJ: Lawrence Erlbaum.

McCloskey, L. A., Figueredo, A. J., and Koss, M. P. 1995. The effect of systemic family violence on children's mental health. *Child Development*, 66, 1239-1261.

McColloch, M. A., Gilbert, D. G., and Johnson, S. 1990. Effects of situational variables on the interpersonal behavior of families with an aggressive adolescent. *Personality and Individual Differences*, 11, 1-11.

McCombs, A., Forehand, R., and Smith, K. 1988. The relationship between maternal problem-solving style and adolescent social adjustment. *Journal of Family Psychology*, 2, 57-66.

McCord, J. 1982. A longitudinal view of the relationship between paternal absence and crime. In J. Gunn and D. P. Farrington (Eds.), *Abnormal offenders, delinquency, and the criminal justice system*. New York: John Wiley.

McCord, J. 1988. Identifying developmental paradigms leading to alcoholism. *Journal of Studies on Alcohol*, 49, 357-362.

McCord, J., and Tremblay, R. (Eds.). 1992. *Preventing antisocial behavior: Interventions from birth to adolescence*. New York: Guilford.

McCoy, J. K., Brody, G. H., and Stoneman, Z. 1994. A longitudinal analysis of sibling relationships as mediators of the link between family processes and youths' best friendships. *Family Relations*, 43, 400-408.

McCrae, R. R., and Costa, P. T. 1990. *Personality in adulthood*. New York: Guilford.

McDermott, D. 1984. The relationship of parental drug use and parents' attitudes concerning adolescent drug use. *Adolescence*, 19, 89-97.

McElroy, E. M. 1987. The beat of a different drummer. In A. B. Hatfield and H. P. Lefley (Eds.), *Families of the mentally ill* (pp. 225-243). New York: Guilford.

McFarlane, A. H., Bellissimo, A., and Norman, G. R. 1995. Family structure, family functioning and adolescent well-being: The transcendent influence of parental style. *Journal of Child Psychology and Psychiatry*, 36, 847-864.

McGee, L., and Newcomb, M. D. 1992. General device syndrome: Expanded hierarchial evaluations at four ages from early adolescence to adulthood. *Journal of Consulting and Clinical Psychology*, 60, 766-776.

McGee, R., Feehan, M., Williams, S., and Anderson, J. 1992. DSM-III disorders from age 11 to 15 years. *Journal of the American Academy of Child and Adolescent Psychiatry*, 31, 50-59.

McGue, M. 1993. From proteins to cognitions: The behavioral genetics of alcoholism. In R. Plomin and G. E. McClearn (Eds.), *Nature, nurture & psychology* (pp. 245-265). Washington, DC: American Psychological Association.

McGue, M., Bacon, S., and Lykken, D. T. 1993. Personality stability and change in early adulthood: A behavioral genetics analysis. *Developmental Psychology*, 29, 96-109.

McGuffin, P., and Gottesman, I. I. 1985. Genetic influence on normal and abnormal development. In M. Rutter and L. Hersov (Eds.), *Child and adolescent psychiatry*, 2nd ed. Oxford: Blackwell Scientific Press.

McGuffin, P., and Katz, R. 1993. Genes, adversity, and depression. In R. Plomin and G. E. McClearn (Ed.), *Nature, nurture & psychology* (pp. 217-230). Washington, DC: American Psychological Association.

McGuffin, P., and Murray, R. 1991. *The new genetics of mental illness.* Oxford: Butterworth-Heinemann.

McGuffin, P., Katz, R., and Rutherford, J. 1991. Nature, nurture and depression: A twin study. *Psychological Medicine*, 21, 329-335.

McGuffin, P. et al. 1994. *Seminars in psychiatric genetics.* London: Gaskell.

McGuire, S., Neiderheiser, J. M., Reiss, D., Hetherington, E. M., and Plomin, R. 1994. Genetic and environmental influences on perceptions of self-worth and competence in adolescence: A study of twins, full siblings, and step-siblings. *Child Development*, 65, 785-799.

McGurk, H. 1992. A comment on child effects in socialization research: Some conceptual and data analysis issues. *Social Development*, 1, 244-246.

McHale, S. M., and Gamble, W. C. 1989. Sibling relationships of children with disabled and nondisabled brothers and sisters. *Developmental Psychology*, 25, 421-429.

McHale, S., and Pawletko, T. M. 1992. Differential treatment of siblings in two family contexts. *Child Development*, 63, 68-81.

McHale, S., Crouter, A. C., McGuire, S. A., and Updegraff, K. A. 1995. Congruence between mothers' and fathers' differential treatment of siblings: Links with family relations and children's well-being. *Child Development*, 66, 116-128.

McKenry, P.C., Everett, J. E., Ramseur, H. P., and Carter, C. J. 1989. Research on black adolescents: A legacy of cultural bias. *Journal of Adolescence Research*, 4, 254-264.

McKeever, P. 1992. Mothering children who have severe chronic illnesses. In A.-M. Ambert, *The effect of children on parents* (pp. 170-190). Binghamton, NY: Haworth Press.

McKinnon, C. E. 1989. An observational investigation of sibling interactions in married and divorced families. *Developmental Psychology*, 25, 36-44.

McLanahan, S., and Booth, K. 1989. Mother-only families: Problems, prospects, and politics. *Journal of Marriage and the Family*, 51, 557-580.

McLanahan, S., and Bumpass, L. 1988. Intergenerational consequences of family disruption. *American Journal of Sociology*, 94, 130-152.

McLanahan, S., and Sandefur, F. 1994. *Growing up with a single parent.* Cambridge, MA: Harvard University Press.

McLanahan, S., Astone, N. M., and Marks, N. F. 1991. The role of mother-only families in reproducing poverty. In A. C. Huston (Ed.), *Children in poverty: Child development and public policy* (pp. 51-78). Cambridge, UK: Cambridge University Press.

McLaren, P. 1995. *Critical pedagogy and predatory culture: Oppositional policies in a postmodern era.* New York: Routledge.

McLeod, J. D. 1995. Social and psychological bases of homogamy for common psychiatric disorders. *Journal of Marriage and the Family*, 57, 210-214.

McLeod, J. D., and Shanahan, M. J. 1993. Poverty, parenting, and children's mental health. *American Sociological Review*, 58, 351-366.

McLoyd, V. C. 1990. The impact of economic hardship on Black families and children: Psychological distress, parenting, and socioemotional development. *Child Development*, 61, 311-346.

McLoyd, V. C., and Wilson, L. 1991. The strain of living poor: Parenting, social support, and child mental health. In A. C. Huston (Ed.), *Children in poverty. Child development and public policy* (pp. 105-135). Cambridge: Cambridge University Press.

McNair, S. 1991. Gender difference in nurturance and restrictiveness in grandparents of young children of teen mothers. In *Grandmothers' lives, grandchildren's lives: An interdisciplinary approach to multigenerational parenting.* Symposium at the Biennial Meeting of the Society for Research in Child Development, Seattle.

McNamara, D. 1988. Do the grounds for claiming that school matters, matter? *British Journal of Educational Psychology*, 58, 557-560.

Mead, M. 1928. *Coming of age in Samoa.* New York: William Morrow.

Mednick, S. A., Moffitt, T., Gabrielli, W., Jr., Hutchings, B. (1986). In D. Olweus, J. Block, J. M. Radke-Yarrow (Eds.), *Development of antisocial and prosocial behavior: Research, theories, and issues* (pp. 33-50). New York: Academic Press.

Medrich, E. A., Roizen, J. A., Rubin, V., and Buckley, S. 1982. *The serious business of growing up: A study of children's lives outside school.* Berkeley, CA: University of California Press.

Meeus, W. 1989. Parental and peer support in adolescence. In K. Hurrelmann and U. Engel (Ed.), *The social world of adolescents: International perspectives* (pp. 141-166). Berlin: Walter de Gruyter.

Mehan, H. 1992. Understanding inequality in schools: The contribution of interpretive studies. *Sociology of Education*, 65, 1-20.

Melby, J. N., and Conger, R. D. 1996. Parental behaviors and adolescent academic performance: A longitudinal analysis. *Journal of Research on Adolescence*, 6, 113-137.

Menaghan, E. G. 1991. Work experiences and family interaction processes: The long reach of the job? *Annual Review of Sociology*, 17, 419-444.

Menaghan, E. G. 1994. The daily grind: Work stressors, family patterns, and intergenerational outcomes. In W. Avison and I. Gotlib (Eds.), *Stress and mental health: Contemporary issues and future prospects* (pp. 115-147). New York: Plenum.

Menaghan, E. G., and Parcel, T. L. 1990. Parental employment and family life: Research in the 1980s. *Journal of Marriage and the Family*, 52, 1079-1098.

Menaghan, E. G., and Parcel, T. L. 1991. Determining children's home environments: The impact of maternal characteristics and current occupational and family conditions. *Journal of Marriage and the Family*, 53, 417-431.

Menaghan, E. G., and Parcel, T. L. 1995. Social sources of change in children's home environments: The effects of parental occupational experiences and family conditions. *Journal of Marriage and the Family*, 57, 69-84.

Mendelson, M. J., and Gottlieb, L. N. 1994. Birth order and age differences in early sibling roles. *Canadian Journal of Behavioural Science*, 26, 385-403.

Merikangas, K. R. 1992. Assortative mating for psychiatric disorders and psychological traits. *Archives of General Psychiatry*, 39, 1173-1180.

Mesquita, P. B. de, and Gilliam, W. S. 1994. Differential diagnosis of childhood depression: Using comorbidity and symptom overlap to generate multiple hypotheses. *Child Psychiatry and Human Development*, 24, 157-172.

Meyer, D. R., and Garasky, S. 1993. Custodial fathers: Myths, realities, and child support policy. *Journal of Marriage and the Family*, 55, 73-89.

Meyer, J. M., Eaves, L. J., Heath, A. C., and Martin, N. G. 1991. Estimating genetic influences on the age-at-menarche: A survival analysis approach. *American Journal of Medical Genetics*, 39, 148-154.

Miller, B. C. 1993. Families, science, and values: Alternative views of parenting effects and adolescent pregnancy. *Journal of Marriage and the Family*, 55, 7-21.

Minton, C., Kagan, J., and Levine, J. 1971. Maternal control and obedience in the two-year-old. *Child Development*, 42, 1873-1894.

Miranda, L. C. 1991. *Latino child poverty in the United States*. Washington, DC: Children's Defense Fund.

Mirande, A. 1991. Ethnicity and fatherhood. In F. Bozett and S. Hanson (Eds.), *Fatherhood and families in cultural context* (pp. 53-82). New York: Springer.

Mishler, E. G., and Waxler, N. E. 1966. Family interaction and schizophrenia: An approach to the experimental study of family interaction and schizophrenia. *Archives of General Psychiatry*, 15, 64-74.

Mitchell, B. A., Wister, A. V., and Burch, T. K. 1989. The family environment and leaving the parental home. *Journal of Marriage and the Family*, 51, 605-613.

Mitchell, J. S., and Register, J. S. 1984. An exploration of family interaction with the elderly by race, socioeconomic status and residence. *The Gerontologist*, 24, 48-54.

Mitman, A. L., and Lash, A. A. 1988. Students' perceptions of their academic standing and classroom behavior. *The Elementary School Journal*, 89, 55-68.

Modell, J., and Goodman, M. 1990. Historical perspectives. In S. S. Feldman and G. R. Elliott (Eds.), *At the threshold: The developing adolescent* (pp. 93-122). Cambridge, MA: Harvard University Press.

Moen, P., and Erickson, M. A. 1995. Linked lives: A transgenerational approach to resilience. In P. Moen, G. H. Elder, Jr., and K. Luscher (Eds.), *Examining lives in context* (pp. 169-210). Washington, DC: American Psychological Association.

Moffitt, T. E., Lynam, D. R., and Silva, P. A. 1994. Neuropsychological tests predicting persistent male delinquency. *Criminology*, 32, 277-300.

Monahan, S. C., Buchanan, C. M., Maccoby, E. E., and Dornbusch, S. M. 1993. Sibling differences in divorced families. *Child Development*, 64, 152-168.

Monroe, S. M., and Simons, A. D. 1991. Diathesis-stress theories in the context of life stress research: Implications for the depressive disorders. *Psychological Bulletin*, 110, 406-425.

Montemayor, R. 1986. Family variation in parent-adolescent storm and stress. *Journal of Adolescent Research*, 1, 15-31.

Montemayor, R., and Hanson, E. 1985. A naturalistic view of conflict between adolescents and their parents and siblings. *Journal of Early Adolescence*, 5, 23-30.

Montgomery, M. J., Anderson, E. R., Hetherington, E. M., and Clingempeel, W. G. 1992. Patterns of courtship for remarriage: Implications for child adjustment and parent-child relationship. *Journal of Marriage and the Family*, 54, 686-698.

Montgomery, R. J. 1992. Gender differences in patterns of child-parent caregiving relationships. In J. W. Dwyer and R. T. Coward (Eds.), *Gender, families, and elder care* (pp. 65-83). Newbury Park, CA: Sage.

Montgomery, R. J. V., and Kamo, Y. 1989. Parent care by sons and daughters. In J. A. Mancini (Eds.), *Aging parents and adult children* (pp. 213-230). Lexington, MA: Lexington Books.

Morgan, S. P., Lye, D. N., and Condran, G. A. 1988. Sons, daughters, and the risk of marital disruption. *American Journal of Sociology*, 94, 110-129.

Morgan, S. P., et al. 1993. Racial differences in household structure at the turn of the century. *American Journal of Sociology*, 98, 798-828.

Morris-Yates, A., et al. 1990. Twins: A test of the equal environments assumption. *Acta Psychiatrica Scandinavica*, 81, 322-326.

Morrison, D. R. 1995. The divorce process and young children's well-being: A prospective analysis. *Journal of Marriage and the Family*, 57, 800-812.

Morrison, T. R. 1994. Toward authentic learning: Reconnecting families and education. In M. Baker (Ed.), *Canada's changing families: Challenges to public policy* (pp. 55-68). Ottawa: The Vanier Institute of the Family.

Mortimer, J. T., Shanahan, M., and Ryu, S. 1994. The effects of adolescent employment on school-related orientation and behavior. In R. K. Silbereisen and E. Todt (Eds.), *Adolescence in context* (pp. 304-326). New York: Springer-Verlag.

Mortimore, P. 1991. School effectiveness research: Which way at the crossroads? *School Effectiveness and School Improvement*, 2, 213-229.

Mortimore, P., et al. 1988. *School matters: The junior years*. Wells, Somerset: Open Books.

Moskowitz, D., and Schwartzman, A. 1989. Painting group portraits: Assessing life outcomes for aggressive and withdrawn children. *Journal of Personality*, 57, 723-746.

Mowbray, C. T., et al. 1995. Motherhood for women with serious mental illness: Pregnancy, childbirth, and the postpartum period. *American Journal of Orthopsychiatry*, 65, 21-38.

Mulkey, L. M., Crain, R. L., Harrington, A. J. C. 1992. One-parent households and achievement: Economic and behavioral explanations of a small effect. *Sociology of Education*, 65, 48-65.

Mullan, M. J., and Murray, R. M. 1989. The impact of molecular genetics on our understanding of the psychoses. *British Journal of Psychiatry*, 154, 591-595.

Muller, C. 1993. Parental involvement and academic achievement. In B. S. Coleman and J. S. Coleman (Eds.), *Parents, their children and schools* (pp. 77-113). Boulder, CO: Westview.

Muller, C. 1995. Maternal employment, parental involvement, and mathematics achievement among adolescents. *Journal of Marriage and the Family*, 57, 85-100.

Muller, C., and Kerbow, D. 1993. Parent involvement in the home, school, and community. In B. Schneider and J. S. Coleman (Eds.), *Parents, their children, and schools* (pp. 13-42). San Francisco: Westview Press.

Mullis, I., et al. 1991. *Trends in academic progress*. Washington, DC: National Center for Education Statistics, U.S. Department of Education.

Mulvey, E. P., Arthur, M., and Reppucci, N. D. 1993. The prevention and treatment of juvenile delinquency: A review of the research. *Clinical Psychology Review*, 13, 133-157.

Munn, P., and Dunn, J. 1988. Temperament and the developing relationship between siblings. *International Journal of Behavioral Development*, 12, 433-451.

Munthe, E. 1989. Bullying in Scandinavia. In E. Roland and E. Munthe (Eds.), *Bullying: An international perspective* (pp. 66-78). London: David Fulton Publishers.

Mutran, E., and Reitzes, D. G. 1984. Intergenerational support activities and well-being among the elderly: A convergence of exchange and symbolic interaction perspectives. *American Sociological Review*, 49, 117-130.

Nagin, D. S., and Land, K. C. 1993. Age, criminal careers, and population heterogeneity: Specification and estimation of a nonparametric, mixed Poisson model. *Criminology*, 31, 327-362.

Nagin, D. S., Farrington, D. P., and Moffitt, T. E. 1995. Life-course trajectories of different types of offenders. *Criminology*, 33, 111-139.

National Institute of Mental Health. 1986. *Client/patient sample survey of inpatient, outpatient, and partial care programs*. Rockville, MD: Department of Health and Human Services. NIMH, Survey & Reports Branch, Division of Biometry.

National Research Council. 1993. *Losing generations: Adolescents in high-risk settings.* Washington, DC: National Academy Press.

Nava, M. 1992. *Changing cultures: Feminism, youth and consumerism.* Newbury Park: Sage.

Neale, M. C., and Cardon, L. C. 1992. *Methodology for genetic studies of twins and families.* Amsterdam: Kluwer.

Needle, R. H., Su, S. S., and Doherty, W. J. 1990. Divorce, remarriage, and adolescent substance use: A prospective longitudinal study. *Journal of Marriage and the Family,* 52, 157-169.

Nelson, B. J. 1984. *Making an issue of child abuse.* Chicago: The University of Chicago Press.

Nelson, K. E., and Landsman, M. J. 1992. *Alternative methods of family preservation: Family-based services in context.* Springfield, IL: Charles C Thomas.

Nesselroade, J. R. 1990. Adult personality development: Issues in assessing constancy and change. In A. I. Rabin et al. (Eds.), *Studying persons and lives* (pp. 41-85). New York: Springer.

Nigg, J. T., and Goldsmith, H. H. 1994. Genetics of personality disorders: Perspectives from personality and psychopathology research. *Psychological Bulletin,* 115, 346-380.

Nitz, K., Ketterlinus, R. D., and Brandt, L. J. 1995. The role of stress, social support, and family environment in adolescent mothers' parenting. *Journal of Adolescent Research,* 10, 358-382.

Nock, S. L., and Kingston, P. W. 1988. Time with children: The impact of couples' work-time commitments. *Social Forces,* 67, 59-85.

Nolen-Hoeksema, S., and Girgus, J. S. 1994. The emergence of gender differences in depression during adolescence. *Psychological Bulletin,* 115, 424-443.

Noller, P. 1994. Relationships with parents in adolescence: Process and outcome. In R. Montemayor, G. R. Adams, and T. P. Gullotta (Eds.), *Personal relationships during adolescence* (Advances in Adolescent Development, vol. 6, 37-77). Thousand Oaks, CA: Sage.

Noller, P., and Callan, V. 1991. *The adolescent in the family.* New York: Routledge.

Norton, A. J., and Moorman, J. 1987. Current trends in marriage and divorce among American women. *Journal of Marriage and the Family,* 49, 3-14.

Nylander, I. 1979. A 20-year prospective follow-up study of 2164 cases at the child guidance clinic in Stockholm. *Acta Paediatrica Scandinavica,* 276, 1-45.

O'Brien, M., Margolin, G., and John, R. S. 1995. Relation among marital conflict, child coping, and child adjustment. *Journal of Clinical Child Psychology*, 24, 346-361.

O'Connor, T. G., Hetherington, E. M., Reiss, D., and Plomin, R. 1995. A twin-sibling study of observed parent-adolescent interactions. *Child Development*, 66, 812-829.

O'Donnell, C. R. 1995. Firearm deaths among children and youth. *American Psychologist*, 50, 771-776.

Office of Disease Prevention and Health Promotion. 1991. *National health promotion and disease prevention objectives* (DHHS Publication no. PHS-9-50212). Washington, DC: U.S. Government Printing Office.

Offord, D., Ostrow, E., and Howard, K. I. 1987. *The adolescent: A psychological self-portrait*. New York: Basic Books.

Ogbu, J. 1987. Variability in school performance: A problem in search of an explanation. *Anthropology and Education Quarterly*, 18, 312-334.

Okagaki, L., and Sternberg, R. J. 1993. Parental beliefs and children's school performance. *Child Development*, 64, 36-56.

O'Keeffe, N. K., Brockopp, K., and Chew, E. 1986. Teen dating violence. *Social Work*, 31, 465-468.

Oldman, D. 1994. Adult-child relations as class relations. In J. Qvortrup et al. (Eds.), *Childhood matters. Social theory, practice and politics* (pp. 43-58). Aldershot: Avebury.

Olweus, D. 1991. Bully/victim problems among schoolchildren: Basic facts and effects of a school-based intervention program. In D. J. Pepler and K. H. Rubin (Ed.), *The development and treatment of childhood aggression* (pp. 411-449). Hillsdale, NJ: Lawrence Erlbaum.

Olweus, D. 1994. Annotation: Bullying at school: Basic facts and effects of a school-based intervention program. *Journal of Child Psychology and Psychiatry*, 35, 1171-1190.

O'Moore, A. M. 1989. Bullying in Britain and Ireland: An overview. In E. Roland and E. Munthe (Ed.), *Bullying: An international perspective* (pp. 3-21). London: David Fulton Publishers.

O'Neill, J. 1993. *The missing child in liberal theory*. Toronto: University of Toronto Press.

Ooms, T., and Figueroa, I. 1992. *Latino families, poverty, and welfare reform*. Washington, DC: AAMFT Research and Education Foundation, Family Impact Seminar.

Oppenheimer, V. K. 1982. *Work and the family: A study in social demography*. New York: Academic Press.

Orleans, M., Palisi, B. J., and Caddell, D. 1989. Marriage adjustment and satisfaction of stepfathers: Their feelings and perceptions of decision making and stepchildren relations. *Family Relations*, 38, 371-377.

Orthner, D. K. 1990. Parental work and early adolescence: Issues for research and practice. *Journal of Early Adolescence*, 10, 246-259.

Osofsky, J. D. 1995. The effects of exposure to violence on young children. *American Psychologist*, 50, 782-788.

Osofsky, J. D., and Fenichel, E. (Eds.). 1994. *Caring for infants and toddlers in violent environments: Hurt, healing, and hope.* Arlington, VA: Zero to Three/National Center for Clinical Infant Programs.

Osofsky, J. D., Weivers, S., Hann, D. M., and Fick, A. C. 1993. Chronic community violence: What is happening to our children? *Psychiatry*, 56, 36-45.

Oyserman, D., Radin, N., and Saltz, E. 1994. Predictors of nurturant parenting in teen mothers living in three generational families. *Child Psychiatry and Human Development*, 24, 215-230.

Pahl, J., and Quine, L. 1984. *Families with mentally handicapped children: A study of stress and of service response.* Report Health Research Unit, UK: University of Kent.

Paikoff, R. L., and Brooks-Gunn, J. 1991. Do parent-child relationships change during puberty? *Psychological Bulletin*, 110, 47-66.

Parcel, T. L., and Menaghan, E. G. 1994. Early parental work, family social capital, and early childhood outcomes. *American Journal of Sociology*, 99, 972-1009.

Parcel, T. L., and Menaghan, E. G. 1994. *Parents' jobs and children's lives.* New York: Aldine de Gruyter.

Pare, D. A. 1995. Of families and other cultures: The shifting paradigm of family therapy. *Family Process*, 34, 1-19.

Parke, R. D. 1994. Epilogue: Unresolved issues and future trends in family relationships with other contexts. In R. D. Parke and S. G. Kellam (Eds.), *Exploring family relationships with other social contexts* (pp. 215-229). Hillsdale, NJ: Lawrence Erlbaum.

Parke, R., and Neville, B. 1987. Teenage fatherhood. In S. Hofferth and C. Hayes (Eds.), *Risking the future*, vol. 2 (pp. 145-173). Washington, DC: National Academy Press.

Parke, R. D., et al. 1994. Family-peer relationships: A tripartite model. In R. D. Parke and S. G. Kellam (Eds.), *Exploring family relationships with other social contexts* (pp. 115-146). Hillsdale, NJ: Lawrence Erlbaum.

Parker, G. 1982. Re-searching the schizophrenic mother. *Journal of Nervous and Mental Disease*, 170, 452-462.

Parkes, C. M., Stevenson-Hinde, J., and Marris, P. (Eds.). 1991. *Attachment across the life cycle.* London: Tavistock/Routledge.

Pasley, K., and Gecas, V. 1984. Stresses and satisfactions of the parental role. *Personal and Guidance Journal*, 2, 400-404.

Patterson, C., Cohn, D., and Kao, B. 1989. Maternal warmth as a protective factor against risks associated with peer rejection among children. *Development and Psychopathology*, 1, 21-38.

Patterson, C. J., Kupersmidt, J. B., and Vaden, N. A. 1990. Income level, gender, ethnicity, and household composition as predictors of children's school-based competence. *Child Development*, 61, 485-494.

Patterson, C. J., Vaden, N. A., Griesler, P. C., and Kupersmidt, J. B. 1991. Income level, gender, ethnicity, and household composition as predictors of children's peer companionship outside of school. *Journal of Applied Developmental Psychology*, 12, 447-465.

Patterson, C. J., Griesler, P. C., Vaden, N. A., and Kupersmidt, J. B. 1992. Family economic circumstances, life transitions, and children's peer relations. In R. D. Parke and G. W. Ladd (Eds.), *Family-peer relationships: Modes of linkage* (pp. 385-424). Hillsdale, NJ: Lawrence Erlbaum.

Patterson, G. R. 1976. *Families of antisocial children: An interactional approach*. Eugene, OR: Castalia.

Patterson, G. R. 1980. Mothers: The unacknowleged victims. *Monographs of the Society for Research in Child Development*, 186.

Patterson, G. R. 1982. *Coercive family process*. Eugene, OR: Castalia.

Patterson, G. R. 1984. Beyond technology: The next stage in developing an empirical base for parent training. In L. L. L'Abate (Ed.), *The handbook of family psychology and therapy*, vol. 2 (pp. 1344-1379). Homewood, IL: Dorset.

Patterson, G. R. 1986. Maternal rejection: Determinant or product of deviant behavior? In W. W. Hartup and Z. Rubin (Eds.), *Relationships and Development*. Hillsdale, NJ: Lawrence Erlbaum.

Patterson, G. R. 1992. Developmental changes in anti-social behavior. In R. D. Peters, R. J. McMahon, and V. L. Quinsey (Eds.), *Aggression and violence throughout the lifespan*. Newbury Park, CA: Sage.

Patterson, G. R., and Capaldi, D. M. 1991. Antisocial parents: Unskilled and vulnerable. In P. A. Cowan and M. Hetherington (Eds.), *Family transitions* (pp. 195-218). Hillsdale, NJ: Lawrence Erlbaum.

Patterson, G. R., and Chamberlain, P. 1994. A functional analysis of resistance during parent training therapy. *Clinical Psychology: Science and Practice*, 1, 53-70.

Patterson, G. R., and Dishion, T. J. 1988. Multilevel family process models: Traits, interactions, and relationships. In R. Hinde and J. Stevenson-

Hinde (Eds.), *Relationships within families: Mutual influences* (pp. 283-310). Oxford: Clarendon.

Patterson, G. R., and Forgatch, M. S. 1990. Initiation and maintenance of process disrupting single-mother families. In G. R. Patterson (Ed.), *Depression and aggression in family interaction* (pp. 209-246). Hillsdale, NJ: Lawrence Erlbaum.

Patterson, G. R., and Stouthamer-Loeber, M. 1984. The correlation of family management practices and delinquency. *Child Development*, 55, 1299-1307.

Patterson, G. R., Bank, L., and Stoolmiller, M. 1990. The preadolescent's contributions to disrupted family process. In R. Montemayor, G. R. Adams, and T. P. Gullotta (Eds.), *From childhood to adolescence* (pp. 107-133). Newburry Park, CA: Sage.

Patterson, G. R., DeBaryshe, B. D., and Ramsey, E. 1989. A developmental perspective on antisocial behavior. *American Psychologist*, 44, 329-335.

Patterson, G. R., Reid, J. B., and Dishion, T. J. 1992. *Antisocial boys*. Eugene, OR: Castalia.

Paulkus, D., and Shaffer, D. R. 1981. Sex differences in the impact of number of older and number of younger siblings on scholastic aptitude. *Social Psychology Quarterly*, 44, 363-368.

Paulson, S. E., Koman III, J. J., and Hill, J. P. 1990. Maternal employment and the parent-child relations in families of seventh graders. *Journal of Early Adolescence*, 10, 279-295.

Pederson, N. L., McClearn, G. E., Plomin, R., and Nesselroade, J. R. 1992. Effects of early rearing environment on twin similarity in the last half of the life span. *British Journal of Developmental Psychology*, 10, 255-267.

Pederson, N. L., Plomin, R., McClearn, G. E., and Friberg, L. 1988. Neuroticism, extraversion, and related traits in adult twins reared apart and reared together. *Journal of Personality and Social Psychology*, 55, 950-957.

Pelletier-Stiefel, J., Pepler, D., Crozier, K., Stanhope, L., Carter, C., and Abramovitch, R. 1986. Nurturance in the home: A longitudinal study of sibling interaction. In A. Fogel and G. F. Nelson (Eds.), *Origins of nurturance*. Hillsdale, NJ: Lawrence Erlbaum.

Pepler, D. J., and Slaby, R. G. 1994. Theoretical and developmental perspectives on youth and violence. In L. D. Eron et al. (Eds.), *Reason to hope: A psychosocial perspective on violence and youth* (pp. 27-58), Washington, DC: American Psychological Association.

Pepler, D. J., Craig, W. M., Ziegler, S., and Charach, A. 1994. An evaluation of an anti-bullying intervention in Toronto schools. *Canadian Journal of Community Mental Health*, 13, 95-110.

Perry, D. G., Kusel, S. J., and Perry, L. C. 1988. Victims of peer aggression. *Developmental Psychology*, 124, 807-814.

Perusse, D., Neale, M. C., Heath, A. C., and Eaves, L. J. 1994. Human parenting behavior: Evidence for genetic influence and potential implication for gene-culture transmission. *Behavior Genetics*, 24, 327-335.

Pervin, L. A. (Ed.). 1990. *Handbook of personality theory and research.* New York: Guilford Press.

Peterson, C. 1992. *Personality*, 2nd ed. New York: Harcourt Brace Jovanovich.

Peterson, G. W., and Rollins, B. C. 1987. Parent-child socialization. In M. B. Sussman and S. K. Steinmetz (Eds.), *Handbook of marriage and the family* (pp. 471-507). New York: Plenum.

Peterson, J. L., and Zill, N. 1986. Marital disruption, parent-child relationships, and behavioral problems in children. *Journal of Marriage and the Family*, 48, 295-307.

Pettit, G. S., Harrist, A. W., Bates, J. E., and Dodge, K. A. 1991. Family interaction, social cognition, and children's subsequent relations with peers at kindergarten. *Journal of Social and Personal Relationships*, 8, 383-402.

Phillips, D. A., McCartney, K., and Scarr, S. 1987. Child care quality and children's social development. *Developmental Psychology*, 23, 537-543.

Phillips, D. A., McCartney, K., Scarr, S., and Howes, C. 1987. Selective review of infant day care research: A case for concern. *Zero to Three: Bulletin of the National Center for Clinical Infant Studies*, 7, 18-21.

Pianta, R. C., Egeland, B., and Erickson, M. F. 1989. The antecedents of maltreatment: Results of the Mother-Child Interaction Research Project. In D. Cicchetti and V. Carlson (Eds.), *Child maltreatment* (pp. 203-253). Cambridge: Cambridge University Press.

Pianta, R. C., Steinberg, M. S., and Rollins, F. B. 1995. The first two years of school: Teacher-child relationships and deflections in children's classroom adjustment. *Development and Psychopathology*, 7, 295-312.

Pickles, A., and Rutter, M. 1991. Statistical and conceptual models of "turning points" in developmental processes. In D. Magnusson et al. (Eds.), *Problems and methods in longitudinal research: Stability and change.* Cambridge, UK: Cambridge University Press.

Piercy, P., and Sprenkle, D. 1990. Marriage and family therapy: A decade review. *Journal of Marriage and the Family*, 52, 1116-1126.

Pillemer, K. 1985. The dangers of dependency: New findings on domestic violence against the elderly. *Social Problems*, 33, 147-158.

Pillemer, K., and Suitor, J. J. 1991a. "Will I ever escape my child's problems?" Effects of adult children's problems on elderly parents. *Journal of Marriage and the Family*, 53, 585-594.

Pillemer, K., and Suitor, J. J. 1991b. Relationships with children and distress in the elderly. In K. Pillemer and K. McCartney (Eds.), *Parent-child relations throughout life* (pp. 163-178). Hillsdale, NJ: Lawrence Erlbaum.

Plomin, R. 1986. *Development, genetics & psychology*. Hillsdale, NJ: Lawrence Erlbaum.

Plomin, R. 1994a. *Genetics and experience: The interplay between nature and nurture*. Thousand Oaks, CA: Sage.

Plomin, R. 1994b. Interface of nature and nurture in the family. In W. B. Carey and S. C. McDevitt (Eds.), *Prevention and early intervention: Individual differences as risk factors for the mental health of children* (pp. 179-189). New York: Brunner/Mazel.

Plomin, R. 1995. Genetics and children's experiences in the family. *Journal of Child Psychology and Psychiatry*, 36, 33-68.

Plomin, R., and Bergeman, C. S. 1991. The nature of nurture: Genetic influences on enviromental measures. *Behavioral and Brain Sciences*, 14, 373-427.

Plomin, R., and Daniels, D. 1987. Why are children in the same family so different from one another? *Behavioral and Brain Sciences*, 10, 1-15.

Plomin, R., and McClearn, G. E. (Eds.). 1993. *Nature, nurture & psychology*. Washington, DC: American Psychological Association.

Plomin, R., and Neiderhiser, J. M. 1992. Quantitative genetics, molecular genetics, and intelligence. *Intelligence*, 15, 369-387.

Plomin, R., and Rende, R. 1991. Human behavioral genetics. *Review of Psychology*, 42, 161-190.

Plomin, R., Chipuer, H. M., and Neiderhiser, J. M. 1994. Behavioral genetic evidence for the importance of nonshared environment. In E. M. Hetherington, D. Reiss, and R. Plomin (Eds.), *Separate social worlds of siblings* (pp. 1-31). Hillsdale, NJ: Lawrence Erlbaum.

Plomin, R., DeFries, J. C., and Fulker, D. W. 1988. *Nature and nurture during infancy and early childhood*. New York: Cambridge University Press.

Plomin, R., DeFries, J. C., and Loehlin, J. C. 1977. Genotype-environment interaction and correlation in the analysis of human behavior. *Psychological Bulletin*, 84, 309-322.

Plomin, R., DeFries, J. C., and McClearn, G. E. 1990. *Behavioral genetics: A primer*, 2nd ed. New York: Freeman.

Plomin, R., Nitz, K., and Rowe, D. C. 1990. Behavioral genetics and aggressive behavior in childhood. In M. Lewis and S. M. Miller (Eds.), *Handbook of developmental psychopathology* (pp. 119-133). New York: Plenum.

Plomin, R., Corley, R., DeFries, J. C., and Fulker, D. W. 1990. Individual differences in television viewing in early childhood: Nature as well as nurture. *Psychological Science*, 1, 371-377.

Plomin, R., Reiss, D., Hetherington, E. M., and Howe, G. W. 1994. Nature and nurture: Genetic contributions to measures of the family environment. *Developmental Psychology*, 30, 32-43.

Plomin, R., McClearn, G. E., Pedersen, N. L., Nesselroade, J. R., and Bergeman, C. S. 1988. Genetic influence on childhood family environment perceived retrospectively from the last half of the life span. *Developmental Psychology*, 24, 738-745.

Plomin, R., McClearn, G. E., Pedersen, N. L., Nesselroade, J. R., and Bergeman, C. S. 1989. Genetic influence on adults' ratings of their current family environment. *Journal of Marriage and the Family*, 51, 791-803.

Plomin, R., et al. 1993. Genetic change and continuity from fourteen to twenty months: The MacArthur Longitudinal Twin Study. *Child Development*, 64, 1354-1376.

Pope, H. G., and Katz, D. L. 1994. Psychiatric and medical effects of anabolic-androgen steroid use: A controlled study of 160 athletes. *Archives of General Psychiatry*, 51, 375-382.

Powell, B., and Steelman, L. C. 1993. The educational benefits of being spaced out: Sibship density and educational progess. *American Sociological Review*, 58, 367-381.

Powers, J. L., and Eckenrode, J. 1988. The maltreatment of adolescents. *Child Abuse and Neglect*, 12, 189-199.

Price, R. A., et al. 1982. Components of variation in normal personality. *Journal of Personality and Social Psychology*, 43, 328-340.

Prior, M. 1992. Childhood temperament. *Journal of Child Psychology and Psychiatry*, 33, 249-279.

Prout, A., and James, A. 1990. *Constructing and reconstructing childhood: Contemporary issues in the sociological study of childhood*. London: Falmer.

Pryor-Brown, L., and Cowen, E. 1989. Stressful life events, support, and children's school adjustment. *Journal of Clinical Child Psychology*, 18, 214-220.

Pulkinen, L., and Tremblay, R. E. 1992. Patterns of boys' social adjustment in two cultures and at different ages: A longitudinal perspective. *International Journal of Behavioral Development*, 15, 527-553.

Pulver, A. E., et al. 1990. Schizophrenia: Age at onset, gender and familial risk. *Acta Psychiatrica Scandinavica*, 82, 344-351.

Putallaz, M. 1987. Maternal behavior and children's sociometric status. *Child Development*, 58, 324-340.

Quine, L., and Rutter, D. R. 1994. First diagnosis of severe mental and physical disability: A study of doctor-patient communication. *Journal of Child Psychology and Psychiatry*, 35, 1273-1287.

Qvortrup, J. 1995. From useful to useful: The historical continuity of children's constructive participation. *Sociological Studies of Children*, 7, 49-76.

Radke-Yarrow, M. 1990. Family environments of depressed and well parents and their children: Issues of research methods. In G. R. Patterson (Ed.), *Depression and aggression in family interaction* (pp. 169-184). Hillsdale, NJ: Lawrence Erlbaum.

Radke-Yarrow, M., and Sherman, T. 1993. Hard growing: Children who survive. In J. Rolf, A. Masten, D. Cicchetti, K. Neuchterlein, and S. Weintraub (Eds.), *Risk and protective factors in the development of psychopathology*. Cambridge: Cambridge University Press.

Radke-Yarrow, M., Richters, J., and Wilson, W. E. 1988. Child development in a network of relationships. In R. A. Hinde and J. Stevenson-Hinde (Eds.). *Relationships within families: Mutual influences* (pp. 48-67). New York: Oxford University Press.

Raine, A., Venables, P. H., and Mark, W. 1990. Relationships between central and autonomic measures of arousal at age 15 years old and criminality at age 24 years. *Archives of General Psychiatry*, 47, 1003-1007.

Reddy, M. T. 1994. *Crossing the color line: Race, parenting and culture.* New Brunswick, NJ: Rutgers University Press.

Regier, D. A., et al. 1990. Comorbidity of mental disorders with alcohol and other drug abuse. *Journal of the American Medical Association*, 264, 2511-2518.

Reid, K. 1985. *Truancy and school absenteeism.* London: Hodder and Stoughton.

Reid, W. J., and Crisafulli, A. 1990. Marital discord and child behavior problems: A meta-analysis. *Journal of Abnormal Child Psychology*, 18, 105-117.

Reiss, A. J., Jr. 1986. Why are communities important in understanding crime? In A. J. Reiss, Jr. and M. Tonry (Eds.), *Communities and crime* (pp. 1-33). Chicago: University of Chicago Press.

Reiss, D. 1993. Genes and the environment: Siblings and synthesis. In R. Plomin and G. E. McClearn (Eds.), *Nature, nurture & psychology* (pp. 417-432). Washington, DC: American Psychological Association.

Reiss, D. 1995. Genetic influence on family systems: Implications for development. *Journal of Marriage and the Family*, 57, 543-560.

Reiss, D., Richters, J. E., Radke-Yarrow, M., and Scharff, D. (Eds.). 1993. *Children and violence*. New York: Guilford Press.

Reiss, D., Plomin, R., Hetherington, M. E., Howe, G. W., Rovine, M., Tryon, A., and Hagan, M. S. 1994. The separate worlds of teenage siblings: An introduction to the study of the nonshared environment and adolescent development. In E. M. Hetherington, D. Reiss, and R. Plomin (Eds.), *Separate social worlds of sibling* (pp. 63-110). Hillsdale, NJ: Lawrence Erlbaum.

Reiss, D., et al. 1995. Genetic questions for environmental studies. Differential parenting and psychopathology in adolescence. *Archives of General Psychiatry*, 52, 925-936.

Rende, R. D. 1993. Longitudinal relations between temperament traits and behavioral syndromes in middle childhood. *Journal of the American Academy of Child and Adolescent Psychiatry*, 32, 287-290.

Rende, R. D., Slomkowski, C. L., Stocker, C., Fulker, D. W., and Plomin, R. 1992. Genetic and environmental influences on maternal and sibling interaction in middle childhood: A sibling adoption study. *Developmental Psychology*, 28, 484-490.

Repetti, R. L. 1987. Links between work and family role. In S. Oskamp (Ed.), *Family processes and problems: Social psychological aspects* (pp. 98-127). Newbury Park, CA: Sage.

Resnicow, K., Ross-Gaddy, D., and Vaughan, R. D. 1995. Structure of problems and positive behaviors in African American youths. *Journal of Consulting and Clinical Psychology*, 63, 594-603.

Rice, G. 1992. Separation-individuation and adjustment to college: A longitudinal study. *Journal of Counseling Psychology*, 39, 203-213.

Richards, M. P. M. (Ed.). 1974. *The integration of a child into a social world*. Cambridge: Cambridge University Press.

Richards, M. P. M., and Light, P. (Eds.), 1986. *Children of social worlds*. Oxford: Polity Press.

Richters, J., and Pellegrini, D. 1989. Depressed mothers' judgements about their children: An examination of the depression-distortion hypothesis. *Child Development*, 60, 1068-1075.

Riese, M. L. 1990. Neonatal temperament in monozygotic and dizygotic twin pairs. *Child Development*, 61, 1230-1237.

Roberts, J. 1995. Lone mothers and their children. *British Journal of Psychiatry,* 167, 159-162.

Roberts, R. E. L., and Bengtson, V. L. 1993. Relationships with parents, self-esteem, and psychological well-being in young adulthood. *Social Psychology Quarterly,* 56, 263-277.

Robin, A. L., Koepke, T., and Moye, A. 1990. Multidimensional assessment of parent-adolescent relations. *Psychological Assessment,* 4, 451-459.

Robins, L. N. 1978. Aetiological implications in studies of childhood histories relating to antisocial personality. In R. D. Hare and D. Schalling (Eds.), *Psychopathic behavior: Approaches to research.* (pp. 255-272). Chichester, UK: Wiley.

Robins, L. N. 1984. Sturdy childhood predictors of adult outcomes: Replications from longitudinal studies. *Psychological Medicine,* 8, 611-622.

Robins, L. N., and McEvoy, L. C. 1990. Conduct problems and predictors of substance abuse. In L. N. Robbins and M. Rutter (Eds.), *Straight and devious pathways from childhood to adulthood* (pp. 182-204). Cambridge: Cambridge University Press.

Robins, L. N., and Ratcliffe, K. S. 1979. Risk factors in the continuation of childhood antisocial behavior into adulthood. *International Journal of Mental Health,* 7, 96-111.

Robins, L. N., Locke, B. Z., and Regier, D. A. 1991. An overview of psychiatric disorders in America. In L. N. Robins and D. A. Regier (Eds.), *Psychiatric disorders in America: The epidemiological catchment area study* (pp. 328-366). New York: Free Press.

Robins, P. V., Mace, N. L., and Lucas, M. J. 1982. The impact of dementia on the family. *Journal of the American Medical Association,* 248, 333-335.

Robins, R. W., John, O. P., Caspi, A., Moffitt, T. E., and Stouthamer-Loeber, M. 1996. Resilient, overcontrolled, and undercontrolled boys: Three replicable personality types. *Journal of Personality and Social Psychology,* 70, 157-171.

Rogers, S. J., Parcel, T. L., and Menaghan, E. G. 1991. The effects of maternal working conditions and mastery on child behavior problems: Studying the intergenerational transmission of social control. *Journal of Health and Social Behavior,* 32, 145-164.

Rogusch, F., Chassin, L., and Sher, F. J. 1990. Personality variables as mediators and moderators of family history risk for alcoholism: Conceptual and methodological issues. *Journal of Studies on Alcohol,* 51, 210-218.

Roland, E., and Munthe, E. (Eds.). 1989. *Bullying: An international perspective*. London: David Fulton Publishers.

Ronka, A., and Pulkinen, L. 1995. Accumulation of problems in social functioning in young adulthood: A developmental approach. *Journal of Personality and Social Psychology*, 69, 381-391.

Roosa, M. W., and Vaughan, L. 1984. A comparison of teenage and older mothers with preschool children. *Family Relations*, 33, 259-265.

Roosa, M. W., Tein, J.-Y., Groppenbacher, N., Michaels, M., and Dumka, L. 1993. Mothers' parenting behavior and child mental health in families with a problem drinking parent. *Journal of Marriage and the Family*, 55, 107-118.

Rose, R. J., and Kaprio, J. 1987. Shared experience and similarity of personality: Positive data from Finnish and American twins. *Behavioral and Brain Sciences*, 10, 35-36.

Rose, R. J., et al. 1988. Shared genes, shared environment, and similarity of adult personality. *Journal of Personality and Social Psychology*, 54, 161-171.

Rosenbaum, J., et al. 1993. Can the Kerner Commission's housing strategy improve employment, education, and social integration for low-income blacks? *North Carolina Law Review*, 71, 1521-1556.

Rosenberg, M. L. 1991. *Violence in America*. New York: Oxford University Press.

Rosenberg, M. S. 1987. Children of battered women: The effects of witnessing violence on their social problem-solving abilities. *Behavior Therapist*, 4, 85-89.

Rosenblatt, P. C., Karis, T. A., and Powell, R. D. 1995. *Multiracial couples: Black and white voices*. Thousand Oaks, CA: Sage.

Rossi, A. S. 1980. Aging and parenthood in the middle years. In P. B. Baltes and O. G. Brim, Jr. (Eds.), *Life-span development and behavior*, vol. 3 (pp. 138-205). New York: Academic.

Rossi, A. S., and Rossi, P. H. 1990. *Of human bonding: Parent-child relations across the life course*. New York: Aldine de Gruyter.

Rowe, D. C. 1981. Environmental and genetic influences on dimensions of perceived parenting: A twin study. *Developmental Psychology*, 17, 203-208.

Rowe, D. C. 1983a. A biometrical analysis of perceptions of family environment: A study of twin and singleton sibling kinships. *Child Development*, 54, 416-423.

Rowe, D. C. 1983b. Biometrical genetic models of self-reported delinquent behavior: A twin study. *Behavior Genetics*, 13, 473-489.

Rowe, D. C. 1986. Genetic and environmental components of antisocial behavior: A study of 265 twin pairs. *Criminology*, 24, 473-489.

Rowe, D. C. 1987. The puzzle of nonshared environmental influences. *Behavioral and Brain Sciences*, 10, 37-38.

Rowe, D. C. 1993. Genetic perspectives on personality. In R. Plomin and G. E. McClearn (Eds.), *Nature, nurture & psychology* (pp. 179-196). Washington, DC: American Psychological Association.

Rowe, D. C. 1994. *The limits of family influence. Genes, experience, and behavior.* New York: Guilford Press.

Rowe, D. C., and Gulley, B. L. 1992. Sibling effects on substance use and delinquency. *Criminology*, 30, 217-233.

Rowe, D. C., and Plomin, R. 1981. The importance of nonshared (E1) environmental influences in behavioral development. *Developmental Psychology*, 17, 517-531.

Rowe, D. C., Rodgers, J. L., and Meseck-Buskey, S. 1992. Sibling delinquency and family environment: Shared and unshared influences. *Child Development*, 63, 59-67.

Rowe, D. C., Rodgers, J. L., Meseck-Buskey, S., and St. John, C. 1989. Sexual behavior and nonsexual deviance: A sibling study of their relationship. *Developmental Psychology*, 25, 61-69.

Rowe, D. C., Woulbroun, E. J., and Gulley, B. L. 1994. Peers and friends as nonshared environmental influences. In E. M. Hetherington, D. Reiss, and R. Plomin (Eds.), *Separate social worlds of siblings* (pp. 159-174). Hillsdale, NJ: Lawrence Erlbaum.

Rubin, K. H., LeMare, L. J., and Lollis, S. 1990. Social withdrawal in childhood: Developmental pathways to peer rejection. In S. R. Asher and J. D. Coie (Eds.), *Peer rejection in childhood* (pp. 217-249). Cambridge: Cambridge University Press.

Rubin, K. H., et al. 1995. Social relationships and social skills: A conceptual and empirical analysis. In S. Shulman (Ed.), *Close relationships and socioemotional development* (pp. 63-94). Norwood, NJ: Ablex.

Rubin, S., and Quinn-Curan, N. 1983. Lost then found: Parents' journey through the community service maze. In M. Seligman (Ed.), *The family with a handicapped child.* New York: Grune and Stratton.

Rubio-Stipec, M., et al. 1991. Children of alcoholic parents in the community. *Journal of Studies on Alcohol*, 52, 78-88.

Rueter, M. A., and Conger, R. D. 1995a. Antecedents of parent-adolescent disagreements. *Journal of Marriage and the Family*, 57, 435-448.

Rueter, M. A., and Conger, R. D. 1995b. Interaction style, problem-solving behavior, and family problem-solving effectiveness. *Child Development*, 66, 98-115.

Ruggles, S. 1994. The origins of African-American family structure. *American Sociological Review*, 59, 136-151.

Rumberger, R. W., et al. 1990. Family influences on dropout behavior in one California high school. *Sociology of Education*, 63, 283-299.

Russell, A., and Russell, G. 1992. Child effects in socialization research: Some conceptual and analysis issues. *Social Development*, 1, 163-184.

Russell, D. A., Matsey, K. C., Reiss, D., and Hetherington, M. 1995. Debriefing the family: Is research an intervention? *Family Process*, 34, 145-160.

Rutter, M. 1979. Protective factors in children's responses to stress and disadvantage. In M. Kent and J. Rolf (Eds.), *Primary prevention and psychopathology*, 3. Hanover, NH: University Press of New England.

Rutter, M. 1985. Resilience in the face of adversity. *British Journal of Psychiatry*, 147, 598-611.

Rutter, M. 1986. The developmental psychopathology of depression: Issues and perspectives. In M. Rutter, C. E. Izard, and P. B. Read (Eds.), *Depression in young people*. New York: Guilford Press.

Rutter, M. 1987. Psychosocial resilience and protective mechanisms. *American Journal of Orthopsychiatry*, 57, 316-331.

Rutter, M. 1989a. Pathways from childhood to adult life. *Journal of Child Psychology and Psychiatry*, 30, 25-51.

Rutter, M. 1989b. Intergenerational continuities and discontinuities in serious parenting difficulties. In D. Cicchetti and V. Carlson (Eds.), *Child maltreatment* (pp. 317-348). Cambridge: Cambridge University Press.

Rutter, M. 1990a. Commentary: Some focus and process considerations regarding effects of parental depression on children. *Developmental Psychology*, 26, 60-67.

Rutter, M. 1990b. Psychosocial resilience and protective mechanisms. In J. Rolf et al. (Eds.), *Risk and protective factors in the development of psychopathology* (pp. 181-214). New York: Cambridge University Press.

Rutter, M. 1991a. Nature, nurture, and psychopathology: A new look at an old topic. *Development and Psychopathology*, 3, 125-136.

Rutter, M. 1991b. Autism as a genetic disorder. In P. McGuffin and R. M. Murray (Eds.), *The new genetics of mental illness* (pp. 225-244). Oxford: Butterworth-Heinemann.

Rutter, M. 1994. Temperament: Changing concepts and implications. In W. B. Carey and S. C. McDevitt (Eds.), *Prevention and early intervention. Individual differences as risk factors for the mental health of children* (pp. 23-34). New York: Brunner/Mazel.

Rutter, M., and Giller, H. 1983. *Juvenile delinquency: Trends and perspectives.* Harmondsworth, UK: Penguin.

Rutter, M., and Pickles, A. 1991. Person-environment interaction: Concepts, mechanisms and implications for data analysis. In T. Wachs and R. Plomin (Eds.), *Conceptualization and measurement of organism-environment interaction* (pp. 105-141). Washington, DC: American Psychological Association.

Rutter, M., and Quinton, D. 1987. Parental psychiatric disorder: Effects on children. *Psychological Medicine*, 14, 853-880.

Rutter, M., and Rutter, M. 1993. *Developing minds. Challenge and continuity across the life span.* New York: Basic Books.

Rutter, M., Quinton, D., and Hill, J. 1990. Adult outcomes of institution-reared children: Males and females compared. In L. Robins and M. Rutter (Eds.), *Straight and devious pathways from childhood to adulthood* (pp. 135-157). Cambridge: Cambridge University Press.

Rutter, M., Bailey, A., Bolton, P., and Le Couteur, A. 1993. Autism: Syndrome definition and possible genetic mechanisms. In R. Plomin and G. E. McClearn (Eds.), *Nature, nurture & psychology* (pp. 268-284). Washington, DC: American Psychological Association.

Rutter, M., Graham, P., Chadwick, J., and Yule, W. 1976. Adolescent turmoil: Fact or fiction? *Journal of Child Psychology and Psychiatry*, 17, 35-56.

Rutter, M., Silberg, J., and Simonoff, E. 1993. Whither behavioral genetics?–A developmental psychopathological perspective. In R. Plomin and G. E. McClearn (Eds.), *Nature, nurture & psychology* (pp. 433-457). Washington DC: American Psychological Association.

Rutter, M., Bolton, P., Harrington, R., and Le Couteur, A. 1990. Genetic factors in child psychiatric disorders. I. A review of research strategies. *Journal of Child Psychology and Psychiatry*, 31, 3-37.

Rutter, M., MacDonald, H., Le Couteur, A., and Harrington, R. 1990. Genetic factors in child psychiatric disorders. II. Empirical findings. *Journal of Child Psychology and Psychiatry*, 31, 39-83.

Rutter, M., et al. 1995. Understanding individual differences in environmental-risk exposure. In P. Moen, G. H. Elder, Jr., and K. Luscher (Eds.), *Examining lives in context* (pp. 61-93). Washington, DC: American Psychological Association.

Rydelius, P. A. 1988. The development of antisocial behavior and sudden violent death. *Acta Psychiatrica Scandinavica*, 77, 398-403.

Sabatelli, R. M., and Anderson, S. A. 1991. Family system dynamics, peer relationships, and adolescents' psychological adjustment. *Family Relations*, 40, 363-369.

Saluter, A. F. 1992. Marital status and living arrangements: March 1991. *Current Population Reports, Population Characteristics* (Series P-20, no. 461). Washington, DC: U.S. Government Printing Office.

Salzinger, S., Feldman, R. S., and Hammer, M. 1993. The effects of physical abuse on children's social relationships. *Child Development*, 64, 169-187.

Salzinger, S., Kaplan, S., and Artemyeff, C. 1983. Mothers' personal social networks and child maltreatment. *Journal of Abnormal Psychology*, 92, 68-76.

Salzinger, S., Feldman, R. S., Hammer, M., and Rosario, M. 1991. Risk for physical child abuse and the personal consequences for its victims. *Criminal Justice and Behavior*, 18, 64-81.

Sameroff, A. J. 1994. Developmental systems and family functioning. In R. D. Parke and S. G. Kellam (Eds.), *Exploring family relationships with other social contexts* (pp. 199-214). Hillsdale, NJ: Lawrence Erlbaum.

Sameroff, A. J., and Chandler, M. 1975. Reproductive risk and the continuum of care taking casualty. In F. Horowitz (Ed.), *Review of child development research*, 4. Chicago: Chicago University Press.

Sameroff, A. J., and Seifer, R. 1990. Early contributors to developmental risk. In J. Rolf et al. (Eds.), *Risk and protective factors in the development of psychopathology* (pp. 52-66). Cambridge: Cambridge University Press.

Sameroff, A. J., Seifer, R., Baldwin, A., and Baldwin, C. 1993. Stability of intelligence from preschool to adolescence: The influence of social and family risk factors. *Child Development*, 64, 80-97.

Sampson, R. J. 1985. Neighborhood and crime: The structural determinants of personal victimization. *Journal of Research in Crime and Delinquency*, 22, 7-40.

Sampson, R. J. 1987. Urban black violence: The effect of male joblessness and family disruption. *American Journal of Sociology*, 93, 348-405.

Sampson, R. J. 1993. The community context of violent crime. In W. J. Wilson (Ed.), *Sociology and the public agenda* (pp. 259-286). Newbury Park, CA: Sage.

Sampson, R. J., and Groves, W. B. 1989. Community structure and crime: Testing social-disorganization theory. *American Journal of Sociology*, 94, 774-802.

Sampson, R. J., and Laub, J. H. 1992. Crime and deviance in the life course. *Annual Review of Sociology*, 18, 63-84.

Sampson, R. J., and Laub, J. H. 1993. *Crime in the making: Pathways and turning points through life*. Cambridge: Harvard University Press.

Sanders, M. R., Dadds, M. R., and Bor, W. 1989. Contextual analysis of child oppositional and maternal aversive behaviors in families of conduct-disordered and nonproblem children. *Journal of Clinical Child Psychology*, 18, 72-83.

Sandler, J. 1980. Social support resources, stress, and maladjustment of poor children. *American Journal of Community Psychology*, 8, 41-52.

Saugstad, L. F. 1989. Social class, marriage, and fertility in schizophrenia. *Schizophrenia Bulletin*, 15, 9-43.

Saunders, B. E. et al. 1992. Child sexual assault as a risk factor for mental disorders among women: A community survey. *Journal of Interpersonal Violence*, 7, 189-204.

Scanlan, C. 1993. New poll finds youths have easy access to guns. *The (Columbia, SC) State*, July 20, 1a.

Scarr, S. 1968. Environmental bias in twin studies. *Eugenics Quarterly*, 15, 34-40.

Scarr, S. 1985. Constructing psychology: Making facts and fables for our times. *American Psychologist*, 40, 499-512.

Scarr, S. 1992. Developmental theories for the 1990s: Development and individual differences. *Child Development*, 63, 1-19.

Scarr, S. 1993. Biological and cultural diversity: The legacy of Darwin for development. *Child Development*, 64, 1333-1353.

Scarr, S. 1994. Genetics and individual differences: How Chess and Thomas shaped developmental thought. In W. B. Carey, and S. C. McDevitt (Eds.), *Prevention and early intervention: Individual differences as risk factors for the mental health of children.* (pp. 170-178). New York: Brunner/Mazel.

Scarr, S., and Carter-Saltzman, L. 1979. Twin method: Defence of a critical assumption. *Behavior Genetics*, 9, 527-542.

Scarr, S., and Kidd, K. K. 1983. Behavior genetics. In M. Haith and J. Campos (Eds.), *Manual of child psychology: Infancy and the biology of development*, vol. 2 (pp. 345-434). New York: Wiley.

Scarr, S., and McCartney, K. 1983. How people make their own environments: A theory of genotype → environment effects. *Child Development*, 54, 424-435.

Scarr, S., Webber, P. L., Weinberg, R. A., and Wittig, M. A. 1981. Personality resemblance among adolescents and their parents in biologically related and adoptive families. *Journal of Personality and Social Psychology*, 40, 885-898.

Schachar, R., et al. 1987. Changes in family function and relationships in children who respond to methylphrenide. *Journal of the American Academy of Child and Adolescent Psychiatry*, 26, 728-732.

Schachter, F. F. 1982. Sibling identification and split-parent identification: A family tetrad. In M. Lamb and B. Sutton-Smith (Eds.), *Sibling relationships: Their nature and significance across the lifespan* (pp. 123-197). Hillsdale, NJ: Lawrence Erlbaum.

Schachter, F. F., and Stone, R. K. 1985. Difficult sibling, easy sibling: Temperament and the within-family environment. *Child Development*, 56, 1335-1344.

Schachter, F. F., and Stone, R. K. 1987. Comparing and contrasting siblings: Defining the self. *Journal of Children in Contemporary Society*, 19, 55-75.

Schaefer, J. A., and Moos, R. H. 1992. Life crises and personal growth. In B. N. Carpenter (Ed.), *Personal coping: Theory, research, and application* (pp. 149-170). Westport, CT: Praeger.

Schaie, K. W. 1994. The course of adult intellectual development. *American Psychologist*, 49, 304-313.

Scheier, M. F., and Carver, C. S. 1985. Optimism, coping, and health: Assessment and implications of generalized outcome expectancies on health, *Journal of Personality*, 57, 1024-1040.

Scheier, M. F., Weintraub, J. K., and Carver, C. S. 1986. Coping with stress: Divergent strategies of optimists and pessimists. *Journal of Personality and Social Psychology*, 51, 1257-1264.

Scheper-Hughes, N. 1987. Introduction: The cultural politics of child survival. In N. Scheper-Hughes (Ed.), *Cultural survival* (pp. 1-29). Dordrecht: D. Reidel Publishing.

Schlegel, A., and Barry, H., III. 1991. *Adolescence: An anthropological inquiry*. New York: Free Press.

Schor, J. B. 1991. *The overworked American: The unexpected decline in leisure*. New York: Basic Books.

Schuerman, L., and Kobrin, S. 1986. Community careers in crime. In A. J. Reiss, Jr. and M. Tonry (Eds.), *Communities and crime* (pp. 67-100). Chicago: University of Chicago Press.

Schulsinger, F., et al. 1986. A prospective study of young men at high risk for alcoholism. *Archives of General Psychiatry*, 43, 755-760.

Schwartz, J. E., et al. 1995. Sociodemographic and psychological factors in childhood as predictors of adult mortality. *American Journal of Public Health*, 85, 1237-1245.

Scott, K. D. 1992. Childhood sexual abuse: Impact on a community's mental health status. *Child Abuse and Neglect*, 16, 205-295.

Scott, J. W., and Perry, R. 1990. Do black family headship structures make a difference in teenage pregnancy? A comparison of one-parent and two-parent families. *Sociological Focus*, 23, 1-16.

Sebald, H. 1992. *Adolescence. A social psychological analysis*, 4th ed. Englewood Cliffs, NJ: Prentice-Hall.

Sedlak, A. J. 1991. *National incidence and prevalence of child abuse and neglect. 1988–Revised report*. Rockville, MD: Westat.

Segal, J., and Yahraes, H. 1979. *A child's journey: Forces that shape the lives of our young*. New York: McGraw-Hill.

Seifer, R., Schiller, M., Sameroff, A. J., Resnick, S., and Riordan, K. 1996. Attachment, maternal sensitivity and infant temperament during the first year of life. *Developmental Psychology*, 32, 12-25.

Seltzer, J. A. 1994. Consequences of marital dissolution for children. *Annual Review of Sociology*, 20, 235-266.

Seltzer, M. M., and Ryff, C. D. 1994. Parenting across the life span: The normative and nonnormative cases. In D. L. Featherman, R. M. Lerner, and M. Perlmutter (Eds.), *Life-span development and behavior*, Vol. 12 (pp. 1-40). Hillsdale, NJ: Lawrence Erlbaum.

Seymore, C., et al. 1990. Child development knowledge, childrearing attitudes, and social support among first- and second-time adolescent mothers. *Journal of Adolescent Health Care*, 11, 343-350.

Seywert, F. 1984. Some critical thoughts on expressed emotion. *Psychopathology*, 7, 233-243.

Shakoor, B., and Chalmers, D. 1991. Co-victimization of African-American children who witness violence: Effects on cognitive, emotional, and behavioral development. *Journal of the National Medical Association*, 83, 233-237.

Shanahan, M. J., Elder, G. H., Jr., and Burchinal, M. (In press). Adolescent earnings and relationships with parents: The work-family nexus in urban and rural ecologies. In J. T. Mortimer and M. T. Finch (Eds.), *Adolescents, work, and family: An intergenerational developmental analysis*. Thousand Oaks, CA: Sage.

Shaw, D. S., and Emery, R. E. 1987. Parental conflict and other correlates of the adjustment of school-age children whose parents have separated. *Journal of Abnormal Child Pyschology*, 15, 269-281.

Shehan, C. L., and Dwyer, J. W. 1989. Parent-child exchanges in the middle years: Attachment and autonomy in the transition to adulthood. In J. A. Mancini (Ed.), *Aging parents and adult children* (pp. 99-116). Lexington, MA: Lexington Press.

Sheley, J. F., and Wright, J. D. 1993. *Gun acquisition and possession in selected juvenile samples*. Washington, DC: Office of Juvenile Justice and Delinquency Prevention, National Institute of Justice.

Sheley, J. F., and Wright, J. D. 1995. *In the line of fire. Youth, guns, and violence in urban America*. Hawthorne, NY: Aldine de Gruyter.

Sherman, L. W., et al. 1991. From initial deterrence to long-term escalation: Short-term custody arrest for poverty ghetto domestic violence. *Criminology*, 29, 821-850.

Shinn, M., Knickman, J., and Weitzman, B. C. 1991. Social relationships and vulnerability to becoming homeless among poor families. *American Psychologist*, 46, 1180-1187.

Sigel, I. E. (Ed.). 1985. *Parental belief systems*. Hillsdale, NJ: Lawrence Erlbaum.

Silbereisen, R. K., Walper, S., and Albrecht, H. T. 1990. Family income loss and economic hardship: Antecedents of adolescents' problem behavior. In V. C. McLoyd and C. A. Flanagan (Eds.), *Economic stress: Effects on family life and child development* (pp. 27-47). San Francisco: Jossey-Bass.

Silliman, R., and Sternberg, J. 1988. Family caregiving: Impact of patient functioning and underlying causes of dependency. *The Gerontologist*, 28, 293-312.

Silverstein, L. B. 1991. Transforming the debate about child care and maternal employment. *American Psychologist*, 46, 1025-1032.

Silverstein, M., and Bengtson, V. L. 1991. Do close parent-child relationships reduce the mortality risk of older parents? *Journal of Health and Social Behavior*, 32, 382-395.

Silverstein, M., Parrott, T. M., and Bengtson, V. L. 1995. Factors that predispose middle-aged sons and daughters to provide support to older parents. *Journal of Marriage and the Family*, 57, 465-475.

Simons, R. L., and Whitbeck, L. B. 1991. Sexual abuse as a precursor to prostitution and victimization among adolescent and adult homeless women. *Journal of Family Issues*, 12, 361-379.

Simons, R. L., Robertson, J. F., and Downs, W. R. 1989. The nature of the association between parental rejection and delinquent behavior. *Journal of Youth and Adolescence*, 18, 297-310.

Simons, R. L., Beaman, J., Conger, R., and Chao, W. 1993. Stress, support, and antisocial behavior trait as determinants of emotional well-being and parenting practices among single mothers. *Journal of Marriage and the Family*, 55, 385-398.

Simons, R. L., Johnson, C., Beaman, J., and Conger, R. D. 1993. Explaining women's double jeopardy: Factors that mediate the association between harsh treatment as a child and violence by a husband. *Journal of Marriage and the Family*, 55, 713-723.

Simons, R. L., Whitbeck, L. B., Beaman, J., and Conger, R. D. (1994). The impact of mothers' parenting, involvement by nonresidential fathers, and parental conflict on the adjustment of adolescent children. *Journal of Marriage and the Family*, 56, 356-374.

Simons, R. L., Whitbeck, L. B., Conger, R. D., and Melby, J. N. 1990. Husband and wife differences in determinants of parenting: A social learning and exchange model of parental behavior. *Journal of Marriage and the Family*, 52, 375-392.

Simons, R. L., Whitbeck, L. B., Conger, R. D., and Wu, C. 1991. Intergenerational transmission of harsh parenting. *Developmental Psychology*, 27, 159-171.

Simons, R. L., Wu, C. I., Conger, R. D., and Lorenz, F. O. 1994. Two routes to delinquency: Differences between early and late starters in the impact of parenting and deviant peers. *Criminology*, 32, 247-276.

Simons, R. L., Wu, C. I., Johnson, C., and Conger, R. D. 1995. A test of various perspectives on the intergenerational transmission of domestic violence. *Criminology*, 33, 141-171.

Sirignano, S. W., and Lachman, M. E. 1985. Personality change during the transition to parenthood: The role of perceived infant temperament. *Developmental Psychology*, 21, 558-567.

Skolnick, A. S., and Skolnick, J. B. 1994. *Family in transition*, 5th ed. New York: Harper Collins College Publishers.

Slater, A. 1995. Individual differences in infancy and later IQ. *Journal of Child Psychology and Psychiatry*, 36, 69-112.

Slavin, R. E. 1994a. *Educational psychology: Theory and practice*, 4th ed. Needham Heights, MA: Allyn and Bacon.

Slavin, R. E. 1994b. *Cooperative learning: Theory, research, and practice*, 2nd ed. Boston: Allyn and Bacon.

Small, S. A., and Kerns, D. 1993. Unwanted sexual activity among peers during early and middle adolescence: Incidence and risk factors. *Journal of Marriage and the Family*, 55, 941-952.

Small, S. A., and Eastman, G. 1991. Rearing adolescents in contemporary society: A conceptual framework for understanding the responsibilities and needs of parents. *Family Relations*, 40, 455-462.

Small, S., and Riley, D. 1990. Toward a multidimensional assessment of work spillover into family life. *Journal of Marriage and the Family*, 52, 51-62.

Small, S. A., Eastman, G., and Cornelius, S. 1988. Adolescent autonomy and parental stress. *Journal of Youth and Adolescence*, 17, 377-391.

Smetana, J. G. 1989. Adolescents' and parents' reasoning about actual family conflict. *Child Development*, 60, 1052-1067.

Smetana, J. G. 1995. Conflict and coordination in adolescent-parent relationships. In S. Shulman (Ed.), *Close relationships and socioemotional development*, Vol. 7 (Human Development), (pp. 155-184). Norwood, NJ: Ablex.

Smith, D. J., and Tomlinson, S. 1989. *The school effect: A study of multi-racial comprehensives*. London: Policy Studies Institute.

Smith, J., and Prior, M. 1995. Temperament and stress resilience in school-age children: A within-families study. *Journal of the American Academy of Child and Adolescent Psychiatry*, 34, 168-179.

Smith, J. P., and Williams, J. G. 1992. From abusive households to dating violence. *Journal of Family Violence*, 7, 153-165.

Smith, M., and Bentovim, A. 1994. Sexual abuse. In M. Rutter, E. Taylor, and L. Hersov (Eds.), *Child and adolescent psychiatry*, 3rd ed. (pp. 230-251). Oxford: Blackwell.

Smith, R. L., and Thomson, L. 1987. Restricted housing markets for female-headed households in U.S. metropolitan areas. In W. van Vliet et al. (Eds.), *Housing and neighborhoods: Theoretical and empirical contributions* (pp. 279-290). Westport, CT: Greenwood.

Smith, T., McGuire, J., Abbott, D., and Blau, B. 1991. Clinical ethical decision making: An investigation of the rationales used to justify doing less than one believes one should. *Professional Psychology Research and Practice*, 22, 235-239.

SmithBattle, L. 1996. Intergenerational ethics of caring for adolescent mothers and their children. *Family Relations*, 45, 56-64.

Smock, P. 1994. Gender and short-run economic consequences of marital disruption. *Social Forces*, 74, 243-262.

Snyder, D. K., et al. 1988. Generalized dysfunction in clinic and nonclinic families: A comparative analysis. *Journal of Abnormal Child Psychology*, 16, 97-109.

Sourkes, B. M. 1987. Siblings of the child with a life-threatening illness. *Journal of Children in Contemporary Society*, 19, 159-184.

Spalter-Roth, R. M., Hartmann, H. I., and Andrews, L. M. 1993. Mothers, children and low-wage work: The ability to earn a family wage. In W. J. Wilson (Ed.), *Sociology and the public agenda* (pp. 316-338). Newbury Park, CA: Sage.

Spaniol, L., Jung, H., Zipple, A. M., and Fitzgerald, S. 1987. Families as a resource in the rehabilitation of the severely psychiatrically disabled. In A. B. Hatfield and H. P. Lefley (Eds.), *Families of the mentally ill: Coping and adaptation* (pp. 167-190). New York: Guilford.

Speare, A., Jr., and Avery, R. 1993. Who helps whom in older parent-child families? *Journal of Gerontology*, 48, S64-S73.

Spitze, G., and Logan, J. R. 1991. Sibling structure and intergenerational relations. *Journal of Marriage and the Family*, 53, 871-884.

Spitze, G., Logan, J. R., Deane, G., and Zerger, S. 1994. Adult children's behavior and intergenerational relationships. *Journal of Marriage and the Family,* 56, 279-293.

Spitzer, A., Webster-Stratton, C., and Hollinsworth, T. 1991. Coping with conduct-problem children: Parents gaining knowledge and control. *Journal of Clinical Child Psychology,* 20, 413-427.

Sprafkin, J., Gadow, K., and Abelman, R. 1992. *Television and the exceptional child: A forgotten audience.* Hillsdale, NJ: Lawrence Erlbaum.

Sprey, J., and Matthews, S. H. 1982. Contemporary grandparenthood: A systemic transition. *Annals of the American Academy of the Political and Social Sciences,* 464, 91-103.

Sroufe, L. A., and Fleeson, J. 1988. The coherence of family relationships. In R. Hinde and J. S. Hinde (Eds.), *Relationships within families: Mutual influences* (pp. 27-47). New York: Oxford University Press.

Sroufe, L. A., and Rutter, M. 1984. The domain of developmental psychopathology. *Child Development,* 55, 17-29.

Stahler, G. H., DuCette, J. P., and Povich, E. 1995. Using research and theory to develop prevention programs for high risk families. *Family Relations,* 44, 78-86.

Starrels, M. E. 1994. Gender differences in parent-child relations. *Journal of Family Issues,* 15, 148-165.

Starrels, M. E., Bould, S., and Nicholas, L. J. 1994. The feminization of poverty in the United States. Gender, race, ethnicity, and family factors. *Journal of Family Issues,* 15, 590-607.

Statistics Canada. 1992. *Lone-parent families in Canada.* Housing, Family and Social Statistics Division. Cat. no. 89-522E, Ottawa.

Stein, A., Gath, D. H., Bucher, J., Bond, A., Day, A., and Cooper, P. J. 1991. The relationship between post-natal depression and mother-child interaction. *British Journal of Psychiatry,* 158, 46-52.

Stein, J. A., Newcomb, M. D., and Bentler, P. M. 1986. Stability and change in personality: A longitudinal study from early adolescence to young adulthood. *Journal of Research in Personality,* 20, 276-291.

Stein, N. 1995. Sexual harassment in school: The public performance of gendered violence. *Harvard Educational Review,* 65, 145-162.

Steinberg, L. 1987. Single parents, stepparents and the susceptibility of adolescents to antisocial peer pressure. *Child Development,* 58, 269-275.

Steinberg, L. 1990. Autonomy, conflict, and harmony in the family relationship. In S. S. Feldman and G. R. Elliott (Eds.), *At the threshold: The developing adolescent* (pp. 256-276). Cambridge, MA: Harvard University Press.

Steinberg, L., and Darling, N. 1994. The broader context of social influence in adolescence. In R. K. Silbereisen and E. Todt (Eds.), *Adolescence in context* (pp. 25-45). New York: Springer-Verlag.

Steinberg, L., and Dornbusch, S. M. 1991. Negative correlates of part-time employment during adolescence: Replication and elaboration. *Developmental Psychology*, 27, 304-313.

Steinberg, L., Dornbusch, S., and Brown, B. 1992. Ethnic differences in adolescent achievement in ecological perspective. *American Psychologist*, 47, 723-729.

Steinberg, L., Fegley, S., and Dornbusch, S. M. 1993. Negative impact of part-time work on adolescent adjustment: Evidence from a longitudinal study. *Developmental Psychology*, 29, 171-180.

Steinberg, L., Lamborn, S., Dornbusch, S., and Darling, N. 1992. Impact of parenting practices on adolescent achievement: Authoritative parenting, school involvement, and encouragement to succeed. *Child Development*, 63, 1266-1281.

Steinberg, L., Darling, N. E., Fletcher, A. C., Brown, B. B., and Dornbusch, S. F. 1995. Authoritative parenting and adolescent adjustment: An ecological journey. In P. Moen, G. H. Elder, Jr., and K. Luscher (Eds.), *Examining lives in context* (pp. 423-466). Washington, DC: American Psychological Association.

Steinberg, L., Lamborn, S. D., Darling, N., Mounts, N., and Dornbusch, S. M. 1994. Overtime changes in adjustment and competence among adolescents from authoritative, authoritarian, indulgent, and neglectful families. *Child Development*, 45, 754-770.

Steinmetz, S. 1988. *Duty bond: Elder abuse and family care*. Beverly Hills, CA: Sage.

Stephenson, P., and Smith, D. 1989. Bullying in the junior school. In D. Tattum and D. Lane (Eds.), *Bullying in schools* (pp. 45-58). Hanley Stoke-on-Trent: Trentham Books.

Sternberg, K. J., Lamb, M. E., Greenbaum, C., and Ciccehetti, D. 1993. Effects of domestic violence on children's behavior problems and depression. *Developmental Psychology*, 29, 44-52.

Stevens, J. H. 1984. Black grandmothers' and black adolescents' knowledge about parenting. *Developmental Psychology*, 20, 1017-1025.

Stevens, R. J., and Slavin, R. E. 1995. The cooperative elementary school: Effects on students' achievement, attitudes, and social relations. *American Educational Research Journal*, 32, 321-351.

Stevenson, D. L., and Baker, D. P. 1987. The family-school relation and the child's school performance. *Child Development*, 58, 1348-1357.

Stevenson, H. W., and Stigler, J. W. 1992. *The learning gap: Why our schools are failing and what we can learn from Japanese and Chinese education.* New York: Summit.

Stevenson-Hinde, J., and Simpson, A. E. 1982. Temperament and relationships. In *Temperamental differences in infants and young children.* Ciba Foundation Symposium 89, London: Pitman.

Stiffman, A. R., and Davis, L. E. (Eds.). 1990. *Ethnic issues in adolescent mental health.* Newbury Park, CA: Sage.

Stocker, C. M. 1994. Children's perceptions of relationships with siblings, friends, and mothers: Compensatory processes and links with adjustment. *Journal of Child Psychology and Psychiatry,* 35, 1447-1459.

Stocker, C., and Dunn, J. 1990. Sibling relationships in childhood: Links with friendships and peer relationships. *British Journal of Developmental Psychology,* 8, 227-244.

Stocker, C., Dunn, J., and Plomin, R. 1989. Sibling relationships: Links with child temperament, maternal behavior, and family structure. *Child Development,* 60, 715-727.

Stoneman, Z., and Brody, G. H. 1993. Sibling temperaments, conflict, warmth, and role asymmetry. *Child Development,* 64, 1786-1800.

Stoneman, Z., Brody, G. H., and Burke, M. 1989. Sibling temperaments and maternal and paternal perceptions of marital, family, and personal functioning. *Journal of Marriage and the Family,* 51, 99-113.

Stoolmiller, M., Duncan, T., Bank, L., and Patterson, G. R. 1993. Some problems and solutions in the study of change: Significant patterns of client resistance. *Journal of Consulting and Clinical Psychology,* 61, 920-928.

Strauss, M. A., and Gelles, R. J. 1990. *Physical violence in American families: Risk factors and adaptation to violence in 8,145 families.* New Brunswick, NJ: Transaction.

Strauss, M. A., and Smith, C. 1990. Family patterns and child abuse. In M. A. Strauss and R. J. Gelles (Eds.), *Physical violence in American families.* New Brunswick, NJ: Transaction.

Strawbridge, W. J., and Wallhagen, M. I. 1991. Impact of family conflict on adult child caregivers. *The Gerontologist,* 31, 770-776.

Strelau, J. 1987. The concept of temperament in personality research. *European Journal of Personality,* 1, 107-117.

Strickland, B. 1982. Perceptions of parents and school representatives regarding their relationship before, during, and after the due process hearing. Doctoral dissertation, Chapel Hill, University of North Carolina.

Strober, M., Lampert, C., Schmidt, S., and Morrell, W. 1993. The course of major depressive disorder in adolescents. I. Recovery and risk of psychiatric and nonpsychiatric subtypes. *Journal of the American Academy of Child Psychiatry*, 32, 34-42.

Strobino, D. M. 1987. The health and medical consequences of adolescent sexuality and pregnancy: A review of the literature. In S. Hofferth and C. D. Hayes (Eds.), *Risking the future*, Vol. 2 (pp. 93-122). National Research Council. Washington, DC: National Academy Press.

Sue, S., and Okazaki, S. 1990. Asian-American educational achievements: A phenomenon in search of an explanation. *American Psychologist*, 45, 913-920.

Suin, R. M. 1993. Practice–It's not what we preached. *The Behavior Therapist*, February: 47-49.

Suitor, J. J., and Pillemer, K. 1991. Family conflict when adult children and elderly parents share a home. In K. Pillemer and K. McCartney (Eds.), *Parent-child relations throughout life* (pp. 179-199). Hillsdale, NJ: Lawrence Erlbaum.

Suitor, J. J., and Pillemer, K. 1994. Family caregiving and marital satisfaction: Findings from a 1-year panel study of women caring for parents with dementia. *Journal of Marriage and the Family*, 56, 681-690.

Sullivan, M. 1989a. Absent fathers in the inner city. *Annals*, 501, 48-58.

Sullivan, M. 1989b. *Getting paid: Youth crimes and work in the inner city*. Ithaca, NY: Cornell University Press.

Sullivan, T. 1992. *Sexual abuse and the rights of children. Reforming Canadian Law*. Toronto: University of Toronto Press.

Super, C. M., and Harkness, S. 1994. Temperament and the developmental niche. In W. B. Carey and S. C. McDevitt (Eds.), *Prevention and early prevention* (pp. 115-125). New York: Brunner/Mazel.

Susman, E. J., et al. 1985. Child-rearing patterns in depressed, abusive, and normal mothers. *American Journal of Orthopsychiatry*, 55, 237-251.

Swift, K. 1990. Contradictions in child welfare: Neglect and responsibility. In C. Baines, C. T. Evans, and S. M. Neysmith (Eds.), *Women's caring: Feminist perspectives on social welfare*. Toronto: McClelland and Stewart.

Sylva, K. 1994. School influences on children's development. *Journal of Child Psychology and Psychiatry*, 35, 135-170.

Tallmadge, J., and Barkley, R. A. 1983. The interactions of hyperactive and normal boys with their fathers and mothers. *Journal of Abnormal Child Psychology*, 11, 565-580.

Tarullo, L. B., Richardson, D. T., Radke-Yarrow, M., and Martinez, P. 1995. Multiple sources of child diagnosis: Parent-child concordance in affectively ill and well families. *Journal of Clinical Child Psychology*, 24, 173-183.

Tarver-Behring, S., and Barkley, R. A. 1985. The mother-child interactions of hyperactive boys and their normal siblings. *American Journal of Orthopsychiatry*, 55, 202-209.

Tate, D. C., Reppucci, N. D., and Mulvey, E. P. 1995. Violent juvenile delinquents. Treatment effectiveness and implications for future action. *American Psychologist*, 50, 777-781.

Taylor, E., Schachar, R., Thorley, G., and Wieselberg, M. 1986. Conduct disorder and hyperactivity: I. Separation of hyperactivity and antisocial conduct in British child psychiatric patients. *British Journal of Psychiatry*, 149, 760-767.

Taylor, R. J., and Chatters, I. M. 1991. Extended family networks of older black adults. *The Journal of Gerontology*, 46, S210-S217.

Taylor, R., and Covington, J. 1988. Neighborhood changes in ecology and violence. *Criminology*, 26, 553-590.

Taylor, R. J., Chatters, L. M., Tucker, M. B., and Lewis, E. 1990. Developments in research on black families: A decade review. *Journal of Marriage and the Family*, 52, 993-1014.

Tellegen, A., Lykken, D. T., Bouchard, T. J., Jr., Wilcox, K. J., Segal, N. L., and Rich, S. 1988. Personality similarity in twins reared apart and together. *Journal of Personality and Social Psychology*, 54, 1031-1039.

Tennant, C. 1988. Parental loss in childhood: A prospective study. *Journal of Abnormal Child Psychology*, 21, 119-134.

Terkelsen, K. G. 1983. Schizophrenia and the family: II. Adverse effect of family therapy. *Family Process*, 22, 191-200.

Terkelsen, K. G. 1987. The meaning of mental illness to the family. In A. B. Hatfield and H. B. Lefley (Eds.), *Families of the mentally ill: Coping and adaptation* (pp. 3-29). New York: Guilford.

Terman, L. M., and Oden, M. H. 1947. *Genetic studies of genius: The gifted child grows up*, Vol. 4. Stanford, CA: Stanford University Press.

Teti, D. M., and Ablard, K. E. 1989. Security of attachment and infant-sibling relationships: A laboratory study. *Child Development*, 60, 1519-1528.

Teti, D. M., Gelfard, D. M., and Pompa, J. 1990. Depressed mothers' behavioral competence with their infants: Demographic and psychosocial correlates. *Development and Psychopathology*, 2, 259-270.

Teti, D. M., Gibbs, E. D., and Bond, A. 1989. Sibling interaction, birth spacing, and intellectual linguistic development. In P. G. Zukow (Ed.), *Sibling interaction across cultures: Theoretical and methodological issues* (pp. 117-141). New York: Springer-Verlag.

Thapar, A., and McGuffin, P. 1995. Are anxiety symptoms in childhood heritable? *Journal of Child Psychology and Psychiatry*, 36, 439-447.

Thomas, A., and Chess, S. 1980. *The dynamics of psychological develop-ment*. New York: Brunner/Mazel.

Thomas, A., and Chess, S. 1986. The New York Longitudinal Study: From infancy to early adult life. In R. Plomin and J. Dunn (Eds.), *The study of temperament: Changes, continuities, and challenges* (pp. 39-52). Hills-dale, NJ: Lawrence Erlbaum.

Thomas, A., and Chess, S. 1989. Temperament and personality. In G. A. Kohnstamm, J. E. Bates, and M. K. Rothbart (Eds.), *Temperament in childhood* (pp. 249-261). New York: John Wiley.

Thomas, D. L., and Carver, C. 1990. Religion and adolescent social com-petence. In T. Gullotta, G. Adams, and R. Montemayor (Eds.), *Adoles-cence and social competences: Advances in adolescent development*, Vol. 4 (pp. 195-219). Thousand Oaks, CA: Sage.

Thomas, L. T., and Cornwall, M. 1990. Religion and family in the 1980s: Discovery and development. *Journal of Marriage and the Family*, 52, 903-992.

Thompson, E. H., Jr., and Doll, W. 1982. The burden of families coping with the mentally ill: An invisible crisis. *Family Relations*, 31, 379-388.

Thompson, L. A., Detterman, D. K., and Plomin, R. A. 1991. Associations between cognitive abilities and scholastic achievement: Genetic over-lap but environmental differences. *Psychological Science*, 2, 158-165.

Thompson, M., Alexander, K., and Entwisle, D. 1988. Household com-position, parental expectations, and school achievement. *Social Forces*, 67, 424-451.

Thompson, R. A., and Wilcox, B. L. 1995. Child maltreatment research. Federal support and policy issues. *American Psychologist*, 50, 789-793.

Thomson, E., McLanahan, S. S., and Curtin, R. B. 1992. Family structure, gender, and parental socialization. *Journal of Marriage and the Family*, 54, 368-378.

Thorne, B. 1993. *Gender play: Girls and boys in school*. New Brunswick, NJ: Rutgers University Press.

Thornton, A. 1991. Influence of the marital history of parents on the marital and cohabitational experiences of children. *American Journal of Sociology*, 96, 868-894.

Thornton, A., Orbuch, T. L., and Axinn, W. G. 1995. Parent-child relation-ships during the transition to adulthood. *Journal of Family Issues*, 16, 538-564.

Thurber, S., and Snow, M. 1990. Assessment of adolescent psychopathol-ogy: Comparison of mother and daughter perspectives. *Journal of Clin-ical Child Psychology*, 19, 249-253.

Tickamyer, A., Bokemeier, J., Feldman, S., Harris, R., Jones, J. P., and

Wenk, D. A. 1993. Women and persistent rural poverty. In Rural Socio-logical Society Task Force on Rural Poverty (Eds.), *Persistent poverty in rural America* (pp. 212-241). Boulder, CO: Westview Press.

Tinsley, B. R., and Parke, R. D. 1983. The person-environment relation-ship: Lesson from families with preterm infants. In D. Magnusson and V. L. Allen (Eds.), *Human development: An interactional perspective* (pp. 93-110). New York: Academic Press.

Toch, H. 1969. *Violent men*. New York: Aldine.

Tolan, P. H., and Thomas, P. 1995. The implications of age of onset for delinquency risk II: Longitudinal data. *Journal of Abnormal Child Psychology*, 23, 157-181.

Tolan, P. H., Guerra, N. G., and Kendall, P. C. 1995. A developmental-eco-logical perspective on antisocial behavior in children and adolescents. Toward a unified risk and intervention framework. *Journal of Consult-ing and Clinical Psychology*, 63, 579-584.

Tompson, M. C., Asarnow, J. R., Goldstein, M. J., and Miklowitz, D. J. 1990. Thought disorders and communication problems in children with schizophrenia spectrum and depressive disorders and their parents. *Journal of Clinical Child Psychology*, 19, 159-168.

Toro, P. A., and Wall, D. D. 1991. Research on homeless persons: Diag-nostic comparisons and practice implications. *Professional Psychology: Research and Practice*, 22, 479-488.

Toro, P. A., Bellevia, C. W., Daeschler, C. V., Owens, B. J., Wall, D. D., Passero, J. M., and Thomas, D. M. 1995. Distinguishing homelessness from poverty: A comparative study. *Journal of Consulting and Clinical Psychology*, 63, 280-289.

Torrey, E. F. 1983. *Surviving schizophrenia: A family manual*. New York: Harper and Row.

Tremblay, R. E., Pagani-Kurtz, L., Mâsse, L. C., Vitaro, F., and Pihl, R. O. 1995. A bimodal preventive intervention for disruptive kindergarten boys. Its impact through mid-adolescence. *Journal of Consulting and Clinical Psychology*, 63, 560-568.

Trepper, T. S., and Barrett, M. J. 1989. *Systemic treatment of incest*. New York: Brunner/Mazel.

Tsuang, M. T., Gilbertson, M. W., and Faraone, S. V. 1991. The genetics of schizophrenia: Current knowledge and future directions. *Schizophrenia Research*, 4, 157-171.

Tucker, B., and Taylor, R. J. 1989. Demographic correlates of relation-ships status among black Americans. *Journal of Marriage and the Family*, 51, 655-665.

Tucker, M. B., and Mitchell-Kernan, C. 1990. New trends in black American interracial marriage: The social structural context. *Journal of Marriage and the Family*, 52, 209-218.

Umberson, D. 1989. Relationships with children: Explaining parents' psychological well-being. *Journal of Marriage and the Family*, 51, 999-1012.

Umberson, D. 1992. Relationship between adult children and their parents: Psychological consequences for both generations. *Journal of Marriage and the Family*, 54, 664-674.

Umberson, D., and Chen, M. D. 1994. Effects of a parent's death on adult children: Relationship salience and reaction to loss. *American Sociological Review*, 59, 152-168.

U. S. Bureau of the Census. 1990. Current Population Reports, Series P-60, No. 168. 1989. *Money income and poverty status in the United States*. Washington, DC: U. S. Government Printing Office.

U. S. Bureau of the Census. 1992a. Poverty in the United States: 1991. *Current Population Reports* (Series P-60, No. 181). Washington, DC: Government Printing Office.

U. S. Bureau of the Census. 1992b. *1990 Census of the Population, Part 1*. Washington, DC: U. S. Government Printing Office.

U. S. Bureau of the Census. 1992c. Workers with low earnings: 1964-90. *Current Population Reports*, Series P-60, No. 178. Washington, DC: U. S. Government Printing Office.

U. S. Bureau of the Census 1993a. Current population reports, Series P60-185. *Poverty in the United States: 1992*. Washington, DC: U. S. Government Printing Office.

U. S. Bureau of the Census 1993b. Fertility of American women, June, 1992. In *Current Population Reports* (Series P-20). Washington, DC: Government Printing Office.

Van den Boom, D. C. 1989. Neonatal irritability and the development of attachment. In G. A. Kohnstamm, J. E. Bates, and M. K. Rothbart (Eds.), *Temperament in childhood* (pp. 299-318). New York: John Wiley.

Vandereycken, W., and Van Vreckem, E. 1992. Siblings as co-patients and co-therapists in eating disorders. In F. Boer and J. Dunn (Eds.), *Children's sibling relationships* (pp. 109-127). Hillsdale, NJ: Lawrence Erlbaum.

Van IJzendoorn, M. H., et al. 1992. The relative effects of maternal and child problems on the quality of attachment: A meta-analysis of attachment in clinical samples. *Child Development*, 63, 840-858.

Vanier Institute of the Family. 1994. *Profiling Canada's families*. Ottawa.

Vasta, R., and Copitch, P. 1981. Simulating conditions of child abuse in the laboratory. *Child Development*, 52, 164-170.

Vaughn, C. E., and Leff, J. P. 1976. The influence of family and social factors on the course of psychiatric illness: A comparison of schizophrenic and depressed neurotic patients. *British Journal of Psychiatry*, 129, 125-137.

Venezky, R., Kaestle, C., and Sum, A. M. 1987. *The subtle danger: Reflections on the literacy abilities of America's young adults*. Princeton, NJ: Educational Testing Service.

Verhulst, F. C., and van der Ende, J. 1992. Agreement between parents' reports and adolescents' self-reports of problem behavior. *Journal of Child Psychology and Psychiatry*, 33, 1011-1023.

Vessey, J. T., and Howard, K. I. 1993. Who seeks psychotherapy? *Psychotherapy*, 30, 546-553.

von Knorring, A. 1991. Annotation: Children of alcoholics. *Journal of Child Psychology and Psychiatry*, 32, 411-421.

Wachs, T. D. 1983. The use and abuse of environment in behavioral genetic research. *Child Development*, 54, 396-407.

Wachs, T. D. 1987a. Specificity of environmental action as manifest in environment correlates of infants' mastery motivation. *Developmental Psychology*, 23, 782-790.

Wachs, T. D. 1987b. The relevance of the concept of nonshared environment to the study of environmental influences: A paradigmatic shift or just some gears slipping? *Behavioral and Brain Sciences*, 10, 41-42.

Wachs, T. D. 1992. *The nature of nurture*. Newbury Park, CA: Sage.

Wachs, T. D. 1993. The nature-nurture gap: What we have here is a failure to collaborate. In R. Plomin and G. E. McClearn (Eds.), *Nature, nurture & psychology* (pp. 375-393). Washington, DC: American Psychological Association.

Wachs, T. D., and Gruen, G. 1982. *Early experiences and human development*. New York: Plenum.

Wachs, T. D., and Plomin, R. (Eds.). 1991. *Conceptualization and measurement of organism-environment interaction*. Washington, DC: American Psychological Association, 1991.

Wadsworth, M. E. J., and Maclean, M. 1986. Parents' divorce and children's life chances. *Children and Youth Services Review*, 8, 145-159.

Wagner, B., Compas, B., and Howell, D. 1988. Daily and major life stressors: A test of an integrative model of psychological stress. *American Journal of Community Psychology*, 16, 189-205.

Wahler, R., and Dumas, J. 1989. Attentional problems in dysfunctional mother child-interactions. *Psychological Bulletin*, 105, 116-130.

Walker, A. J., Pratt, C. C., and Oppy, N. C. 1992. Perceived reciprocity in family caregiving. *Family Relations*, 41, 82-85.

Wallerstein, J. S., Corbin, S. B., and Lewis, J. M. 1988. Children of divorce: A ten-year study. In E. M. Hetherington and J. Arasteh (Eds.), *Impact of divorce, single parenting, and stepparenting on children*, (pp. 198-214). Hillsdale, NJ: Lawrence Erlbaum.

Wampler, R., et al. 1993. Young adult offspring and their families of origin: Cohesion, adaptability, and addiction. *Journal of Substance Abuse*, 5, 195-201.

Ward, R., Logan, J., and Spitze, G. 1992. Coresidence and parent and child needs. *Journal of Marriage and the Family*, 54, 209-221.

Warr, M. 1993. Age, peers, and delinquency. *Criminology*, 31, 17-40.

Warr, M., and Stafford, M. 1991. The influence of delinquent peers: What they think or what they do? *Criminology*, 29, 851-866.

Wartofsky, M. 1983. The child's construction of the world and the world's construction of the child: From historical epistemology to historical psychology. In F. S. Kessel and A. W. Siegel (Ed.), *The child and other cultural inventions: Houston symposium 4* (pp. 188-215). New York: Praeger.

Wasserman, G. A., Brunelli, S. A., and Rauh, V. A. 1990. Social supports and living arrangements of adolescent and adult mothers. *Journal of Adolescent Research*, 5, 54-66.

Waters, H. F. 1993. Networks under the gun. *Newsweek*, July 12, 64-66.

Watkins, M. P., and Meredith, W. 1981. Spouse similarity in newlyweds with respect to specific cognitive abilities, socioeconomic status, and education. *Behavior Genetics*, 11, 1-21.

Watson, D., and Clark, L. A. 1992. On traits and temperament. General and specific factors of emotional experience and their relation to the five-factor model. *Journal of Personality*, 60, 441-476.

Waxler, N. E. 1974. Parent and child effects on cognitive performance: An experimental approach to the etiological and responsive theories of schizophrenia. *Family Process*, 13, 1-22.

Weatherall, D. 1992. *The Harveian oration: The role of nature and nurture in common diseases: Garrod's legacy.* London: The Royal College of Physicians.

Webster, D. W. 1993. The unconvincing case for school-based conflict resolution programs for adolescents. *Health Affairs*, 12, 126-141.

Webster-Stratton, C. 1989. The relationship of marital support, conflict, and divorce to parent perceptions, behaviors, and childhood conduct problems. *Journal of Marriage and the Family*, 51, 417-430.

Webster-Stratton, C. 1990. Stress: A potential disruptor of parent perceptions and family interactions. *Journal of Clinical Child Psychology*, 19, 302-312.

Webster-Stratton, C., Hollingsworth, T., and Kolpacoff, M. 1989. The long-term effectiveness and clinical significance of three cost-effective training programs for families with conduct-problem children. *Journal of Consulting and Clinical Psychology*, 57, 550-553.

Weisman, M. M., Fendrich, M., Warner, V., and Wickramaratne, P. 1992. Incidence of psychiatric disorder in offspring at high and low risk for depression. *Journal of the American Academy of Child and Adolescent Psychiatry*, 31, 640-648.

Weiss, B., and Weisz, J. R. 1995. Relative effectiveness of behavioral versus nonbehavioral child psychotherapy. *Journal of Consulting and Clinical Psychology*, 63, 317-320.

Weiss, R. S. 1990. *Staying the course: The emotional and social lives of men who do well at work*. New York: Fawcett Columbine.

Weissman, M. M., Gammon, G. D., John, K., Merikangas, K. R., Warner, V., Prusoff, B. A., and Sholomskas, D. 1987. Children of depressed parents. *Archives of General Psychiatry*, 44, 847-853.

Weisz, J. R., and Weiss, B. 1993. *Effects of psychotherapy with children and adolescents*. New York: Sage.

Weisz, J. R, Donenberg, G. R., Han, S. S., and Weiss, B. 1995a. Bridging the gap between laboratory and clinic in child and adolescent psychiatry. *Journal of Consulting and Clinical Psychology*, 63, 688-701.

Weisz, J. R., Weiss, B., Han, S., Granger, D. A., and Morton, T. 1995b. Effects of psychotherapy with children and adolescents revisited: A meta-analysis of treatment outcome studies. *Psychological Bulletin*, 117, 450-468.

Weisz, J. R., Martin, S. L., Walter, B. R., and Fernandez, G. A. 1991. Differential prediction of young adult arrests for property and personal crimes: Findings of a cohort follow-up study of violent boys from North Carolina's Willie M Program. *Journal of Child Psychology and Psychiatry*, 32, 783-792.

Weisz, J. R., Donenberg, G. R., Han, S. S., and Kauneckis, D. 1995. Child and adolescent psychotherapy outcomes in experiments versus clinics: Why the disparity? *Journal of Abnormal Child Psychology*, 23, 83-106.

Wentzel, K. R. 1991. Social competence at school: Relations between social responsibility and academic achievement. *Review of Educational Research*, 61, 1-24.

Werner, E. 1985. Stress and protective factors in children's lives. In A. R. Nichol (Ed.), *Longitudinal studies in child psychology and psychiatry* (pp. 335-355). New York. John Wiley and Sons.

Werner, E., and Smith, R. 1982. *Vulnerable but invincible.* New York: McGraw-Hill.

Werner, E. E., and Smith, R. S. 1992. *Overcoming the odds: High risk children from birth to adulthood.* Ithaca, NY: Cornell University Press.

Werner, E. E. 1990. Protective factors and individual resilience. In S. J. Meisels and J. P. Shonkoff (Eds.), *Handbook of early childhood education.* Cambridge, U.K.: Cambridge University Press.

Werry, J. S., and Taylor, E. 1994. Schizophrenic and allied disorders. In M. Rutter, E. Taylor, and L. Hersov (Eds.), *Child and adolescent psychiatry,* 3rd ed. Oxford: Blackwell.

Werthamer-Larsson, L., Kellam, S. G., and Wheeler, L. 1991. Effect of first-grade classroom environment on shy behavior, aggressive behavior, and concentration problems. *American Journal of Community Psychology,* 19, 585-602.

Wertsch, J. V. 1984 (Ed.). *Children's learning in the "zone of proximal" development.* San Francisco: Jossey-Bass.

Wharf, B. 1994. Families in crisis. In M. Baker (Ed.), *Canada's changing families: Challenges to public policy* (pp. 55-68). Ottawa: The Vanier Institute of the Family.

Whipple, E. E., Fitzgerald, H. E., and Zucker, R. A. 1995. Parent-child interactions in alcoholic and nonalcoholic families. *American Journal of Orthopsychiatry,* 65, 153-159.

Whitbeck, L. B., Hoyt, D. R., and Huck, S. M. 1994. Early family relationships, intergenerational solidarity, and support provided to parents by their adult children. *Journal of Gerontology: Social Sciences,* 49, S85-S94.

Whitbeck, L. B., Simons, R. L., and Conger, R. D. 1991. The effect of early family relationships on contemporary relationships and assistance patterns between adult children and their parents. *Journal of Gerontology: Social Sciences,* 46, S330-S337.

Whitbeck, L. B., Simons, R. L., and Kao, M. Y. 1994. The effects of divorced mothers' dating behaviors and sexual attitudes on the sexual attitudes and behaviors of their adolescent children. *Journal of Marriage and the Family,* 56, 615-621.

White, K. R., Taylor, M. J., and Moss, V. D. 1992. Does research support claims about the benefits of involving parents in early intervention programs? *Review of Educational Research,* 62, 91-125.

White, L. 1994. Coresidence and leaving home: Young adults and their parents. *Annual Review of Sociology,* 20, 81-102.

White, L., and Peterson, D. 1995. The retreat from marriage: Its effect on unmarried children's exchange with parents. *Journal of Marriage and the Family*, 57, 428-434.

White, L. K., and Riedmann, A. 1992. When the Brady bunch grows up: Step/half- and fullsibling relationships in adulthood. *Journal of Marriage and the Family*, 54, 197-208.

Widom, C. S. 1989. Does violence beget violence? A critical examination of the literature. *Psychological Bulletin*, 106, 3-28.

Widom, C. S. 1990. The intergenerational transmission of violence. In N. A. Weiner and M. E. Wolfgang (Eds.), *Pathways to criminal violence* (pp. 137-201). Newbury Park, CA: Sage.

Wilkie, C. F., and Ames, E. W. 1986. The relationship of infant crying to parental stress in the transition to parenthood. *Journal of Marriage and the Family*, 48, 545-550.

Wilkin, D. 1981. A task-oriented approach in the assessment of the distribution of the burden of care, levels of support, and felt needs in the family. In B. Cooper (Ed.), *Assessing the handicaps and needs of mentally retarded children*. London: Academic Press.

Wille, D. E. 1991. Relation of preterm birth with quality of infant-mother attachment at one year. *Infant Behavior and Development*, 14, 227-240.

Williams, H., and Carmichael, A. 1985. Depression in mothers in a multiethnic urban industrial municipality in Melbourne: Aetiological factors and effects on infants and preschool children. *Journal of Child Psychology and Psychiatry*, 26, 277-288.

Williams, L. M., and Finkelhor, D. 1995. Paternal caregiving and incest: Test of a biosocial model. *American Journal of Orthopsychiatry*, 65, 101-113.

Williams, T. H., and Handford, A. G. 1986. Television and other leisure activities. In T. H. Williams (Ed.), *The impact of television: A national experiment in three communities* (pp. 143-213). Orlando, FL: Academic Press.

Wilson, J. Q., and Herrnstein, R. J. 1985. *Crime and human nature*. New York: Simon & Schuster.

Wilson, W. J. 1987. *The truly disadvantaged: The inner city, the underclass, and public policy*. Chicago: University of Chicago Press.

Wilson, W. J. 1991a. Studying inner-city social dislocations: The challenge of public agenda research. *American Sociological Review*, 56, 1-14.

Wilson, W. J. 1991b. Public policy research and "the truly disadvantaged." In C. Jencks and P. E. Peterson (Eds.), *The urban underclass*. Washington, DC: Brookings Institution.

Winokur, G., et al. 1995. A family study of manic-depressive (bipolar I) disease. *Archives of General Psychiatry*, 52, 367-373.

Wintre, M. G., Yoffe, M., and Crowley, J. 1995. Perception of parental reciprocity scale (POPRS): Development and validation with adolescents and young adults. *Social Development*, 4, 129-148.

Wolf, R., and Pillemer, K. 1989. *Helping elderly victims: The reality of elder abuse*. New York: Columbia University Press.

Wolking, S. N., and De Salis, W. 1982. Infant temperament, maternal mental state and child behaviour problems. In *Temperamental differences in infants and young children*. Ciba Foundation Symposium 89, London: Pitman.

Yoshida, R. et al. 1978. Parental involvement in the special education pupil planning process: The school's perspective. *Exceptional Children*, 44, 531-533.

Yoshikawa, H. 1994. Prevention as cumulative protection: Effects of early family support and education on chronic delinquency and its risks. *Psychological Bulletin*, 115, 28-54.

Youngblade, L. M., and Belsky, J. 1995. From family to friend: Predicting positive dyadic interaction with a close friend at 5 years of age from early parent-child relations. In S. Shulman (Ed.), *Close relationships and socioemotional development* (pp. 35-61). Norwood, NJ: Ablex.

Youniss, J. 1980. *Parents and peers in social development*. Chicago: University of Chicago Press.

Youniss, J., and Smollar, J. 1985. *Adolescent relations with mothers, fathers, and friends*. Chicago: University of Chicago Press.

Youniss, J., and Smollar, J. 1989. Adolescents' interpersonal relationships in social context. In T. J. Berndt and G. W. Ladd (Eds.), *Peers' relationships in child development* (pp. 301-316). New York: John Wiley and Sons.

Youniss, J., McLellan, J. A., and Strouse, D. 1994. "We're popular, but we're not snobs": Adolescents describe their crowds. In R. Montemayor, G. R. Adams, and T. P. Gullotta (Eds.), *Personal relationships during adolescence* (pp. 101-122). Thousand Oaks, CA: Sage.

Yutrzenka, B. A. 1995. Making a case for training in ethnic and cultural diversity in increasing treatment efficacy. *Journal of Consulting and Clinical Psychology*, 63, 197-206.

Zahn-Waxler, C., et al. 1990. Antecedents of problem behavior in children of depressed mothers. *Development and Psychopathology*, 2, 271-291.

Zahner, G. E. P., et al. 1992. Children's mental health service needs and utilization patterns in an urban community: An epidemiological assessment. *Journal of the American Academy of Child and Adolescent Psychiatry*, 31, 951-960.

Zaslow, M. J. 1989. Sex differences in children's response to parental divorce: 1. Samples, variables, ages and sources. *American Journal of Orthopsychiatry*, 59, 118-141.

Zelkowitz, P., Papageorgiou, A., Zelazo, P. R., and Weiss, M. J. S. 1995. Behavioral adjustment in very low and normal birth weight children. *Journal of Clinical Child Psychology*, 24, 21-30.

Zigler, E. F. 1995. Meeting the needs of children in poverty. *American Journal of Orthopsychiatry*, 65, 6-9.

Zigler, E., and Glick, M. 1986. *A developmental approach to adult psychopathology*. New York: Wiley.

Zigler, E., and Styfco, S. J. 1993. Strength in unity: Consolidating federal education programs for young children. In E. Zigler and S. J. Styfco (Eds.), *Head Start and beyond: A national plan for extended childhood intervention* (pp. 111-145). New Haven, CT: Yale University Press.

Zill, N. 1988. Behavior, achievement, and health problems among children in stepfamilies: Findings from a national survey of child health. In E. M. Hetherington and J. D. Arasteh (Eds.), *Impact of divorce, single parenting, and stepparenting on children* (pp. 325-368). Hillsdale, NJ: Lawrence Erlbaum.

Zill, N., and Coiro, M. J. 1992. Assessing the condition of children. *Children and Youth Services Review*, 14, 119-136.

Zill, N., and Nord, C. W. 1994. *Running the place: How American families are faring in a changing economy and an individualistic society*. Child Trends, Inc.

Zill, N., and Rogers, C. C. 1988. Recent trends in the well-being of children in the United States and their implications for public policy. In A. Cherlin (Ed.), *The changing American family and public policy* (pp. 31-115). Washington, DC: Urban Institute Press.

Zill, N., Morrison, D. R., and Coiro, M. J. 1993. Long-term effects of parental divorce on parent-child relationships, adjustment, and achievement in young adulthood. *Journal of Family Psychology*, 7, 91-103.

Zimmerman, S. L. 1992. *Family policies and family well-being: The role of political culture*. Newbury Park, CA: Sage.

Zingraff, M. T., Leiter, J., Johnsen, M. C., and Myers, K. A. 1994. The mediating effect of good school performance on the maltreatment-delinquency relationship. *Journal of Research in Crime and Delinquency*, 31, 62-91.

Zinn, M. B. 1992. Family, race, and poverty in the eighties. In B. Thorne and M. Yalom (Eds.), *Rethinking the family, 2nd ed.* (pp. 71-90), Boston: Northeastern University Press.

Zinneker, J. 1990. What does the future hold? Youth and sociocultural change in the FRG. In L. Chisholm, P. Bücher, H.-H. Krüger, and P. Brown (Eds.), *Childhood, youth and social change: A comparative perspective* (pp. 17-32). London: Falmer Press.

Zucker, R., Boyd, G., and Howard, J. (Eds.). 1994. *The development of alcohol problems: Exploring the biopsychosocial matrix of risk.* NIH Publication No. 94-3495. Rockville, MD: National Institute on Alcohol Abuse and Alcoholism.

Zuckerman, M. 1987. All parents are environmentalists until they have their second child. *Behavioral and Brain Sciences,* 10, 42-44.

Zuckerman, M. 1991. *Psychobiology of personality.* New York: Cambridge University Press.

Zuckerman, M. 1995. Good and bad humors: Biochemical bases of personality and its disorders. *Psychological Science,* 6, 325-332.

Zuckerman, M., Miyake, K., and Elkin, C. S. 1995. Effects of attractiveness and maturity of face and voice on interpersonal impressions. *Journal of Research in Personality,* 29, 253-272.

Zuo, J. 1992. The reciprocal relationship between marital interaction and marital happiness: A three-wave study. *Journal of Marriage and the Family,* 54, 870-878.

Author Index

Note: When there are four or more co-authors, only the first author is indexed.

Subject Index

Order Your Own Copy of
This Important Book for Your Personal Library!

PARENTS, CHILDREN, AND ADOLESCENTS
Interactive Relationships and Development in Context

_____ in hardbound at $59.95 (ISBN: 0-7890-6034-5)

_____ in softbound at $24.95 (ISBN: 0-7890-0181-0)

COST OF BOOKS_____

OUTSIDE USA/CANADA/
MEXICO: ADD 20%_____

POSTAGE & HANDLING_____
_(US: $3.00 for first book & $1.25
for each additional book)
Outside US: $4.75 for first book
& $1.75 for each additional book)_

SUBTOTAL_____

IN CANADA: ADD 7% GST_____

STATE TAX_____
_(NY, OH & MN residents, please
add appropriate local sales tax)_

FINAL TOTAL_____
_(If paying in Canadian funds,
convert using the current
exchange rate. UNESCO
coupons welcome.)_

☐ **BILL ME LATER:** ($5 service charge will be added)
(Bill-me option is good on US/Canada/Mexico orders only;
not good to jobbers, wholesalers, or subscription agencies.)

☐ Check here if billing address is different from
shipping address and attach purchase order and
billing address information.

Signature_____

☐ **PAYMENT ENCLOSED: $**_____

☐ **PLEASE CHARGE TO MY CREDIT CARD.**

☐ Visa   ☐ MasterCard   ☐ AmEx   ☐ Discover

Account # _____

Exp. Date _____

Signature _____

Prices in US dollars and subject to change without notice.

NAME _____

INSTITUTION _____

ADDRESS _____

CITY _____

STATE/ZIP _____

COUNTRY _____ COUNTY (NY residents only) _____

TEL _____ FAX _____

E-MAIL_____
May we use your e-mail address for confirmations and other types of information? ☐ Yes   ☐ No

Order From Your Local Bookstore or Directly From
The Haworth Press, Inc.
10 Alice Street, Binghamton, New York 13904-1580 • USA
TELEPHONE: 1-800-HAWORTH (1-800-429-6784) / Outside US/Canada: (607) 722-5857
FAX: 1-800-895-0582 / Outside US/Canada: (607) 772-6362
E-mail: getinfo@haworth.com
PLEASE PHOTOCOPY THIS FORM FOR YOUR PERSONAL USE.

BOF96